MEDIA POWER,
PROFESSIONALS AND POLICIES

The work of Jeremy Tunstall, one of the founding fathers of British media studies, is the inspiration behind *Media Power, Professionals and Policies*. In this collection of new work, leading international contributors address the central themes of Tunstall's work: the history, structures and practices of the international media industry; the relationship between media and government; and the sociology of media professionals in the communications industry.

Divided into themed sections, *Media Power, Professionals and Policies* explores:

- aspects of media policy, from the history of press reform to merger mania in the United States
- the idea of media power, tracing the development of mass communications research and addressing contemporary issues such as digital communication, the production of knowledge and the changing public sphere
- the management of the media, from the emergence of information policing in the seventeenth century to Labour's reform of Downing Street press practices, the use of negative political advertising and the role of news media in contemporary conflicts
- the role of journalists, their professional autonomy and their relationship with newspaper and broadcasting proprietors
- international media operations, from international news agencies and satellite television, to the impact of information technology in the US on audience knowledge of the outside world.

Howard Tumber is Professor of Sociology and Dean of the School of Social and Human Sciences at City University, London.

MEDIA POWER, PROFESSIONALS AND POLICIES

Edited by Howard Tumber

London and New York

First published 2000 by Routledge
11 New Fetter Lane, London EC4P 4EE

Simultaneously published in the USA and Canada
by Routledge
29 West 35th Street, New York, NY 10001

Routledge is an imprint of the Taylor & Francis Group

Typeset in Bembo by Keystroke, Jacaranda Lodge, Wolverhampton.
Printed and bound in Great Britain by St Edmundsbury Press,
Bury St Edmunds, Suffolk

British Library Cataloguing in Publication Data
A catalogue record for this book is available from the British Library

Library of Congress Cataloging in Publication Data
Media power, professionals, and policies / edited by Howard Tumber.
p.   cm.
Includes bibliographical references and index.
1. Mass media—Political aspects. 2. Journalism. 3. Communication, International.
I. Tumber, Howard.
P95.8 .M3934 2000
302.23—dc21
99–054955

ISBN 0–415–19668–X (hbk)
ISBN 0–415–19669–8 (pbk)

To Jeremy Tunstall

CONTENTS

CONTENTS

CONTENTS

TABLES

CONTRIBUTORS

Oliver Boyd-Barrett, Professor of Communications, California State Polytechnic University

James Curran, Professor of Communications, Goldsmiths College, University of London

Winston Fletcher, Chairman, Advertising Standards Board of Finance, UK

Simon Frith, Professor of Film and Media, University of Stirling

Hanno Hardt, Professor of Journalism and Mass Communication and Communication Studies, University of Iowa and Professor of Communications, University of Ljubljana

Michael Harris, Senior Lecturer in History, Birbeck College, University of London

Stephen Hess, Senior Fellow, The Brookings Institution, Washington, DC

Bo Hellgren, Professor of Management, Linkoping University

Gladys Engel Lang, Professor Emerita of Communications, Political Science, Sociology, University of Washington

Kurt Lang, Professor Emeritus of Sociology and Communications, University of Washington

Stuart Macdonald, Professor of Information and Organisation, University of Sheffield

Denis McQuail, Professor Emeritus of Communications, University of Amsterdam

David E. Morrison, Professor of Communications Research, University of Leeds

Michael Palmer, Professor of International Communications, CRIFEME, Université Paris III Sorbonne Nouvelle

Herbert I. Schiller, Professor of Communication, University of California, San Diego

Philip Schlesinger, Professor of Film and Media, University of Stirling

Colin Seymour-Ure, Professor of Government, University of Kent

Hugh Stephenson, Professor of Journalism, City University

Christopher H. Sterling, Professor of Telecommunication, George Washington University

Rodney Tiffen, Associate Professor of Government and International Relations, University of Sydney

Howard Tumber, Professor of Sociology, City University, London

David Walker, Analysis Editor, *The Guardian*

Rex Winsbury, Consultant Editor, *Intermedia*

INTRODUCTION
Academic at work

Howard Tumber

In 1962 Jeremy Tunstall published his first book *The Fishermen*. Some fifteen books later, in 1999 his latest study *The Anglo-American Media Connection* was published. Tunstall's work as an academic has been substantial. As James Curran writes (see Chapter 2): 'He will be remembered primarily as a sociologist and one of the founding fathers of British media studies.' This collection of pieces by scholars and media practitioners, mainly from the United States and Britain, forms a tribute to the contribution that Tunstall has made to the field of mass communication research and also reflects the personal respect and esteem in which he is held.

After finishing a social anthropology degree at Cambridge University in the late 1950s, Jeremy Tunstall went to Hull University to pursue his growing interest in sociology and begin his first research project. At that time sociology was an emerging discipline beginning to become fashionable but there were only a few sociology departments in UK universities. Hull had only two sociology lecturers, Peter Worsley and Gordon Horobin.[1] One of Tunstall's influences as he began his study of the fishermen of Hull was Young and Willmott's *Family and Kinship in East London* (1957). Tunstall used to write to authors and ask if he could go and talk to them. He went to Bethnal Green in London on two or three occasions to look round and talk to Young and Willmott, and since there were very few people doing sociological research at that time they did not object to conversing with a budding sociologist.

The Fishermen was based on a household survey and observation on-board ship. Tunstall spent nine weeks at sea, quite a long while if you are there all the time, day and night. He was not immune to seasickness. The research was challenging, exploring a romanticised world that was actually an extremely tough existence. Apart from observation at sea, Tunstall developed the diplomatic interviewing skills he employed throughout his career by interviewing the fishermen's wives while their spouses were at sea.[2]

The study that issued in *The Fishermen* was one of the factors that fed Tunstall's interest in the media. One of the remarkable things about the fishing industry at that time was that it was very good at public relations and the trawler owners – the British Trawlers' Federation – had an effective public relations campaign, which had developed through the conflicts with Iceland over fishing rights. The owners of the companies emphasised the heroism of the trawlermen of Britain in their portrayal of the industry and paid for advertisements supporting the fishermen. Tunstall realised that the campaign was a fabrication of the truth. In reality, despite their lauding of the trawlermen, the owners treated their workers appallingly.

Tunstall's growing media interest developed further when at the University of Manchester (as research fellow) he shared a flat with an old Cambridge colleague who had become a *Guardian* journalist. Tunstall would accompany him regularly to the pub behind the *Guardian*'s offices in Manchester and was introduced to journalists' culture. He met lots of hacks and drank loads of beer. Tunstall's media fascination was secured when he returned to London and worked in an advertising agency, which (together with subsequent interviews) led to his book *The Advertising Man* (1964).

Tunstall then moved to the London School of Economics where he was employed on a study of elderly people under the direction of Peter Townsend. The study, funded by the National Institute for Mental Health in the United States, involved national sample surveys in three countries – the US, the UK and Denmark. Tunstall was given considerable autonomy to examine a sub-group of the main study. He decided to look at isolated old people and conducted around 200 interviews in four areas of the country, gaining access through general practitioners' records. Subsequently Peter Townsend was appointed head of the sociology department at the new University of Essex, and Tunstall's appointment switched to Essex. It was here that Tunstall applied for and received the first of several research grants – for what turned out to be a pioneering and famous study on journalists. *Journalists At Work* (1971) was the first major social science study of specialist journalists in the UK. The intention behind the original proposal was to conduct a study about the occupation and profession of journalism. He decided to concentrate on specialists, and conducted a survey of over 200 journalists and undertook direct observation and unstructured interviews with newspaper editors, advertising and circulation managers, sub-editors and provincial journalists.[3]

In planning the study Tunstall was influenced by previous sociological studies of occupations. He was particularly keen on the work of Everett Hughes (1958) and persuaded him to write an Introduction to the advertising book. He was impressed by Hughes' irreverent approach about the latter's study of medical students, 'The Boys in White', in contrast to that of Robert Merton *et al.* (1957) whose work on student doctors had come out at the same time but was much more reverential, referring to the subject-group as 'student physicians'. Bernard Cohen's *The Press and Foreign Policy* (1963) was also influential. Tunstall was fascinated by the manner in which Cohen had talked to foreign and diplomatic correspondents in Washington. He was influenced, too, by the survey studies conducted in the US by Leo Rosten, particularly *The Washington Correspondents* (1937).

Before the publication of *Journalists At Work* Tunstall produced a reader – *Media Sociology* (1970). This was one of two readers that came out around this time, the other being Denis McQuail's *Sociology of Mass Communications* (1972). Tunstall was asked to edit the reader for Constable. Media research was a developing field in the UK, and both these readers stand as important milestones in the development of the field. Following the successful publication of the reader, Tunstall offered both the *Journalists At Work* book and a proposal for a new series on media to Constable. Both were accepted. The Constable series became a major platform for young scholars in this newly emerging field.[4]

Following the completion of the journalists' study at Essex, Tunstall moved to a permanent position as head of the sociology division at the Open University. Together with colleagues Tunstall wrote the sociology material for the first-year general social science course and a second-year course entitled 'sociological perspectives'. The material was produced for students in a number of books, and in addition to these Ken Thompson and Tunstall edited a Penguin reader – *Sociological Perspectives* (1971).[5] Before leaving the Open University Tunstall developed the idea for a third-year course on the mass media. He started producing outlines for the course but the whole process of approval proved to be extremely slow. Courses at the Open University are relatively expensive to generate as they involve the production of television programmes, books and other course material. Other media academics were invited to meetings to discuss the course. Tunstall had very little to do with the writing of the course since by that time he had moved to City University as professor of sociology. But his legacy was an important one in establishing the idea and gaining approval for its development.

One of Tunstall's other involvements in the development of media courses in Britain was for the Council for National Academic Awards (CNAA), the organisation that validated courses for the UK's polytechnics. Following the path of Central London Polytechnic (now the University of Westminster), the first institution to develop a media studies degree, other institutions all over the country produced similar courses.[6]

Jeremy Tunstall was appointed in 1974 to the Chair of Sociology at City University, London, where he resides today.

MEDIA AND POLICY

The first part of the book is concerned with media policy, an area of media research that began to emerge in a substantial way in the early and mid-1980s as the deregulation policies of the Reagan presidency spread to Britain and the rest of Europe. One of Tunstall's qualities as a communications specialist is to spot trends and then to embark on a voyage of empirical discovery. Tunstall's initial interest in policy began during his work for the Royal Commission on the Press (1974–7). This continued during the writing of *The Media in Britain* (1983), a detailed and comprehensive account of the British media. Tunstall characterises the British tradition of policy making as one of minimalist legislation and the voluntary principle. He shows how, unlike Europe and the United States, Britain exhibited hostility towards a single media ministry or a single set of strategic national goals. This fragmentation and compartmentalisation in Britain was further demonstrated through a detailed analysis of policy making in a comparative study that Tunstall conducted with Michael Palmer. *Liberating Communications* (1990) focuses on French and British communications policy during the 1980s.[7]

Denis McQuail in the opening essay acknowledges Tunstall's characterisation of the press as a non-policy area. McQuail considers the proposition that not only the press but communications in general are increasingly non-policy areas, and he examines the longer term prospects for media policy in general. Writing on communications policy some years ago, Tunstall and others stressed the fragmentation of policy making and regulation. But, as McQuail points out, the trend towards convergence makes it increasingly problematical to maintain traditional compartmentalisation of media sectors. McQuail seeks to examine the possibility of a new media policy paradigm. The supposed causes of death of old policy contours vary. Sometimes it is the new liberal political–economic climate in the world; sometimes the new (and converging) technologies that undermine the foundations and purpose of media policy; sometimes it is the globalisation that challenges national control. Tracing some of the history and developments of communications, McQuail suggests that it is difficult to represent the emerging paradigm in a single framework due to the uncertainties that still exist. However, while one may assume that the general goal of policy is still to serve the public interest, it is the balance of component values shaping the definition of public interest that has changed.

James Curran concentrates on one important aspect of policy: the British press. Acknowledging that in the UK there is a cultural infrastructure of reform encompassing broadcasting, Curran asserts that no such dynamic exists for the press. Examining eighty years' history of press reformism, Curran pronounces it a 'study of failure', arguing that a mutually reinforcing combination of publishers' power, press-freedom rhetoric and reform movement weakness has inhibited change. Curran also illuminates the failing of the Press Council in the training of journalists. Despite calls by Royal Commissions on the Press for a national streamlined training scheme, the professionalising of journalism remains undeveloped. Unlike the US, where the project had the support of publishers and universities played an important role in sustaining a professional culture, in Britain antipathy to critical media theory and media studies courses by press employers began at the outset and remains today. This led to a strongly humanities' influenced definition of media courses and a neglect of press research.

In *Newspaper Power* (1996) Tunstall credits the 1960s with planting the seeds of hope that British journalism was moving towards professionalisation, but by the 1990s such efforts to raise standards, control entry and improve education had receded (1996: 141).[8] In a later piece in Part I Hugh Stephenson surveys the history of attempts to regulate British press behaviour and examines some of the factors inhibiting the efforts to shift British journalism in a professional direction. He looks at whether recent attempts to establish a code of conduct, particularly in relation to matters of privacy, represent an 'ethical sea-change' towards an enforced professional order. Decades of failure by reformers in Britain, though, may paradoxically, as Stephenson points out, be overturned by the incorporation into UK law of the European Convention of Human Rights.

Tunstall was one of the first British academics to examine recent United States' communications policy making. He spent 1983–4 in Washington, DC, primarily researching the major deregulation period 1975–85. In *Communications Deregulation* (1986) Tunstall highlights the revolutionary nature of the change in US communications, arguing that it was produced by the combination of running technology on 'fast forward' while running regulation on 'fast backward'.[9] It was an interesting period to witness because the divestiture of AT&T was coming to a conclusion. An important aspect of the book is the uncovering, for the benefit of those outside of the system, of the intense political conflicts involved in communications policy making. Tunstall reveals the degree of commercial lobbying that obtains and the role that the courts and Congress play in the process.

Christopher Sterling looks at recent events in United States communications. In particular he examines whether the huge merger and consolidation trend over the last few years is the result of the 1996 United States Telecommunications Act's encouragement of the restructuring of the industry into a small number of large companies. Sterling traces the history of ownership policies prior to 1996 and shows how Congress sought specifically to sweep away previous Federal Communications Commission ownership regulations. Echoing Tunstall's illumination of political lobbying, Sterling tells of congressmen being bombarded with industry data to support the view for diminished regulatory controls. Providing empirical data to show the media merger mania that followed, Sterling argues that the 1996 Act accelerated the urge to merge but had not created it; nor has technology been a driving factor. The main reasons are fear, awareness of the importance of being a global player and in some cases the wish to enter the Internet world.

Simon Frith focuses on the familiar theme of the British music industry. In reflecting on his early engagement with the sociology of rock Frith acknowledges his debt to Tunstall who had facilitated his book (Frith 1978) twenty years ago. Frith empathised with Tunstall's kind of sociology and was delighted to have the opportunity to explore his own favourite niche. In this piece he looks at the government's interest in the music industry, tracing the history of music policy and practice in Britain over the last twenty-five years in order to focus on the peculiarities of music as a mass medium and as a culture industry. Frith examines the new Labour government's interest in the music industry and suggests that different research questions should be asked now from those he posed twenty years ago. In particular he calls for the abandonment of the production of culture and gatekeeper models of the music industry. He sees the current music industry as one organised primarily around the politics and economics of rights, but also one that historically exhibits continuity in its adaptation of technology and its renegotiation with cinema and radio. If anything is anomalous in music industry history it is the emergence of rock. Frith sees this anomaly in rock's defiance of industrial constraints, and its mark on academia, on cultural commentary and on government policy.

MEDIA POWER

A constant if sometimes understated theme throughout Tunstall's work is the notion of media power. In the three chapters in Part II different aspects of power are examined. Philip Schlesinger, in a lucid exposition, explores a line of discourse in social and political theory. He posits that despite the range of conceptual languages used in the ideas and work from Deutsch to Castells there are indications that recurrent assumptions underlie much of the work on the relationship between nation and communication. Social communication theories are traditionally limited to thinking in terms of communications and the nation with the formation or maintenance of the interior of the national communicative space the main priority. In the light of the impact of transnational and global changes Schlesinger reassesses the implication that the sovereign nation–state is the vessel for communicative space. He offers the European Union as a bell jar within which to examine the possibility of a supra-national public sphere and for illuminating the communicative relations between nation–states and supra-national entities.

Herbert Schiller paints a depressing picture of corporate power in the communications sphere. He tackles the theme of US dominance but extends this to the new world of cyberspace. He acknowledges Jeremy Tunstall as one of the few people to describe perceptively the manner in which the United States' notion of the free flow of communication had been built into the structure of UNESCO. Not only did this doctrine consolidate US advantages in foreign markets, but it acted as a propaganda weapon during the Cold War. Tunstall's work on the American media considers these developments, and though the salience of a few of these issues has diminished most remain urgent areas for study and policy making. As Schiller remarks, Tunstall's original and critical analyses are as useful today as they were courageous and far-seeing twenty years ago. In the latter part of his chapter Schiller shows how the digitization of the communications economy coupled with the end of the Cold War has led the US to adjust the terms of the free flow doctrine but not its objectives. Part of the 'new' digitized arena is the commodification of information and the battle over rights culminating in what Schiller sees as the corporate enclosure of intellectual property.

David Morrison tackles a different aspect of power – the production of knowledge. Examining the political struggle involved in cultural production he traces the development of early communications research in America, and explains why the first major work on television was produced in Britain and not America, as might have been expected. He highlights the role that philanthropic foundations played in the development of mass communications research. In particular he provides a small historical study of the beginnings of modern mass communications research, most notably the part that the Rockefeller Foundation played in establishing radio research in the early 1940s.

MEDIA MANAGEMENT

The third part of the book brings together four pieces that deal with different aspects of the dynamics of access to the construction of news and image. Recent work on the relationship between sources and journalists reconsidered earlier formulations of ideological hegemony and attempted to explore differences and competition within dominant power blocks. A further theme is an analysis of battles over the interpretation of events and also of conflicts over the conditions for the functioning of a public sphere.

It was Jeremy Tunstall's *Journalists At Work* that first showed that source confidentiality and the parliamentary lobby system was a researchable subject. *The Westminster Lobby Correspondents* (1970) was the result of a sociological study of national political journalism. Tunstall collected information from thirty-nine lobby correspondents, providing an important account of political journalism at work. Tunstall returned to this area over twenty-five years later in a chapter in *Newspaper Power* (1996).

In the first chapter of this part Colin Seymour-Ure looks at how the Blair government introduced new principles into Downing Street's news operations. Not only has the new Labour administration brought new techniques and practices, but more seriously it has disturbed such long-established principles as civil service non-partisanship and ministerial responsibility. Blair's news operations in the first six months after May 1997 involved the use of a partisan Downing Street press secretary, partisan ministerial press

secretaries, a downgrading of the traditional civil service style of departmental information work, increased centralisation of government media
management, a challenge to traditional confidential lobby briefings and the
designation of a (*de facto*) minister for media relations. Seymour-Ure argues
that the cumulative impact may amount to a qualitative change, tantamount
to the operation of new principles rather than more efficient practices.

While Seymour-Ure concentrates on the management of information
by governments, Winston Fletcher assesses the use and effectiveness
of political advertising. Providing a brief historical trawl through recent
political advertising campaigns in the US and Britain, Fletcher analyses why
negative advertising is more common in political campaigning than in
product marketing. An accepted explanation for this is that the public's
opinion of politicians is now so poor that only derogatory and pejorative
words (and presumably images) will resonate with the public. Fletcher
suggests another six contributory factors for the use of negative political
advertising, including the death of ideological difference among political
parties and less regulation than for product advertising. The effectiveness
of political advertising is hard to measure. Testing is difficult because of its
discontinuity and inability to adopt controls. Fletcher contends that most
political advertising is intended to bolster existing support and that voter
antipathy to negative advertising does not appear to be reflected in the ballot
box. As politicians get involved only at elections, they tend to be amateurs in
the art of advertising.

Michael Harris provides an historical perspective on politicians' attempts
to control information, in this case policing the medium of print prior to
1750. Since the early seventeenth century government interests have been
served by the formation of information networks in which selected material
was redirected into the public sphere through the publication of news serials.
Because governments have been unable to suppress the flow of news and information a series of official publications was established containing the official
version of events. Harris provides an analysis of the policy and organisational
structure that emerged during the seventeenth century and, in particular,
the role the *London Gazette* played in relation to both government and the
wider community. Government obsession with the gathering and control
of information led to informers being paid to report on the identity of
those responsible for writing, printing and publishing material considered
outside the bounds of legitimate comment. Records were seized and people
prosecuted. These state activities, Harris argues, were only part of a more
generalised web of interventions that involved not only political interests but
commercial ones by booksellers in their attempts to establish collective
dominance over the structures of publication.

In the final chapter in Part III Rodney Tiffen concentrates on the varying
role of the news media in different types of contemporary conflict – inter-
party, intraparty, industrial, between pressure groups and social movements,

ethnic, and international. Tiffen's piece complements the work on sources by comparing behaviour in different conflicts. He analyses whether news coverage of these socio-political conflicts conforms to a particular pattern and if the media play a consistant role in these various conflicts. His conclusion, echoing some of the recent work on source behaviour, suggests that in cases where the news media perceive approximate parity between sources and between audiences, as in the case of inter-party conflicts, there is more balanced reporting. Overt partiality, in contrast, occurs where viewpoints are not strongly represented in either sources or audiences, as in international conflicts. A number of variables are also identified that affect the behaviour of sources, in particular publicity requirements and publicity capability.

MEDIA PROFESSIONALS

Part IV of the book examines media professionals, a key feature of Tunstall's work. From the pioneering *Journalists At Work* (1971) through *Television Producers* (1993) to *Newspaper Power* (1996) he has focussed on the individuals working in media organisations and their degree of autonomy.[10] Tunstall has conducted over 1,000 interviews with media professionals during his career, and many a time he has regaled colleagues with stories and anecdotes from his adventures in media land. In the Preface to *The Westminster Lobby Correspondents* (1970: ix) he was particularly frank about his methods. Explaining that he deliberately adopted a discursive essay-writing approach, he states:

> Neutral social science is in any case an impossibility; the sociologist who ventures among journalists travels especially heavily laden with values. Perhaps by wearing some of these values on his sleeve, he will assist both his readers and himself.

Stephen Hess claims that Tunstall became his teacher after he had read *The Westminster Lobby Correspondents* and *Journalist At Work*. Hess used Tunstall's work as a methodological and spiritual guide for the study he conducted on Washington reporters in 1978 (Hess 1981). Hess here reconsiders the news from Washington twenty years later. He attempted a replication of part of his original research, even managing to interview sixteen of the sixty-five journalists who are still plying their trade in Washington. The main changes have been the use of new technology and the speeding up of the editorial process. While the media landscape has changed dramatically – Internet, multi-channel cable, talk radio, CNN – the early evening network news programmes still exceed the number of viewers that the cable community can deliver. However the content of these news programmes as well as the newspapers surveyed twenty years ago have shown a decline in Washington stories and a consequent trend towards local news.

9

Hanno Hardt provides a pessimistic account of current newsroom culture. Hardt argues that over the course of the last century the idea of journalism as an independent fourth estate has been replaced by a commercial solution. As media interests have merged with the politics of mass society, journalism as cultural practice has been considerably diminished and trivialised. Traditional ideas of journalistic practices free from a business-oriented paternalism have been eroded by the rise of corporate power and its control over journalists' role and function. Hardt is critical of public journalism and civic journalism – the new crusade for responsive journalism. Far from seeing them as the salvation of journalism, their development is, he claims, a new partisanship for the patrons of business offering democracy as private enterprise rather than public commitment. Hardt sees support for the 'new' journalism by the media foundations as demonstrating their institutional power in shaping press policies.

David Walker gives an insider's view of the crisis of confidence in British journalism. Walker believes that metropolitan journalism is all at sea and points to a trend in the retreat from intellectual and cultural standards. He cites a loss of confidence by journalism that has lost touch with its societal and cultural moorings. The internal segmentation in newspapers, far from providing a structure for the reaffirmation of journalistic autonomy, is increasing a sense of alienation on the part of journalists as they become more distanced from the central values of the newspapers. Walker believes that part of the crisis results from a neglect of self reflection and a failure to engage with social scientists such as Tunstall. The reluctance of journalists to explain their working practices is similar to that shown by other professionals, including academics.

Rex Winsbury confirms the reticence of journalists to reveal trade secrets to academics. Like Walker, Winsbury has direct experience of working in Fleet Street for famous newspaper proprietors. While his experiences did not provide him with evidence for the theory of a free press, Winsbury highlights an 'enabling role' that proprietors have exercised. By having enough financial muscle proprietors can distance themselves from government. To illustrate this Winsbury examines the press in Kenya, where he was employed for four years on *The Nation*. He shows how three newspapers, each owned by a 'foreign' proprietor, survived under the Moi regime and played a part, albeit circumscribed, in moving the country towards a more open and democratic regime while escaping the genocide witnessed in other countries in Africa.

In the final piece in Part IV Stuart Macdonald and Bo Hellgren also touch on the professional–academic relationship. They examine the use of the interview as an empirical tool for researchers and suggest some ways for the journalist to present the findings. The authors argue that the importance of fieldwork to management research lies not so much in the gathering of information as in satisfying the requirements of those who fund the research – a legitimising process showing that research funds are being well spent. In

10

discussion of the interview in theory and practice they acknowledge the wealth of information on the organisation that the interview may provide, but this is tempered by the constraints it imposes, in particular the influence the organisation may have or demand over the research results. By entering the arena of an organisation with an unfamiliar culture, the researcher runs the risk of encountering difficulties. Macdonald and Hellgren identify how the interview in particular has become an increasingly important component of research in management studies, because the organisations themselves have become the primary customers of the research. Increasingly research is being directed towards satisfying the immediate demands of specific users, while less research is performed as a public good, publicly funded.[11]

INTERNATIONAL MEDIA

The final part of the book is devoted to international media flow, another favourite Tunstall theme. Michael Palmer looks at the relationship between the historian and the news agency. He examines how the historian of news agencies approaches the various logics that fashion the production, transmission and distribution of copy by news-agency journalists. Several news-agency historians have both explored the 'corporate records' of news organisations and consulted the 'news product', as preserved in public and private archives – such as collections of the Correspondence Havas in the Bibliothéque Nationale de France. Palmer stresses that certain questions arise from juxtaposing material accessible from archives that contain information concerning the history of the news agencies and issues that may arise during observation – in this case a month-long 'observer-participation' study of AFP, based in its Paris headquarters. He argues that the premise or the starting-point is that ongoing concerns about the writing of history of news agencies and of the news flow are influenced by the present environment in which the news media operate – however careful historians may be to guard against anachronism.

Kurt and Gladys Lang examine why a real knowledge-deficit exists among Americans about the real world and why it continues to exist in a highly developed information society. Providing a detailed schematic look at how the new technology has affected the view of the world from America, they address the limits to the acquisition of new knowledge via an overview of the flow of information through four levels: the production of information about other countries, which determines how and where information about them originates; the distribution of such information, namely how it is screened and selectively transmitted; its utilisation by audiences with varying access to information and communicative competence; and the refraction in the imagery of other countries as a result of these processes.

Oliver Boyd-Barrett provides the final chapter in Part V. Through an ethnographic observation of the feasibility planning for a new Pan–Arab satellite venture based in Dubai, he attempts to illuminate the dynamics of identity construction, in particular to issues of audience and programming. The objectives of the new Pan–Arab channel, apart from profit, were to provide a family service and to promote Dubai. In a detailed account Boyd-Barrett explores the negotiations that took place in an attempt to meet these objectives. The case study shows the potential of non-western satellite television to assuage early critical arguments of satellite television and cultural imperialism. But this is not sufficient reason, Boyd-Barrett argues, to be optimistic about the future. Although western media influences have been reduced, structured inequalities still exist. While the overall concept can be described as *Arab*, western programming formats are still likely to play a part, as also are heavy reliance on western and Japanese technology.

Tunstall has travelled a long road – from his social-anthropological study of the fishermen of Hull to his analysis of the new communications environment. In his latest book[12] *The Anglo-American Media Connection*[13] he illuminates the advances in media and communications globalisation. The book demonstrates the dominance of the American media and the role that it plays in providing support for other areas of American international leadership. For example, the consumer media have promoted and exported the popular culture of which they are a part; the news media have supported American commercial deregulation and financial services; and Hollywood (a favourite Tunstall preoccupation), as well as selling entertainment, is part of a wider communications business, elements of which have military connections.

In *The Media Are American* (1977) he argued that the mass media have been packaged into shape to fit US conditions and market preferences. He viewed the Anglo-American media connection then as 'imperialism, British Imperialism' (1977: 63). The current book examines the British media and their place in the wider international context. It argues that Britain has attempted to remain a globally significant player in world media, striving to be the Number 2 to the United States. The main focus of the book is the period from 1980 onwards, taking into account the Reagan and Thatcher deregulation and privatisation years. Britain's slippage into media dependence during this period and its generally subservient role to major elements of the US media are shown to parallel the political, diplomatic and military Anglo-American connection. The study as a whole provides evidence of the British media's claim to be world players and significant Number 2s in news flow, factual television, popular music, book publishing and advertising.

Tunstall's contribution to the debates on globalisation and the 'old' themes of media and cultural imperialism continue. His output shows no sign of abating. Indeed a number of projects are planned for the future, and their outcomes awaited with eager anticipation.

NOTES

1 Among its third-year students was Anthony Giddens.
2 Tunstall, reflecting on his work, sees it partly as an unmasking of occupations, but a relatively sympathetic kind of unmasking.
3 Tunstall was joined in the study by a research assistant – Oliver Boyd-Barrett.
4 Among the authors who published in the series which ran from 1971 until 1984 were Philip Elliott (1972), Colin Seymour-Ure (1974), Stan Cohen and Jock Young (1973), David Murphy (1976), Philip Schlesinger (1978), George Boyce, James Curran and Pauline Wingate (1978), Herbert Gans (1980) and Simon Frith (1978).
5 This reader had numerous printings, selling a huge number of copies and providing a good income for the Open University.
6 James Curran and Nick Garnham were the main instigators of the course at Central London, and presented details of the course to the CNAA committee that, among others, included Tunstall, Denis McQuail, Philip Elliott, Colin Seymour-Ure and Jay Blumler. Soon after the degree was validated Curran and Garnham became members of the committee that approved degrees in other institutions.
7 According to Tunstall the original the idea was to conduct a comparison of the US, Britain and France, but this was quite a difficult project to do. In his usual disarming way Tunstall, describing Michael Palmer as originally a nineteenth century historian and himself as a fairly messy kind of sociologist, acknowledges the difficulty of conducting a comparative policy study. In fact the research produced three books – *Liberating Communications* (1990) and *Media Moguls* (1991), both together with Michael Palmer, and *Communications Deregulation* (1986).
8 Curran and Tunstall, among others involved at the outset in the development of media studies courses in the UK, experienced this hostility directly.
9 In conversation, Tunstall remarked how the scale and complexity of the Washington policy arena can be overwhelming – the number of committees, the amount of documents it produces, the size of the staffs, the length of the hearings and coverage on C-span television. It was during this trip that he met Christopher Sterling who aided his passage through the labyrinth of the Washington policy arena. A first draft of the book was made on Kurt Lang's old electric typewriter in Stonybrook – Tunstall had exchanged houses that summer with the Langs.
10 Tunstall views the individual journalist as having more freedom within the larger structure than some Marxists would argue. In *Journalists At Work* he found that senior specialist reporters largely decided on their own stories, particularly in the more serious papers. This is due partly to the bureaucracy, the desk people, not knowing enough to constrain them and also being reluctant to inhibit people they had appointed.
11 Tunstall's main method in interviewing is the semi-structured one. On occasions he tried to go for a total sample. For example in *Journalists At Work* (1971) and *Television Producers* (1993) he attempted to cover everyone in each category. In the latter study the rule for himself and his research assistants was to watch

at least one but preferably several of the programmes made by the person to be interviewed.

12 Written with David Machin.

13 The title is similar to *Anglo-American Media in the World*, the subtitle of *The Media Are American* (1977).

REFERENCES

Boyce, G., J. Curran, and P. Wingate (eds) (1978) *Newspaper History from the Seventeenth Century to the Present Day*, London: Constable.

Boyd-Barrett, O., C. Seymour-Ure and J. Tunstall (1977) *Studies on the Press*, London: HMSO for Royal Commission on the Press.

Cohen, B. (1963) *The Press and Foreign Policy*, Princeton, NJ: Princeton University Press.

Cohen, S. and J. Young, (eds) (1973) *The Manufacture of News*, London: Constable.

Elliott, P. (1972) *The Making of a Television Series*, London: Constable.

Frith, S. (1978) *Sociology of Rock*, London: Constable.

Gans, H. (1980) *Deciding What's News*, London: Constable.

Hess, S. (1981) *The Washington Reporters*, Washington, DC: Brookings Institution.

Hughes, E. (1958) *Men and Their Work*, Glencoe, IL: Free Press.

McQuail, D. (ed.) (1972) *Sociology of Mass Communications*, Harmondsworth: Penguin Books.

Merton, R. K., G. G. Reader and P. L. Kendall (eds) (1957) *The Student Physician: Introductory Studies in the Sociology of Medical Education*, Cambridge, MA: Harvard UP.

Murphy, D. (1976) *The Silent Watchdog*, London: Constable.

Palmer M. B. and J. Tunstall (1990) *Liberating Communications*, Oxford: Blackwell.

Rosten, L. (1937) *The Washington Correspondents*, New York: Harcourt Brace.

Schlesinger, P. (1978) *Putting 'Reality' Together*, London: Constable.

Seymour-Ure, C. (1968) *The Political Impact of Mass Media*, London: Constable.

Thompson, K. and J. Tunstall (eds) (1971) *Sociological Perspectives*, Harmondsworth: Peguin.

Tunstall, J. (1962) *The Fishermen*, London: MacGibbon & Kee.

—— (1964) *The Advertising Man*, London: Chapman & Hall.

—— (1966) *Old and Alone*, London: Routledge & Kegan Paul.

—— (1970) *The Westminster Lobby Correspondents*, London: Routledge & Kegan Paul.

—— (ed.) (1970) *Media Sociology*, London: Constable.

—— (1971) *Journalists At Work*, London: Constable.

—— (1977) *The Media Are American*, London: Constable and New York, Columbia University Press.

—— and D.Walker (1981) *Media Made in California*, New York: Oxford University Press.

—— (1983) *The Media in Britain*, London: Constable.

—— (1986) *Communications Deregulation*, Oxford: Blackwell.

—— and M. B. Palmer (1991) *Media Moguls*, London: Routledge.

—— (1993) *Television Producers*, London: Routledge.

—— (1996) *Newpaper Power*, Oxford: Clarendon Press.

—— and D. Machin (1999) *The Anglo-American Media Connection*, Oxford: Oxford University Press.

Young, M. and P.Willmott (1957) *Family and Kinship in East London*, London: Routledge & Kegan Paul.

Part I

MEDIA POLICY

1

MEDIA POLICY

Premature obsequies?

Denis McQuail

At some point early in my association with Jeremy Tunstall, around the time of the Third Royal Commission on the Press (1974–7), when we were both engaged as researcher–advisers, I took particular note of one of his famous *obiter dicta*. This was to the effect that 'the press is a non-policy area'. The precise reference and words now escape me, but the thought has always remained with me, as a mental sparring partner if not necessarily as received wisdom. The final *Report* of the RCP (1977) certainly seemed to confirm the judgement, and it put an end, for a generation at least, to any realistic expectations that public policy could effectively intervene in the British newspaper system on behalf of some more or less political version of the public good. Looking further afield, it seems that by the end of the 1970s much the same situation applied also in other countries. In Canada, the Royal Commission on Newspapers (1982) largely followed the British example in defining the problems of loss of competition and inadequate public information, and in much the same way. It also commissioned a great deal of empirical research to back up the *Report*, which effectively did nothing to change things. In other European countries, including Germany, The Netherlands, Sweden and France we can observe a similar pattern of political concern followed by public debate and evidence gathering and, ultimately, *stasis* on the part of powerless political elites and unwilling political parties.

The outcome can be considered either a failure of political will and defeat for the public interest or the rescue of the newspaper press, which was saved from the threat of drastic intervention in its market freedom. The explanation may well lie embedded in Jeremy Tunstall's succinct remark which can be unpacked as suggesting that the goal of reforming the press was always illusory, politically naïve and ahistorical, in the sense of failing to take account of the history of the press.

My own understanding of the proposition is that it sums up the following points. First, that there is no sufficiently agreed goal or acceptable means for intervening with the rights of free publication enjoyed by newspaper owners.

Even if some general principles of freedom and diversity can be found as a common basis for policy, any means to promote independence from the organised power of owners would involve some measure of state control. Any effective move to ensure newspaper diversity of content and ownership would involve some limits on the freedom to publish and would distort the market. Second, any attempt to implement effective control over the press would face such powerful resistance from the press that the risks, real or imagined, would seem to render the effort suicidal or fatally divisive for any political party or administration. Third, the history of the press as enshrined in its own mythology and belief, as well as in various established rights and privileges, simply could not accommodate the kind of government control or regulation which would deliver 'reform', assuming one agreed on the goals. It would be impossible to find an acceptable redefinition of the relationship between a free press and political power that could satisfy the aspirations of would-be reformers of the press.

Although there are strong commonsensical underpinnings for the view that the press is beyond the scope of policy, one could make an equally strong case for the view that the press remains very much within the scope of politics and in some sense is inescapably politicised. We might even coin an aphorism to the effect that a politics-free press is unthinkable. This could be a response to those who seriously pursue the goal of a depoliticised press under a variety of banners, including the aspiration to objectivity of news and comment, the establishment of broadcasting systems without political commitments, the triumph of the market over all other values. The fact that democratic political systems cannot effectively restrain the newspaper press by way of a framework of policy does not so much demonstrate the independence of the press from politicians as it reflects the total penetration and interconnection between the practice of the press and the world of politics. The press is a policy-free zone precisely because it is so entwined with politics. There is a distinct paradox here, and it is useful to expose it at the outset of any attempt to foresee the shape of the media politics to come, which is the aim of this essay.

THE CONTINUING DEBATE

Despite these remarks, which generally support the independence of the press from policy, and despite the experience of non-interventionism which has characterised the last two decades in Britain and elsewhere, there remain strong impulses in society 'to do something' about the alleged failings of the press and about its vulnerability in the face of market forces and global capitalism. These failings are not especially novel in kind. They refer to reduction of choice for readers, tendencies of sensationalism and personalization (together, 'tabloidization'), decline of attention to serious issues and displacement of serious journalism by gossip and entertainment. Intertwined with the simple logic of the argument that maximising profits inevitably requires minimising the costs of good reporting – and also appealing to simpler minds and baser instincts – was the criticism of increased concentration of ownership within and between media sectors. Tendencies towards monopoly were associated with less concern for readers, for abstract ideals and for professional standards of performance.

In the background, there was still a general anxiety about the relative failure of the press to dispel public ignorance (Lacey and Longman 1997) and to make a fair and useful contribution to the electoral process. On the wider European scene, the undoubted trend towards a more commercialised television landscape has also stimulated debate in the European Union and the Council of Europe about the options for *European* policy that would promote or protect diversity in the newspaper press.

These introductory remarks have sketched a scenario in which proponents of active and interventionist press policy appear to meet with conclusive defeat in the political arena, without the case being lost, on any but pragmatic grounds. The arguments on public interest grounds have remained strong, and have even been strengthened by events in global media developments, but the prospect of the attainment of policy goals has receded. Some observers would readily link all of this with the decline of public broadcasting (and thus public policy for broadcasting), giving rise to the argument that not only the press but the media in general constitutes (increasingly) a non-policy area. The underpinnings for this proposition are somewhat different from the arguments against intervention in the press, since they are derived from observation of deregulatory tendencies at work in broadcasting and telecommunications over the last decade-and-a-half. They also reflect the increasing scope of the free market in all matters to do with communications driven by global entrepreneurial ambitions.

FROM PRESS POLICY TO MEDIA POLICY

Although this chapter begins with remarks about the newspaper press in Britain, it has the wider purpose of considering the longer term prospects for media policy in general (somewhat less than all communications policy, although the two are inseparable). The main point is to examine the proposition that not only the press but communications in general are increasingly non-policy areas, especially because of trends towards *convergence* which make it increasingly difficult to maintain the traditional compartmentalisation of media sectors for purposes of policy and regulation. In the present context 'policy' refers specifically to projects of government and public administration which have particular goals and a certain legitimation in terms of the wider 'public interest'. Beyond this, policy projects are characterised by deploying

21

certain means in the form of regulatory or administrative measures that are legally binding, nationally or internationally.

The discussion that follows will largely leave to one side issues of property and other individual rights that are not specific to media and communication but have a much wider range (for instance, questions of copyright, privacy, damage to reputation). There is no claim that such matters are declining in importance, perhaps, indeed, the contrary. The proposition of decline in the range of media policy refers to matters of public purpose and society-wide impact. Its main import is that such policy projects are steadily less necessary, legitimate and practicable than they used to be. In relation to such a proposition three basic responses seem possible. One is to support by further argument and evidence, with indications of what will remain. Another is to reject it as an ideological assertion that, whether or not by design, can only further the interests of those who are opposed to public policy constraints on their activities, especially large commercial media concerns. A third possibility is to reject the proposition as a guide to future developments on the grounds that it has no general validity, but simply reflects the circumstances of time and place, and is descriptive rather than analytic. This will be the position taken here.

In order to take the matter further we need to sketch briefly the conventional, and widely received, version of the development and varied application of communication policy as it relates to established liberal democracies. This is most clearly to be found stated in Pool (1983) where a distinction is made between three regulatory 'regimes' applying to different spheres, defined primarily by communications technology. The first is that of print media, which is governed by guarantees of freedom of expression (absence of censorship in particular), subject only to other law. The print sector (books, newspapers, magazines, etc.) is characterised by voluntarism and private initiative, with the role of government or other authority kept to a minimum. In general, within this framework (which should really not be referred to as a 'regime'), neither the quality and the amount of what is published nor the structure and organisation of publishing are directly the concern or responsibility of government. The main purpose of public policy in relation to print media is to safeguard the right to freedom of publication. As we shall see, this particular role has given rise to some legitimate grounds for intervention in the economic and structural arrangements of the newspaper press. This version of communication policy is strongly associated with the rise of democratic politics, and it reflects the historic part played by print media in challenging social, economic and ecclesiastic hegemony.

The second sphere of communications policy identified by Pool concerns what is now referred to as the telecommunications sector. In its early phase, in the late nineteenth and the early twentieth century, it comprised of telegraphy, wireless and telephony. These means of communication were also generally defined as 'common carriers', along the model established even earlier by postal services. They were essentially technologies of transmission made available to private (or public) users for their own purposes of communication. Public policy was concerned with regulation of ownership, structure, rights of access and public availability, but not with content. The goals of policy were mixed, but included mainly the speedy development of efficient communication services, especially for purposes of the state and for business. The communication services based on these new electronic technologies were treated generally in the same way as the public utilities of water and power that rapidly came to be regarded as necessities for cities. They also shared some of the attributes of 'natural monopolies', that is to say, most efficient for the consumer when organised on a monopoly basis.

The third regulatory regime (in this case an appropriate term) applied first to wireless broadcasting in the 1920s and later to television. Despite differences between national versions of the regimes and changes over time, broadcasting policy retains many of the features of its early manifestations. There is strict regulation of access to communicators by way of licensing or franchising supervised by some government-appointed agency, restricted freedom of expression, usually some form of monopoly of organisation of provision, often rights of intervention and control retained by the state. Unlike the case with press or telecommunication, the content of what is broadcast has generally been considered to be in principle a matter of the public interest. However, the grounds of legitimation for broadcasting policy have always been mixed and variable. They include elements from both the earlier models relating to print and wireless/telephony, for instance the need to regulate natural monopoly, the wish to secure the widest possible availability of services and to allocate access in a fair and democratic manner. They were also motivated by efforts to secure benefits to the state and society from the enormous and varied potential of the communication media.

By comparison, somewhat new in the underpinnings of broadcasting policy were ideas of protecting society from potential harm as a result of undesirable media influences which could be amplified by the scale of distribution and the believed impact of the audio-visual media in particular. The origins of these widely held ideas are probably to be found both in the experience of another medium, the film, and also in the uses being made of the then (early twentieth-century) new means of 'mass' communication for propaganda, advertising and mass entertainment. The factor of 'massification' was an essential ingredient in the perception of media during the early twentieth century, and its influence has not yet been extinguished, despite the alleged decline of mass media.

Although this tripartite division and delineation of policy frameworks has proved useful in describing the media landscape in a summary way, and to some extent in analysing trends, it has its limitations. It does not account adequately for important variations between countries and historical circumstances, nor does it distinguish between different uses and purposes of the different media. It does not really have a logic of progression from one 'stage' or 'phase' to another. As Winseck (1998) argues, the 'divergence' of media policy regimes, although seeming to follow demarcation lines based on technology with some logic, is not actually a *consequence* of technology. There is no intrinsic reason for the variations in the degree of freedom, which mattered so much to Pool, or for the strict allocation of different means of communication to different types of control mechanism. Accident and historical circumstance rather than conscious policy seem to account for the separating out of policy regimes. This is not to say that there is no logic or rationale for some fundamental differences (for instance between the freedom of broadcasters and newspapers to express their views), only that there is no single logic and certainly not a technological one.

A FRAMEWORK FOR POLICY

It is useful to consider different media within a common framework, according to a variety of possible policy objectives and in their different component activities. For instance, the three main kinds of media discussed above comprise at least three main elements. There are elements of infrastructure (physical plant, equipment, etc.); there are organised processes of distribution, in which issues of access as senders and receivers arise, as well as questions of efficiency and scale; there are different kinds of service (essentially matters of the content carried). Looked at in this way, the lines between the technologies are not so clear, and they are becoming less clear or justifiable, as Pool (1983) observed. It has become commonplace to speak of a growing 'convergence' of technologies, especially because of the ubiquity and multi-purpose character of computer-driven telecommunications media. In a discussion of policy we should also note the variation in objectives as far as the general public or the wider interest of society is concerned.

In their proposal for a new and more integrated general model for communications policy, Van Cuilenburg and Slaa (1993) distinguished, along the lines indicated above, between infrastructure, transport services (essentially distribution systems) and 'information services'. The latter refer generally to all kinds of content, ranging from data through news to entertainment of all kinds. They also suggested that 'information services' should be distinguished by the mode of communication involved and not just by the 'function' as seen by the user (e.g. information, education, entertainment). The modes of communication proposed are based on the earlier model of Bordewijk and Van Kaam (1986) which identified four different kinds of information traffic flow. These are:

- *allocution*, meaning all forms of centre–peripheral distribution of messages, typified by 'mass communication', and thus including both the newspaper press and broadcasting;

- *consultation*, referring to information sources that are accessed selectively by 'users' in search of specific kinds of information, with a primary reference to electronic sources, but also overlapping with some traditional media, such as newspapers;
- *conversation*, meaning all kinds of interactive media, but especially telephone-based services and other interactive forms using computers, cable or satellite; and
- *registration*, referring to the central collection of data about information flows and other uses in a given network.

This way of classifying information services breaks the traditional link made for purposes of regulation between certain kinds of content and function of communication on the one hand and certain means of distribution ('transport services') and certain technologies on the other.

The message is not so much that media are converging on any one form, although that is one often heard prediction for the future, but that they are diversifying in their means of delivery as well as multiplying in their form and in the services they can offer. In these circumstances, the struggle to 'police' them effectively for some goal of public policy seems destined to fail, since the instruments of policy cannot focus clearly either on a technology, or on a particular use, or even on a particular definition of user (e.g. a private person or a public body).

The general aim of public policy is to serve some version of the public interest or public good. Not surprisingly there are alternative versions of what this consists in, and insofar as any consensus can be reached on the matter within the political arena, this changes over time. It is useful, here, to refer also to Van Cuilenburg and Slaa's 1993 triparpite division of the public interest into issues of political welfare, social and cultural welfare and economic welfare, respectively. Each of these can be defined in different ways, but in general the first refers to the communications requirements of the democratic system including freedom of expression, the second to social integration, identity and expression, while the third relates to efficiency in delivering services and producing wider economic benefits in terms of employment and profit. The relative importance attaching to these issues is often contested and the balance of argument has shifted from time to time. Advances in technology and changes in social communication systems continually shift the content of goals, the criteria for attainment and the terms of policy debates (Van Cuilenburg and McQuail, 1998).

PHASES OF POLICY

In the earliest phase of communications policies, especially as they related to telegraph and wireless telephony, the political functions of communications were largely unrecognised and unregulated. The assumption was that the medium for overtly political communication should be the printed newspaper, for which there was no policy (at least, not in North America and the more liberal European regimes) except freedom from censorship and subjection to the rule of law. Very soon after its emergence in the mid 1890s, the cinema was subject to regulation and generally treated in a similar way to the theatre and other public entertainments and shows. The main aim of public policy for the cinema was to prevent the potential harm to morals and the young by way of various forms of censorship and control, often operated on a local or city basis. Pressure groups of churches and concerned citizens led the way. This was the forerunner of much subsequent social–cultural policy.

Policy in relation to the electric telegraph, telephony and wireless, on the other hand, from the start had a primarily economic character, although it was mixed with statist, hence also political, goals. In the United States, the telegraph rapidly developed into a private monopoly, largely owned by Western Union. Telephony, when it arrived, was also all but monopolised (Sussman 1997). Aside from brief wartime intervals, this model of government-regulated private monopoly was the core of early communications policy in the United States. The emphasis was on private ownership, and regulation was prompted more by general anti-trust sentiment and support for competition rather than by a vision of service to the public interest. What was good for capitalism was good for America. The main alternative model was to be found in Europe. In Britain, all telegraph services were reserved by law for the Post Office as early as 1868 and a similar pattern was followed in Germany, France, The Netherlands and Sweden. Aside from minor experiments and deviations, much the same can be said of telephony. The European policy was to make the telegraph and telephony, along with postal services, a public monopoly and effectively a branch of government. Wireless communication, in its turn, followed the same path, in the early twentieth century.

Even in countries firmly dedicated to capitalism, state monopoly was regarded as the best way to serve the national interest (as defined by the state itself). The electronic media were seen as engineering and infrastructure too strategically essential to the state and to industry to be left to the uncertainties of the free market, and not at all as elements in a consumer society. They were also generally regarded as either 'non-political' or outside the realm of democratic political debate, a perception supported by their status as branches of the civil service. Despite important differences, both the US and the European model shared certain broad features, especially when the medium of wireless broadcasting in its early (pre-Second World War) form is included in the picture.

First of all, different branches of media (film, press, telephony, broadcasting, wireless–telegraphy) were kept apart and subjected to medium-specific regulation. Second, some media were treated as branches of industry and regulated on economic grounds, while others were treated as primarily social–cultural in function (although America and Europe divided on this). Third, all communications media were treated as in some respect of strategic importance (including their potential for propaganda) and were subordinated to considerations of national interest. Although the situation changed with respect to radio in the 1930s, the field of communications policy was treated mainly according to either a technical–administrative or a commercial logic, rather than as something for democratic political debate. The policy terrain was effectively depoliticized.

A new phase of media and communications policy can be said to have opened after the Second World War and it was dominated by socio-political rather than economic concerns. There are several origins for this turn. One is the more collectivist and socially conscious spirit of the times, stimulated in part by a reaction to the Depression and the War, but also to a maturation of social democratic political tendencies. This maturation process involved a more adequate evaluation of the significance of mass media for political and social life in 'mass democracy'. Early twentieth-century experience taught lessons about the power of propaganda not only in totalitarian society but also in capitalist societies dominated by large companies with 'press barons' as their allies.

In respect of broadcasting, the spirit of social reform, encouraged by post-war reconstruction, emphasised the positive social benefits of broadcasting run for public service goals, as well as offsetting the unfair political bias of capitalist newspapers. On the continent of Europe, the end of the Second World War provided the opportunity and sometimes the necessity for reconstructing the entire media system on more democratic lines after war, occupation and dictatorship. Even the once-sacred print medium could legitimately be brought within the scope of policy. The general spirit of the time was favourably disposed to progressive change and to social planning in all spheres of life.

The ideas needed to give shape to policy were already available, especially in the form of earlier democratic theories of the press, including a critique of monopoly capitalist control. The early phase of public service broadcasting, which emphasised social and cultural objectives rather than entertainment or profit, helped considerably to extend the scope of policy. Further ideas were provided by the influence of the 1947 American Commission on Freedom of the Press (Hutchins 1947). This made a clear link for the first time between freedom of the press and 'social responsibility', meaning an obligation to provide trustworthy and relevant news and information as well as opportunities for diverse voices to be heard in the public arena (Siebert et al. 1956). The idea that freedom of expression carried some kind of social duty was controversial and resisted by newspaper owners, but it was nevertheless influential in affecting the longer term climate of opinion. In the United States this made it easier for the controlling body of broadcasting, the FCC, to impose the requirements of fairness and diversity. The promotion of the virtues of 'freedom' in the context of the Cold War and the global battle for hearts and minds also made the notion of a democratic and public-spirited policy more acceptable within an ideology of free enterprise.

In Europe, the traditional political bias of newspapers coupled with growing tendencies towards economic concentration in the post-war period provided the incentive for scrutinising the press, for example by the Royal Commission on the Press, 1947–9, in Britain or the Swedish Press Commission of 1972–5 (Hulten 1979). In several countries, pressure was brought to bear (by various means, including legislation) to promote diversity of ownership and content, limit monopoly and deal more effectively with complaints against the press. An emphasis on the *positive* freedom of the press was an important element in what Picard (1985) described as a 'democratic socialist theory of the press'.

Broadcasting was extremely controlled in its structure and content. For three decades after the Second World War, most European countries operated a public monopoly of radio and broadcasting, with Britain the only significant (though partial) exception. Decisions about the expansion of broadcasting and its broad tasks were political decisions, and broadcasting became publicly accountable for the nature and quality of the services it provided, despite often having considerable editorial independence. The obligations laid on public service broadcasting generally involved the following elements:

- a commitment to universal service;
- diversity and representativeness of content in political, social and cultural terms;
- democratic accountability;
- public financing and non-profit goals.

Broadcasting policy began to change from the mid-1970s. It became increasingly preoccupied with the financing and viability of public broadcasting, with preserving or removing its monopoly status and with the problems of incorporating new media developments into existing systems of regulation (McQuail and Siune 1986).

In the post-war phase, media policy had largely bypassed the common carrier/conversational media. The dominant media policy paradigm was shaped by normative concerns relating especially to the needs of democracy. Policy was also national in character, bounded in its range by the territory of the state and the sovereign within it. Far-reaching government intervention was justified by social, cultural and political needs, as democratically decided. The emphasis was on the role of the media and communications in public life, and substantive issues of content were considered within the boundaries of debate.

It is becoming more and more apparent that this phase of policy is over, although there is no final date to be assigned to it and important elements of social–cultural policy are still in force and have even been transferred to the international level. The key steps in the transition have been:

- a process of deregulation spreading from the USA to Europe and further;
- the commercial exploitation of significant new media and key elements of old media (broadcasting in particular);
- deregulation and privatisation of telecommunications monopolies;
- ramifying tendencies of the globalization of media structures and flows.

The fall of communism made its own significant contribution to a changed global climate concerning communications policy, since the Third World lost one of the supports in its resistance to global capitalist media. Many of the changes have been contested in the spirit of normative expectations about the political and cultural roles of the media. However, the ground has shifted too far and it is widely agreed that policy has (once again) to be dominated by technical and economic considerations, with an inevitable geo-political dimension (McQuail and Siune 1998). The post-war era can be seen not as an aberration but maybe as exceptional in terms of the relative stability of national societies and the world-order as well as stable in terms of technology. It witnessed the steady rise to maturity of two dominant and nation-based communications media – the newspaper press and television broadcasting – and its conclusion coincides with their decline.

TOWARDS A NEW POLICY PARADIGM?

The historical sketch just offered of policy changes in terms of successive periods might seem an invitation to sketch a third 'phase' that we have now entered and which can, in turn, be characterised in terms of its key elements. However, it would be mistaken to suppose that there is any clear logic to the transition from one phase to another that could guide such an exercise. But the accumulation of experience over a century does present us with some guidelines concerning the components of any new paradigm and how they will be related to the politics of communications. In particular, it has been instructive to look back at the earlier, pre-normative, phase of development of 'telecommunications'. In some respects, the early history has had to be replayed, but against an entirely different background, with new political ideas and social values. Once again there are new and powerful technologies with unclear potential for development, vast commercial and industrial interests at stake, governments struggling to keep abreast of change. Again, it has become appropriate to let the market drive development itself, while politics tries to hold the reins of the market in this sector.

Currently, governments are generally very aware of (national) interests in exploiting the employment and revenue benefits of the expanding markets in hardware and software. Globalisation is helping to drive expansion but has not significantly reduced the role of national communications policies, since national governments, along with national and multinational corporations, are still the main actors in the policy arena. Corporations want to develop new international markets and also to expand and merge by crossing old regulatory frontiers. Governments are retreating from regulation where it interferes with market development and giving increasing priority to economic over social–cultural and political welfare when priorities have to be set. The weakening and transformation of normative commitment can proceed only as far as the political system allows, but there is a good deal of evidence to show that economic pragmatism and the re-evaluation of costs and benefits by political actors have given much room for change.

The emerging policy paradigm does not lack normative elements but they cover a wider range of values and are less exclusively supported by the normative underpinnings of democratic theory. The relevant norms are in fact noticeably more 'communicative' and less 'political' and 'cultural' in character. This remark depends on the conventional meanings of those terms, in which *culture* refers to the traditional art and language of a nation, region or group, while *politics* is defined in terms of the established political institution (especially public communication supports for elections, law-making and the practice of government).

The values that have been added to the spectrum of relevant norms, or given greater prominence, include especially:

- *openness* and *transparency* concerning private ownership and public control and regulation; *access* and *participation* in (interactive) communication flows;
- *choice* for users/consumers (instead of a guarantee of a basic minimum of universal provision);
- *competition* and *innovation* in technology and services;
- protection of *privacy* and *confidentiality*.

If one so chooses, one can interpret these 'new' values simply as extensions of older ones, especially those of freedom and equality. Certain other important principles have also kept their place in the spectrum of policy discourse. These include the principle of *accountability*, in the sense that virtually all forms of public communication are subject to scrutiny, debate and evaluation, even if formal mechanisms for accounting are absent or weak. Again, there is still likely to be an appeal to *national interest*, or claims made on its behalf, often with reference to cultural as well as material or strategic matters. There is no very good reason to suppose that under conditions of threatened or actual international conflict, communications systems would not be subject to supervision or intervention on grounds of national security. Fortunately, the conditions have not arisen to any significant degree in leading industrial countries. Furthermore, despite a steady erosion of taboos and a relaxation of standards in many aspects of sexual morality and its representation in media, there remain strong public and political pressures to maintain some powers of control, especially on areas where the welfare of minors is involved. Something similar can be said of the area of human rights, where racism or other forms of prejudice or symbolic harm are involved. Finally, the value placed on *diversity* of structure (ownership, control and content) has not diminished, although the dynamic of the expanding communications system on its own appears to make for considerable diversity.

There are also changes, and some older values are losing force. The main area of growing deficit in value terms seems to be in respect of 'social responsibility', public service and altruism (non-profit goals). The 'public interest' is being significantly redefined to encompass economic and consumerist values. At least from the perspective of political activists and the political elite, the media in general seem to be less inclined to respect and service the political process. The dominance of 'serious' political journalism and international reporting in the hierarchy of media esteem has diminished and the loss is often regretted by articulate and critical observers as well as by insiders. This particular change seems to go with a more widely observed phenomenon of disengagement from political activism and the decline of ideology. Together, these trends are likely to encourage the view that the media are escaping from the reaches of any effective 'policy'.

It is not easy to represent the emerging paradigm in a single framework. This is not only because the path of development of communications is still uncertain: it is because of the continuing contradictions and unresolved dilemmas facing policy making, not to mention the general uncertainty about the viability of *any* coherent national communications policy under present conditions. In addition, as I have noted, processes of convergence and divergence are at work, making it impossible to effectively compartmentalise the range of media or to single out any one sector, such as 'broadcasting' or the 'press', for special treatment.

This discussion has presupposed that the general goal of policy is still to serve the public interest, but what has mainly changed is the balance of component values that shapes the definition of the public interest. In general, it can be suggested that economic welfare has risen in salience in comparison with political welfare and that social cultural welfare has been redefined with greater reference to values that touch on the communications process itself, its opportunities and its potential consequences. These include more equal chances to participate in communication flows, protection from the dangers of intrusion, loss of confidentiality, openness to manipulation and even surveillance. In relation to democratic politics, the emphasis has shifted from trying to safeguard the vertical flows of politicians to electors or the horizontal flows of political elites to encouraging active and more autonomous flows with citizen groups and from citizens to potential leaders.

31

The quandaries and unanswered questions that arise for policy makers include the following:

- whether to promote market dynamics or stability:
- what balance to maintain between the roles and the extents of public and private sectors;
- how to finance whatever public sector;
- which policy instruments to use for what purpose (as between economic interventions, legal/regulatory moves, public and political pressure, self-regulation and other initiatives generated by the system itself);
- whether and how far to direct policy and control at content or at structure;
- whether to seek a coherent policy for all sectors or to redraw the map in a new way;
- whether to concentrate or disperse regulatory power (and policy making itself);
- whether to maintain the national policy or to enter into wider – international – regulation agreements;
- how to maintain ultimate political control without government intervention.

Only when the answers to some of these questions of choice become clearer in a given context will it be possible to be precise about the policy paradigm that is likely to apply in a given country. No doubt there will be several variants, depending on such factors as size, the relative share of the information and communications sector in the national economy and the general political climate. It is likely that countries related culturally or economically, for instance by membership of the European Union, will have similar policy projects.

The issue of whether policy will or should converge, following the logic of technology, by choosing the same goals and applying the same principles and means, within some sort of unified regulatory apparatus (as suggested, e.g., by Collins and Murroni 1996) will probably not be answered by a simple Yes or No. There are reasons for redrawing boundaries, but not an imperative to have only one regime for different kinds of service. There are also reasons for having a coherent set of principles (especially on matters to do with freedom and diversity), but this does not mean that all kinds of content (advertising, art, news, pornography, etc.) have to be treated equally. Distinctions of content and audience reached remain. It is also possible, even necessary, to use different means for different purposes. It is important in the interests of freedom not to concentrate too much power over communication in any single body, and there must always be exceptions and alternative routes to follow, as well as different courts of appeal.

CONCLUSION

As was emphasised at the outset, there is a paradoxical interaction between politics and policy. Any sphere of social life as crucial as communications is likely to be extensively politicised in one way or another. Certainly, there will be intense debate, and policy projects will form part of the struggle between opposing interest groups – which, one hopes, encompass also the needs of ordinary citizens. But apparent gaps or failures in policy can also reflect the intensity of political struggle. The lighter regulation of many of the emerging media and communications activities is just as much a reflection of politics at work as was the rather effective and complete framework of policy for electronic media that we seem to be leaving behind. The outcome of this excursion is to deny any axiomatic or universal status to the view that the media constitute a non-policy area. Sometimes this will apply, but public communication is never going to be a non-political area, however much it seems to diverge from the older model of the politicised system that characterised the newspaper press.

REFERENCES

Bordewijk, J. L. and Van Kaam (1986) 'Towards a new classification of tele-information services', *Intermedia* 14(1): 11–21.

Collins, R. and C. Murroni (1966) *New Media: New politics*, Cambridge: Polity Press.

Hulten, O. (1984) *Mass Media and State Support in Sweden*, Stockholm: Sweden Books.

Hutchins, R. (1947) *A Free and Responsible Press: Commission on Freedom of the Press*, Chicago: University of Chicago Press.

Lacey, C. and D. Longman (1997) *The Press as Public Educator*, Luton: University of Luton Press.

McQuail, D. and Siune, K. (eds) (1986) *New Media Politics*, London: Sage.

McQuail, D. and Siune, K. (eds) (1998) *Media Policy: Convergence, Concentration and Commerce*, London: Sage.

Picard, R. G. (1985) *The Press and the Decline of Democracy*, Westport, CT: Greenwood Press.

Pool, I. de Sola (1983) *Technologies of Freedom*, Cambridge, MA: Harvard University Press.

Royal Commission on the Press (1977), *Report*, Cmnd 6180, London: HMSO.

Royal Commission on Newspapers (1982) *Report*, Ottawa: Canadian Government Publishing Centre.

Siebert, F. S., T. Patterson and W. Schramm (1956) *Four Theories of the Press*, Urbana: University of Illinois Press.

Sussman, G. (1977) *Communication, Technology, and Politics in the Information Age*, Thousand Oaks, CA: Sage Publications.

Van Cuilenberg, J. J. and D. McQuail (1998) 'Media policy paradigm shifts' in R. Picard (ed.) *Evolving Media Markes*, Turku, Finland: the Economic Research Foundation for Mass Communication, 57–81.

Van Cuilenburg, J. J. and P. Slaa (1993) 'From media policy towards a national communications policy', *European Journal of Communication* 8(2): 149–76.

Winseck, D. (1998) 'Pursuing the Holy Grail: information highways and media reconvergence in Britain and Canada', *European Journal of Communication* 13(2): 337–74.

2

PRESS REFORMISM 1918–98

A study of failure

James Curran

INTRODUCTION

The history of *broadcast* reformism in Britain could well be subtitled a 'study of success' (Curran 1998). In contrast, the record of press reformism has been one of failure. This chapter examines what press reformers have sought to achieve over an eighty-year period; how their aspirations have been mediated by public enquiries; and, above all, why their efforts have been frustrated at almost every turn.

LIBERTARIAN LEGACY

The politics of the press is strongly influenced by a selective understanding of its past. Especially in the early twentieth century, it was commonplace for popular books about the *contemporary* press to refer back to an heroic struggle against the state, beginning with the battle against print censorship and ending gloriously with the abolition of the 'taxes on knowledge' in the nineteenth century (e.g. Dibblee 1913; Symon 1914). This simple view of the past – now widely contested by historians[1] – celebrated the press' emancipation from official control. From this was derived a simplistic conclusion: the freedom of the press is constituted by the absence of government restraint.

The other foundation-stone of the libertarian tradition is a view of the press as a public champion or fourth estate. The press had won special legal privileges in the nineteenth century by presenting itself as a 'popular' institution in Britain's emergent democratic system. This self-portrayal had sometimes assumed a grandiose form, in which it was claimed that the press was more representative than was parliament, and the market was more democratic than the elective system (Boyce 1978). While fustian versions of this theory never really took hold, a residual version did. This argued simply that the press holds governments to account through the disclosure of information and the expression of public opinion (again, an over-simple view that is regularly contested or qualified in the sociology of the press).[2]

From these two sources, political theory and history, there emerged a composite perspective. This asserted both that a free press empowers the people and that government has always been the enemy of press freedom. These two arguments passed into the bloodstream of British political culture. For example they were invoked, in the period 1940–3, not only in protest meetings and the annual conference of the TUC but in the debates of the civil service, parliament and even the cabinet (Curran and Seaton 1997). These two themes appealed to different groups, for different reasons. They reflected a dissenting tradition suspicious of established authority. They were under-written by orthodox Whig history. They were supported by the cautionary experience of totalitarian repression abroad. They related to folk memories of the struggle for mass democracy. In short, these two arguments cannot be dismissed simply as the self-regarding discourse of journalists who wanted to view themselves as tribunes of the people; nor can they be discounted as merely the special pleading of an institution which sought a privileged constitutional status as 'untouchable'. They had roots in libertarian–radical as well as libertarian conservative thought, and resonated in the culture and collective experience of British society.

Out of this tradition emerged a political consensus that the best press policy was to have no policy. In this way, it was argued, the press could be insulated from the dangerous attentions of government. Indeed, even an utterance of public criticism of the press was viewed with suspicion as a possible prelude to 'political interference'. 'Attacks, open and veiled, on the Press', warned the respected liberal journalist, A. J. Cummings, 'are an essential part of a general campaign in high places against liberty of thought' (Cummings 1936: 122).

CONTESTED LEGACY

The 'no policy' consensus prevailed throughout the inter-war period, sustained by press propaganda. But while the press was the principal source of ideas about itself, its fourth-estate rhetoric was challenged from four different directions.

Much the most damaging attack came from Stanley Baldwin, when he was the leader of the Conservative opposition. It was caused by the growing dealignment between the Conservative press and the Party, which had resulted in formerly loyal papers not only campaigning against Baldwin but backing right-wing protest groups and a new political project, the United Empire Party. In set-piece speeches in 1930–1, Baldwin denounced the 'harlot' press barons, Beaverbrook and Rothermere, as political adventurers who were corrupting the press (Jenkins 1988; Middlemas and Barnes 1969). The newspapers under their command, he declared, were 'engines of propaganda for the constantly changing policies, desires, personal wishes, personal likes and dislikes of two men', and employed 'direct falsehood, misrepresentation, half-truths . . . alteration . . . and suppression . . . ' to further their capricious purpose (*The Times*, 18 March 1931 cited PEP 1938: 179).

Baldwin's attacks caused a sensation, and passed into collective political memory. However, they were a targeted and contained assault, not on the press as an institution but on two prominent publishers. Significantly, his criticisms were not linked to a political programme of press reform. Moreover, the open hostilities that had prompted the attacks gave way to a more harmonious relationship between the press and the Conservative leadership (Koss 1984), culminating in the tacit co-option of much of the press in support of the Conservative government's appeasement policies in the late 1930s (Cockett 1989). One key source of press criticism was thus mollified.

The other significant institution to criticise the press was the Labour movement. Its central theme was that the press was owned by millionaires, who used newspapers to support 'the interests of the capitalist class' (Labour Research Department 1922: 47). However, O'Malley argues, in an illuminating essay, that its fundamentalist criticism was combined with weak solutions. The main ways, he claims, that the Labour movement hoped to change the press were by raising educational standards, so that people would demand something better, and through 'voluntary activity by Labour movement supporters and journalists' (O'Malley 1997: 138).

This is to overlook an influential group within the Labour Party, which was committed to major legislative reform. It included Beatrice and Sidney Webb (1920) who argued that individual and joint-stock ownership of the press should be replaced by consumer co-operative ownership under democratic management; Sir Norman Angell (1933) who advocated the establishment of a publicly owned press corporation; and Kingsley Martin (1947: 141) who argued that newspapers should be 'not commercial institutions but public concerns'. These were not fringe figures. Sidney Webb (later Lord Passfield) was a member of the first two Labour cabinets; Sir Norman Angell was a Labour MP who won the Nobel Peace Prize; Kingsley Martin was the editor of *New Statesman* for twenty-nine years. They were part of a formidable force on the Left, then publicly committed to a new form of social organisation of the press.

However, the leadership of the Labour movement opted for a more direct approach. The TUC bought the *Daily Herald* in 1922, and joined forces with a commercial publisher, Odhams, in 1929 to turn it into a mass circulation newspaper; the Co-operative movement acquired *Reynolds News* in 1929; and, in the 1940s, Labour won the support of two mass newspapers, *Daily Mirror* and *Sunday Pictorial*, without a dominant shareholder. Labour's excursion into mass journalism gave rise to a deflating internal debate about how socialism could be reconciled with what people wanted to read (Richards 1997). It also changed Labour's relationship with the press, making Labour a stakeholder in the system. In 1918, Labour had been confronted by an overwhelmingly hostile national press: by 1947, it was both a substantial publisher and had powerful press allies.

The third key source of criticism came from the 'progressive centre'. This challenged not the democratic credentials of the press but the shortcomings of its performance. Its main concern was that creeping commercialisation was leading to sensationalism, irresponsibility and the erosion of civic information. This was expressed in a number of publications written by senior journalists (e.g. Wickham Steed 1938; Harris 1943). However, its most powerful exposition came in a book-length report by Political and Economic Planning (PEP 1938), which stands out both because of its intellectual quality and because it was published by an influential think-tank.

The report's reformist premiss was that 'the press, like the Bank of England, can only be defended as a private institution on condition that it acts in practice as a public one' (PEP 1938: 276). However, the press was not fulfilling its public role adequately. This led PEP to consider a number of legislative schemes, only to reject them on the grounds that 'if the ideal is accepted of a free press . . . then the press must be allowed to develop on its own lines . . . ' (PEP 1938: 268). This posed the problem of what to do with an institution that was partly failing but should not be regulated. The report's answer was to argue that

> progress depends far more upon such intangibles as better education and a heightened sense of responsibility than upon any structural or mechanical changes which can be given effect by national legislation or by administrative measures.
>
> (PEP 1938: 268)

However, recognising that verbal uplift was not enough, PEP came up with the idea of a voluntary press tribunal to hear readers' complaints, plus proposed improvements in the recruitment and training of journalists. It was a portent of things to come.

The other significant source of attack on the press was more unexpected. It took the form of criticism expressed through the National Union of Journalists (NUJ). The NUJ represented only a minority of journalists in the inter-war period (Christian 1980), but it was then a more effective campaigning organisation than it was to be later. The NUJ responded to the rise of the newspaper chains (and the insecurity it created among its members) by publicly attacking press concentration, the decline of independent papers and the debasement of journalistic standards (Mansfield 1943). Small but noisy, with a network of influential journalist MPs, it played a strategic role in securing the appointment in 1947 of the Royal Commission on the Press (Bundock 1957; O'Malley 1997).

This was the first official general enquiry into the press in the twentieth century, and it was greeted with angry protests from Fleet Street as an attack on press freedom. The 'above-politics' status of the press, its exclusion from public accountability, had been repudiated.

PROFESSIONALISING MOMENT

The 1940s was a period when the prestige of the professional middle class, and the associated belief in disinterested public service, were consolidated (Perkin 1989). This belief suffused the work of the first Royal Commission on the Press (RCP 1949). The other key factor influencing it was the desire of the new Labour administration to mitigate press hostility by appointing reassuring figures to serve on the Commission. This included people about whom even the strongly Conservative press baron Lord Camrose (1947: 2–3) enthused.

'Free enterprise', declared the Commission, 'is a prerequisite of a free press' (RCP 1949: 177). It opposed all reform proposals that 'interfered' with the free market, apart from an increased overseeing of press concentration. However, the Royal Commission was critical of some aspects of the press' performance. Its solution was to adopt a professionalising strategy. The quality of the press, it reasoned, depended on the quality of individual journalists: make them better educated, and they will produce more intelligent journalism. Foster a culture of public service, and the press will be less inaccurate, biased and irresponsible.

The Commission's principal way of engineering these changes was to recommend the establishment of a 'General Council of the Press', deriving its 'authority from the press and not from statute' (ibid.: 173). In view of what transpired, it is worth recording how this proposed new body was conceived. It was to be a dynamic centre of reform that would 'encourage the growth of a sense of responsibility and public service among all engaged in the profession of journalism' (RCP 1949: 174). Only one of its many functions would be to adjudicate public complaints. The Council would also improve methods of recruitment, education and training for journalists. It would offer professional leadership by censuring undesirable types of journalistic behaviour and developing a code of professional conduct. It would initiate, encourage and promulgate press research. It would concern itself with a wide variety of issues (including even journalists' pensions) affecting the quality, independence and integrity of the press. It would represent the press in the public arena. As an authoritative and independent body, its chairman would be appointed by the Lord Chief Justice and a senior law lord.

This professionalising strategy became part of a new political consensus. The idea of the 'Press Council' had come from the progressive centre, and had been endorsed by the NUJ. It was supported in 1949 by both the Labour government and the Conservative opposition. Even the Labour Left was, in a sense, in step with this professionalising approach. 'Creating a profession of journalism' was generally the main objective of its social ownership proposals (Martin 1947: 142; cf Webb and Webb 1920: 271).

However, a professionalising strategy clashed with the libertarian culture of the press, which insisted on freedom from restraint,[3] even in a voluntary form. Controllers of the press simply ignored the clamour for reform, until a private member's Bill for a statutory press authority was moved in 1952 (Levy 1967). The Press Council was set up, unwanted by the industry, in 1953.

Every single public body that has examined the Press Council (and its successor) has been scathingly critical. In 1962, the second Royal Commission on the Press (1962: 101) reached the damning conclusion that 'the Council as now constituted has not been able . . . to make any significant contribution to the solution of the broad problems which we are called upon to consider'. The third Royal Commission on the Press (1977: 198–9) reported: 'it is unhappily certain that the Council has so far failed to persuade the knowledgeable public that it deals satisfactorily with complaints against newspapers', a view that took account of the critical report of the Committee on Privacy (1972). In 1990, yet another Committee on Privacy (1990: 77) declared: 'we consider that the Press Council's poor image derives from its ineffectiveness'. Sir David Calcutt's follow-up enquiry (Calcutt 1993: 63) into its successor body, the Press Complaints Commission (PCC), argued that it 'has not proved itself to be an effective regulator', and went on to list a catalogue of failures.

Underlying these indictments were three basic problems. First, the Press Council and the PCC were ineffective because they lacked authority. They did not have the legal power to require evidence, impose fines or insist on the publication of corrections. They also lacked the moral authority needed to command compliance. This was because they were viewed by a significant part of the press industry as organisations whose main function was to placate politicians, and so prevent a still more serious assault on press freedom. This absence of consent gave rise to a recurrent cycle in the development of self-regulation: belated reform in response to external pressure, falling short of what was needed to be effective, followed by further criticism, pressure and ineffectual reform (RCP 1962; RCP 1977; Robertson 1983; Calcutt 1993; Tulloch 1998).

The second problem was that the Press Council and its successor were never fully independent. Their funding, procedures and appointments were controlled by the press, and favoured the press. Public (i.e. non-journalist) members were not introduced until 1963, and parity between public and press membership was delayed until 1978. Even then 'public' appointees continued to be selected by the industry.

Attempts to make the Press Council more autonomous in the late 1970s and the 1980s foundered due to press resistance. Some senior journalists took the view that non-professionals, with personal axes to grind, had no business making judgements about their work. By the 1980s, a number of leading newspapers were not only flouting but also ridiculing the Press Council's judgements (Chippendale and Horrie 1990; Committee on Privacy 1990).

The reinvention of the Press Council as the PCC in 1991 marked the abandonment of the attempt to make the Press Council more representative of the general public. The new body was set up, as both Tunstall (1996) and Tulloch (1998) argue, as an attempt to engineer a pact between the press and the powerful. Its members in 1997 consisted of four lords (connected, respectively, to the three main political parties and Buckingham Palace), three knights, one professor and one senior medical man. While the PCC upheld few complaints (a derisory 1 per cent in 1995), these included a significant number from prominent figures.

The third shortcoming of the Press Council was that it failed to play a formative role in fostering a public-service culture (in the sense of promoting an active commitment to the public interest, transcending the sectional concerns of press employers or employees). It played no part in the development of journalism training and education; nor did it systematically monitor the general performance of the press. It took thirty-seven years to publish a general code of conduct. All that the Press Council did, other than to adjudicate public complaints, was to develop from the 1960s onwards a low-key corporate role that included occasional pronouncements on ethical and freedom issues. Even this was largely abandoned when the Press Council was reincarnated as the PCC in 1991. It became simply a customer complaints' service, a far cry from the professionalising vocation to which it had been called with such wide-eyed hope by the first Royal Commission on the Press.

The other element of the public-service mission that the Commission advocated, in 1949, was a larger dose of education for journalists. Its arguments were repeated, with small variations, by the third Royal Commission on the Press in 1977 (RCP 1977). Both bodies thought that there should be more journalists who were university graduates, and both wanted journalists' training to be better organised. Above all, both wanted the training to have an educational element, and for it to fulfil professional, not merely industrial, objectives.

The Commissions' hopes of a streamlined national training scheme were never realised. The National Council for the Training of Journalists (NCTJ) was set up in 1952, but presided over a piecemeal and improvised system. The Printing and Publishing Industry Board, the third Commission's chosen instrument of reform, achieved little before it was closed down. Training provision actually became more fragmented in the 1990s (Bromley 1997). The NCTJ qualification did not become a universally respected yardstick of competence, as the third Commission had expected. Today it is possessed by only a minority of journalists (Delano and Henningham 1996).

Journalism training was not recast in a professional mould. Press employers steadfastly opposed the introduction of critical 'media theory', a liberal education or even the learning of creative skills. What they wanted was training that imparted basic skills (shorthand), relevent knowledge (law) and an unquestioning attitude. What they wanted was largely what they got (McBarnet 1979: Boyd Barrett 1980), until the student-led expansion of media studies at universities in the 1980s and 1990s.

This expansion was neither anticipated nor desired by the Royal Commissions (RCP 1949: 166; RCP 1977: 178), and was not managed to achieve a professionalising goal. Most people involved in the development of media studies, apart from ex-journalists teaching journalism practice, gave little thought to what might contribute to the improvement of the press.[4] Their main concern was with what was educationally 'sound', conceptually interesting and effective in recruiting students.

This version of planning gave rise to an innovative definition of media studies that was strongly influenced by the humanities, centred on the study of popular culture and non-vocational in orientation. It powerfully influenced the development of media studies around the world. But this positive outcome also had a negative side. Research into the press was neglected in favour of other media. Limited resources were allocated to journalism training (and where this happened at universities, it tended, to judge from Thomas' survey (1998), to ape the narrowness of training in technical colleges). Both media studies' departments and their graduates also encountered hostility from the press, with one respected organ declaring 'this paper regards a degree in media studies as a disqualification for the career of journalism' (*Independent*, 31 October 1996). Thus, a major investment was made in university media education without the participating universities acquiring an accepted role in supporting and interpreting the ideals of the profession of journalism.

Only the first and third Royal Commissions' hope that more journalists would be university educated was fulfilled (Tunstall 1996). Yet, their respective expectations of what would result from this were disappointed. Both Commissions, but especially the first, had exaggerated ideas of what education could achieve because they tended to view the shortcomings of the press as the product of the failings of individual journalists. What they failed to appreciate was the extent to which individual journalists are subject to pressures and constraints beyond their control.

This was partly, perhaps, because the first Royal Commission investigated the press at a time when commercial pressures had been greatly eased by newsprint rationing. These pressures returned when newsprint rationing was lifted, in 1956, and they have intensified as a consequence of the almost continuous decline in national newspaper circulation since 1957. They were given a further competitive edge by the launch of new papers in the 1980s, while the increasing casualisation of employment in the 1990s' made organisational demands more difficult to resist. Anti-professional tendencies also became stronger in the regional press due to editorial cost cutting, falling sales and the rise of freesheets (Franklin and Murphy 1991 and 1997).

The general consensus of the specialist literature is that editorial standards fell, especially in the 1980s (McNair 1996; Tunstall 1996, Curran and Seaton 1997; Franklin 1997; Franklin and Murphy 1997). This view is shared by the general public. In 1993, only 10 per cent thought that journalists could generally be trusted to tell the truth. This was a drop of almost half by comparison with ten years' earlier, and placed journalists at the bottom of fifteen groups in terms of public credibility, well below even politicians (Worcester 1998).

There can scarcely be a more telling indictment of the Press Commissions' professionalising project. Its failure is in striking contrast to what happened in the United States, where an approximately comparable body to the first Royal Commission on the Press, also in the 1940s, urged the press to perform 'a public service of a professional kind' (Commission on the Freedom of the Press 1947: 92). Its report set in motion an influential reform process that significantly changed the American press.

One key difference is that the professionalising project obtained the support of leading publishers in the United States, unlike Britain. This high-level sponsorship is reflected in the fact that about half of American newspapers now issue ethics' codes to their journalists (Jaehnig 1998). A second key difference is that most leading newspapers in the United States are local monopolies, whereas in the UK they compete in a cut-throat (if oligopolistic) national press. A public-service orientation was consequently easier to accommodate in the American market system (even though it was subject to commercial erosion in the 1990s) than in the British one. A third key difference is that American universities played a significant role in sustaining a professional culture in the American press, in contrast to their counterparts in Britain. American universities generated more informed press research; they seemed to be more successful in combining journalism training with education; and they developed a reciprocal dialogue with journalists.

All these different factors brought into being a rich literature of critical reflection about the American press. It is supported by brilliant historical scholarship (Schudson 1995), incisive legal analysis (Baker 1989), insightful sociology (Hallin 1994), influential insider attacks (Fallows 1996), thoughtful debate about the purpose of journalism (Glasser and Craft 1998) and admirable journals of self-criticism (*Columbia Journalism Review*). These reflect – and sustain – in the United States a vibrant public culture of journalism of a kind that reformers in Britain have failed to achieve.

SOCIAL MARKET MOMENT

If the first Royal Commission on the Press launched a professionalising strategy which faltered in Britain, the second Royal Commission (1961–2) offered a new beginning. It was appointed at the tail-end of the 'one-nation' Conservative ascendancy, when there was a shift towards greater market intervention by the government (Pollard 1969; Clarke 1996). This was supported by the growing influence of radical Keynsian analysis which argued that further intervention was needed in order to avert or reverse market failure.

The second Royal Commission drew heavily upon this analysis in its report, and in turn provided the data for a celebrated Keynsian essay (Reddaway 1963). The Commission's central argument was that the newspaper business has an inbuilt disposition towards closure and concentration due to the importance of scale economies in its production process. Typically, a large circulation newspaper can outspend its smaller rival on its 'first copy' (by employing, for example, more journalists), and yet spend less per copy sold due to its ability to spread its costs over a larger volume of production. This competitive advantage helps the strong to drive the weak to the wall. In addition, the local advertising market usually operates in a way that weakens the position of the market loser. 'The natural tendency', concluded the second Royal Commission (1962: 113), 'of the economic and financial factors affecting production and sale is to diminish the number of newspapers wherever competition is close . . . '. This explains why the trend since 1949 had been towards fewer newspapers, and increased press concentration.

The Commission almost split over what to do about this problem. The minority, consisting of the chairman and vice-chairman, believed that any subsidy scheme designed to help vulnerable newspapers was 'divorced from the political realities of a free society' (RCP 1962: 98), while the majority thought that there might come a time when selective intervention would be necessary. However, all agreed that this was best avoided in the short term due to 'the dangers of governmental interference with the Press which we think would follow from . . . artificial attempts to regulate the incidence of market forces' (RCP 1962: 98).

The third Commission (RCP 1974–7) replicated its predecessor's analysis, though with a different emphasis. There was, it concluded, an inbuilt tendency towards market instability in the press that had resulted in the acceleration of local press concentration. This was due partly to the importance of multi-title economies, and the competitive advantages of established press groups in launching successfully new publications (Hartley, Gudgeon and Crafts 1977), both arguments that had not featured strongly in its predecessor's report. On the other hand, the third Commission stressed that scale economies could be offset by market specialisation and corporate subsidy. New technology could also lower costs, although it would not alter the unequal relationship between weak and strong titles.

Although the third Commission was more optimistic than its predecessor, it was less adept at reconciling its disagreements. A minority of two members recommended a National Printing Corporation and a Launch Fund to assist the launch of new publications. The large majority opposed all support schemes, including those proposed by the Labour Party (1974) and radicals like Jeremy Tunstall (1977) and Hirsch and Gordon (1975), for preserving or extending press diversity. The Commission's objection was framed partly in terms of a libertarian principle which, if applied generally, would have required the privatisation of television, radio, libraries and education, as well as a counter-revolution in arts' and film policy (Curran 1978).

However, both the 1962 and 1977 *Reports* opposed the view that the best press policy was to have no policy. The 1962 Commission argued that special measures were needed because the press was central to the democratic process, and concentration of ownership had become a serious problem. This led to the introduction of a press monopoly law in 1965, which was subsequently incorporated into the 1973 Fair Trading Act. This requires government consent for all transfers of newspaper ownership if the total paid-for circulation of both parties concerned is more than 500,000. The third Press Commission argued that this law should be strengthened, but its advice was ignored.

Since press anti-monopoly legislation has been in existence for over thirty years, it is possible to make an informed assessment of its effectiveness. Between 1965 and 1993, 151 transfers of newspaper ownership gained approval, and only four (all relatively minor) were stopped.[5] Every major acquisition, such as Murdoch's purchase of *The Times* and *Sunday Times*, and the *Guardian's* purchase of the *Observer*, was waived through. Governments were reluctant to antagonise powerful media groups by blocking their expansion, and allowing an acquisition to go ahead often seemed the best way of saving an ailing newspaper.

More success initially attended attempts to limit media cross-ownership. Economic ties between press, television and radio were reduced as a consequence of successive franchise awards, a process formalised by the relatively strict controls that were established by the 1990 Broadcasting Act. However, progress was thrown into reverse when the largest press publisher in Britain, Rupert Murdoch, was allowed to win control of the merged British satellite broadcaster, BSkyB, in 1990 on the specious grounds that it was a non-domestic satellite service. Lobbying by the Media Industry Group, representing the major media corporations, secured subsequently a relaxation of cross-ownership rules through the deregulating 1996 Broadcasting Act. This led in turn to increased joint-ownership of press and television.

In brief, the social market approach did not work in Britain. It resulted in press anti-monopoly legislation that was ineffective and cross-media ownership controls that were lowered in response to industrial pressure. However, it cannot be inferred from this that policies designed to make press markets work in the public interest are inherently flawed. Again, what is striking is that an approach which failed in Britain nonetheless succeeded elsewhere.

In Sweden, economists drew upon the same radical Keynsian theory – especially Penrose (1959) – as the second Royal Commission on the Press to make a broadly similar case that there is an inbuilt disposition towards contraction and concentration in the press industry. This work provided the rationale for the introduction of a selective subsidy system in 1970 (Gustafsson 1980 and 1995). This now takes the form, primarily, of a graduated production subsidy for newspapers, with a less than 40 per cent penetration of their respective markets, and financial support for rival newspapers that cut costs by sharing distribution.

This support system has succeeded in preserving a vigorous minority political press and, in 1997, a choice of local paper in twenty regions of Sweden (Gustafsson and Hulten 1997). One reason why it has been more successful than the British approach is that it has addressed the *cause* of market failure, the unequal competitive relationship between newspapers, rather than merely treating its *symptoms* through monopoly controls.[6] While this has involved a greater degree of market intervention than has been acceptable in Britain, it has not resulted in government control of the Swedish press. The Swedish Press Subsidies Board has representatives from all the major parties; it allocates subsidies according to agreed, automatically applied, critieria; and these help to preserve critical papers on the Right as well as the Left. The system – initially viewed with suspicion when it was introduced by a Social Democratic government – now enjoys consensual support in Sweden.

Yet, this is merely one variant of a selective subsidies' approach that has been introduced to sustain press diversity in France, Norway, Finland, Austria and The Netherlands, among other countries (Santini 1990; Host 1991; Lichtenberg 1995; Humphreys 1996; Brants and McQuail 1997; Skogerbo 1997; Murschertz 1998). Arguably, the most successful of these is that in Norway because it has encouraged the establishment of new papers. Instead of functioning solely as a life-support machine for a threatened minority press, it has helped to introduce new blood.

CONSERVATIVE MOMENT

The *Report* of the third Royal Commission on the Press (1977) was framed at the tail-end of liberal corporatism, when a Labour government had largely abandoned Keynsian management (Panitch and Leys 1997), and the public had moved to the Right (Crewe 1988). Yet, even from the outset, the Commission gave every indication of going nowhere. Its early meetings, recalled Jeremy Tunstall, a senior academic adviser, were 'rambling and uninformed', and usually took place on Friday afternoons, 'not perhaps the most wide-awake time of the week' (Tunstall 1980: 137–8). 'At the centre of operation', continues Tunstall, 'was an atmosphere of shoulder-shrugging' in which the Commission failed to define policy objectives that could be explored and researched. In the event, the Commission followed uncertainly in the footsteps of its predecessors, supporting both a professionalising and an anti-monopoly strategy. As we have seen, it was no more successful in doing this than they had been.

The third Commission's only original contribution was to propose a press charter that was intended to secure, initially through voluntary agreement, a press environment which would foster freedom of expression. The charter arose from a publishers' campaign against the union closed-shop, and contained detailed prohibitions against union influence. However, in one important respect the Commission did not follow the publishers' line: it acknowledged in principle that journalists should have some protection from publishers. This propelled the Commission into deep waters from which it hastily retreated. Internal democracy, it declared, was 'a complex and disputed subject' about which it was unable to 'express a view' (RCP 1977: 227).

The Commission's press charter was quietly dropped, partly perhaps because it was not totally orthodox. In effect, it questioned whether press freedom resides exclusively in the property rights of publishers and is secured solely through freedom from government restraint. Press freedom also had something to do, it suggested, with the freedom of people who edit and work on newspapers. The Commission did not fully clarify its own position in relation to this, nor think through its implications. But other people have explored this idea further, and have advanced detailed proposals for changes in the law, management structure or economic organisation of the press designed to increase editors' and staffs' freedom and control (Williams 1966: Ascherson 1978; Baistow 1985; Keane 1991; Curran 1995; Curran and Seaton 1997). In effect, the third Commission flagged up – but failed to develop – a third main strategy of press reform.

REACTION

No Royal Commission on the Press has been appointed in the last two decades. This reflects a sea-change in British politics that has diminished the opportunities for press reform.

Between 1979 and 1997, successive Conservative governments were elected that were committed to free-market policies. When the pendulum eventually swung back to Labour, it was to a reformed Party committed to a pro-market approach. The ascendancy of neo-liberalism thus curtailed the prospect of social-market reform (save perhaps in the form of disbursement of Lottery money).

The introduction of new print technology in the mid-1980s also eased concern about press concentration. It increased the profitability of newspapers, and led to the launch, between 1985 and 1988, of six new national titles.[7] However, all of these either closed down or were acquired by a large press group. Press concentration remained more advanced in Britain than in any other country of the European Union, apart from Ireland (European Commission 1992). But an impression was cultivated that the market had loosened up, and no longer needed repair.

Wider changes extinguished the weak impetus towards internal democratisation of the press. The 1980s and 1990s strengthened the 'right to manage'. The main bodies contesting this right – trade unions – were decisively defeated in the press (Tunstall 1996), as they were in the economy as a whole (Kavanagh 1987). The chain of events that had led to the 1977 Bullock Report, *Industrial Democracy*, belonged to a vanished era when trade unions were part of a corporatist system of government, and the climate of opinion at least cautiously entertained (but did little to advance) the idea of participation in the workplace (Crouch 1982).

Yet, as we have seen, the professionalising strategy for reform of the press had been sidelined. Indeed the reform approach that seemed most likely to succeed for a time was the introduction of new legal controls over the press, in a possibly authoritarian form. There was growing public dissatisfaction with tabloid intrusion and inaccurate reporting, which found expression in the 1980s and 1990s in private members' Bills for the right to reply or for privacy protection. To this public indignation were added the fears and resentments of politicians who were on the receiving end of a sustained press attack on their probity and private lives during the mid-1990s. Just how potentially restrictive this mixture of elite fear and public anger could be was indicated by the Calcutt Report (Calcutt 1993). This proposed the establishment of a press tribunal, made up of government appointees, which would have the power to exercise pre-publication censorship of the press in accordance with a professional code which they drew up. Fortunately, this proposal was rejected in the end by all political parties.

There also developed in the 1990s a growing reaction against the authoritarianism of the Thatcherite period. This found a voice in a constitutionalist movement, mobilised by Charter 88, which advocated the introduction of new checks on executive power. Strengthened press freedom was viewed as part of this strategy (Seaton 1991).

The politics of the press thus came to be shaped by two opposed currents in the late 1990s, seeking both to diminish and to extend legal controls on the press. These will result in a new legal settlement for the press. The Labour administration elected in 1997 is publicly committed to incorporating the European Convention on Human Rights into British law, and introducing a Freedom of Information Bill. The first measure will provide qualified protection for privacy, while the second will increase access to currently restricted public information. In effect, freedom of the press will contract in one area and be extended in another.

CAUSES OF FAILURE

The most striking thing about press reforming activity in Britain is how little it has accomplished. It has not successfully fostered a public-service culture among journalists comparable to that in the United States. Nor has it brought into being a subsidy system for minority publications, as in much of northern Europe. All that has been achieved so far is a system of self-regulation which does not work and press monopoly legislation that is ineffectual.[8]

This failure is not simply a consequence of the Conservative political dominance of the 1980s and early 1990s. It is a failure that both predates and postdates this ascendancy, and is to be explained by the conjunction of a number of factors that go back in time.

Publishers have been implacably opposed to most kinds of press reform most of the time. Their opposition has been fired by a righteous libertarianism which has equated their freedom from constraint with public liberty. This has become the central idea shaping the regulatory environment of the press because publishers and their staffs have been the principal disseminators of ideas about the press.

Publishers have dominated the discourse of press politics partly because they have been united. Left-leaning publishers have made common cause with right-wing publishers on most issues of press policy. They have also encountered little resistance from within the press itself. Although press trade unions have been formally committed to press reform, their energy and resources have been largely confined to pursuing narrowly defined industrial objectives. While numerous individual journalists have been critical of the conduct of the press, they have been more outspoken in pubs than in print or on public platforms. The weakness of internal dissent is best illustrated (not in a critical way) by the record of two indomitable institutions, the Campaign for Press and Broadcasting Freedom (CPBF) and the *British Journalism Review*. The CPBF was set up originally by the print unions, following a conference of the Institute of Workers Control, and immediately received the support of numerous unions including the NUJ (Richardson and Power 1986). Its key activists, until they lost their jobs, were print workers. They were replaced primarily by recruits from the expanding sectors of media studies and independent television production. This prompted the CPBF to switch its attention from the press to the media more generally.

In contrast to the proletarian origins of the CPBF, *British Journalism Review* was launched with the backing of celebrated journalists and Rowntree money in 1989. Its opening editorial attacked the 'contagious outbreak of squalid, lazy and cowardly journalism', and announced its intention to rectify British journalism's 'lack of a reflective and analytical culture' (Anon. 1989: 2–3). In 1998 the BJR, edited by a retired journalist, Geoffrey Goodman, had a subscription of less than 1,000.

An effective challenge to the press' self-definition did not emerge from the political parties. Baldwin's celebrated assault on press barons (greatly assisted by the speech-writing skills of his cousin Rudyard Kipling) has not been repeated by a politician of equivalent standing and eloquence. The Conservative Party made its peace with the press, from which it has generally received strong support. The Labour movement edged towards a more critical position, especially after it ceased in the 1960s to be a press proprietor. However, it was not until 1974 that the Labour Party developed an official policy on the press, and not until the 1983 and 1987 general elections that it incorporated this policy into its manifesto. This was in its wilderness years. Its commitment to curbing press monopolies and assisting new papers was quietly dropped as part of the revision that made it 'electable' in the 1990s.

No effective consumers' group was formed to give voice to public dissatisfaction. Due to the lack of developed press policy, the civil service has not become a centre of press-policy expertise. Universities have also failed to make good this deficit. As the chairman of the last Royal Commission, with some justification, complained: 'Over its [the Commission's] very wide terms of reference, knowledge was patchy and unsystematic, policy choices were ill-defined and academic study of the press had not advanced far enough to be of much assistance' (McGregor 1980: 154). This relative absence of countervailing knowledge helps to explain, in turn, why the press industry was so influential in shaping the contents of successive public enquiries into the press.

In short, the key to the failure of press reformism is the way in which the power of publishers, the traditional rhetoric of press freedom and the weakness of reform movements coalesced. It was not simply that publishers were a powerful vested interest well able to defend themselves and to inflict injury. It was not just that they wrapped around their shoulders the mantle of liberty in a way that sowed doubt about the desirability of reform. It was not even that the wider environment offered so little support for press reform. It was the mutually reinforcing *combination* of these three things that has constituted an enormous obstacle to change.

This explains, in turn, the caution with which reformist politicians approached press reform. Clement Attlee was initially against the idea of having a Royal Commission on the Press. The Callaghan government buried the Royal Commission's 1977 recommendation for tough-press monopoly controls because it did not want to open up a new front when it was beset with economic and political difficulties. Even in its radical wilderness phase, Labour rejected proposals for regulation of the press modelled on public-service broadcasting as being outside the realm of practical politics.[9] This wariness switched to outright pragmatism when Labour, under Tony Blair, attacked the Conservative government for failing to lift the ban on publishers, with more than 20 per cent of national circulation, buying commercial TV companies. Large publishers, according to the Labour spokesman John Cunningham, were being 'treat[ed] unfairly in their access to broadcasting markets' (HMSO 1996: 275 (84) col. 551). It was clearly understood in internal policy meetings of the Labour Party during this period that the framing of press policy had to take account of the need to gain press support.

The politics of press and television thus have different dynamics. Public regulation of television is defended by the resources, accumulated expertise and prestige of major organisations, not least the BBC. It is supported by a political consensus and sustained by a public culture in which individual broadcasters actively participate. Out of this critical public culture emerge, from time to time, new initiatives (such as Channel 4) that renew the tradition of public service broadcasting. It is precisely this cultural infrastructure of reform that has been lacking in the case of the press.

This is partly what makes Jeremy Tunstall important. He will be remembered primarily as a sociologist and one of the founding fathers of British media studies, whose many books became key texts for teaching and research. But he has also a wider public significance. Jeremy Tunstall is one of the very first people to examine systematically the organisation, public policy and content of the British press. He is a pioneer of that critical tradition whose absence has been one of the reasons for the failure of press reformism in Britain. His importance lies not only in what he has achieved but it also lies in what he has begun.

NOTES

1 For example, Williams (1998); see also Boyce (1978); Cockett (1989); Curran and Seaton (1997), among others. They point to the persistence of economic, ideological or party controls in the period after the abandonment of state regulation.

2 For instance, Tiffen (1989), Franklin and Murphy (1991), Protess *et al.* (1991), Tunstall (1996), Eldridge, Kissinger and Williams (1997), McNair (1998), among others. These all argue, either implicitly or explicitly, that a fourth estate view of the press fails to take adequate account of the way in which the press is linked to structures of power in liberal-democratic societies.

3 It was accepted only that the press, like other forms of communication, should be subject to laws upholding human rights (including the right to security, reputation and a fair trial). The press generally held these to be overly restrictive.

4 I cannot recall ever giving conscious thought to what might contribute to the welfare of the press when advising on media studies curricula development during the 1980s and early 1990s, until being re-educated as an external examiner to

overseas universities. Maybe other 'theory' lecturers in the UK were different, though in my experience most were not.

5 Information derived from the Department of Trade and Industry, and supplied by Jake Ecclestone.

6 This is not to suggest that we should reproduce the Swedish press subsidies' system in Britain. This is geared to preserving a local political press that has largely disappeared in Britain, and is therefore not directly applicable to the British context.

7 This does not include the *Sport* or the *Sunday Sport* since they are specialist newspapers.

8 For a different and engaging perspective, see O'Malley (1998) who argues that reformism succeeded in discursive terms. It established the principle of public accountability, and secured a more progressive framework of debate. This does not seem to me to be a big pay-off after eighty years of reformist lobbying.

9 Thus, radical proposals from Michael Meacher, Chris Mullin and others for public-service regulation of the press were kicked into touch. Neil Kinnock, the then labour leader, was also dissuaded from floating the idea of an EU citizenship requirement for newspaper ownership, comparable to that for terrestial television.

REFERENCES

Angell, N. (1933) *The Press and the Organisation of Society*, Cambridge: Gordon Fraser.

Anon. (1989) 'Why we are here', *British Journalism Review* 1(1).

Ascherson, N. (1978) 'Newspapers and internal democracy', in J. Curran (ed.) *The British Press: A Manifesto*, London: Macmillan.

Baistow, T. (1985) *Fourth-Rate Estate*, London: Commedia.

Baker, C. E. (1989) *Human Liberty and Freedom of Speech*, New York: Oxford.

Boyce, G. (1978) 'The fourth estate: the reappraisal of a concept', in G. Boyce, J. Curran and P. Wingate (eds) *Newspaper History*, London: Constable.

Boyd-Barrett, O. (1980) 'The politics of socialisation: recruitment and training for journalists', in H. Christian (ed.) *The Sociology of Journalism and the Press*, Sociological Review Monograph 29, Keele: University of Keele.

Brants, K. and D. McQuail (1997) 'The Netherlands', in Euromedia Research Group, *The Media in Western Europe*, (2nd edition), London: Sage.

Bromley, M. (1997) 'The end of journalism? Changes in workplace practices in the press and broadcasting in the 1990s', in M. Bromley and T. O'Malley (eds) *A Journalism Reader*, London: Routlege.

Bundock, C. J. (1957) *The National Union of Journalists, 1907–1957*, London: Oxford University Press.

Calcutt, D. (1993) *Review of Press Self-Regulation*, London: HMSO.

Camrose, W. E. B. (Lord) (1947) *British Newspapers and Their Controllers*, London: Cassell.

Chippendale, P. and C. Horrie (1990) *Stick it Up Your Punter*, London: Heinemann.

Christian, H. (1980) 'Journalists' occupational ideologies and press commercialisation', in H. Christian (ed.) *The Sociology of Journalism and the Press*, Sociological Review Monograph 29, Keele: University of Keele.

Clarke, P. (1996) *Hope and Glory*, London: Allen Lane.

Cockett, R. (1989) *Twilight of Truth*, London: Weidenfeld & Nicholson.

Commission on the Freedom of the Press (1947) *A Free and Responsible Press*, Chicago: University of Chicago Press.

Committee on Privacy (1972) *Report*, Cmnd 5012, London: HMSO.

Committee on Privacy and Related Matters (1990) *Report*, Cmnd 1102, London: HMSO.

Crewe, I. (1988) 'Has the electorate become Thatcherite?', in R. Skidelsky (ed.) *Thatcherism*, London: Chatto and Windus.

Crouch, C. (1982) 'The peculiar relationship: the party and the unions', in D. Kavanagh (ed.) *The Politics of the Labour Party*, London: Allen & Unwin.

Cummings, A. J. (1936) *The Press*, London: Bodley Head.

Curran, J. (1978) 'Introduction', in J. Curran (ed.) *The British Press: A Manifesto*, London: Macmillan.

—— (1995) *Policy for the Press*, London: Institute for Public Policy Research.

—— (1998) 'The crisis of public communication: a reappraisal', in T. Liebes and J. Curran (eds) *Media, Ritual and Identity*, London: Routledge.

—— and J. Seaton (1997) *Power Without Responsibility* (5th edition) London: Routledge.

Delano, A. and J. Henningham (1996) *The News Breed: British Journalists in the 1990s*, London: London Institute.

Department of National Heritage (1995) *Media Ownership*, London: HMSO.

Dibblee, G. B. (1913) *The Newspaper*, London: Williams and Norgate.

Eldridge, J., J. Kissinger and K. Williams (1997) *The Mass Media and Power in Britain*, Oxford: Oxford University Press.

European Commission (1992) *Pluralism and Media Concentration in the Internal Market*, Brussels: Commission of the European Communities.

Fallows, J. (1996) *Breaking the News*, New York: Pantheon.

Franklin, B. (1997) *Newszak and News Media*, London: Arnold.

—— and D. Murphy (1991) *What News? The Market, Politics and the Local Press*, London: Routledge.

—— and D. Murphy (1997) 'The local rag in tatters? The decline of Britain's local newspapers', in M. Bromley and T. O'Malley (eds) *A Journalism Reader*, London: Routledge.

Glasser, T. and S. Craft (1998) 'Public journalism and the search for democratic ideals', in T. Liebes and J. Curran (eds) *Media, Ritual and Identity*, London: Routledge.

Gustafsson, K. (1980) 'The press subsidies of Sweden: a decade of experiment' in A. Smith (ed.) *Newspapers and Democracy*, Cambridge, MA: MIT Press.

—— (1995) 'Origins and dynamics of concentration', in K. Gustafsson (ed.) *Media Structure and the State*, Gothenberg: Gothenberg University Press.

—— and O. Hulten (1997) 'Sweden', in Euromedia Research Group, *The Media in Western Europe* (2nd edition), London: Sage.

Hallin, D. (1994) *We Keep America on Top of the World*, London: Routledge.

Harris, W. (1943) *The Daily Press*, Cambridge: Cambridge University Press.

Hartley, N., P. Gudgeon and R. Crafts (1997) *Concentration of Ownership in the Provincial Press*, Royal Commission on the Press Research Series 5, London: HMSO.

Hirsch, F. and D. Gordon (1975) *Newspaper Money*, London: Hutchinson.

HMSO (1996) *Parliamentary Debates*, Broadcasting Bill (Lords) (16 April), London: HMSO.

Host, S. (1991) 'The Norwegian newspaper system: structure and development', in H. Ronning and K. Lundby (eds) *Media and Communication*, Oslo: Norwegian University Press.

Humphreys, P. (1996) *Mass Media and Media Policy in Western Europe*, Manchester: Manchester University Press.

Independent (1996) 'How not to be a journalist' (leader), 31 October.

Jaehnig, W. (1998) 'Kith and sin: press accountability in the USA', in H. Stephenson and M. Bromley (eds) *Sex, Lies and Democracy*, London: Longman.

Jenkins, R. (1988) *Baldwin*, London: Collins.

Kavanagh, D. (1987) *Thatcherism and British Politics*, Oxford: Oxford University Press.

Keane, J. (1991) *The Media and Democracy*, Cambridge: Polity.

Koss, S. (1984) *The Rise and Fall of the Political Press in Britain*, vol.2, London: Hamish Hamilton.

Labour Party (1974) *The People and the Media*, London: Labour Party.

Labour Research Department (1922) *The Press*, London: Labour Publishing.

Lichtenberg, L. (1995) 'The Dutch model of press policy', in K. Gustafsson (ed.) *Media Structure and the State*, Gothenberg: Gothenberg University Press.

Levy, H. (1967) *The Press Council*, London: Macmillan.

McBarnet, A. (1979) 'Disciplining the journalist; an investigation of training methods', *Media, Culture and Society* 1(2).

McGregor, O. (1980) 'The Royal Commission on the Press, 1974–7: a note', in M. Bulmer (ed.) *Social Research and Royal Commissions*, London: Allen & Unwin.

McNair, B. (1996) *News and Journalism in the UK* (2nd edition), London: Routledge.

—— (1998) *The Sociology of Journalism*, London: Arnold.

Mansfield, F. (1943) *Gentlemen. The Press!*, London: W. H. Allen.

Martin, K. (1947) *The Press the Public Wants*, London: Hogarth Press.

Middlemas, K. and J. Barnes (1969), *Baldwin*, London: Weidenfeld & Nicholson.

Murschetz, P. (1998) 'State support for the daily press in Europe: a critical appraisal', *European Journal of Communication* 13(3).

O'Malley, T. (1997) 'Labour and the 1947–9 Royal Commission on the Press', in M. Bromley and T. O'Malley (eds) *A Journalism Reader*, London: Routledge.

—— (1998) 'Demanding accountability: the press, the Royal Commissions and the pressure for reform, 1945–77', in H. Stephenson and M. Bromley (eds) *Sex, Lies and Democracy*, London: Longman.

Panitch, L. and C. Leys (1997) *The End of Parliamentary Socialism*, London: Verso.

Penrose, E. (1959) *The Theory of the Growth of the Firm*, Oxford: Blackwell.

Perkin, H. (1989) *The Rise of Professional Society*, London: Routledge.

Political and Economic Planning (PEP) (1938) *Report on the British Press*, London: PEP.

Pollard, S. (1969) *The Development of the British Economy* (2nd edition), London: Arnold.

Protess, D., F. Coook, J. Doppelt, J. Ettema, M. Gordon, D. Leff and P. Miller (1991) *The Journalism of Outrage*, New York: Guildford.

Reddaway, W. (1963) 'The economics of newspapers', *Economic Journal* 73.

Richards, H. (1997) *The Bloody Circus*, London: Pluto.

Richardson, A. and M. Power (1986) 'Media freedom and the CPBF', in J. Curran, J. Ecclestone, G. Oakley and A. Richardson (eds) *Bending Reality*, London: Pluto.

Robertson, G. (1983) *People Against the Press*, London: Quartet.

Royal Commission on the Press 1947–9 (1949) *Report*, Cmnd 7700, London: HMSO.

—— 1961–2 (1962) *Report*, Cmnd 1811, London: HMSO.

—— 1974–7 (1977) *Final Report*, Cmnd 6810, London: HMSO.

Santini, A. (1990) *L'Etat et la presse*. Paris: Litec.

Schudson, M. (1995) *The Power of News*, Cambridge, MA: Harvard University Press.

Seaton, J. (1991) *Media and the Constitution*, London: Charter 88.

Skogerbo, E. (1997) 'The press subsidy system in Norway', *European Journal of Communication* 12(1).

Symon, J. (1914), *The Press and its Story*, London: Seeley, Service & Co.

Thomas, B. (1998) 'Teaching ethics to journalists in the United Kingdom', in H. Stephenson and M. Bromley (eds) *Sex, Lies and Democracy*, London: Longman.

Tiffen, R. (1989) *News and Power*, Sydney: Allen & Unwin.

Tulloch, J. (1998) 'Managing the press in a medium-sized European power', in H. Stephenson and M. Bromley (eds) *Sex, Lies and Democracy*, London: Longman.

Tunstall, J. (1977) Unpublished evidence to Royal Commission on the Press 1974–7, Royal Commission on the Press Papers.

—— (1980) 'Research for the Royal Commission on the Press 1974–7', in M. Bulmer (ed.) *Social Research and Royal Commissions*, London: Allen & Unwin.

—— (1996) *Newspaper Power*, Oxford: Clarendon.

Webb, B. and S. Webb (1920) *A Constitution for the Socialist Commonwealth of Great Britain*, London: Longmans.

Wickam Steed, H. (1938) *The Press*, Harmondsworth: Penguin.

Williams, K. (1998) *Get Me a Murder a Day!*, London: Arnold.

Williams, R. (1966) *Communications* (revised edition), London: Chatto & Windus.

Worcester, R. (1998) 'Demographics and values; what the British public reads and what it thinks about its newspapers', in H. Stephenson and M. Bromley (eds) *Sex, Lies and Democracy*, London: Longman.

3

US COMMUNICATIONS INDUSTRY OWNERSHIP AND THE 1996 TELECOMMUNICATIONS ACT

Watershed or Unintended Consequences?

Christopher H. Sterling

In the years since the passing of the 1996 Telecommunications Act, many US policymakers and critics have expressed surprise and dismay at what appears to be a signal outcome of that legislation – a massive merger and consolidation trend among American electronic media and telecommunications industries. Major takeovers were underway within days of the new law taking effect, and have continued to be announced almost daily since. Critics were soon blaming the law's provisions for encouraging (if not actually mandating) the substantial restructuring of the industry into a small number of huge companies.

Is the expanding American 'merger mania' an *intended* result of the 1996 legislation? What *other* factors are also driving the urge to merge? This chapter briefly explores how, to what extent, and why US communications industry ownership is undergoing such a dramatic consolidation in the late 1990s.

As in other industries, there are two major types of concentration communication – vertical integration and horizontal concentration. The former implies control of the means of production, distribution, and exhibition, as with the old Hollywood studio system, which owned theater chains to distribute and exhibit studio productions, or a newspaper owning paper mills. Horizontal concentration means control of multiple outlets of the same type and 'level,' such as commercial television stations or local cable systems. Merger activity in the 1990s reflected increases in both types.

OWNERSHIP POLICIES BEFORE 1996

American communications industry ownership policy is rooted in the 1934 Communications Act, which created the Federal Communications Commission (FCC) and remains, in amended form, the bedrock of American telecommunications regulation. Based on both the technology and economic thinking of the time, telephone service was regulated as a monopoly with resulting common carrier regulation – control of rates and conditions of service, but not of content. Radio (and later television) broadcasting, on the other hand, was seen as a competitive service with, ideally, one station per owner, who would be responsible for all content broadcast. The Act did not, however, include a specific limitation on the number of stations any owner could control. The telephone and broadcast businesses were perceived as dramatically different in what they did, the technologies they used, and in their ownership – and thus in how and why they were regulated. For several decades rules governing electronic media ownership remained remarkably stable. By 1953, the FCC had established a '7–7–7 rule,' allowing any single owner to control up to seven AM, seven FM, and seven television stations nation-wide, not more than five of the latter to be VHF outlets (Sterling 1982: 328). By the 1980s, therefore, even the largest group owners controlled no more than twenty-one stations, though three-quarters of the country's television stations were by then owned by such groups (Sterling 1984: 60).

There was a parallel local market ownership goal as well – 'one to a customer' – though existing AM–FM or even AM–FM–TV combinations established prior to the rule were allowed to persist until sold. So, despite the idealistic goal, by the 1980s the majority of AM and three-quarters of all FM radio stations were held in co-owned AM–FM pairs (Sterling 1984: 58). In station sales, the FM typically was tossed in as an extra to the AM station which determined the price.

Attempts to regulate cable television system (horizontal) ownership, however, generally came to nothing. While overall national limits on the proportion of cable subscribers controlled by one entity were often considered (generally to parallel existing caps on broadcast television), none was adopted. In the two decades from the mid-1970s to the mid-1990s, concentration levels in cable sharply increased. The largest multiple system operator (MSO), TCI by the 1990s, grew from controlling 8.5 percent of subscribers to 21 percent; the largest four firms collectively rose from 24.5 percent to nearly half of all subscribers, and the largest eight companies rose from 36.4 percent to 63.6 percent (Chan-Olmsted 1996: 32). In a euphoria of perceived convergence potential, regional Bell telephone company Bell Atlantic announced a takeover of TCI in 1993, issuing plans to merge the best of telephone, data, and cable communications for a '500-channel' future. But the deal fell apart early in 1994 over policy and ego-driven disagreements, leading to assessments that the two quite different industries were not yet ready to dance to the same tune.

Worries about cable's vertical integration were more pervasive. Again, arguments about the same entity controlling both cable networks and cable systems had been around for years. The Cable Act of 1992 required the FCC to develop rules defining how many cable networks could be controlled by multiple system operators – in other words, how many program channels of any system could be occupied by programmers in which the multiple system operator held a financial interest. A year later, the commission finally decided that 40 percent would be the limit of such vertical control (Ahn and Litman 1997: 473). A related concern, about the degree to which cable network programming might be made available to competing services – chiefly direct broadcast satellite or terrestrial MMDS services – was hotly debated in the halls of a Congress increasingly worried about cable's local monopoly grasp on two-thirds of American TV households.

A number of FCC *cross-media* ownership limits were in place by the 1970s:

- neither a local television station nor a telephone company could own a co-located cable television system;
- a local newspaper could not control a co-located broadcast station (again, the many extant combinations could remain until sold – while only a handful of radio stations were so owned, nearly one-third of television stations had press ownership); and
- broadcast networks could not control cable systems anywhere in the country.

By the mid-1980s, the overall proportion of newspaper-owned television stations had stabilized at about 30–33 percent, while same-market cross-ownership was dropping (Howard 1985). The FCC's rules clearly were designed to enforce the perception that different media should have different owners to encourage diversity of viewpoint and allow for competing advertising markets.

Even with these regulations, a healthy number of stations changed hands annually – by the early 1980s, an average of 400–500 radio and 30 television stations (Sterling 1984: 45). Rising station prices indicated continuing demand for most urban outlets even as satellite-delivered multi-channel cable services offered increasing competition by dividing the audience into smaller segments. Faced with that demand and an expanding industry, the FCC eased its admittedly arbitrary national ownership limits in 1985, to allow owners to control twelve broadcast stations of each type, later (1992) raising AM and FM radio limits still further to eighteen each and finally to twenty in 1994 (US Dept. of Commerce 1997: 2).

One other aspect of electronic-media ownership was subject to policy decisions in this period – attempts to increase the proportion of stations held by ethnic minorities. Beginning in the late 1970s, the FCC developed several means of encouraging more minority-owned stations, among them distress sale and tax certificate policies whereby minorities could obtain stations at lower-than-market prices. But the real problem for minority groups was obtaining sufficient capital to either build stations or enter the bidding wars. Despite industry attempts to assist, this problem was never sufficiently resolved. While the FCC's policies were initially promising, by the 1990s minority ownership totals stabilized far below the incidence of minority groups in the population. From a 1972 total of fifty-one radio and television stations (only eight were TV outlets), minority-controlled stations increased to 178 in 1982, 330 a decade later, and had risen to 337 (thirty-two of them television) by 1998 (Sterling 1984: 46; *Broadcasting & Cable* (1998a: 28)). The rate of minority ownership growth was basically flat in the mid-1990s. To make matters worse, Congress (angered by one multi-million dollar tax deal) repealed the tax certificate policy in 1995, and several other FCC race-based policies were under increasing pressure from the courts concerned with equity across all groups.

As for ownership policy in the telephone industry, the picture was very simple for decades. More by tradition than formal regulation, the policy-makers' assumption until 1982 was of a single local telephone carrier or utility per market, and (until competition began to crop up in the early 1970s) a single national long-distance carrier, AT&T. Indeed, AT&T controlled 80 percent of the local telephones in the nation, allowing it to perform much as a PTT, though under private ownership and operating at a profit. But the forced divestiture of the local Bell Operating Companies in 1984 arbitrarily divided the industry into monopoly (local exchange) and competitive (manufacturing, value-added, and long-distance service) sectors. The latter, including AT&T, MCI, Sprint and other long-distance carriers, and all manufacturing, was largely deregulated while the former remained closely controlled as to both conditions of service provided and rates charged.

But technology, so often a driver of policy change in communications, was again laying the foundation for major regulatory shifts. Increasing digitalization of transmission and equipment in both the telephone and electronic media industries by the 1980s called into question old policies created for two industries once perceived to be fundamentally different. The pressure for change was not all technical in nature. By the late 1980s it became increasingly apparent that the forced separation of the telephone business into monopoly and competitive sectors was not effective. It placed inefficient limitations on what carriers could offer and what customers could demand. Limiting competition led merely to higher prices and often poorer service. But only action by Congress could overturn the many court orders dividing the industry.

1996: WHAT CONGRESS INTENDED

Despite widespread agreement that US communications laws had long needed fundamental updating – especially those dividing the telephone business – it took several years for legislation to result. Involved and highly technical or economic issues, the shift in control of Congress from Democrat to Republican dominance (and thus a need to educate new committee chairmen and staff members), long intervening budget-based debates, and the deeply entrenched positions of different parts of the industry all served to delay action (Sterling 1996: 143–4). The final law taking up more than 100 pages of tiny government print (Telecommunications Act 1996), plus another 100 pages of description (US House of Representatives 1996), focused primarily on the telecommunications industry and marked several fundamental policy shifts. Competition was to be encouraged, not only in long-distance service where it already existed, but in local exchange and cable television service as well.

The most contentious sections of the law were those that dictated the conditions of transition from traditional monopoly to forthcoming competitive market structure (Telecommunications Act 1996: sections 251–7, 271–2). These became the subject of complex FCC rulemakings and controversial lower-court rulings which culminated in a Supreme Court decision, AT&T v. Iowa Utilities Board in January 1999, which largely upheld the Act and related FCC decisions. As to telephone company ownership questions, while the new law did not specifically mandate changes, it did set the stage for possible modifications by terminating the 1982 legal agreement that had broken up AT&T (ibid.: section 601). By removing US district court judge Harold Greene from his dozen years of determining policy under provisions of that agreement, the Act freed the Regional Bell Operating Companies to pursue new structures and partners.

More specifically, however, the Act required the FCC to drop most restrictions on radio station ownership. Licenses were extended from seven to eight years (section 203), existing licensees were all but guaranteed renewal (section 204), and national radio station ownership limits were to be abolished. Further, single entities could now own multiple radio outlets in the same market – up to as many as eight stations in the largest cities (section 202).

Television licenses were also extended, in this case from five to eight years. The existing FCC ownership cap (no more than twelve television stations collectively reaching no more than 25 percent of the nation's audience) was raised to include any number of stations, as long as their total 'reach' did not exceed 35 percent of the population. (There was one important loop-hole here: the FCC counted UHF stations as reaching only half their potential audience and thus, if an owner's portfolio included such outlets, their overall national 'reach' might extend well above the 35 percent ceiling.) And cross-ownership rules limiting or banning broadcast networks' control of cable systems or co-located telephone carriers and local cable were also eliminated (section 202).

Ironically, the Act would have two opposing impacts on minority ownership. On the one hand, relaxing of many ownership limits was clearly going to increase station prices, making minority purchases that much harder to fund. On the other, the Act called for the creation of a Telecommunication Development Fund to 'provide a source of loans and investment capital to small communications businesses' (US Dept. of Commerce 1997: 5). While not specifically aimed at ethnic minorities, the Fund may prove useful to their attempts to broaden electronic media ownership.

With these provisions, decades of traditional FCC ownership regulation were swept away. Many remaining rules were at least questioned – the law required the Commission to study the easing of existing local television cross-ownership or *duopoly* (owning no more than one station of a type in the same market) rules, and in mid-1999 the FCC ended television duopoly restrictions. And the outright takeover of cable systems by co-located telephone carriers was not allowed. The overall *intent* of Congress was quite clear, however: to take into account the increasing number of media options available to most Americans – and thus to encourage the FCC to eliminate restrictive ownership rules where at all possible (US House of Representatives 1996: 163). Overall, Congress sought less governmental oversight and control of communications industry generally, and fewer ownership rules specifically. During countless hearings and lobbying exchanges, congressmen were bombarded with industry data (showing both the continued growth in the number of stations plus the growing variety of other news and entertainment media becoming available to more Americans), supporting their argument that such diversity argued for looser or lessened regulation – and thus a freer hand for media owners.

1996–9: THE URGE TO MERGE

Passage of the Act unleashed a host of merger activity, which greatly surpassed what anyone had projected. It began almost immediately, and rapidly accelerated.

Telephone mergers

Within days of the Act's passage, SBC, one of the seven Bell Operating Companies, announced it was taking over Pacific Telesis (Pactel), another RBOC – a move Judge Greene would never have allowed under the old MFJ. A few weeks later, Bell Atlantic announced an even larger merger (long rumored, it later turned into a takeover) with NYNEX – and the seven RBOCs were about to become five. Several layers of state and federal regulatory approval required for both actions were, after some months of discussion and compromise, forthcoming (Rosenberg 1997).

Soon other telephone firms were in merger play, led by long-distance carrier MCI. In a series of short-lived partnerships, MCI was seemingly captured by British Telecom (in what would have been the first major American tele-communications carrier to fall under the control of a foreign firm), then an alternate US suitor (GTE), and finally a relatively new US inter-exchange company few had even heard of – Worldcom, based in Jackson, Mississippi. After regulatory approvals and divestiture of extensive Internet trunks to Cable & Wireless, the MCI Worldcom merger became final in September 1998. A further merger with Sprint was announced in late 1999.

Already digesting Pactel, SBC in mid-1998 announced plans to expand further with a $62 billion take over of Ameritech, followed a few weeks later by plans to take over SNET, the independent company which controls most telephones in Connecticut, giving SBC a truly national reach. Indeed, to some alarmists, it appeared that the San Antonio, Texas-based SBC was to a large degree reassembling the old AT&T monopoly. But they were not alone.

In July 1998, Bell Atlantic and GTE (the biggest non-RBOC local carrier) announced a nearly $53-billion merger covering operations in thirty-nine states and thirty foreign countries. The resulting entity became the second-largest telephone carrier after only AT&T. The country's eight largest local service carriers (seven RBOCs and GTE) in 1996 consolidated into half that number in about three years ('Dial M' 1998).

Merger rumors continued to swirl around AT&T, both Bell South and US West (the remaining Regional Bell Companies), and such international players as Cable & Wireless. In mid-1998, after rumors of a take-over of Internet service provider America On-Line, AT&T revived the idea of combining cable television and telecommunications concerns with its announced complex takeover of cable giant TCI (Schiesel 1998a). The $32-billion purchase was intended to provide the long-distance giant with an effective means of re-entering local telephone service while expanding its relatively small piece of the growing Internet market.

Radio mergers

Gaining almost as much attention were the convulsions of the once fairly calm radio industry. Where companies had been restricted to owning no more than twenty AM and twenty FM radio stations, 'Within a month of the law's passage, the two largest national radio group owners had 52 . . . and 46 stations respectively. . . . By mid-year, merger activity led to the first group owner with more than 100 stations' (Sterling 1996: 4). At the same time, station trades and sales led to some companies owning up to eight stations in the largest cities. Three major group owners – CBS, Westinghouse and Infinity – merged to become what was briefly the largest radio station group

Table 3.1 Top radio group owners: January 2000

	Number of stations		Total audience reach		Total annual revenue	
	#	Rank	Millions	Rank	$ billions	Rank
Clear Channel	959	1	108	1	3.1	1
Cumulus	303	2	7	–	0.2	–
Citadel	176	3	8	–	0.2	–
Infinity	161	4	56	2	1.6	2
Entercom	91	5	12	4	0.3	4
Cox	71	–	10	5	0.3	5
ABC	43	–	13	3	0.4	3

Note: [a] – indicates a figure out of top five ranking.

Source: *Who Owns What?* (January 10, 2000: 1–2).

owner in the nation in terms of audience and revenue. Several radio group owners held close to 200 stations by early 1998 – and more than twice that number later the same year. But as seen in Table 3.1, the number of stations owned (a rapidly changing list) can be misleading. Measuring the top five radio companies in terms of number of stations owned, total audience reach, and annual revenues, offers quite different pictures of the industry. Infinity, for example, which includes the stations of the former Westinghouse and CBS chains, holds stations primarily in major markets, explaining why the smaller number of stations ranks so high in total audience and revenues. The major market concentration of stations' factor also boosts ABC and Cox into upper rankings despite their far fewer stations.

Several factors drove this radio frenzy, including 'an eye toward economies of scale, such as the use of a single advertising sales force for several stations' (Frieden 1998: 49). Bigger groups of stations can more efficiently program their outlets by offering satellite-delivered program services (often co-owned) to large numbers of stations. FM stations (with their larger audiences and advertising revenues) are driving radio's merger train, with AM stations often simply thrown in as part of the deal (a total reversal of conditions two decades ago). The overall state of a thriving economy – and thus ease in finding capital for expansion – clearly contributes as well.

But amid all this merger euphoria, traditional regulatory concerns about excessive concentration have reappeared. By mid-1998 at least two FCC commissioners were arguing that the agency needed a clear policy on how to handle the wave of mergers, and should not simply approve them assuming the Justice Department would take action on any egregious problems. For, as FCC oversight diminished, the Justice Department's Antitrust Division had become more active. The Division first challenged several radio mergers or station purchases within months of the 1996 law's passage. By 1998 the Division appeared to be heading toward a *de facto* single-owner control limit of no more than 40 percent of any one market's radio advertising revenue (McConnell 1998a). When Clear Channel purchased AMFM for $23.5 billion late in 1999, the company had to *sell* about 100 outlets, worth $1 billion, to meet FCC and Justice Department requirements. Still, a lack of joint FCC–Justice Department goals or co-operation was evident. Part of the FCC's problem was that the wave of change included more than radio.

Television and cable mergers

'In 1996, the total market value of terrestrial broadcast, cable, and satellite television and radio sales amounted to $80.1 billion, which was a 75 percent increase over 1995' (Frieden 1998: 49). Likewise, the largest 25 group owners of television stations expanded their portion of TV outlets from 25 percent in 1996 to 36 percent by early 1998, a sharp rise in only two years (Brown 1998). Those groups collectively controlled some 432 stations. Small and formerly little-known companies expanded their station ownership to cover more of the country. For example, as shown in Table 3.2, by 1999 Paxson Communications owned fifty television stations serving more than 30 percent of the nation's TV homes.

The same concentration is evident in cable television where, 'in 1994, the 10 largest operators controlled roughly 45 percent of cable subscribers. That's now up to 74 percent' (Broadcasting & Cable 1998c). The top four MSOs alone controlled a high and still growing proportion of the industry's total subscribers.

Table 3.2 Top television group owners: January 1999

| | Number of stations | | Total audience reach[b] | |
	#	Rank	Proportion	Rank
Sinclair	56	1	13.8	–
Paxson	50	2	29.2	3
Hearst-Argyle	32	3	16.0	–
Hicks Muse	27	4	7.9	–
Fox	23	5	35.3	1
Tribune	20	–	27.6	4
CBS	14	–	30.8	4
NBC	13	–	26.6	5

Notes:
[a] – indicates a figure outside of the top four ranking. Revenue figures are not available as several of these firms (Fox, Tribune, and CBS, for example) are but branches of larger companies where revenue includes many other entities.
[b] Measured in terms of the potential proportion of the national television audience reached collectively by all the stations owned.

Source: *Broadcasting & Cable* (1999).

Evidence of the growing convergence between the film and television industries could be seen in the Disney studio's 1996 takeover of the ABC Network, or the mid-1980s' creation of the Fox Network, combining stations (formerly the Metromedia Group) with the movie studio. In 1995 both the Paramount and Warner Brothers' studios have established fledgling television networks.

Finally, in 1999–2000, the quest for greater cable and Internet access fuelled some of the largest mergers of all, and at the same time demonstrated growing convergence across media. AT&T broke out of its traditional telephone mode with the purchase of the largest cable multiple system operator, TCI , in a $32-billion deal in mid-1998, followed by a take-over bid for MediaOne, still under regulatory review early in 2000. Taken together, these purchases make AT&T the largest MSO with just under a third of all cable homes. And the driver of these deals is not cable *television*, but rather cable as a broadband means of providing faster Internet access in addition to more traditional services. Whether AT&T could make its Internet strategy work or not – and if so, how quickly – was very much up in the air at the turn of the century.

In September 1999, Viacom announced its intended takeover of CBS in a deal valued at about $80 billion, the largest media deal to date. The merged entity would control major cable networks, a top-ranked radio station owner (Infinity), the largest television group, Paramount Pictures, extensive production and syndication facilities, publishing, theme parks and several Internet services. Early in 2000 came the biggest media-related deal of all (indeed, for the moment, the biggest corporate take-over in American history) when Internet service provider America on Line (AOL) announced its take-over of the Time-Warner conglomerate (the number two cable system operator) in an all-stock deal worth about $165 billion. While various regulatory approvals were also necessary here, the deal was scheduled to close late in 2000. It marked the first time one of the newer and fast-rising information-age companies (AOL was founded in 1985) had taken over a giant traditional media-based company. And it increased pressure on other firms, telecommunications, media, and information, to find their own partners to create entities providing content as well as varied distribution channels.

WATERSHED?

Anyone assessing the pros and cons of media or telephone company ownership must determine whether who owns these firms matters. Looking first at content implications, a half-century ago Steiner (1949) concluded that monopoly ownership of radio stations might actually *encourage* diversity of content as the one owner sought as much total audience for his multiple stations as possible. The Rand Corporation undertook the most intensive study of this issue a generation ago, and concluded that research showed little discernible impact of media ownership patterns on the diversity of content provided (Baer 1974). Nearly a decade later, and despite a continuing trend to further consolidation, the same research-based bottom line seemed to hold (Compaine *et al*. 1982: 494). Just two years later another Rand study noted 'it appears that there is no connection between group ownership [of TV stations] and the diversity of viewing fare provided by a station, although there is only limited evidence on this point' (Besen and Johnson 1984). Later research showed little change in results. Despite all these rather benign findings, however, critics of the consolidation trend – and the 1996 Act that seemed to trigger it – were loudly evident.

While critics' arguments often spoke to content concerns, the 'other' or economic side of merger and acquisition activity strengthened the negative arguments. And here the evidence is both longer run and more compelling. Tracing back to decades-old newspaper studies, it is quite clear that monopoly urban dailies charge far more for advertising and other services than do competing newspapers in the relatively few markets where they survive (Compaine *et al*. 1982: 69). Likewise, where stations and newspapers share local ownership, discount advertising prices for sponsors buying both media serve to squeeze out possible competing stations or papers. End user costs – newspaper (or cable system) prices – are also usually higher.

The frenetic pace of merger and takeover activity crowded into the first three years since the 1996 Act's passage suggest that the legislation *has* been a prime contributor to consolidation. Specific legislative provisions clearly opened the way for the wave of acquisitions in the radio industry. Even here, however, the new law's impact was in part a matter of fortuitous timing. In the mid-to-late 1990s, the American economy was roaring to new high levels as reflected in rising stock prices and high investor confidence. The head of the Federal Reserve noted that the American economy was the strongest he had seen in a half-century. Merger activity in many sectors of the economy merely reflected such confidence.

More specifically, however, the Republican-controlled Congress was inclined to allow the trend to consolidation across the economy (banking, transport, and other sectors) to continue unabated. They were persuaded, in part, by arguments that American firms needed to be larger, with more economic resources on which to draw, in order to effectively compete in a worldwide information marketplace. Further, significant entry barriers to new companies (no frequencies for new stations in major markets, and the cost of starting a newspaper when facing an entrenched monopoly paper, for example) increased interest in and prices for successful existing firms. So did various tax laws. Looked at in this context, the 1996 legislation can be seen more as an amplifier than as a sole cause of the many take-overs.

Within months of the Act's passage – and more so as time went on – a growing number of congressmen expressed concerns about what they argued was an unintended impact of their handiwork. While most clearly wanted to lift many media controls, they did not foresee a total restructuring of the industry that seemed increasingly likely to cost rather than serve consumers. Consumer costs (for cable service, for example, where the Act terminated most rate regulation, and eliminated the remainder early in 1999) were rising, not falling as had been predicted (based on industry testimony and intensive lobbying) when members voted for the Act. The law that many congressmen expected to expand competition seemed instead to promote growing merger activity.

Critics of the perceived, proven, or predicted impacts of consolidation – especially among news media – continue to argue the social and economic drawbacks of greater concentration (Bagdikian 1993; Barnouw 1998). Their concerns center on the decline in diversity of viewpoint as well as economic concentration, as more and more outlets fall within the ownership orbit of fewer owners. A widely noted parallel was the 'malling of America,' with huge indoor shopping malls featuring the same chain stores everywhere – and leading to the decline and disappearance of smaller shops and traditional downtown shopping areas. The bottom line in both cases – less choice and the threat at least of higher prices with the decline in competition. In communications, many blamed the 1996 Act for encouraging this trend.

But while the 1996 Act accelerated the urge to merge, it did not create it. Nor has technology been the primary driver in most mergers – the motive is usually fear. The 'if I don't do it, my competitors will' line of thought seems to dictate the many boardroom mergers. The feeling is strategic – that size *does* matter in developing global competition (Schiesel 1998b). Yet in the end, technology may provide the final word on the ownership debate. By 2000, policy focus was shifting to a new topic – public access to the wildly-popular Internet and World Wide Web. Valuable for both information and entertainment, Internet use is increasingly taking home viewers away from traditional media services (and even the telephone), usage levels of which are dropping uniformly. As nobody 'owns' the Web, some argue that questions of traditional communications industry 'ownership' policy will soon not matter. On the other hand, recent mega-deals, such as the 1998 AT&T-announced take-over of TCI, and the huge AOL/Time Warner merger early in 2000, were in large part driven by the desire to gain a stronger Internet foothold.

The federal government demonstrated its own concerns with the filing of two massive anti-trust suits within weeks of each other in mid-1998. In the first, against Microsoft, the Justice Department argued that the firm's integrated Windows operating system and Internet Explorer browser were a threat to open public access to the Internet. (That case went to trial in October 1998 and led to a late-1999 finding that Microsoft *had* violated anti-trust laws.) Shortly thereafter the Federal Trade Commission filed an action against Intel, arguing that its dominance of the PC-chip market was a hardware threat parallel in impact to the concern about Microsoft. The outcome of these complex cases may determine the future of 'ownership' policy concerns.

Despite the growing evidence of consolidation, the FCC continued its plans to lift some ownership regulations by the end of 1998. Their ban on newspaper ownership of radio (but not of television) stations was likely to be lifted in the top twenty-five markets, with more than thirty 'voices' (media outlets) existing. Also likely was a relaxing of rules to allow co-owned television stations whose 'Grade B' signals overlapped. (These would not be co-located stations, but could involve markets within a 100 miles of each other.) Among several other rule changes under consideration, the Commission also appeared likely to formally establish a long-discussed national limit of 30 percent of cable subscribers 'passed' (not necessarily served) by any single owner (McConnell 1998b).

In any case, future communications owners will be fewer but larger – controlling multiple media and information businesses. Whether or not this result is socially 'good' will continue to be both a critical social and academic debate – but one with little likely bottom-line impact on the marketplace or its regulators. Barring unforeseen events, a media world made up largely of single-owner media (or owners focused on a single medium) will not reappear. The economic stakes have grown too large.

REFERENCES

Ahn, H. and B. R. Litman (1997) 'Vertical integration and consumer welfare in the cable industry,' *Journal of Broadcasting & Electronic Media* 41: 453–77.

Baer, W. S., H. Geller, J. A. Grundfest and K. B. Possner (1974) *Concentration of Mass Media Ownership: Assessing the State of Current Knowledge*, Santa Monica, CA: Rand Corporation.

Bagdikian, B. (1993) *The Media Monopoly* (4th edition), Boston, MA: Beacon Press.

Barnouw, E. (1998 *Conglomerates and the Media*, New York: The New Press.

Bates, B. J. (ed.) (1998) 'Economic impacts of the 1996 Telecommunications Act,' *Journal of Media Economics* (special issue) 11(3): 1–64.

Besen, S. M. and L. L. Johnson (1984) *Regulation of Media Ownership by the Federal Communications Commission*, Santa Monica, CA: Rand Corporation.

Broadcasting & Cable (1998a) 'Few and Far Between' (October 5): 28–34.

—— (1998b) 'Television's Revamped Leadership' (April 6) : 46–68.

—— (1998c) 'Cable's 57 Million Sub Club' (April 20): 28–38.

—— (1999) 'Television's Top 25' (January 25): 44–64.

Brown, S. (1998) 'The big get bigger,' (April 6): 8.

Chan-Olmsted, S. M. (1996) 'Market Competition for Cable Television: Reexamining its Horizontal Mergers and Industry Concentration.' *Journal of Media Economics* 9(2): 25–41.

Compaine, B. M., C. H. Sterling, T. Guback and J. K. Noble Jr (1982) *Who Owns the Media? Concentration of Ownership in the Mass Communications Industry* (2nd edition), White Plains, NY: Knowledge Industry Publications.

Compaine, B. M. and D. Gomery (2000) *Who Owns the Media?* (3rd edition), Mahwah, NJ: Lawrence Erlbaum.

Frieden, R. M. (1998) 'Comment: The Telecommunications Act of 1996: predicting the winners and losers,' *Hastings Communications and Entertainment Law Journal* 20(1): 11–57.

Gomery, D. (2000a) 'Television: broadcast, cable and satellite,' Chapter 5 in Compaine and Gomery.

—— (2000b) 'Radio broadcasting and the music industry,' Chapter 6 in Compaine and Gomery.

Howard, H. H. (1985) *Group and Cross-Media Ownership of Television Stations: 1985*, Washington, DC: National Association of Broadcasters.

McConnell, B. (1998a) 'Justice studies more radio mergers,' *Broadcasting & Cable* (May 25): 19.

McConnell, B. (1998b) 'FCC moving, cautiously, on ownership,' *Broadcasting & Cable* (November 16): 27–42.

Media Studies Journal (1996) 'Media mergers' 10(2–3) spring–summer.

New York Times (1998) 'Dial M for Merger' (July 28): D6.

Rosenberg, E. A. (1997) *Telecommunications Mergers and Acquisitions: Key Policy Issues and Options for State Regulators*, Columbus, OH: National Regulatory Research Institute.

Schiesel, S. (1998a). 'With cable deal, AT&T makes move to regain empire,' *New York Times* (June 25): 1.

Schiesel, S. (1998b) 'Phone mergers: a heated game of musical chairs,' *New York Times* (July 28): D1.

Steiner, P. (1949) 'Workable competition in the radio broadcasting industry,' Harvard University dissertation published by Arno Press, *Dissertations in Broadcasting* (1979).

Sterling, C. H. (1982) 'Television and radio broadcasting,' and 'Cable and pay television,' Chapters 6 and 7 in Compaine *et al.* (1982): 299–450.

Sterling, C. H. (1984) *Electronic Media: A Guide to Trends in Broadcasting and Newer Technologies, 1920–1983*, New York: Praeger.

Sterling, C. H. (1996) 'Changing American telecommunications law: assessing the 1996 amendments,' *Telecommunications and Space Journal* 3: 141–65.

Sterling, C. H. (1997) 'Radio and the Telecommunications Act of 1996: an initial assessment,' *Journal of Radio Studies* 4: 1–6.

The Nation (1998) 'Who Controls TV?' (June 8): 11–38.

United States Congress (1996) *Telecommunications Act of 1996* Public Law 104–104.

US Department of Commerce (1997) *Minority Commercial Broadcast Ownership in the United States*, Washington, DC: Minority Telecommunications Development Program, National Telecommunications and Information Administration.

US House of Representatives (1996) '*Joint Explanatory Statement of the Committee of Conference*,' Report 104–458 (January 31).

Who Owns What (weekly).

4

POWER AND POLICY IN THE BRITISH MUSIC INDUSTRY

Simon Frith

Sometime in 1971 or 1972 I received a letter from Jeremy Tunstall asking me if I had any book ideas for a series he was editing for Constable on the theme of *communication and society*. I did not know Jeremy then, but I had read his books on fishermen and London advertising agencies, and thought he did the sort of sociology I wanted to do – nosey, systematic, sympathetic. (And later, when I met him, Jeremy struck me as being like an advertising man himself, sharp but a little distrait, a contemporary sociologist as imagined by Michael Frayn.)

He had got my name from Leo Lowenthal, who taught me the sociology of culture in graduate school at Berkeley, regarding me as a European theoretical ally against the phalanx of bright young American number-crunchers. What neither Lowenthal nor Tunstall knew was that I had another life as a rock fan, that I had fallen in with the new kind of music critic emerging from the interstices of the underground, pop and political presses. Jeremy's letter gave me the idea of – and the opportunity for – applying sociological order to this new cultural field. I proposed what became *The Sociology of Rock* (1978) and my subsequent academic career was determined.

Just as it is difficult now to remember what The Beatles' 'Love Me Do' really sounded like when I first heard it, so I find it difficult to remember how I understood the rock industry when I first started to study it. It was, to begin with, little studied. The record industry was of no interest to media sociologists (who focused on television, advertising and the press); it was rarely covered by cultural or business journalists. In British universities rock was first taken seriously as text rather than institution: it was first analysed as a new cultural phenomenon by literary and music critics like Christopher Ricks and Wilfrid Mellers. There was some US social science commentary (pioneered by R. Serge Denisoff and Richard A. Peterson), and in the pages of the new American rock magazines like *Rolling Stone* and *Crawdaddy* one could find a casual version of the Frankfurt School's critique of the cultural industry. Rock was interpreted as a reproach to pop. The music industry in itself was obviously a bad thing; rock ideology drew on both art and folk's contempt for commerce. Rock was something new and different in American popular culture – the first academic American rock histories were free with terms like 'revolution'.

I was saved from such naïvety, from the peculiar idea that rock was somehow anti-commercial, by more measured British studies that combined academic research with the enthusiasm of long-time pop fans, a journalistic eye for the new rock readership and, most strikingly, a pragmatic rather than idealistic view of music business. Charlie Gillett's *Sound of the City* (1971), which remains an astonishingly informative account of the origins of rock'n'roll in terms of local urban history, also first laid out what became a familiar account of the economic and ideological role of 'independent' record companies in popular music history (Gillett went on to run his own independent label, Oval Records). Dave Laing's *Sound of Our Time* (1970), the first rock book to draw on continental theory, Sartre, Barthes *et al*, was as fascinated by rock as business (Laing went on to be press officer for IFPI – the International Federation of Phonogram Industries – and to co-found the *Financial Times'* music business newsletter *Music and Copyright*).

In the mid-1970s, then, when I started my own research, there was a marked gap between academic and journalistic accounts of rock: academics, whether in early versions of youth subcultural theory or influenced by Marcuse's Marxist romanticism, tended to see a struggle between the forces of creativity (musicians, fans) and the standardising machinations of commerce; journalists were more likely to understand rock as the effect of a necessary negotiation between art and commerce. Their heroes were not youth stylists or hip poets but the small-scale entrepreneurs and eccentric hucksters of rock-and-roll history; and, for a writer like Gillett, 'making it' was a triumph rather than a sell-out (even if individual creativity was unlikely to survive corporate routine). Writing in the cusp between the academy and the music press I tried (with the help of the then-flourishing and now-unthinkable Marxist Rock Critics Circle) to integrate the two positions. My analytic breakthrough came when I realised (somewhat belatedly) that I was dealing not with a manufacturing but with a rights' industry, with a power structure that could not easily be mapped in terms of bosses and workers.

What was the British music business like when I began to interview industry personnel and scour the trade press? It was, to begin with, still a British industry (and, more particularly, a London industry), but one in the midst of a rather messy process of Americanisation – the unexpected success of 1960s' British 'Beat' in the US market had led the major American record companies to open offices in the city. The licensing deals which had brought American records to UK (and, through the UK, to European) consumers, thus seeing-off local cover versions, were no longer enough. CBS and WEA now wanted to sign UK acts for global exploitation for themselves. This was part of the broader Beatles' effect, which meant a shift in the centre of gravity of the industry from the routine servicing of the classical and pop markets to the development of the new market for rock. My immediate sense was of an industry, once gentlemanly, conservative and slightly seedy, becoming fashionable, professional and brash (a change marked by a rapid generational turnover of senior executives).

Two aspects of this were particularly interesting in terms of the industry's power structure. First, record companies' symbiotic relationships with other media – radio, television, the music press, the cinema – were having to alter because of independent changes in those media (commercialism, the reorganisation of BBC Radio, the new concern for the youth market). The music industry, that is to say, was having to restructure anyway because the post-war settlement of entertainment was breaking up – hence, in this period, the declining significance of the old music publishers, the rising importance of young A&R teams, and the emergence of key new players, the managers and agents, the independent producers and production companies who understood rock talent in ways that the established companies did not (and who had often developed their skills on a new showbiz site, the ENTS offices of university students' unions). But there were also ways in which the industry hadn't been changed by rock. The Performing Rights' Society still organised the collection and distribution of performing rights' income according to long-established if opaque views of musical value. Rock musicians themselves were still treated as if their careers would be short-lived, a matter of fashion, the dominant industry characters were still showbiz legends like Lew Grade and Dick James.

The fact was that the music industry expanded so rapidly between 1968 and 1978 that new and old ways of doing things ran alongside each other (which resulted in the routine sight of the patrician bosses of EMI and Decca posed uneasily for their annual company reports with their arms round their latest long-haired million-sellers). On the one hand, then, a new independent rock sector was established – Island, Chrysalis, Virgin, companies that weren't just the 'little labels' of rock-and-roll history but themselves brought together different rock sectors (management, distribution, retail, production). On the other hand, vertical integration continued apace as major companies like EMI used their profits to consolidate their interest in every part of the music-making process, from musical instruments to dance halls to record pressing plants. The crunch came in 1978 when a slow-down in the growth of record sales, coupled with the increase in production costs brought about by the rising price of oil (and vinyl), meant that the US music industry (on which the UK's profitability had become increasingly dependent) faced an unexpected economic crisis. (My study of an industry in expansion – with EMI as the central success story – came out after it was clear that the industry in general, and EMI in particular, were in crisis.)

I had also missed out on punk, which at the time was treated as a revolutionary return to real rock ways but in retrospect marked the end of the rock era in British music industry history. The problem was that British punk musicians simply didn't have the export earnings that the old rock farts had (and still have), and, in the event, the music industry was 'saved' by hardware rather than software, by digital technology and the brilliantly effective campaign to persuade people to replace their vinyl records with CDs. A new Beatles, it turned out, was unnecessary; the old Beatles could be sold all over again. The fallout from this technological revolution was, though, significant. Digital developments were led by Phillips in Holland, by Japanese electronic companies; Britain had become a follower rather than leader of leisure changes, and in the resulting reorganisation of entertainment into global electronics and publishing corporations British companies were swallowed up, leaving EMI as the only significant UK player in the international music business (and a player unlikely long to survive the new century). Britain is still important in the way the international music industry works, as a source of certain sorts of management and production skills and contacts, and global companies still have significant if not their central offices here. But neither as a market nor as a source of talent is the UK as important as it was twenty-five years ago (in terms of setting international sales' trends, for example), and to research the music industry now is to research a rather different business than the one I first examined.

I would characterise the changes under three overlapping headings: corporatism; globalism; professionalism. By *corporatism* I mean primarily size – record company executives today work for bigger companies in bigger offices in bigger buildings. But there's also a change in style, which reflects, I think, a centralisation of decision-making power. There are undoubtedly more small music-related businesses scattered about (for reasons I'll come to) but they seem to be more focused than they were in the 1970s, more dependent on their place in broader strategic decisions about release schedules, marketing campaigns and so forth. This reflects in part the collapse of a significant independent sector. The large independents like Island and Virgin have been absorbed into the global majors; the small independents are for the most part locked into major ways of doing things in licensing deals, joint-ventures and co-ownership deals. The majors' view of the business has thus become the dominant view.[1]

In this context the corporate view could be said to have three elements:

1 *control* exercised through budgeting and accounting processes – 'artistic decisions', that is to say, are taken in the context of agreed annual turnover and profit targets;

2 an emphasis put on overarching company *strategy* as the context in which artists are signed, release dates and promotional packages planned, etc.;

3 an increasing emphasis on management as *co-ordination* (rather than leadership), making sure that all the people involved with a particular title are working to the same timetable which, in turn, makes sense according to everyone else's timetables too.

To describe this a different way, corporate thinking means rationalising the process that links the two key moments of irrationality (the signing of an act, the purchase of a record), a process which becomes ever more complex as new technologies increase the opportunities for cross-media promotion, multi-media exploitation and so forth.

In some ways, as Keith Negus' work has shown, this process has also opened up new fault lines, new kinds of power struggle within the music industry itself. In *Producing Pop* (1992) Negus describes how tensions develop between A&R and marketing departments, each blaming the other when an act fails, each having a different idea of what success would mean. Both a cause and an effect of the resulting tensions is that these departments also tend to employ people with different skills, but also different musical backgrounds and tastes. In his more recent work, Negus points to a different sort of tension, between corporations' national and international sectors – why should the UK division of, say, EMI, go out of its way to help make a product of EMI France a UK hit? – and between the different divisions of the corporate portfolio (as rock and pop, dance and classical, rap and country compete for resources, attention, time). (See Negus 1999.)

The effect of such structural tensions has been to *professionalise* music industry roles, roles that didn't strike me as very professionally treated in the 1970s. Again, there are a number of different facets here. While the record industry still likes to see itself as running on instinct, passion and risk-taking (its senior personnel still don't wear suits), management science has made its mark, if not in the recruitment process then through training courses and on-the-job jargon. Two aspects of this are striking to an outsider: first, there is a much clearer differentiation of roles than there used to be (which means that co-ordination needs to be formalised); second, the knowledge – of the market, of the music – that one must deploy in what has become the increasingly competitive pursuit of backing for particular projects has become much more systematised. This is particularly noticeable in the rise of market research, hardly mentioned when I was doing my 1970s study but now (as in the television industry) a crucial component of 'creative' decisions. And organised knowledge has become equally important at the other end of the process, in the management of talent and a record company's relationship with such managers. Managers are, I suppose, the last music business people to display something of the wildness and unpredictability of their charges. But they, too, are now organised in the International Management Forum, and, as Mike Jones (1998) has shown, these days the manager's role is less about representing the artist to the company (injecting a spirit of anarchy into the office) than representing the company to the artist, through their access to strategic corporate knowledge (knowledge denied to the musicians themselves). The manager's central role, in other words, has become the management of a bureaucratically determined career path – the case of Oasis is a nice example of how this works, even for a supposedly 'difficult' band on an independent label.

Professionalisation is also a useful way, I think, to describe one of the more striking changes in the British music industry over the last twenty-five years, the move away from the ideal of vertical integration (major companies doing everything inhouse) to a system in which the majors consolidate their control of the distribution of music and the exploitation of their musical rights through horizontal integration, while, at the same time, depending on a network of specialist service providers – sleeve designers, record producers, radio pluggers, concert promoters, etc. – to bring their stars to the public. In this system professionalism is the basis of trust, trust that is especially important for independent companies with no market clout, and the result (just as in 1990s' broadcasting) is that there is little room left for mavericks or innovators. They must now operate outside the 'legitimate' business altogether.[2]

As a result of both corporatism and professionalism contemporary record company executives have to operate in a far more varied context than did their predecessors – varied in terms of the media deals that need to be done; varied in terms of the countries in which they find themselves doing those deals. Which brings me to the context for these developments, *globalism*, and the fact that the cultural territory in which the executive must now work is the globe (even if those executives are in a charge of a local–national division). Two mutually reinforcing tendencies – the increasing impossibility of a national market the size of Britain sustaining the investment now needed to produce and promote an act; and the increasing costs of promotion involved in covering the global marketplace (symbolised by the sales' role of MTV and the promotional video) – have meant that not even a small independent label can now avoid getting involved in international deals. At the same time, the resulting international flow of music is not just one way: it is not so easy now as it was twenty years ago to think of 'global music' as simply another description of Anglo-American cultural imperialism. 'World music' describes a different sort of flow – from south to north and east to west – and increasingly the major corporations see their biggest growth potential in non-English speaking markets anyway, in the growth of worldwide Spanish or Chinese pop media, for example.

If nothing else, then, the global music industry now shapes everyday music business practice, whether we're describing a small dance-record producer weaving together a network of licensing deals, territory by territory, around the world, or the international trade body, IFPI, engaging in ceaseless lobbying to persuade governments and trade regulators to harmonise (and enforce) copyright protection, or local divisions of major corporations calculating which deals with what national rights' fee-collecting agencies will maximise their returns. There were ways in the 1970s in which British music industry figures were distinctly provincial; these days they most certainly are not.

Given all this, I would now ask rather different research questions than those I asked in 1972.[3] First of all, while it is now commonplace even in the academy to describe the music industry as a rights' industry, we still have a very limited understanding of what this means, either economically or politically. In terms of the *economics of rights* there are at least four kinds of question which need answering.

1   How can we measure the flow of rights' income? Who holds what sort of power in the negotiations that determine how rights' fee incomes are distributed?
2   What are the relative returns from different sorts of license, from primary and secondary rights and how do these affect investment decisions? (It is sometimes suggested by industry observers, for example, that the income from the sales of records to individual consumers is now less than that from other licensed uses. The significance of consumer sales is increasingly, therefore, as a form of promotion, affecting the media musical decisions which will bring even bigger returns – which is to put into new perspective current debate about the potential decline of retailing with the rise of down loading services on the Net).
3   What are the cost–benefits of the different license-fee-collecting societies and collecting methods? Are the transaction costs involved justifiable in terms of the returns to the majority of musicians? Who benefits most from existing copyright regimes?[4]
4   How much money is really being lost by whom as a result of piracy?

The reason why research is needed on these questions is not that we know nothing about record industry income but that the details of its internal distribution (and the power structure that determines it) are opaque, and in providing such data the industry has its own agenda (on piracy, for example). Which brings me to the *politics of rights.* The economic interest of the copyright regime is that it is a regulated rather than a free market, and the details of regulation – how (and for how long) rights are defined, protected and rewarded – is a matter of legislation, state and inter-state policies. The question thus becomes how are such regulatory decisions taken? How do copyright laws get changed? And what is the lobbying role of the industry in such decision making? In the global music economy this is a complex issue, involving small local companies seeking state protection against global 'invasion' as well as the global companies themselves, seeking copyright harmonisation and 'fair' global trade agreements.[5] Two aspects of this lobbying process are particularly interesting: first, how the industry presents itself as an interest group, how it legitimises its policy demands to different governments; second, how certain musical actors – like pirates – are through this process defined as illegitimate (so that, for example, it is not a legitimate option for the dance music sector in Britain to forswear copyright deals, licensing and so forth, even though this may well be in its economic interest, given that it is focused less on products than on events).

A second set of questions follows from this, questions about *the culture of the firm*. My original research questions – What sort of business is the music business? Producing what? – have in some ways now been answered. The music business is a rights' business. It manages rather than creates talent. It avoids rather than takes risks. But what researchers like Keith Negus have gone on to show is that while the music industry can therefore be analysed using conventional organisational terms ('portfolio management', for example), it remains distinct from other industries in terms of the kind of information and trust on which its different sectors depend.[6] Knowledge of markets, trends and cultures, that is to say, varies greatly according to the music involved – as Negus suggests, what's at stake here is not the way a global corporation imposes its management culture on a musical form like rap or salsa, but the way in which the cultures of rap and salsa have to be taken account of in the network of relationships through which rap and salsa artists and sounds reach markets.

If nothing else, then, it is clear that the 'production of culture' and 'gatekeeper' models that for so long dominated accounts of the music business should now be dropped. What is much more pertinent is an understanding of the ways in which A&R teams establish trusting relationships with the divisional executives above them and with the artists and managers with whom they must deal; of the ways in which small and independent operators establish licensing deals, trusted partners, preferential supplier status. Different kinds of music produce different kinds of business culture because they involve relationships between different kinds of people with different kinds of background, contact and expertise. Negotiating the terms of a deal with a contemporary classical composer like James MacMillan is a process very different from negotiating the terms of a deal with a contemporary indie band like Bis, even if they involve representatives of the same major corporations meeting in adjoining Glasgow hotel rooms.

If the music industry is a rights' industry and a talent industry it is primarily, then, a deals' industry, an industry depending on an endless series of legal and financial negotiations between players who have shared interests and are yet in a zero-sum game: a good deal, that is to say, is one that will increase the size of the cake for everyone, but it can be negotiated only in terms of who is going to get what cut. The peculiarity from the corporate side is that while marketing may be the key to success, branding is not possible, or, rather, 'branding' describes stars not labels: people may buy a Blur record because it is by Blur; they don't buy an EMI record because it's EMI.

One conclusion I would draw from this is that what we have now is not a single industry (on the old major–indie model) but a number of separate industries (at least in terms of cultures and networks – compare jazz, folk, dance, classical) organised around the central unifying focus of rights (even the 'illegitimate' sector is defined by its treatment of rights, by its unlicensed raves and broadcasts and samples). The networks at issue here are both local –

as live bands, for example, circulate around familiar venues and audiences, and global – as a great variety of transnational deals are done. What is problematic from this perspective is the attempt to describe a *national* music industry. It is a problem that can be clarified, I think, from a historical perspective.

The description that I would now give of the music industry – as a set of industries organised around the politics and economics of rights, dependent on local and global networks of knowledge and trust, constantly adapting to technological change and renegotiating their deals with music-using media such as radio and the cinema – is, in fact, a description of the industry as it has developed over the twentieth century rather than the last decade. In other words, what I've been describing in terms of change – how the industry at the end of the 1990s is different from the industry at the beginning of the 1970s – could also be described in terms of continuity. Look at the industry at the beginning of the century, for example, and we find a global spread of phonograph technology depending on a network of locally trusted suppliers of phonogram recordings to suit particular local markets; we find the perceived urgent need for changes in copyright laws to take account of the new technology and the need for international copyright regulation and enforceable deals between license-fee-collecting agencies; we find the power structure in the industry determined by rights' structures (whether we're talking about Edison's control of his patents or the ways in which black and other 'folk' musicians were excluded from the control of their own compositions); we find an intimate relationship between record companies and radio stations, between music publishers and the cinema industry, in terms of deals, investment and ownership; we find, in short, from the inception of the industry – contributing, indeed, to the way in which the industry was defined – that lawyers and contracts were as significant as were entrepreneurs and hucksters, that 'independents' were always in fact 'dependent', dependency being determined not by direct ownership but by an indirect chain of obligations.

From this perspective, it was the moment in music industry history I originally studied (*c*. 1965–75) – the rock moment, the youth moment, the UK moment – which was anomalous, with its sense of a music bursting through the industrial constraints (defying the gatekeepers), springing spontaneously, as it were, from utopian-minded youth in Britain to reach utopian-minded youth everywhere else. Rock was anomalous, in other words, because it could be understood, however briefly, as a commercial music successful despite rather than because of the music industry. But it is also an anomaly that has left its mark on academic study (rock is still taken to be the model for the music section of media and cultural studies courses), on cultural commentary[7] and on state music policy.

There is one strand of policy, of course, to which this argument does not apply, namely the industry's continuing concern with rights' protection, for which it needs legal support. Technological change always has the effect of making obsolete existing copyright laws, always raises the question of whether or not courts will interpret the new situation in the industry's interests. And so the digital revolution which 'saved' the music industry at the end of the 1970s was also a threat, offering new possibilities for both home-taping and piracy. In its pursuit of legislative change on these issues, the industry had both to temper its swashbuckling account of itself as an untrammeled free market (piracy was now the enemy) and to improve its image as an industry, to shake off the publicly perceived 1970s' excesses of sex and drugs and rock-and-roll. More problematically, because it was trying to persuade national governments to pass national legislation, it also had to sell itself as a national industry (in terms of earnings, exports, etc). To that end, in the 1980s the British industry's trade body, the BPI, employed political lobbyists and invested in a City Technological School, the British School of Music and the Performing Arts (CTSs were one of Margaret Thatcher's pet projects). As it turned out, the industry failed to get a home-taping levy (it is instead now lobbying the European parliament to this end) but it did get the protection it sought against digital piracy in the 1988 Copyright Act, and established its place at the industrial high table, as it were.

Meanwhile, local policy makers were reacting to technological change in a different way, drawing on rock ideology in the context of (restricted) local state power in response to the decline of manufacturing industries and the new emphasis on the service sector. The local state sector developed specific 'music policies' along four (sometimes contradictory) strands:

- *youth policy*, initially as a matter of keeping young people off the street and giving them something useful and 'empowering' to do (this was a particularly significant policy for 'minority' youth and the source of a surprising number of successful music projects) but increasingly in terms of the provision of skills that might be relevant for employment;
- *cultural industries' policy*, in which new forms of local industry were encouraged by judicious investment (particularly in space); musical resources like recording studios were therefore provided to meet the needs (including training needs) of new kinds of music industry worker – producers and engineers as well as musicians and would-be performers;
- *community policy*, in which arts-and-recreation policy was adapted to the needs of a multicultural community and local government began to support a range of expressive activities which included the 'low' as well as the 'high';
- *tourist policy*, in which music was used as a way of drawing visitors to a locality (examples would be Liverpool's Beatles Museum, Manchester's 'Madchester' club promotion, and, now, Sheffield's National Centre for Popular Music).

These policies were developed by Labour local authorities under a Tory government, but at national level, too, Britain's rock reputation began to be treated as part of our 'heritage', and the Arts Coucil in the 1990s certainly became more populist in its account of which arts should be available to whom. But in general terms national music policy (or, rather, the lack of it) ran against the thrust of local activities. The Conservatives' deregulation of the media and rejection of European moves towards cultural protectionism (content quotas, for example) made the UK an important base from which US media companies got a foothold in the European media market,[8] but also undermined the idea of national media industries. At the level of Westminster policy making there was little sense of a national music interest to match local state claims about local music interests. (One reason, I suspect, why the industry failed to get parliamentary support for a blank-tape levy. Its adoption in other European countries was as much to do with policies of supporting national music cultures as it was with accepting the industry's claim that it was being 'robbed' by home-tapers.)

Enter, in May 1997, Chris Smith as Minister of Culture, Media and Sport, and a government with an unprecedented interest in the business of music. Read Smith's speeches on music (and follow the recommendations of his Creative Industries' Task Force and National Music Forum), and it is clear that at least part of his cultural strategy was to rework in national terms the 1980s and 1990s' concerns of Labour municipal authorities (Smith 1998). New Labour music policy thus has three strands:

- *rights' protection*, which is seen as a necessary way of protecting music industry profitability and its contribution to national wealth; the aim here is to promote the UK's creative industries, to ensure that we are at the forefront of the increasingly important global trade in intellectual property.
- *training*, to ensure both that young people have fair access to music industry careers, and the right preparation for such employment, and that there will be sufficient talent available for the industry to exploit in the future;
- *community*, by which I mean an arts policy designed to give everyone in a multicultural society access to a means of making or having their voices heard, with music taken to be one of the most important ways in which the nation represents itself to itself (and to the rest of the world).

The problem here is the slippage between the various accounts of the national interest: what is good for the music industry (which isn't really national, anyway) is equated with what is good for the nation economically (in terms of employment, investment and exports); and what is good for the nation economically is taken to be good for the nation culturally (in terms of uplift and identity) – as if sales success is, in itself, a defining characteristic of psychic health. This is, of course, the standard argument made by the music industry itself (whether in campaigning for rights' protection and/or celebrating itself at the Brit Awards), and the BPI has become, in effect, the national lobbying agency of a global industry, persuading a receptive New Labour of the idea that 'Britpop' can take its place alongside other creative activities (Young British Art, say) as a 'brand' in the global marketplace, an effective way of both encouraging inward investment and maintaining export sales.

The confusion here is symbolised by the March 1999 opening of the National Centre for Popular Music in Sheffield.[9] The NCPM is an appropriate memorial – if nothing else, it is a stunning building – to probably the most sophisticated and successful example of municipal cultural industries' policy. Starting from an investment in Red Tape Studios, a technical and training resource for local musicians, Sheffield Council built a Cultural Industries' Quarter which has been quite successful in meeting its aims – giving support to new (or inward-moving) small cultural service businesses, providing employment and training opportunities and drawing in leisure vistors. If it seems odd that a national music centre should be based in Sheffield, it is actually an appropriate setting: not because of the recent history of Sheffield music (from Human League, Heaven 17 and ABC to Warp Records and Pulp) but because Sheffield had the commitment and the energy to pursue the idea of the Centre in the first place (raising funds from the Lottery, Europe, tourist boards and a variety of sponsors).

In October 1999 it was announced that NCPM had debts of more than £1 million and that its projected visitor figures had been wildly over-optimistic. Insolvency advisors had been called in; a new chief executive recruited from Madame Tussaud's (for whom he had developed the London Rock Circus). The NCPM is likely now to become less arty, more vulgar, with closer ties to the music industry. The problems of arts' policy and professionalism that this crisis reveals are important in themselves. How should the Arts Council fund a commercial concern? How does local politics shape a national institution? What is the role of management consultants in shaping Lottery bids? But my point here is this. However drastically the NCPM changes its exhibition policy, it will necessarily remain, for so long as it survives, a celebration of British popular music in terms of a particular kind of rock romance. Visitors will be invited to delight in this small land's ability to have a world musical impact quite disproportionate to its population headcount. The overwhelming effect of a trip to the NCPM, for all its up-front use of new technology, is nostalgic (and this feeling is likely to be intensified if the Centre now, as seems likely, moves into memorabilia). It can be argued that popular music is by its nature nostalgic, that its pleasure comes from its ability to recall the optimism for the future that is rooted in the past. But the NCPM is specifically nostalgic: for rock, for spectacular youth subcultures, for the days when international British pop success was both surprising and a matter of course. I'm touched by such nostalgia, too, of course: nostalgia for the days when the British music industry did indeed seem both adventurous and innocent. But what I learned from Jeremy Tunstall all those years ago was to be sceptical of the ways in which media professionals make sense of themselves. The British music industry has never been quite what it seems. It has always been implicated just as much in failure as in success; it has always been driven as hard by the forces of conservatism as by the impulse to innovate.

NOTES

1 I observed this directly, ten years ago, when I was organising annual seminars for the John Logie Baird Centre. Among the regular contributors were the then managing directors of BMG (UK), a major, and Rough Trade, an independent. For the first couple of years they had very different accounts of how their companies were organised; by the third year Rough Trade was echoing BMG in its concern to find a good 'overseas marketing manager'.

2 The interesting comparison here is between punk and dance labels. See David Hesmondhalgh (1997 and 1998).

3 What follows is drawn from the music industry research undertaken by Ruth Towse and Millie Taylor of Exeter University, Keith Negus of Leicester University and Roger Wallis and his team at City University for projects on the ESRC's Media Economics and Media Culture Programme.

4 For discussion of these issues see Taylor and Towse (1998).

5 For discussion of these issues see Wallis *et al.* (1999).

6 For discussion of these issues see Negus (1999).

7 My favourite recent example of this is Jonathan Glancey's review of the National Centre for Popular Music. Without even thinking about it, Glancey assumes that 'popular music' means rock'n'roll, and that 'rock'n'roll is at heart and groin, the stuff of sex, drugs, sweat and rebellion . . . ' (1999: 12).

8 I'm drawing here on Jeremy Tunstall's research on the Anglo-American media connection for the ESRC Media Economics and Media Culture Programme. See Tunstall and Machin (1999).

9 I should declare an interest here. I wrote the original feasibility study for the Centre, and served on its Board of Directors.

REFERENCES

Gillett, C. (1971) *Sound of the City*, London: Souvenir Press.

Glancey, J. (1999) 'Rock without a role', *Guardian* (Friday Review, 12 February).

Hesmondhalgh, D. (1997) 'Post-punk's attempt to democratise the music industry: the success and failure of Rough Trade', *Popular Music* 16(3).

—— (1998) 'The British dance music industry: a case study of independent cultural production', *British Journal of Sociology* 49(2).

Jones, M. (1998) 'Organising pop – why so few pop acts make pop music', PhD thesis, Liverpool: Institute of Popular Music, University of Liverpool.

Laing, D. (1970) *Sound of Our Time*, London: Sheed & Ward.

Negus, K. (1992) *Producing Pop*, London: Edward Arnold.

—— (1999) *Music Genres and Corporate Cultures: Strategy and Creativity in the Music Business*, London: Routledge.

Smith, C. (1998) *Creative Britain*, London: Faber & Faber.

Taylor, M. and R. Towse (1998) 'The value of performers' rights: an economic approach', *Media Culture and Society* 20(4).

Tunstall, J. and D. Machin (1999) *The Anglo-American Media Connection*, Oxford: Oxford University Press.

Wallis R., G.-M. Klimis and M. Kretchner (1999) 'Contested collective administration of intellectual property rights in music: the challenge to the principles of *reciprocity* and *solidarity*', *European Journal of Communication* 14(1).

5

BRITISH PRESS AND PRIVACY

Hugh Stephenson

> In the consensual 1960s British journalism was far from being
> an established profession; but it was moving in a 'profes-
> sionalizing' direction – with various attempts being made to
> raise occupational standards, to control entry, and to improve
> educational levels. . . . But by the 1990s all this had changed
> and in terms of 'professionalization' had gone backwards.
>
> (Tunstall 1996: 141)

Much of Jeremy Tunstall's prolific output has concerned itself with how
journalists behave. It is now well over twenty-five years since the publication
of his *Journalists at Work*. In that time journalism in the United Kingdom,
as in all industrial countries, has been taken over almost entirely by men
and women who by upbringing and education (and increasingly by social
background) are indistinguishable from those who go into recognised
professions, such as medicine and the law. For ten years now, almost without
exception, journalists hired by national newspapers, the BBC, commercial
television and radio, and by the magazine industry have been educated at
university. In regional and local newspapers also the trend is strongly in the
same direction. It is, therefore, a paradox that, over a period when those going
into journalism came more and more from a *professional* culture, as Jeremy
Tunstall has observed *professionalisation* has gone backwards.

One of the essential elements of the traditional professions is that they
produce agreed codes of behaviour, require that those claiming the benefits of
membership should abide by them and impose effective sanctions on those
who are caught out not doing so. This chapter looks at the history of efforts
to improve the quality of the professional self-regulation of the British press,
and then examines some of the reasons why these efforts have failed so
conspicuously to shift British newspaper journalism in a truly professional
direction.

Concern in this century about ethical standards in British journalism was
raised first and most persistently by the National Union of Journalists (NUJ),
founded in 1907. The president of the NUJ at the end of the First World War
was F. J. Mansfield. He was on the staff of *The Times* from 1914 to 1934 and a

visiting lecturer on the pioneer university journalism course run at King's College, London, between the wars. His history of the NUJ, *Gentlemen of the Press!* (1943), is evidence that debate about ethical behaviour and the need for an effective professional code of practice has a long and repetitive history.

Mansfield's account of the events that led to the NUJ adopting its first code of professional conduct in 1936 has an entirely contemporary resonance. The catalogue of charges of sensational or trivialising journalism, of invasions of privacy and of intrusions into private grief might, with the dates changed and the language slightly modernised, be taken from any critical analysis of the misdeeds of the press in the last ten years. A contemporary resonance is also to be found in the arguments advanced in favour of proactive self-regulation:

> Although the Code was now 'on the record' it was not a time for the Union to sit back at ease. During 1937 the storm continued full blast, and the President (F. G. Humphrey) was the leader of an active campaign. He proclaimed that if this cult of sensationalism was allowed to proceed until vast numbers of people were affronted, a first-class case would be presented to the people who demanded the restriction of Press freedom. . . . Alarm and disgust [at the activities of 'a ghoulish minority of the Press'] were registered at the 1937 ADM [Annual Delegate Meeting], which foresaw that, if they continued, legislative control might come, which would be inimical to the interests of journalists and a menace to the freedom of the Press. In a resolution sent to the Government and the newspaper proprietorial bodies, the NEC [National Executive Committee] noted with satisfaction the commendation which had been expressed and offered the fullest co-operation with efforts to stamp out the malpractices of a small minority in the collection of news.
>
> (Mansfield 1943: 528–9)

The outbreak of war in 1939 suppressed the debate about ethical and professional conduct, though it is of passing interest, in the light of current concern about intrusion by journalists into personal grief or shock, that in 1940 the NUJ's National Executive Committee sent union branches a letter 'expressing its opinion that the interviewing of persons who had lost near relatives through the war would not necessarily be an intrusion into private grief' (Mansfield 1943: 531).

Debate on these issues resumed, however, once the war was over. The 1949 *Report* of the first Royal Commission on the Press clearly had a professional model, like the General Medical Council, in mind when it called for the setting up of a 'General Council of the Press'. It saw two problems of outstanding importance for such a General Council to tackle, both critical to the notion that journalism should develop as a responsible profession. One was to do with the recruitment and training of journalists. The other was 'the problem of formulating and making effective high standards of professional conduct' (Royal Commission 1949: 165).

The second post-war Royal Commission on the Press, chaired by Lord Shawcross, severely criticised the feeble record of the industry-financed and industry-dominated Press Council, which had been set up in 1953 as the newspapers' delayed, grudging and partial response to the 1949 recommendations. The *Report*'s general conclusion was that the newspaper industry and its Press Council be given a finite period within which to prove its ability to reform itself into an effective body capable of reassuring the general public that it could uphold acceptable professional and ethical standards: otherwise statutory regulation should take its place (Royal Commission 1962: 325). The message was clear: so far as continued self-regulation was concerned, the newspaper industry was 'drinking in the Last Chance Saloon'. (The Shawcross Royal Commission did not, of course, use this actual phrase. For those precise words the newspaper industry had to wait until David Mellor, as Secretary of State for National Heritage in John Major's government, used them in issuing an almost identical 'final warning' some thirty years later.)

The same basic theme tune was re-played ten years later in the *Report* of the departmental Committee of Inquiry on Privacy, chaired by former Labour minister Sir Kenneth Younger (HMSO 1972: 189). The Younger *Report* called specifically for the Press Council to codify its adjudications so that they could be more apparent to journalists and the public alike and for it to keep such a code up to date. The same tune was played yet again by the third Royal Commission on the Press, chaired by Lord McGregor. Its *Report*, published in 1977, found the record of the Press Council in enforcing professional standards to be lamentably wanting:

> It is unhappily certain that the Council has so far failed to persuade the knowledgeable public that it deals satisfactorily with complaints against newspapers, notwithstanding that this has come to be seen as its main purpose.

In the Commission's view, the Press Council had to stop seeming to be concerned more with protecting newspapers from politicians and the public than with raising the standards of newspapers in the public interest. It had to draw up and promulgate a code of conduct. It had to develop more effective sanctions against newspapers and journalists who flouted its rulings. The report concluded that 'willingness on the part of the Press to accept and conform to the rulings of the Council is the only alternative to the introduction of a legal right of privacy, and, perhaps, of a statutory Press Council' (Royal Commission 1977: Chapter 20).

The next thirteen years were not good ones for those who believed in the capacity and willingness of British national newspapers, their owners, their editors and their journalists to pay more than lip-service to the need for ethical standards. The National Union of Journalists had long since switched from being a professionally oriented organisation with concern for standards to concentrating, more or less effectively, on its role as a white-collar industrial union, fighting for higher pay and better conditions for its members and, where possible, the closed shop. While Rupert Murdoch's downmarket tabloid the *Sun* did more than any other single paper to damage the ethical reputation of Fleet Street in the eyes of the general public, responsibility for bringing the Press Council into serious disrepute was much more widely shared. For example, when the editor of the *Sunday Express*, John Junor, was reprimanded by the Press Council for including a racial slur in his signed column, he repeated the offending words and described the Council as being made up of 'po-faced, pompous, pin-striped, humourless twits' (*Sunday Express*, 3 September 1978). John Junor was knighted for his services to journalism by Mrs Thatcher in 1980.

A yet more widespread and flagrant example of contempt for the Press Council's authority centred on Fleet Street's scramble in 1981 to buy exclusive arrangements with the wife of the mass-murderer Peter Sutcliffe, the 'Yorkshire Ripper', and others of his family circle. The *Daily Express*, the *News of the World*, the *Yorkshire Post*, the *Daily Star* and the *Daily Mail* were all found to a greater or lesser extent to have broken the long-standing Press Council guidelines on 'chequebook' journalism, designed to stop convicted criminals, their families and close associates from making money by selling their stories. Most importantly, the Council's subsequent report on the episode, *Press Conduct in the Sutcliffe Case* published in 1983, revealed that the editors involved had failed to co-operate with its subsequent enquiry, hiding behind partial answers, direct evasions and straight lies. The *Daily Mail* and its editor Sir David English were picked out for special censure. English simply refused to come to the oral hearing of the Press Council's complaints committee. The Council said that its investigation had been materially hampered by the *Daily Mail*'s failure to disclose information of obvious relevance. The paper was censured for 'gross misconduct'. Sir David's response was contained in a signed article in which he described these findings as 'short-term, short-sighted and smug' and as proving 'yet again that the Press Council still does not understand the concept of a Free Press' (*Daily Mail*, 4 February 1983). The damage done to the Press Council's professional standing by the *Daily Mail* and its editor was particularly severe because, as Jeremy Tunstall has correctly observed: 'The editorship of David English at the *Daily Mail* was the most influential London editorship in the final one-third of the twentieth century' (Tunstall 1996: 112). In 1982, even while the Press Council was investigating the Sutcliffe case and drafting its report, David English was knighted by Mrs Thatcher for his services to journalism.

Although *Press Conduct in the Sutcliffe Case* (Press Council 1983) was by far the most robust attempt by the Press Council to assert its authority as a self-regulating body concerned with upholding a code of professional conduct, it also marked a low point for its authority, from which it struggled in vain to recover. Seven years later the departmental Committee on Privacy and Related Matters, under the chairmanship of David Calcutt QC, went round the circle once more. The Calcutt Committee declared the Press Council to be terminally inadequate to its professional task. It called for a new, authoritative, independent and impartial Press Complaints Commission, promulgating and enforcing a written code of conduct. Indicating the extreme scepticism of many of its members, including in particular its chairman, as to whether self-regulation could ever be the basis for professional conduct, the *Report* said:

> Should the press fail to set up and support the Press Complaints Commission, or should it at any time become clear that the reformed non-statutory mechanism is failing to perform adequately, this should be replaced by a statutory tribunal with statutory powers and implementing a statutory code of practice.
>
> (HMSO 1990: 16.9)

At that moment an actual move by the government to impose a statutory regime to regulate press behaviour was indeed closer than ever. The Calcutt Committee had given the press its 'final' final warning. When asked by the government in the summer of 1992 to review the performance of the new Press Complaints Commission in keeping order in the Last Chance Saloon, (now) Sir David Calcutt, working this time without a committee, concluded that the press had run out of time, and called unequivocally for a statutory Press Complaints Tribunal, answering to parliament and with powers to call for documents and persons, to order corrections and apologies, to award legal costs and to impose substantial fines (Review of Press Self-Regulation 1993). In 1993, for good measure, the House of Commons' National Heritage Select Committee also joined the fray, calling for legislation making a new civil wrong of infringement of privacy for which damages could be sought through the courts (HMSO 1993a); and the Lord Chancellor, Lord Mackay, published a Consultation Paper, *Infringement of Privacy* (HMSO 1993b), asking for views but not concealing between the lines the fact that he personally was in favour of such a new tort.

In the event this particular crisis for press self-regulation passed. The new Press Complaints Commission (PCC) gave every appearance both of wanting to take seriously its ethical responsibilities and of having the full support of newspaper owners and editors alike. Sir David English – now editor-in-chief and chairman of Associated Newspapers, the owners of the *Daily Mail* – became a key figure in the campaign to make the PCC a credible institution in terms of self-regulation and the maintenance of professional standards. He accepted an invitation to become a member of the Commission, in 1993, and actively chaired its code revision committee until his death in 1998. His conversion to the side of self-regulation's angels and the eagerness with which the PCC forgave and forgot his past record on professional ethics were measures of how seriously the press was by then taking the perceived threat of statutory regulation. In a much-publicised incident in 1995, designed to show how the ethical climate had changed, Rupert Murdoch, as chairman of News International and thus publisher of the *News of the World*, accepted a finding by the PCC that the paper and its editor, Piers Morgan, had been guilty of a severe and calculated breach of the code of conduct in printing a story, complete with pictures taken without permission by telephoto lens, about the drink and health problems of Countess Spencer, then wife of the brother of the Princess of Wales. Murdoch's statement read:

> While I always support worthwhile investigative journalism as a community responsibility, it is clear that in this case the young man (Mr Morgan) went over the top. Mr Morgan has assured me that his forthcoming apology to Countess Spencer on this matter is sincere and without reservation. I have no hesitation in making public this remonstration and I have reminded Mr Morgan forcefully of his responsibility to the Code to which he as editor – and all our journalists – subscribe in their terms of contract
>
> (*News of the World*, 14 May 1995: 4)

Although Mr Morgan was conspicuously not sacked or demoted for this 'severe and calculated' breach of a Code that was part of his terms of employment, nonetheless it seemed that the need for new ethical standards was at last being accepted by Britain's most powerful newspaper proprietor.

By this time, also, the Major government (1990–7) had become beset by scandals of one sort and another. This enabled those in Whitehall who argued that government mechanisms to control the content of the written press were wrong in principle to add their voice to those who argued that, if, in the run up to a general election, the government introduced statutory curbs on the press, it would look as if the Tories were simply taking revenge and seeking to reduce potential future political embarrassment. After two years of internal Whitehall debate and re-drafting, the outcome was a White Paper (HMSO 1995) which came out unequivocally against further statutory controls on the press.

Those who hoped that all this truly marked a new departure by the written press in the direction of professionalism and ethical standards were further encouraged by way in which the death of Diana, Princess of Wales, in August 1997 affected relations between the press and its public. The initial hysterical reaction was undoubtedly that the Princess had been hounded to her death by the media. Even when this was replaced by more reasoned analysis, it remained the case that her death crystalised a mass of hostility towards the press, particularly towards the national tabloids, and that journalists experienced a genuine sense of collective shame. The editor of the *Daily Telegraph* expressed the feeling thus:

> [We] have a blind spot – we do not seem to understand what people are saying and thinking about *us*. Even when Lord Spencer [the Princess's brother, in his funeral oration] stands up in Westminster Abbey and says it to two billion people, we still find it difficult to understand. The message is very simple: people think newspapers, particularly London-based tabloid newspapers, are dishonest, intrusive and cruel. Since the death of Diana, Princess of Wales, this feeling has risen to the level of outrage.
>
> (*Daily Telegraph*, 18 September 1997)

In the aftermath of Diana's death the PCC's code was strengthened, notably in respect of harassment by reporters and photographers and of reporting about children. The re-drafted code came into effect on 1 January 1998. Further, proprietors of national newspapers and their editors all adopted, with more or less conviction, the rhetoric of concern for ethical standards. The sixty-four-dollar question, however, is whether New Years Day 1998 will in due course be seen as the start for British newspapers of a new era of concern for ethical standards, reinforced by effective mechanisms for professional self-regulation. As we have seen, the evidence of history is not encouraging.

The idea that the PCC is presiding over an ethical sea-change relies heavily on the belief that its revamped code of practice can be the basis of a new and effectively enforced professional order. In particular, what the code says about (and how the PCC adjudicates on) questions of privacy is a key pressure point. The rest of this chapter is therefore concerned with this contentious issue.

Privacy is at once a simple and a fraught concept. Most people would readily enough accept the general proposition, first developed by the American lawyers Warren and Brandeis in 1890, that the individual has an inherent 'right to be let alone' (*Harvard Law Review* 1890: 193–220). However, the moment that one also accepts the proposition that the proper role of the media in a democratic society is to 'inform, educate and entertain', it is clear that performance of this role will involve the publication of material that someone, somewhere, will regard as an invasion of personal privacy, giving rise to conflicting opinions as to where the lines should be drawn. As the 1993 Consultation Paper recognised,

> privacy is a highly complex subject. Different people may need (or want, or have) different amounts of privacy. The same person will need (or want, or have) different amounts of privacy at different times. Sometimes, like Greta Garbo, we want to be alone; sometimes, like Mae West, we do not.
>
> (HMSO 1993b: 3.10)

The PCC code now includes a strong statement on the principle of privacy (based, in anticipation of the passage of the Human Rights' Act into United Kingdom law, on Article 8 of the European Convention of Human Rights). It says (clause 3):

> Everyone is entitled to respect for his or her private and family life, home, health and correspondence. A publication will be expected to justify intrusions into any individual's private life without consent.

Much of the rest of the code of practice is also taken up with detailed and practical defences of individual privacy: for example, prohibitions of the use of long-lens photography for taking pictures of people in private places and on the use of clandestine listening devices; prohibitions on intimidation, harassment or persistent pursuit by journalists; guidelines on intrusion where persons are in grief or shock; restrictions on talking to, photographing or publishing material about children and persons still at school; and guidelines to protect children involved in sex cases.

This all represents a serious effort by the PCC on behalf of the newspaper industry to establish ethical guidelines as to where the privacy line should be drawn in specific instances. How it works out in practice will depend critically on two questions. The first concerns what has become known as the 'public interest' defence. The second concerns the political will of the PCC itself.

The code, in common with most statutory restrictions on the freedom of the media to publish or broadcast, recognises that there may be exceptions to its general prohibitions. These are defined as instances in which activity *prima facie* in breach of the code 'can be demonstrated to be in the public interest'. The 'public interest' is then further defined as including the detection or exposure of crime or serious misdemeanour, the protection of public health and safety, and the prevention of the public from being misled by some statement or action of an individual or organisation. In the debate about 'privacy' and the 'public interest defence' much effort has gone into trying to draw a clear distinction between published material that raises issues 'of public interest' and material which is merely 'of interest to the public'. The PCC has sought to establish the position that newspaper activity in breach of the various privacy provisions of the code can be justified only if the editor concerned can show specifically 'how the public interest was served', or, in cases involving children, how an 'exceptional public interest [over-riding] the normally paramount interest of the child' was served.

In a traditional profession, with a code of conduct covering its members that included analogous provisions, such a code could and does provide the basis on which a body of professional 'case law' is established and developed over time. In the case of the newspaper industry there is no evidence since 1990 that the PCC has been any more successful than was the Press Council before it in the process of establishing a real dividing line between personal material which throws light on matters affecting the public interest (which can, therefore, legitimately be published) and personal material of a merely curious kind (which should, therefore, not be published, if doing so would cause significant distress to those involved).

For the sake of the argument, at this point I shall leave out of account stories that have appeared in the press in clear breach of the privacy of members of the Royal Family or of elected politicians. In the case of all or most of the published stories in this category some kind of 'public interest' justification can be made, even if it has often seemed in fact to be a pretty inadequate fig leaf. For example, it is hard to see what real 'public interest' was served by publishing the verbatim transcript of a long and sexually intimate telephone conversation between the Prince of Wales and Mrs Camilla Parker Bowles (*The People*, 17 January 1993), though it unquestionably excited wide public interest and was picked up and used by most of the rest of the media. A similar conclusion applies to a 'Royal world exclusive' (*Sun*, 8 October 1996), which accepted as genuine what purported to be an amateur video of Princess Diana in deshabillé frolicking with Captain James Hewitt. (The following day the video was proven to be a hoax, but not before the story had been covered by other newspapers and a clip of the video shown for real on ITV's *News at Ten*.)

Confining the argument to what has been published about non-Royals and non-politicians, the evidence is that in the matter of writing about the private lives of individuals in an intrusive way, even where no 'public interest' issue is involved, things have remained pretty much 'business as usual'. To some extent, even, the practice has spread in the sense that there is an increasing tendency for the whole press, including now the broadsheets, to follow up and develop a personal interest story after it has been broken by one of the tabloids. Taking stories almost at random from the past three years, the following are examples of *prima facie* breaches of the PCC Code for which no real public interest defence was available:

- details of the private life of the banker, Amschel Rothschild, who committed suicide in Paris (*Guardian*, among others, 12 July 1996);
- the disclosure that the playwright Harold Pinter and the television personality Joan Bakewell had an affair in the 1960s (*Daily Telegraph*, and others, 23 September 1996);
- details of the breakdown of the marriage of Glenn Hoddle, the England football manager (*Daily Star*, 15 October 1997)
- details of the sex life of television personality Anthea Turner, involving her husband, her lover and her lover's wife (*Sunday Mirror*, *News of the World*, 4 January 1998);
- the disclosure that BBC TV's sports' presenter Des Lynam had had an affair with a woman (*News of the World*, 27 September 1998); and
- the disclosure that a retired and widowed admiral, Sir James Eberle, had had a relationship with a prostitute (*News of the World*, 4 October 1998).

All the examples above involve figures with some public reputation. It is more difficult to gauge the reaction of 'ordinary people' when the media spotlight happens to fall on them. However, the words attributed by the *Press Gazette* (28 November 1997) to the son of a helicopter winchman, Bill Deacon, who died saving the lives of the crew of the wrecked ship *Green Lily*, on Orkney, indicate that the media trauma associated with the death of Diana Princess of Wales had not had any obviously lasting effect:

> Since my dad died we haven't been given a minute's peace or been allowed the privacy to grieve. We now understand what people like Princess Diana and her family have had to put up with for so many years. Media journalism is not an honourable occupation and none of you would deserve to kiss my dad's feet.

Much of the analysis of why newspapers continue to behave intrusively and to publish articles (more often than not centred on sex) that invade the privacy of individuals without raising public interest issues has concentrated on the economic aspects. All the marketing evidence indicates that, however critical the public may be of the ethical standards of newspapers in the matter of invasion of privacy, the same public is eager to buy and read the resulting articles. In a highly competitive market sector like national newspapers, according to this argument, it is not reasonable to expect newspapers to refrain from publishing what their public wants to read.

While there is some force in this argument, it misses two much more fundamental aspects, undermining any hope that the newspaper industry through the PCC can draw and defend a line between what is genuinely 'of public interest' and what is merely 'of interest to the public'. The first is that the agenda of the newspaper-reading public has changed over the years. The second is that the PCC, being the creature of the newspaper industry, has never shown real intention of developing an ethical standard based on this distinction.

The reasons why newspaper agendas have changed are many and various, and this is not the place to describe or analyse them. In summary, however, journalism (including broadsheet journalism) is now less exclusively concerned with public affairs and is more concerned to explore the realms of lifestyle, relationships and the emotions. The media-consuming public wants and expects strong human-interest perspectives in how the world and society are presented to it. Over the last twenty years or so, the reticence about exposing or discussing in the media the private aspects of life has hugely decreased. In many ways the 'personal' has now become both 'public' and 'political'. In such a changed climate the range of what the newspaper-reading public considers of legitimate interest for publication has changed out of all recognition. Certainly if, hypothetically, newspapers were suddenly to refrain totally from publishing any personal or private material to which anyone directly involved objected, unless a clear 'public interest' justification could be advanced, their readerships would find them decidedly old-fashioned.

There is no evidence, in fact, that the PCC has sought actively to develop case law in relation to invasions of privacy in line with the apparently clear meaning of its code. None of the apparent breaches of its code listed above, for example, resulted in a ruling by the Commission. A flow of such rulings would be necessary to build up the kind of case law that could establish a new ethical regime in this field. The main reason for this lack of activity is that the PCC from the outset adopted a general rule that it would not entertain complaints about published articles from 'third parties'. In the majority of cases where, in theory, the PCC might find that material had been published which unjustifiably invaded someone's privacy, the person wronged has no interest in bringing a complaint. To do so would only increase and prolong the distress involved. The PCC has accordingly remained silent in these cases.

Significantly, the few occasions when the PCC has departed from its self-denying ordinance about acting only on the basis of direct complaints have concerned the Royal Family. In June 1992, when the *Sunday Times* serialised Andrew Morton's book, *Diana – Her True Story*, the PCC's chairman, Lord McGregor, first privately sought assurances from the Queen's Private Secretary that the Princess had not authorised the revelations about the breakdown of her marriage, and then issued a deliberately emotive statement condemning journalists for 'dabbling their fingers in the stuff of other people's souls'. (It rapidly emerged that, in fact, the Princess had herself cooperated fully with the author.) Then, in November 1993, when the *Sunday Mirror* published pictures taken clandestinely of the Princess of Wales exercising in a private gym, Lord McGregor, without having received a complaint or heard evidence, roundly condemned the editor's justification of the article as one of the most hypocritical breaches of the code that he had ever encountered and, even more surprisingly, called for advertisers to boycott the paper. In 1995 the PCC's chairman, now Lord Wakeham, was proactive in seeking to obtain voluntary agreements from the newspaper industry not to carry stories about Prince William at school at Eton. The then code limited only interviews with and photographs of children under the age of 16. The revised code that came into force on 1 January 1998 extended this protection by stipulating: 'Young people should be free to complete their time at school without unnecessary intrusion.' This provision, of course, applied to all young people, but Lord Wakeham did not conceal the fact that his main motivation in pressing for the change was to protect the position of the Princes William and Harry at Eton (see, for example, the report of a speech to the London Press Club, in the *Press Gazette*, 12 September 1997).

It is difficult to avoid the conclusion, from this survey, that the PCC has been concerned less with developing new ethical guidelines for the newspaper industry and more with its role as broker between the newspaper industry and government. In this role its operating brief has been to do all that is necessary to keep at bay the threat of further statutory press regulation. This perception has been heightened since 1995 under the chairmanship of Lord Wakeham, who as John Wakeham was Chief Whip in the House of Commons from 1983 to 1987 in Mrs Thatcher's government and subsequently Leader of the House of Lords from 1992 to 1994 in the Major government. His skills and experience are those of a gifted political fixer, and at the PCC he has certainly carried through the brief with which he was charged. Whatever the continuing political or public criticisms of ethical standards in the newspaper industry, the threat of regulatory legislation is no longer in the air.

Paradoxically, just at the stage when the threat of further legislation to regulate the print media has lifted a potential revolution is upon us. The Human Rights Act, incorporating the European Convention of Human Rights into UK law, is giving us privacy legislation by the back door. The principle enshrined in Article 8 of the Convention (respect for private and family life, home and correspondence) will now have to be taken into account by judges in all their rulings. They will, of course, now also have to take into account Article 10 of the Convention, which underpins the right to freedom of expression. The courts will have to strike a balance between these two conflicting considerations in deciding cases involving the media with, for example, the law on trespass, breach of contract or harassment and in any judicial reviews that may come to cover PCC rulings themselves. The judicial process involved is likely to prove altogether more muscular than the PCC's own efforts to date to draw a line between invasions of privacy that can be justified on public interest grounds and those that can not.

REFERENCES

HMSO (1949) *Royal Commission on the Press, 1947–1949 Report*, Norwich: HMSO.
—— (1962) *Royal Commission on the Press, 1961–1962 Report*, Norwich: HMSO.
—— (1972) *Report of the Committee on Privacy*, London: HMSO.
—— (1977) *Royal Commission on the Press: Final Report*, Norwich: HMSO.
—— (1993a) *Privacy and Media Intrusion: Fourth Report of the National Heritage Select Committee*, London: HMSO.
HMSO (1993b) *Infringement of Privacy*, London: HMSO.
—— (1995) *Privacy and Media Intrusion: The Government's Response*, London: HMSO.
Mansfield, F. J. (1943) *Gentlemen of the Press!*, London: W. H. Allen.
Press Council (1983) *Press Conduct in the Sutcliffe Case*, London: Press Council.
Robertson, G. (1983) *People Against the Press*, London: Quartet Books.
Tunstall, J. (1971) *Journalists at Work*, Constable, London: Sage.
—— (1996) *Newspaper Power*, Oxford: Clarendon Press.

Part II

MEDIA POWER AND DEMOCRACY

6

THE NATION AND COMMUNICATIVE SPACE

Philip Schlesinger

THE ARGUMENT

This chapter explores a remarkably persistent line of argument in social and political theory. In the sketch that follows, I trace an underlying filiation that, in the post-Second World War period, stretches from the social communication theory of Karl Deutsch to the anatomy of the information age in the work of Manuel Castells.[1] Despite the diverse conceptual languages used in this influential body of work, there are recurrent underlying assumptions about how the relationship between the nation and communication might be theorised. I first give a brief statement of my argument and then go on to demonstrate it in more detail.

The *social communications* approach evidently has considerable heuristic value – so much so that it appears to be an almost reflexive starting-point for quite disparate influential scholars who, in one way or another, concern themselves with how national communicative spaces are constituted. (One might add, indeed, that social communications' ideas appear also to infuse and underpin much of our everyday thinking as well as governmental policy assumptions about nationhood and nationality.)

Characteristically, the emphasis in this approach falls upon the highly functional relation between the nation and modes of social communication. Consciously or unconsciously social communication thinking is an expression of the cultural geography of the nation–state in a world of sovereign states. Its functionalism produces an image of a strongly bonded communicative community. Under present conditions, clearly, this needs to be revised given the increased attention afforded the 'globalisation' of communication – especially the border-circumventing flows resulting from the rapid transformation of electronic media and of information and communication technologies.

However, the new wave of concern with global interconnectedness should not make us now envisage the world as definitively 'post-national'. The continuing strong links between modes of social communication and national political spaces remain fundamental for conceptions of collective identity. That said, if social communication thinking is to adapt productively to changing circumstances, it does now need to offer an explanatory grasp of the increasingly evident contradictions between various levels of culture and identity that are tending to decouple state and nation. Recent theorising about the European Union is used to illustrate this argument.

THE NATION AND SOCIAL COMMUNICATION

Karl W. Deutsch (1966) articulated one of the most explicit and wide-ranging theorisations of the role of communication in nationalism. His theoretical work *Nationalism and Social Communication* – paradoxically little read these days though talismanically invoked as a matter of routine – is marked by its sense of an end to European colonialism, an awareness of the forced migrations in Europe during the Second World War and after, and the dramatic national conflicts in the Indian subcontinent and the middle east.[2] A preoccupation with Nazism as the exemplar of nationalism gone wrong is ever-present in the text. The deportation and annihilation of most of European Jewry is counterpointed by an appreciation of the United States as a country relatively successful in assimilating immigrants. Deutsch provides an exile's take on the topic and seeks to shed light on 'some of the conditions and prospects of national or supranational integration' (Deutsch 1966: 189). Given his deeply post-Habsburgian sensibility, he assumes as a matter of course that *peoples* may become *nations* as political space is redrawn. This sense of a changing geo-politics, of the widespread non-coincidence of states and nations, is exceedingly relevant to present-day Europe.

In his introduction to the second edition of *Nationalism and Social Communication*, Deutsch (1966: 4) highlighted a cardinal theme that remains pertinent for current debate: he observed that the nation–state was 'still the chief political instrument for getting things done', and underlined his view that supranational integration had inherent limits given the resilience of nationality. The key proposition of Deutsch's theory is this:

> The essential aspect of the unity of a people . . . is the comple-
> mentarity or relative efficiency of communication among individuals
> – something that is in some ways similar to *mutual rapport, but on a
> larger scale.*
>
> (1966: 188; emphasis added)

Deutsch sees a *people* as providing the basis for the forging of a nationality. This, in turn, is distinct from *nation statehood*, where political sovereignty is harnessed to the pursuit of a group's cohesion and the continuity of its identity. Without expressly naming it, the theory therefore entertains an idea – that of *the nation without a state* – that has of late become increasingly significant both as an analytic category and as a political project aimed at redefining the autonomy of national groups within the existing international system of states (cf. Nairn 1997; McCrone 1998). For Deutsch (1996: 75), the eventual exercise of national power relies upon 'the relatively coherent and stable structure of memories, habits and values', which in turn 'depends on existing facilities for social communication, both from the past to the present and between contemporaries'.

Social communication is therefore very broadly understood: it is akin to an all-embracing anthropological notion of culture as a way of life, an interactively sustained mode of being that integrates a given people and provides it with singularity (Deutsch 1966: 96–7). This idea is otherwise represented as a principle of coherence for a community, and has a basis in the 'facilities for storing, recalling, and recombining information, channels for its dissemination and interaction, and facilities for deriving further information' (Deutsch 1966: 75). Much influenced by the pioneers of information theory, after being regarded as rather unfashionable for some years, Deutsch's half-century-old idiom has a striking contemporaneity in the era of the so-called information society.

Social communication theory embraces the ways in which socio-cultural groups cluster and how forms of cohesion affect institutions and socio-cultural interaction. Communicative integration has a key significance because it produces social closure. Consequently, Deutsch (1966: 95) stresses the well-worn sociological distinction between 'community' and 'society', keenly aware that a society may contain quite different ethno-cultural communities that speak to themselves and therefore cannot find a common overarching code – or mode of social communication.

Central to the argument is the view that nations and nation–states are strongly bounded by their socially communicative structures of interaction: 'Peoples are held together "from within" by this communicative efficiency, the complementarity of the communicative facilities acquired by their members' (1966: 98). Nationality therefore becomes an objective function of communicative competence and belonging. Although Deutsch acknowledges the analytical place of such ideas as *national consciousness* and *national will*, the symbolic level of national self-awareness – what in today's idiom would be termed 'national identity' – is seen as an outcome of the structural cohesion that comes about through social communication.

One key implication is that the communicative practices of nations lead to the exclusion of foreigners. 'Ethnic complementarity' (which, for Deutsch, broadly equates to nationality) sets up 'communicative barriers' and engenders '"marked gaps" in the efficiency of communication' relative to other groups (1966: 100). Although some nations, those based on immigration and openness to assimilation, are well adapted to the integration of new members, others may throw the process into reverse by expulsion or even extermination.

A further consequence is that the creation of wider collectivities via, for instance, supranational political arrangements such as federation or confederation, is inherently difficult to achieve, especially where communicative complementarity is weak or does not exist. In a negative anticipation of the techno-utopia of the global village, Deutsch argues that the construction of a universal communication system is impossible in a non-uniform world (1966: 176). Deutsch is therefore more struck by the likely persistence of the nation–state than by its disappearance. As he neatly puts it, 'the present distribution of sovereign states' is 'necessary in its essential features, though not in its accidents' (1966: 187).

This functionalist conception of cultural integration has a decisive weakness when the level of analysis shifts *outside* the nation–state. There is no general principle for analysing the interaction between communicative communities, for assessing cultural and communicative flows in a global system – matters of central concern to contemporary cultural and media studies – because that is not where the theoretical interest lies. Social communication theory is therefore internalist. At root, it is about how shared cultural and communicative practices strengthen the identity of a group by creating boundaries.

HIGH CULTURES, IMAGINED COMMUNITIES, BANAL NATIONALISMS

Deutsch's underlying conception of social communication – if not his theoretical idiom – lives on strongly, mostly half-recognised at best, in more contemporary work, such as, for instance, Ernest Gellner's noted *Nations and Nationalism* (1983), which has become the lodestar exposition of the 'modernist' conception of nationalism. Like Deutsch, Gellner displays a *Mitteleuropäisch* exilic strand in his work, and – no accident, this – his thinking about Europe was also especially marked by the post-Habsburg legacy of non-congruence between states and nations in central Europe.[3]

Gellner argues that the formation of nation–states is the inevitable outcome of industrialisation, with its concomitantly complex division of labour. The social relations created by industrial society mean that to function effectively one needs to be able, in principle, to do anything, and that requires 'generic training'. This transmission of know-how necessitates a universal, standardised system of education, using a standardised linguistic medium. It is this process that brings about an inevitable 'deep adjustment in the relationship between polity and culture', namely nationalism, which is 'the organization of human groups into large, centrally educated, culturally homogeneous groups' (Gellner 1983: 35). Gellner's theory, then, connects the explanatory motor of industrialisation to a quintessentially Deutschian conception of social communication.

Gellner takes culture to refer to 'the distinctive style of conduct and communication of a given community', which in the modern world takes the modal form of a nation–state. For the members of such political formations 'culture is now the necessary shared medium' (1983: 37–8). Cultural boundaries become defined by national cultures, which diffuse a literate 'high culture', in which the key agency is a national education system. In this account, the culture of a nation is broadly identified with official culture. The theory is less focused on sources of internal differentiation and conflict than it is concerned with what makes the nation cohere. Consequently, like Deutsch's theory, Gellner's is mainly an analysis of how a national culture comes to be created, rather than concerning itself with how it is maintained and renewed. It likewise stresses the self-containedness of nation–state-protected cultures. So, although Deutsch is mentioned only en passant, as the springboard for Gellner (1983: 126) to think briefly about the role of media in the national culture, his influence actually runs rather far deeper than it seems.

Whereas contemporary media and cultural theories are especially concerned with cultural flows and relations of dominance within the global communications order (cf. e.g. Sreberny-Mohammadi et al. (eds) 1997; Thussu (ed.) 1998) this is not a key interest for Gellner, any more than it was for Deutsch. In a way still quite characteristic of most sociological theorising, mass-mediated communication is dealt with as a relative triviality.[4] Gellner (1983: 127) argues, in a cryptic passage, that it is not the content of such communication that matters, but rather

> the media themselves, the pervasiveness and importance of abstract, centralized, standardized, one to many communication, which itself automatically engendered the core idea of nationalism, quite irrespective of what in particular is being put into the specific messages transmitted. The most important and persistent message is generated by the medium itself, by the role which such media have acquired in modern life. The core message is that the language and style of the transmissions is important, that only he who can understand them, or can acquire such comprehension, is included in a moral and economic community, and that he who does not and cannot, is excluded.

Echoing Marshall McLuhan, Gellner therefore argues in part that the media are the message. But the formula is modified to take account of 'language and style', of how common codes invite the audience to consider and understand themselves to be members of a given community. The media therefore function as a categorial system: widespread public identification with the national space is held to be an effect of this form of cultural organisation.

Media are boundary markers, intimately related to the 'political roof' that caps a culture and makes it into a nation–state. It is their function in sustaining a political community that is of prime interest for Gellner, and it is therefore not a problem to think of them as univocal.

Although persuasive, this argument overstates the point. 'Language and style' are about more than the medium that transmits them: they are closely related to the question of 'content'. This is of cardinal interest for the cultural industries that produce it. Moreover, the attitude of the state to its own *national* content is frequently a matter of high importance in international cultural trade and often embedded in national communication policies. Hence, Gellner's rendition of social communication theory reproduces the original Deutschian fixation on what is internal to the communicative community rather than considering the import of what lies outside and how it may be addressed. It ignores the *otherness* that may well substantially condition any given national identity.

This internalist line of argument also runs through another pivotal text of recent years, Benedict Anderson's *Imagined Communities* (1983), whose approach on the face of it takes its distance from Gellner.[5] Since Anderson's work appeared, his title has turned from a pithy descriptor of nationhood into a sociological and journalistic cliché.[6] In his account of the emergence of European nations, Anderson, like Deutsch and even more than Gellner, takes mediated communication to be of central importance in the formation of a nationalist consciousness (or, as we now say, national identity):

> What, in a positive sense, made the new communities imaginable was a half-fortuitous, but explosive, interaction between a system of production and productive relations (capitalism), a technology of communications (print), and the fatality of human linguistic diversity.
>
> (Anderson, 1983: 46)

Whereas for Gellner national systems of education that produce cultural affines (a community of 'clerks') take centre-stage, Anderson's key contention is that '[p]rint-language is what invents nationalism, not *a* particular language per se' (1983: 122). Thus, what is highlighted is the importance of the media of communication in the construction of an imagined community, given the appropriate material conditions.

According to Anderson, 'print language' was the means whereby given vernaculars became standardised, being disseminated through the market for books and newspapers. His account is resolutely Gutenbergian: the impact of electronic media is not addressed.[7] Mechanically reproduced print-languages unified fields of linguistic exchange, fixed *national* languages, and created new idioms of power. The 'nationalist novel' (its plot enacted in a socially recognised common space) together with the newspaper, with 'calendrical consciousness' as its principle of organisation, were, Anderson argues, the two key vehicles in shaping national consciousness. By co-ordinating time and space these could address an imagined national community even before it had been formed into a nation–state.

Hence, the collective consumption of mediated communication serves to create a sense of national community. Like Gellner, from whom he would differentiate his approach, Anderson actually understands the confines of the nation to be inescapably implicit in the way that media categorise reality and address their audiences. Strikingly, like Deutsch, who writes of large-scale 'mutual rapport', Anderson speaks of the nation's 'deep, horizontal comradeship' (1983: 16).

Subsequently, Anderson (1991: 184) has considered how the national story has been told in post-colonial states by way of the cultural institutions of the census (enumerator and sorter of populations), the map (definer of the political boundaries) and the museum (vehicle for the establishment of legitimate ancestry). Although (unlike Gellner) Anderson makes no reference to Deutsch's work, his approach is still unmistakably located in a social communication framework: the imagined community is situated within the socio-cultural and communicative space of the nation–state and it is the internal processes of nation-formation that are of predominant interest.

Anderson's argument about the 'imagined community' has been taken up, with a distinctive twist, by Michael Billig (1995: 70) who rightly observes that this increasingly overworked slogan can be illuminating, but only when 'it is realised that the imagined community does not depend upon continual acts of imagination for its existence'. This line of interpretation is of a piece with his general argument about nationalism's 'banality': namely, the demonstrable proposition that a great deal of nationalist practice is embedded in the rituals and practices of everyday life. Billig takes as one paradigm case the daily saluting of the flag in US schools. This activity has become so 'natural' that even most social scientists have failed to interrogate its significance. And although those who salute may have various relationships to the act of saluting itself, they are participating in a common rite.

Billig argues that in the contemporary world, entire peoples are simply embedded in their national deixes. Their flags flutter diurnally, largely unnoticed as adornments to public buildings; the news categorises some events as home affairs and distinguishes these from foreign reports; the weather forecast reinforces the awareness of political geography; sporting heroes embody national virtues and mobilise collective loyalties; moments of crisis – especially war – produce patriotic addresses from political leaders; national languages and histories, through their transmission, constitute a sense of communality. And so forth. Thus are the internal props of national identity routinely and unremarkably reproduced. In line with Gellner and Anderson, Billig's analysis fills in the space of 'communicative complementarity' and underscores its tenacious grip on how we categorise the world.

But, notably, unlike his precursors, Billig is interested less in the question of nation-formation than in that of nation-maintenance.

Billig largely concurs with Gellner's insight that it is largely impossible to think of oneself as *other* than a national and have a place in the contemporary world. And that is because we live a world of states – often officially represented, however inaccurately, as *nation*–states – whose boundaries impose the requirement that we belong to some juridically recognised collectivity. Billig certainly recognises the pressure of global culture and international relations as needing to be negotiated by banal nationalisms, which continue to provide anchorages for collectivities. Consequently, his position is resolutely resistant to the postmodern claims that our collective identities have become free-floating signifiers, or, alternatively, that we have entered a stage of post-national tribalism. Rather, it is insisted, rightly, that whatever the transformative impact of 'globalisation' might be, it has not neutralised national attachments. But this proper acknowledgement of the shaping impact of the extra-national (based in Billig's engagement with current media and cultural studies) is still largely subordinate to offering an account of how, as Deutsch would say, nations are held together 'from within'.[8]

All the above theories share a notion of the prototypically modern – i.e. national – communicative community as strongly bounded. Deutsch's work emphasises the communicative 'gaps' between peoples, this being the dark side of relatively cosy insider efficiency and complementarity. Gellner and Anderson, too, stress the role of a common culture based in a standardized language and cultural institutions in making a common people; whereas Billig underscores the often unnoticed daily 'flagging' of a common identity.

THE NATION AS DELIBERATIVE SPACE

Social communication theories, then, all partake of a broad interest in how nations speak to themselves, mark themselves off as different from others. This theme is also central to the work of Jürgen Habermas, whose work is widely recognised as premised on a theory of communication, but is less well understood to be also concerned with the *nation* addressed as a political community. Habermas' theory, expounded in *The Structural Transformation of the Public Sphere* (1989) has exerted a profound influence in recent debate about the role and quality of political communication and the mediation of civic deliberation. The *public sphere* – another sociological trope of our time – refers to the whole domain of debate in an institutional space that exists outside the state, but which engages all who are concerned with matters of public interest. The presence of this domain is central to the freedom of expression commonly associated with democracy; it is necessarily a space in which communication takes place.

Even when the Habermasian version of the public sphere has been an object of criticism (see Calhoun (ed.) 1992; Schudson 1992) it has still been the starting-point for much recent discussion of the role of media in democracies (cf. Curran 1991; Dahlgren 1995). What tends widely to have been presumed to be natural rather than examined critically is the necessary co-extensiveness of political public space with the boundaries of nation statehood. Perhaps this is not surprising, as the formation of the classic public sphere coincided with the growth of nationalism and nation–state formation. In line with this, Habermas' theory in its earliest formulation emphasises that public communication remains pre-eminently tied to the structures of meaning of nation–states – although these have long been subject to international flows of information and cultural products.

OVER THE NATIONAL BOUNDARY

Thus far, it has been argued that social communication theories have two key limitations:

1 a tendency to think in terms of a close functional fit between communication and the nation; and
2 an overwhelming concern with the interior of the national communicative space, whether this be in respect of its formation or its maintenance.

This internalism may, at times, acknowledge how nations are defined by their positions in the relations of an interstate world, but that is of secondary interest. Taken together, therefore, these positions carry a major implication: that the politically salient container for communicative space is the sovereign nation–state.

Critical deliberation within national spaces, however, is not adequate to the global changes that presently face us. Decision making about key matters that affect nation–states is commonly located extra-territorially: in the boardrooms of transnational corporations, inside international organisations of various descriptions, within the cabinets of regional military, political and economic groupings, in the various centres of global finance. If national publics are to become involved in deliberation about what concerns them, national communicative spaces need to be complemented by those that enable the formation of publics with a transnational, even global, scope.

As various commentators have argued, it is important to ask questions about the impact of transnational and global changes on what are still largely nation–state-bound systems of communication. What do these imply both for the possibility of a supranational public sphere as well as for new forms of communication emanating from the self-organisation of civil society (Keane 1991: 142–6; Garnham 1994: 372)? The European Union (EU) offers a

107

particularly apt laboratory test for those interested in the communicative relations between nation statehood and supranationalism. In the EU, for instance, the nation–state is being squeezed from above and below: from above, by a process of *Europeanisation* that circumscribes and redefines conceptions of sovereign action by member states in the fields of economics, defence, social affairs, communication and, increasingly, foreign policy; and simultaneously from below, by the growth of a more autonomous regionalism within nation–states, which is especially significant when regions are also stateless nations.

To what extent is the classical framework of communication theories of nationalism – focused, as we have seen, almost exclusively on the level of the nation–state – transposable to an emergent supranational entity in which substate regions are acquiring increased political visibility?

Deutsch (1966: 3–4) doubted that a common communicative space could easily emerge in the then European Community because of the continuing strength of the nation–state. Some thirty years later, in sharp contrast, Habermas (1994: 21) has maintained that the 'classic form of the nation–state is presently disintegrating'. For him, the European Union now offers scope for a new, wider, conception of citizenship with a correlatively broader framework of public communication. He has thus transposed the national public sphere to the supranational level, assuming a diminished hold by the nation–state and nationality on collective loyalty and identification. By this account the eventual European political community would be linked not by means of common symbols but rather through a less emotionally compelling framework of rules. As Habermas (1994: 27) puts it:

> [The] political culture must serve as the common denominator for a constitutional patriotism which simultaneously sharpens an aware-ness of the multiplicity and integrity of the different forms of life which exist in a multicultural society.

Is such political rationality enough to make an extended and variegated collectivity cohere? Certainly, it offers a strong point of contrast to the symbol-rich, affectively connected and routinised national life-form depicted by the first wave of social communication theory. In his more recent thinking, Habermas expressly conceives of the public sphere as potentially *unbounded*, as having shifted from specific locales (such as the nation) to the virtual co-presence of citizens and consumers linked by media. A European public sphere, on this model, would be open-textured, since its communicative connections would extend beyond whatever expedient political form the EU happens to take; indeed such connections would extend beyond the European continent altogether. Of course, this makes a certain sense: contemporary communication flows and networks ensure that no – or hardly any – political community can remain an island. However, to the extent that this perspective implies, too, that we somehow belong also to a global village, it inevitably raises questions about *which* communicative boundaries continue to be *most* significant for the development of a distinctive political identity and political culture in the EU. In other words, we are compelled to ask are there *specific* communicative processes that might contribute to the Union's social cohesion?

Habermas envisages a liberal and egalitarian European political culture in which decision-making bodies are open to scrutiny. He assumes that there will be intensified networking across national boundaries and sets out an ideal interplay between 'institutionalised processes of opinion and will formation' and 'informal networks of public communication' (1994: 31). Moreover, it is postulated that a radical form of popular involvement in public affairs will act as the essential corrective to professionalised politics. Since parliamentary democracy is as indispensable at the European level as at that of the nation–state, what is needed is 'a discursive structuring of public networks and arenas in which anonymous circuits of communication are detached from the concrete level of single interactions' (Habermas 1997: 171). In other words, a *European* communicative space is required. Note, though, that entwined with the argument about the sphere of public deliberation is another, about how long-term social interaction produces forms of solidarity. While this is quite understated, it is analytically distinct and begins to offer a quite plausible social-interactionist account of *supra-nation-building* alongside the more procedural–deliberative level of action summed up as *constitutional patriotism*.

This somewhat shadowy sociology of solidarity needs to be foregrounded, as otherwise the consequence of unbounding the national public is to insert us into 'a highly complex network that branches out into a multitude of overlapping international, national, regional, local and subcultural arenas' (Habermas 1997: 373–4). This complete opening out of communication, the globalisation of the public sphere in effect, sits somewhat uneasily alongside Habermas' thinking about the supersession of the nation–state and its *bounded* reconstitution at the federal European level with a political culture to match. While, by definition, the global communication network thus conceived has no necessary boundaries, arguably a European polity does. It is hard to see how a discursively linked community could develop a collective political loyalty and identity if completely unbounded. A European political community without some distinctive communicative boundary-markers simply cannot be imagined as a sociological possibility.

This relates to the general problem of an emergent European collective identity. Habermas offers a federalist model of political involvement by Europeans in which the content of their collective identities is different at each level. At the level of the nation–state it is 'thick' and articulates with a national political culture elaborated within a highly institutionalised public sphere. At the level of Union Europe, it is 'thin' and legalistic, and overwhelmingly refracted through the medium of nation–state politics. Behind this characterisation of two levels of collective identification lies the unresolved broader issue of what makes collectivities cohere, and whether any conceivable constitutional patriotism ultimately presupposes a hinterland of *non-rationalistic* assumptions and sentiments in order to make its civic appeal work (Schlesinger 1997: 385–8).

For Habermas, therefore, the potentially transformative impact on communities of communication technologies is subordinate to an argument about the need for a public sphere and, so far as the European Union is concerned, how an appropriate new communicative space might be constituted. His latest formulations make some minor play with the concept of *the network*. This is much more developed in the work of Manuel Castells (1996; 1997; 1998), for whom the radical impact of communication technologies is held to have contributed to the formation of an altogether new kind of society, the *informational*.

Castells (1996: 3) argues that as 'patterns of social communication come increasingly under stress' we now need to think of communicative relations on the model of the network: 'Our societies are increasingly structured around a bipolar opposition between the Net and the Self.' From this perspective, to the extent that our anchorage in social structure is weakened, we are supposedly increasingly the authors of our identities.[9] Castells' post-nationalism does indeed acknowledge its Deutschian provenance (Castells 1997: 31), which is evidently adaptable enough to take account of the transformation of the nation–state.

Like Habermas, Castells considers the European Union's form to be of especial interest. But it is not public sphere concerns that preoccupy Castells, so much as his view that the EU is the precursor of a new political order, of new forms of association and loyalty. For him, the emerging Euro-polity epitomises what he terms 'the network state'. Although the diagnosis is squarely in line with much contemporary political science and constitutional thinking (e.g. Schmitter 1996; Weiler 1996), there is a distinctive twist, inasmuch as Castells sees the emergent Euro-state not only as a political-economic zone but, by virtue of privileging its network character, as a specific kind of *communicative* space.[10]

For Castells, just like the world order itself, the EU has different 'nodes' of varying importance that together make up a network. Regions and nations, nation–states, European Union institutions, therefore together constitute a framework in which authority is shared. In Castells' account of the Euro-matrix (unlike that of Habermas) the stateless nation is judged to be of especial significance as a prototype of potentially innovative forms of post-nation–state affiliation. This comes out most clearly, perhaps, in his account of his native Catalonia, which – like the EU, but on a different level – is taken to be an exemplar of flexible networking and as offering multiple identities and allegiances to its inhabitants.[11] Nations are defined as distinct from the state, being characterised as 'cultural communes constructed in people's minds by the sharing of history and political projects' (1997: 51).

This fits into a more general diagnosis in which Castells (1997: 354) avers that '[b]ypassed by global networks of wealth, power and information, the modern nation–state has lost much of its sovereignty'. The result is a 'dissolution of shared identities', ostensibly producing a split between global elites that consider themselves citizens of the world and the resistance of those who have lost economic, political and cultural power who 'tend to be attracted to communal identities' that either cut across the nation–state or operate somewhere below the nation–state level (ibid. 356). The EU is an instance of the former; Catalonia and Scotland, examples of the latter. For Castells (1998: 318), European integration represents 'at the same time a reaction to the process of globalization and its most advanced expression'. It is hailed as the harbinger of a new type of society.

In terms of Castells' wider theory, much as with Habermas, we might ask what gives *boundaries* to the putative European communicative space? The answer is one curiously reminiscent of Deutsch's argument about cultural complementarity and communicative efficiency. It resides in the nexus of political institutions that constitute Union Europe and the dealings between them and it involves also the growing criss-crossing of 'subsidiary' horizontal linkages at all levels across the member states (Castells 1998: 330–1). This coincides exactly with Habermas' argument. In short, a form of Deutschian 'communicative complementarity' emerges out of what Keith Middlemass (1995) has called the 'Euro-civilising process', namely the informal processes of state making. Thus, the potentially globalising pull of communication technologies is countered by emergent patterns of social interaction in the European Union's space that are polyvalent: simultaneously, they knit together diverse actors economically, politically and communicatively. Thus, a supra-national network on the European Union's scale comes to develop a specific interactive intensity that favours internal communication and creates a referential boundary that can co-exist with global networking.

In broad explanatory terms, then, social communication theory is capable of discarding its national shell and, indeed, its tight functionalism. However, although it can produce an account of distinct and intersecting levels of communicative space above, at and below the level of the nation–state, the theory is still characteristically centred on how specific forms of communication induce patterns of cohesion. Moreover, to develop social communication theory by invoking the model of the network does not resolve the knotty questions of how contradictions of interest, identity and loyalty, or structured inequalities of power, are handled within the more complex account of communicative space that latterly has been elaborated.

CONCLUDING REMARKS

Theoretical arguments about social communication and contemporary policy developments are intimately connected. Take, for instance, the EU's attempts to define a 'European' cultural identity and common communicative space in the 1980s and 1990s, which took place in the context of global industrial competition, most especially with the United States and Japan. Heightened invocations of a common European culture accompanied efforts to protect European audiovisual production from the impact of US film and television imports during the concluding phase of the GATT negotiations in 1993, and this remains a live issue (cf. van Hemel *et al.* 1996). The emphasis on defending 'Europeanness' and the need to treat films and television programmes as protectable cultural goods has reflected official concern about the extent to which the globalisation of communication had undermined the cultural sovereignty of nation–states and, by extension, that of the intergovernmental European Union itself.

In global cultural trade, the EU has made efforts to represent itself as a coherent cultural entity. However, that is only its outward face, since internally the EU demonstrates acutely the tensions between supra-nationalism and nationalism. Where diversity of language and culture are crucial symbols of collective identity, supra-national Euro-goals encounter national resistances. To complicate things further, the EU-endorsed recognition of regional differences within member states – the so-called 'Europe of the Regions' – has reinforced autonomist, even secessionist, tendencies, particularly in the territories of stateless nations.[12] Hence, state-endorsed national culture may not only contradict the demands of 'Europeanisation' but European nation–states may simultaneously find themselves challenged from another direction by claims made for cultural and communicative recognition on the part of national, ethnic and linguistic minorities.

Such arguments about the impact of cultural flows and the reconfiguration of politico-cultural spaces are one way of thinking about identity construction. Another is to consider the obstacles in the way of the long-term process of quasi-state-building that is being undertaken in Europe. As Ernest Gellner (1997: 50) has observed in proferring a neat metaphor for uneven development, we might consider the European continent as though it were a set of 'time zones' with 'belts of territory running from north to south, within which the pattern is roughly similar, but which differ from one zone to another'. Therefore, despite the asynchronicity of present-day conditions in different parts of the continent, the 'Euro-civilising process' may well ultimately result in sychronic convergence: the longer term outcome could be the creation of a new political culture that sustains a distinct level of European identity and citizenship (cf. Schlesinger and Kevin [forthcoming]). To date, however, the Union's intermittent expansion to embrace such diverse states has produced a knotty cultural problem: its instability has provoked a continual rethinking of forms of governance and also has made it difficult to establish a stable basis for collective identification across and 'above' the level of the nation–state.

Contemporary developments suggest, therefore, that social communication theory, with some adaptation, is likely to inform how we think about future European developments, as it has in the past. Having now abandoned the homologous coupling of nation and communication, its exponents are bound to analyse both the contradictions and congruences of at least three political levels at which communicative space is elaborated: the supra-national, the nation–statal, and the subnation–statal. This shift of theoretical focus is the very least that is needed to keep pace with growing complexity.

NOTES

1 This discussion is part of an intended short book. In the present text, I have revisited and substantially developed some earlier considerations (cf. Schlesinger 1991).

2 Only a brief introduction was added to the second edition in 1966. There is complementary material in Deutsch's later work but the essentials of the argument do not change from its first formulation.

3 Just how much so has latterly emerged in his posthumous work (notably Gellner 1998). I hope to deal with the Habsburg matrix and some of its intellectual consequences in future work.

4 Alvin Gouldner (1976) was one mainstream sociologist who recognised the importance of communication in constructing public (national) discourse. More recently, from the standpoint of social theory, John Thompson (1995) has tried also to integrate the findings of media research into an analysis of the public sphere.

5 As I pointed out some years ago: 'Anderson distinguishes his position from that of Gellner, whom he describes as "so anxious to show that nationalism masquerades under false pretences that he assimilates "invention" to "fabrication" and "falsity", rather than to "imagining" and "creation".' (Schlesinger 1991: 163). As is plain, the deep structure of their arguments is much closer than Anderson thinks.

6 Characteristically enough, it has been probed for analytical shortcomings, though these have not yet shaken the fashionableness of the slogan. (cf. Balakrishnan 1996; Chatterjee 1996; Tamir 1995.)

7 A point latterly acknowledged by Anderson (1994: 320–1) who has recognised the boundary-crossing impact of electronic media but without explaining what that might be.

8 Billig's sole reference to Deutsch is both cryptic and mistaken in its emphasis on his developmentalism (Billig 1995: 43). Again, here is an author evidently unconscious of a key conceptual debt.

9 My purpose here is not to take issue with this postmodern vision, which I do not share, and which is hardly consistently adhered to by the author himself.

10 I have argued along similar lines myself, albeit from within a different theoretical framework. (cf. Schlesinger and Kevin [2000].)

11 Castells takes issue with both Gellner and Anderson for their modernism (on defensible historical grounds) and for what (mistakenly, I believe) he takes to be their treatment of nationhood as lacking any 'real existence'. Castells takes Gellner's stress on 'invention' and Anderson's on the 'imagined' aspects of community to be denials of the nation's material reality. I understand them to be talking about the production of beliefs or consciousness or identities that both express and designate an actually existing collectivity. So far as the historical critique of modernism goes, there are powerful echoes of this in Scotland, a case analogous to Catalonia in many respects (cf. Ferguson 1998).

12 I have begun to explore the impact of these processes on communicative spaces in Scotland, in Schlesinger 1998.

Acknowledgment

This study is based on research carried out as part of the 'Political Communication and Democracy' project in the ESRC's 'Media Economics and Media Culture Programme' (Reference No. L126251022). The author is grateful to the Council for its support.

REFERENCES

Anderson, B. (1991) *Imagined Communities: Reflections on the Origin and Spread of Nationalism*, London: Verso Editions (1983).

—— (1994) 'Exodus', *Critical Inquiry* 20(2): 314–27.

Balakrishnan, G. (1996) 'The national imagination', in G. Balakrishnan (ed.) *Mapping the Nation*, London: Verso, 198–213.

Billig, M. (1995) *Banal Nationalism*, London: SAGE Publications.

Calhoun, C. (ed.) (1992) *Habermas and the Public Sphere*, Cambridge, MA: MIT Press.

Castells, M. (1996) *The Rise of the Network Society*, Malden, MA: Blackwell Publishers Inc.

—— (1997) *The Power of Identity*, Malden, MA: Blackwell Publishers Inc.

—— (1998) *End of Millennium*, Malden, MA: Blackwell Publishers Inc.

Chatterjee, P. (1996) 'Whose imagined community?', in G. Balakrishnan (ed.) (1996), 214–25.

Curran, J. (1991) 'Rethinking the media as a public sphere', in P. Dahlgren and C. Sparks (eds) *Communication and Citizenship: Journalism and the Public Sphere*, London and New York: Routledge.

Dahlgren, P. (1995) *Television and the Public Sphere: Citizenship, Democracy and the Media*, London: SAGE Publications.

Deutsch, K. W. (1996) *Nationalism and Social Communication: An Inquiry into the Foundations of Nationalism*, Cambridge, MA; and London: MIT Press (1953).

Ferguson, W. (1998) *The Identity of the Scottish Nation: An Historic Quest*, Edinburgh: Edinburgh University Press.

Garnham, N. (1992) 'The media and the public sphere', in Calhoun (ed.) *Habermas and the Public Sphere*, 359–76.

Gellner, E. (1983) *Nations and Nationalism*, Oxford: Basil Blackwell.
—— (1997) *Nationalism*, London: Weidenfeld & Nicolson.
—— (1998) *Language and Solitude: Wittgenstein, Malinowski and the Habsburg Dilemma*, Cambridge: Cambridge University Press.
Gouldner, A. W. (1976) *The Dialectic of Ideology and Technology: The Origins, Grammar and Future of Technology*, London and Basingstoke: MacMillan Press.
Habermas, J. (1989) *The Structural Transformation of the Public Sphere: An Inquiry into a Category of Bourgeois Society*, Cambridge: Polity Press (1962).
—— (1994) 'Citizenship and national identity', in B. van Steenbergen (ed.) *The Condition of Citizenship*, London: SAGE Publications, 20–35.
—— (1997) *Between Facts and Norms*, Cambridge: Polity Press.
Keane, J. (1991) *The Media and Democracy*, Cambridge: Polity Press.
McCrone, D. (1998) *The Sociology of Nationalism: Tomorrow's Ancestors*, London and New York: Routledge.
Nairn, T. (1997) *Faces of Nationalism: Janus Revisited*, London: Verso.
Middlemas, K. (1995) *Orchestrating Europe: The Informal Politics of European Union 1973–1995*, London: Fontana Press.
Schlesinger, P. (1991) *Media, State and Nation: Political Violence and Collective Identities*, London, Newbury Park and New Delhi: SAGE Publications.
Schlesinger, P. (1997) 'From cultural defence to political culture: media, politics and collective identity in the European Union', *Media, Culture and Society* 19(3): 369–91.
—— (1998) 'Scottish devolution and the media', in J. Seaton (ed.) *Politics and the Media: Harlots and Prerogatives at the Turn of the Millennium*, Oxford: Blackwell Publishers.
—— and D. Kevin (2000) 'Can the European Union become a sphere of publics?', in Eriksen, E. O. and J. E. Fossum (eds) *Democracy in Europe*, London and New York: Routledge, 206–29.
Schmitter, P. (1996) *Is it Really Possible to Democratize the Euro-Polity?*, Working Paper 96/11, Oslo: ARENA.
Schudson, M. (1992) 'Was there ever a public sphere? If so, when? Reflections on the American case', in C. Calhoun (ed.), 143–63.
Sreberny-Mohammadi, A., D. Winseck, J. McKenna and O. Boyd-Barrett (eds) (1997) *Media in Global Context: A Reader*, London: Arnold.
Tamir, Y. (1995) 'The enigma of nationalism', *World Politics* 47(2): 418–40.
Thompson, J. B. (1995) *The Media and Modernity: A Social Theory of the Media*, Cambridge: Polity Press.
Thussu, D. K. (ed.) (1998) *Electronic Empires: Global Media and Local Resistance*, London: Arnold.
van Hemel, A., H. Mommaas and Smithuijsen (eds) (1996) *Trading Culture: GATT, European Cultural Policies and the Transatlantic Market*, Amsterdam: Boekman Foundation.
Weiler, J. H. H. (1996) *Legitimacy and Democracy of Union Governance: The 1996 Intergovernmental Agenda and Beyond*, Working Paper 96/22, Oslo: ARENA.

7

DIGITISED CAPITALISM

What has changed?

Herbert I. Schiller

In the transformation of the world's capitalist system, and its communication component, in recent decades, a few features stand out.

There is, visibly and palpably, a gargantuan concentration of capital, best illustrated by, but by no means exclusive to, the United States. The corporate sector, which in pre-Second World War years already was a dominating presence, came out of the war a behemoth. There is simply no comparing, for example, a corporation like General Electric, with current assets of $200 billion, with its prewar status. It is not a concluded process and the pyramidisation of assets proceeds feverishly. The outcome, though we are unable to predict it with specificity, will certainly be a handful of global economic giants in the various sectors of the world economy.

In the communication sphere, the concentration has been occurring at an intensifying tempo over the last twenty years, spurred on by a gale of new technologies and, more importantly, by the systemic requirements of the transnational corporate order which is heavily reliant on communication for its global operations and its worldwide marketing efforts. It follows that new investments in telecommunications have become significant percentages of the economy's total investment, and that the communication sector has become the pacemaker of the entire economy.

This enhanced corporate sphere has focused its attention, in its drive for ever-greater profitability, on the destruction of the state's social services' activity and role, created during the Depression of the 1930s and expanded briefly in the 1960s. Confident of its growing strength, capitalism no longer is willing to accept limitations, especially those placed on it during earlier crisis times. It is more dismissive still of social measures aimed at alleviating the distress of that part of the population discarded or unutilized by the business system.

The banner of capital, in its push toward total social unaccountability, proclaims 'deregulation.' With deregulation, one sector of the economy after another is 'liberated' to capital's unmonitored authority. The very existence of a reality called 'the public interest' is contested. Public functions are weakened or eliminated.

This occurs in most industrial states, at varying speeds, with minimal resistance. Opposition where it develops, e.g. in France, seems to be no more than a delaying action. The rampaging juggernaut of transnational capital is, moreover, abetted by the powerful cultural industries and especially the mass media. A modest case in point comes from the publishing field.

A new economics text offers this perspective of current economic activity: the author

> teaches that increases in government spending crowd out private capital, producing higher interest rates. Higher thrift and greater savings produce lower interest rates and higher economic growth. Unemployment is caused not by greedy industrialists, but by minimum wage laws, collective bargaining, unemployment insurance and other regulations that raise the cost of labor.
>
> Skousen (1997)

This new primer, *Business Week* notes, 'will play a big role in shaping public opinion about how the economy works' (Coy 1997: 44).

It will also inform the new generation that the general efforts of working people to improve their lives over the last two centuries have been misguided. It will claim that the dismantlement of social protection is liberatory. And, it will insist that the 'principles of economics' it presents have universal applicability.

Deregulation and concentration of capital have been facilitated by the stream of new information technologies, many derivative of America's enormous Cold War military expenditures on research and development. These technologies, beyond their obvious military purposes, have served the operational needs of transnational capital, as it undertakes production and distribution in multitudinous global sites.

Vast electronic and telecommunication networks have been organized which are indispensable to corporate global activities. The circuits serve also to open up new markets and transmit, along with business data, the cultural products and especially the advertising of the global companies. The combination of deregulation of industry, concentration of capital and worldwide instantaneous communication are the essential pillars of a massive globalisation of capital in recent decades. It is also the source of the ever-diminishing power of the nation–state, excluding – for the time being only – the most powerful nation–state, the United States.

It is the globalisation of capital also that serves as the battering ram that relentlessly attacks working people's living standards. And it is especially ruthless to national efforts on social protection. Though some still see the Internet, for example, as a democratic structure for international individual expression, it is more realistic to recognize it as only the latest technological vehicle to be turned, sooner or later, to corporate advantage – or advertising, marketing and general corporate aggrandisement.

Today, the increasingly integrated communication system in most parts of the world is firmly in the hands of Big Capital. Capital investments in telecommunication, for example, run into hundreds of billions of dollars annually. It is a system in which investment and production decisions are made less and less by national figures, more and more by transnational corporations and investors and their global institutions, e.g. the World Bank, IMF, WTO, etc. Some of the effects of the corporate control of communications are already manifest.

CAPITAL'S INSATIABILITY

What is becoming increasingly clear is the fierce and insatiable drive of capital to roll back as many of the social measures as possible that have been struggled for over the last two centuries. All of the tales of a reformed capitalism – a capitalism with a human face, a people's capitalism – have been repudiated. As vast new pools of labor from India, China, Indonesia and the rest of the poor world, enter the world economy, the balance between labor and capital, never equal in the past, becomes grossly tilted in favor of capital. The new communication technologies enable the world business system to dip into these new reserves of labor power to the great disadvantage of working people in the already industrialised and, at least partially, unionised labor force.

Takeover of public property and services

In this wildly misaligned distribution of power, there is no social or public space or activity that is either not appropriated for commodity production and profitability or, failing that, left to wither away. In the United States, for example, the public school system is under siege and the various schemes to privatise schooling are treated with respect and credulity in the mass media. The progressive income tax, adopted more than eighty years ago following strong popular demand, is all but a memory. The people's political representatives talk of substituting blatantly regressive taxes, i.e. the flat tax or a sales tax, for what remains of the income tax.

To those who regard *any* publicly supported activity as unacceptable, the arts as well are in the target zone. The National Endowment of the Arts has been under constant attack, and its – never adequate – budget has been reduced to a meagre hand-out.

Another feature of unrestrained capitalist onslaught is less visible but no less threatening to a democratic order: the ongoing transfer of social services into for-sale transactions, if unchecked, will leave people totally enmeshed in market relationships, losing every vestige of their communality. Private (for-pay) childcare centers, run by corporate chains, provide another instance of this growing phenomenon (Davis 1997). Health care, too, has become, in the language of the day, 'a profit center.' Imagine, for-profit hospitals! Yet these are not fanciful projects. They exist and proliferate.

The press

Then there is the press itself, a private institution from the beginning, in the west at least. Freedom of the press is defined – by the press, naturally – as based on the private ownership of the press properties. This definition has been incorporated by the sacred texts of American capitalism, and no less so in Great Britain as well.

With this elemental grounding of the press, there has never been a mystery about which side – labor or capital – the media have been on. They are capital. But in the age of voracious capitalism, the managers and directors of the press – newspapers, radio and television – go one step further. Now, the alleged age-old separation of editorial and business departments is being scrapped. The media are unashamedly offering their news and content to the big advertisers and sponsoring corporations for review. What once was a variably nuanced management perspective has become full obeisance. This overt aggression against reliable information is reported in different accounts, of which the following is representative:

> The *Los Angeles Times* announced a big step in its much-debated reorganization today. Its editor, Shelby Coffee 3rd, resigned and the newspaper named a new editorial team that will further dismantle the wall that has traditionally separated the news and business sides at most major newspapers.
>
> (Sterngold 1997: C-5)

Perhaps the one positive aspect of these developments is that they allow an easier recognition of what earlier had been an unacknowledged condition.

The concentration of capital reaches its apogee in the communication sector of the economy, and a no-holds-barred atmosphere permits the creation of giant cultural–media–communication predators. These have led a monumental looting of the public domain.

The radio spectrum, that part of the physical universe that offers the means – the frequencies – to transmit radio, television and other signals, has been the latest target of the privatisers and capital accumulators. From their earliest use, the air waves were recognised as inalienable public property, no less a part of the national patrimony than air and water, and later, national parks and lands.

No longer! In a series of auctions, wide chunks of the spectrum have been sold off to corporations who already own the circuitry of the country's information system. Under previous arrangements, parts of the spectrum were given, free of charge, to broadcasting interests, but always with the proviso that ultimate control and disposition were vested in the state. Actually, the supervisory agency, the Federal Communications Commission (FCC), left matters in the hands of the private spectrum holders. But the principle, if not the practice, of accountability, remained in place.

Sale of the spectrum removes that ultimate social authority and confers on the new owners property rights in perpetuity. The unwillingness of unleashed corporate enterprise to acknowledge any limits, to either its demands or its efforts to eliminate social space, is a distinctive feature of post-Cold-War capitalism.

DISAPPEARANCE OF THE THIRD WORLD

Another characteristic of this new age, is the literal disappearance of what used to be called 'the Third World.' The poor ex-colonial states have metamorphosed, under the spell and the blandishments of Wall Street investors, into 'emerging markets.' What formerly were struggling, mostly unindustrialized, states have become the locus of huge investment flows from the capital-rich nations in western Europe, the United States and Japan.

The leadership of these nations, with few practical alternatives after the demise of the Soviet system, have opted – some enthusiastically, others reluctantly – for the American 'model':

- privatization of their main industries, especially communication;
- concessions to foreign capital;
- opening of commerce and culture to free trade; and
- the free flow of information.

Third World demands, expressed twenty-five years ago, for a new international economic order and a new international information order have been interred. There *is* a new economic and a new information order. But these are domains that instead of conferring equity, reciprocity, and redistribution – the earlier objectives – impose inequality, enrichment of a new, limited, middle class, huge profits for the ownership stratum, domestic and foreign, and harsh working conditions for those employed. For the rest, a very sizeable portion of the population, there is continuing deep impoverishment. The model is on view on all continents.

No less a source than the *Wall Street Journal* informs about the Mexican experience:

> The Fund (International Monetary Fund] and the US Administration keep bragging about the Mexican model. . . . After two years Mexico is now growing again in peso terms, but what the braggarts seldom note is that every Mexican worker took a 50% pay cut in world purchasing power terms, that inflation decimated the rising middle class, and that political instability is now on the uptick.
>
> (*Wall Street Journal* 1997: A–22)

In Latin America, Mexico, Brazil, Argentina, and Chile are given special attention. In Asia, until the recent financial collapse in Thailand and across the area, South Korea, Indonesia, Malaysia, Thailand, and China especially, are viewed as attractive areas for capital investment. Eastern Europe – Czechoslovakia, Hungary and Poland, and Russia itself – gets high marks from transnational corporations and international investors. Washington, London, Paris, Tokyo, and, most of all, Wall Street, find these areas attractive sites for their speculative capital.

Yet beyond the flashy expenditures of the new and modest-sized consuming classes, the creation of a wrenching economic and social divide characterises each of these societies. Not only do the earlier poverty and social distress endure and deepen, the new model brings with it all the cultural control mechanisms of its progenitors – the United States.

Twenty-five years ago, the ex-colonial states and other poor nations sought an information order which would allow diversity, openness, mutuality, diminished commercialisation, and monopolistic control of cultural creation. Today, the 'emerging markets' are swamped with the cultural–media outputs of the western cultural industries. The very notion of cultural autonomy has disappeared into the maw of free trade and market imperatives.

Replacing the quest for a free, balanced, non-commercial information flow, is the creation of satellite transmissions and digital networks, more dominated than ever by a few transnational corporate groups. Paradoxically, these technologies are promoted, and accepted, as advanced means to escape backwardness and impoverishment.

THE FUSION OF CULTURAL–SYMBOLIC PRODUCTION AND THE GENERAL ECONOMY

Another feature of contemporary capitalism is its enfolding of cultural–symbolic production into the systemic core. The expansion of the cultural–communication industries has become crucial to the functioning of a globalised market economy. Media, publishing, advertising, public relations, opinion polling, accounting, consultancy, and market research today constitute an essential protective ring around the activities of the goods and services production center.

The transnational corporate drive for markets is dependent on the use of saturation advertising in the targeted areas. Opinion polling affords political governors the capability to monitor minutely the sentiments of their people, enabling the appropriate public relations to be applied to the problems at hand, be they elections, corruption, military adventures. However, it must be emphasized that this arsenal of communication services at the disposal of the controllers is by no means a guarantee of frictionless stability. It aims at this condition but cannot overcome numerous and unexpected sources of resistance.

Not surprisingly, these relatively newly developed fields are staffed by the most highly trained and capable members of the labor force. They have quickly become an important element of governing power.

The film and television industries, important since their inception as providers of popular diversion and the dominant ideology, have become economic heavyweights as well, exporting billions of dollars' worth of symbolic product. These exports are now second only to those of the aerospace industry.

The increasing value of information and the digitised networks that transmit it, confer still more importance on the communication sector. US primacy in this field, perhaps only temporary but presently very considerable, is seen by some in the political and military leadership as an indisputable basis for an American-led twenty-first century (Nye and Owens 1996: 20–36 and Rothkopf 1997: 38–53).

Domestically, one is overwhelmed by the continuous barrage of commercial messages, trivial news broadcasts and endless sports programming. Watching television, it seems that America is made up of models, celebrities, grasping politicians, and athletes. Along with the Third World, working people have disappeared from view.

In October 1997, there was a short press report that Henry Kissinger, former Secretary of State and long-time Poo-Bah of the foreign policy establishment, had been hired as a consultant by the Walt Disney Company, one of the country's largest cultural–media conglomerates. What better indication could there be of the fusion of economics, politics and culture? 'Michael Eisner, the chairman of Disney,' the account notes, 'has hired Mr Kissinger as an adviser in the company's dealings with China. . . . Disney views China as a potentially powerful market for films, videos, company stores, and even a theme park. Accordingly, the call was made to Kissinger' (Weinraub 1997: B–7).

In truth, the government and the State Department in particular, historically have represented the economic interest of American companies around the world. The Disney gambit can be seen as the company seeking extra insurance. Still, a former Secretary of State shilling for Disney offers witness to the current melding of the symbolic and the commercial cultures.

THE EMERGENCE OF THE NOTION OF
FREE ELECTRONIC COMMERCE

A very special feature of digital capitalism is its transformation of what was once the cornerstone of US foreign-cultural policy, the free flow of information doctrine, into a newly minted 'free flow of electronic commerce.'

The free-flow doctrine served US policy well in the post-Second World War period. Its advocacy, and promotion, to world-principle status opened up markets to American film, and later TV programs, news and publications. It provided, at the same time, the ideological club with which to pummel the non-market societies. This was so because their efforts to develop their economies outside of the dominant world system of necessity had to be restrictive and exclusive of goods, services, and some kinds of cultural product.

Jeremy Tunstall was one of the few who perceptively described this process. 'The free flow of communication,' he wrote, 'a basically American notion, was built into the structure of UNESCO. . . . UNESCO has propagated such American notions as the "free information," which inevitably favours the major media exporting nations' (Tunstall 1977: 138 and 205).

Throughout the Cold War, the free-flow doctrine served, on one hand, to consolidate American advantages in the global flow of information and cultural product, and, on the other hand, as a propaganda weapon against the Evil Empire. Now, with the Cold War concluded, and the United States rushing to gain global advantage by computerising its economy, the terms of the free-flow doctrine – though not its objectives – are also being adjusted.

This adjustment was begun through a series of international US-initiated agreements which unobtrusively substituted the phrase 'trade in services' for, among other items, exports of information–media–cultural products. With the new terminology, exports of services – financial, film, TV programs, news, advertising, and others – are aggregated simply as trade items, governed by agreed rules of trade and economic exchange.

Automatically, under this designation, measures to protect national cultural industries, for example, are ruled unacceptable infringements of 'free trade.' Informational and cultural creations are made indistinguishable from commercial goods and are treated as such. This fits nicely with the needs of American cultural conglomerates, but it is not exactly a popular idea in many parts of the world. Only the strength of the US economy, and the threat of the closure of its huge market to recalcitrant states, overcomes most opposition.

A more sweeping effort to extend the free-flow doctrine into the new digital age, was announced by the White House in July 1997. A presidentially endorsed document, *Framework for Electronic Commerce*, set forth the new terms of free flow and, at the same time, made very clear what was at stake. It gave this appraisal:

World trade involving computer software, entertainment products (motion pictures, videos, games, sound recordings), information services (databases, online newspapers), technical information, product licenses, financial services, and professional services (business and technical consulting, architectural design, legal advice, travel services etc.), has grown rapidly in the past decade, now accounting for well over $40 billion dollars of US exports alone [and] an increasing share of these transactions occurs on line.

(White House 1997)

Desire to protect and enlarge this digitised commercial product, which has been growing spectacularly from year to year, accounts for the appearance of the framework document. This is made quite explicit:

[G]overnments must adopt a non-regulatory, market-oriented approach to electronic commerce, one that facilitates the emergence of a transparent and predictable legal environment to support global business and commerce. . . . The US Government supports the broadest possible free flow of information across international borders. This includes most informational material now accessible and transmitted through the Internet . . .

(Ibid.)

In short, other nations are instructed to take no actions that might be deemed protective of their economic viability or cultural independence. The free-flow doctrine, in its cyberspace reincarnation, is no less a unilateralist assertion of American digital advantage than its predecessor doctrine was, and remains, an assertion in favor of the pre-digital cultural industries' product. How long this formula for inequality will survive depends mainly on the capability of the US corporate system to maintain its present edge in high-tech mastery and its economic dominance.

Free flow of electronic commerce may be the policy of the American cultural industries and their Washington representatives, but no effort is being spared, at the same time, to ensure that this commerce is not 'free' in the customary sense of the word.

It is in this context that the issue of ownership of intellectual property has risen to a new level of prominence. A genuine free flow of information would suggest a loosening of intellectual property laws and an increased general and free accessibility to creative work wherever it appeared. Far from it! Lester Thurow, a sometimes populist economist, explains the new situation: 'Intellectual property lies at the center of the modern company's economic success or failure. . . . Increasingly, intellectual property is becoming central to strategic battle plans' (Thurow 1997: 96).

Thurow sees the emerging digital period following a historical progression:

The Industrial Revolution began with an enclosure movement that abolished common land in England. The world now needs a socially managed movement for intellectual property rights or it will witness a scramble among the powerful to grab valuable pieces of intellectual property, just as the powerful grabbed the common lands of England three centuries ago.

(Thurow 1997: 101)

What we are witnessing, in fact, *is* a corporate enclosure of intellectual property, a process that can hardly be called 'socially managed.' Intellectual property rights are being strengthened and extended, and new means are being devised to ensure that these rights are unable to be breached.

Most of this activity is justified on the once-valid notion of protecting the rights of individual creators–authors–designers–artists–film makers, and to provide continuing incentives for their creative work. Though such individual work continues, the larger share of intellectual–artistic creation today is produced under corporate auspices, with the individual talent and skills, under contract to huge research and cultural factories. Individual incentives in this environment are laughable.

The big publishers, conglomerated film and TV producers, and corporate research labs are intent that their outputs, which they want to circulate on the Internet, are easily available *but not for free*. To this end, relief and joy were expressed when Digital Object Identifiers were unveiled at the Frankfurt Book Fair in October 1997. 'It's one of the most important events in publishing for this century, and I don't think I'm saying too much,' the chief executive of Axel Springer Verlag, the German publishing giant, explained (Carvajal 1997: C-11).

This awkwardly named technology is an electronic branding technique that enables intellectual property to be numbered, identified, and monitored as it hurtles through cyberspace, thus guaranteeing that it will not be appropriated without some specified payment.

With this technology in place, the transformation of the Internet into a predominantly commercial venue will be at last realisable. Business expectations of the Net for commercial use will be fulfilled. The early optimism that cyberspace was a new public common space dissipated.

In the emerging digital era, the corporate owners of intellectual property will charge for any and all, use of their holdings. The flow of electronic 'commerce' – which now includes human and social creativity – will be sold in domestic and global markets, at the same time that older forms of social usage, i.e. 'fair use,' are limited if not eliminated, and another pillar of social public space crumbles. The free flow of electronic commerce, in concert with strengthened intellectual property rights, constitute the underpinning of the new global corporate information order.

CONCLUSION

The international communication field that Jeremy Tunstall wrote about twenty years ago, is still recognisable. Despite astonishing technological developments, industrial concentration; and mergers, new global alliances, and additional communication voices, the world information order remains for the large part still American. Cyberspace has been added to familiar communication terrain, but the transmitters with few exceptions continue to be corporate voices, mostly from a handful of countries. Advertising, more than ever remains the fount that finances the bulk of the global media's cultural flow. There are more sub-centers of media and data production, but ultimately they are subordinate to the central producers. And, as Tunstall had earlier observed, though it is more evident today than then, there is not one medium of domination, but a multi-media–multi-communication facility enterprise, horizontally and vertically integrated.

With deregulation imposed across all continents, the state has a reduced capability to intervene and socially manage the system. A worldwide capitalist presence throughout cultural–media space grows apace, squeezing out the social sphere. Will this process reach its ultimate destination – a form of global corporate feudalism? The jury – 6 billion people – is still to be heard from.

REFERENCES

Carvajal, D. (1997) 'Electronic branding receives accolades at the Frankfurt Book Fair,' *New York Times* (October 20).

Coy, P. (1997) 'Let's not take feel-good economics too far,' *Business Week* (October 20): 44.

Davis, S. (1997) 'Space jam and family values in the entertainment city,' *Proceedings of the American Studies Annual Meeting*, Washington, DC.

Nye, J. S. Jr and W. A. Owens (1996) 'America's information edge,' *Foreign Affairs* (March/April): 20–36.

Rothkopf, D., (1997) 'In praise of cultural imperialism?', *Foreign Policy* no. 107: 38–53.

Skousen, M. (1997) 'Keynesianism defeated,' *Wall Street Journal* (October 9).

Wall Street Journal (1997) 'Socialist International' (December 17): A-22.

Sterngold, J. (1997) 'Editor of Los Angeles Times quits amid shake-up,' *New York Times*, (October 10): C-5.

Thurow, L. (1997) 'Needed: a new system of intellectual property rights,' *Harvard Business Review* (September/October): 95–103.

Tunstall, J. (1977) *The Media Are American*, New York: Columbia University Press.

Weinraub, B. (1997) 'Disney hires Kissinger,' *New York Times*, (October 10): B-7.

White House, (1997) *The Framework for Global Electronic Commerce*, Washington, DC, July.

8

THE LATE ARRIVAL OF TELEVISION RESEARCH

A case study in the production of knowledge

David E. Morrison

Cultural production invariably involves political struggle, as a battle either to have one's understanding gain acceptance or to have one's area of enquiry accepted as legitimate, valued and appropriate. As often as not this latter area of struggle involves scholarship in direct confrontation with power arrangements outside the academy. For those who engage in expensive large-scale empirical social research, then, from the outset operating tensions are built into research practice. Research monies must come from somewhere, and unless one is the beneficiary of some massive endowment, that 'somewhere', to varying degrees, enters the research operation as more than pure financial support. One may have direct operational interference, or one may have framing interference.

What I attempt to do is examine one area of funding that is normally considered 'pure' or 'free money' – namely, foundation money – and show how political pressures influenced the manner and patterns of operation within mass communication research. In particular I aim to explain why the first major study of television was conducted in England and not, as might have been expected, given the development of the field, in America. Indeed, Charles Wright, in his report for UNESCO on American mass communication research in the mid-1950s found the absence of a major work on television by American scholars puzzling:

> In reviewing the recent history, one is struck by the absence of material on what is perhaps the most salient development in the mass media in the United States during this period; that is, television. There has been no major sociological study of the new medium to date.
>
> (Wright 1956: 83)

The first major work on television came from England in the form of Himmelweit, Vince and Oppenheim's study, *Television and the Child*, which appeared in 1958. It was not until three years later that Schramm, Lyle and Parker's *Television in the Lives of Our Children*, appeared in America. What is interesting is that Schramm in the Preface to the latter work saw fit to complain about the lack of money for their research, and contrasted their situation with that of Himmelweit, 'who knew in advance the amount of their support, and could therefore plan the entire study before they gathered any data'. Himmelweit had been exceptionally well funded in Britain by the Leverhulme Trust.

FOUNDATIONS: THEIR EARLY POSITION

To understand the absence of foundation money to support early research on television it is necessary to understand the position of the foundations themselves, both historically and at the time when entry into television research might have been expected.

Despite antecedents in other periods and in other cultures, the modern philanthropic foundation is a peculiarly American and an essentially twentieth-century, institution.[1] As William Whyte Jr notes:

> The concept of a private foundation for public progress is a very American development and a fairly recent one. Up until the late nineteenth century, businessmen used to give largely for the alleviation of misfortune, rather than prevention of it. But capitalism kept piling up more and more personal surpluses. Even with Newport chateaux, yachts and heirs, there was more left to give than they could give intelligently.

From the very beginning suspicion hovered over the motives of the donors, since on the surface such generosity did not fit with their other public behaviour.[2] Leaving aside for the moment the motivation of the donors, the fact is, as Lindeman (1936: 9) notes: 'The distinction between ordering private charity and large scale philanthropy is the difference between a small and a large surplus. The former may remain on a personal level, but the latter involves organisation.' Philanthropy was thus put on the same entrepreneurial footing as the donors' industrial and commercial empires. However, if foundations provided an organisational solution to the problem of rationalising the distribution of large-scale personal wealth, they were not always greeted with universal applause. This lack of acclaim stemmed in part from recognition of the dubious nature of the source and the methods which had facilitated such endowments. Fosdick (1952: 19) in his history of the Rockefeller Foundation, notes that such wealth was made 'under conditions unique in the history of the country and not infrequently by methods which, if permissible at that time, no longer accord with social conscience or the requirements of the law'. Quite apart from the spectre of 'tainted money', a particular suspicion hanging over the early foundations was that their founders would use them to resist change and support their own economic views and practices. Thus there were two strands to the early suspicion of foundations, one associated with the sources of endowment, and the other with the uses to which such monies might be put.

FOUNDATIONS AND THE SHAPE OF KNOWLEDGE

Prior to the First World War, apart from such endowments as those of the Smithsonian and Carnegie Institutions, foundations in general had not engaged actively in supporting research in any of the sciences. In terms of the social sciences, then, it is true, as Oberschall (1972: 218) points out, that the flowering of the social survey movement in the decade around 1919 owed much to the establishment of the Russell Sage Foundation in 1907, but it was not until the late 1930s and the Second World War that the survey technique was methodologically perfected and systematically applied in professionally directed scientific research projects. As late as 1920 only the physical and natural sciences were receiving any appreciable foundation support.[3]

If support for the social sciences was absent before the First World War – and there was little enough shortly afterwards – matters changed in the 1920s, as Hollis (1938: 116) notes: 'the natural and physical sciences have continued to receive about the same proportion of the expanding philanthropic budget but the social sciences have received an ever-increasing proportion and are clearly the dominant foundation interest for the 1921–30 decade, as well as for the succeeding half decade'. It was the climate of opinion produced by the war that began to run in favour of foundation intervention in areas that had previously been closed to them. In terms of support for the social sciences, then, although the assistance given by the social sciences to government in the course of the First World War can be seen as a dress-rehearsal for the assistance during the Second World War, the benefits attendant upon social science research were clearly visible after the First World War. As Lyons (1969: 31) notes:

> the wartime use of intelligence testing set a precedent elsewhere in government and especially in private industry. Indeed, the research work that psychologists had performed for the military was called 'a war gift to industry'; private companies began to use psychologists, consulting firms were organised and new techniques established.

It was within this improved atmosphere that Beardsley Ruml, as head of the Laura Spelman (Rockefeller) Memorial, spent $14 million of the foundation's money over 1922–9 'in order to put the social sciences on the academic map' (Macdonald 1956: 24). However, if the aim was to put the social sciences 'on the academic map' then the cartography was certainly that of empirical enquiry. In fact, the earliest support for the social sciences in any significant amount was provided by foundations. Donald Young (1969: xv), Director General of the Russell Sage Foundation, in viewing foundation activity observed: 'In the years prior to World War Two it was practically impossible to write a text in any of the social sciences without relying on findings financed by the private foundations.'

Viewed historically, the importance of the foundations' contribution to the social sciences rests not so much in any individual piece of work that they supported as in the strain or style of academic endeavour that they encouraged and gave emphasis to. If America was not the home of quantification, but the recipient of a European export, then it certainly adopted those techniques on a large scale. A not insignificant part was played in aiding this adoption by the willingness of the foundations to provide the necessary funds for such expensive research. Not only were they prepared to support such quantitative work but, perhaps more importantly from the point of view of propagation, they supported and encouraged the requisite institutional forms within which such work could flourish and expand: namely, research institutes, centres, bureaux and similar offices. In fact the driving idea behind Ruml's giving of the Spelman Memorial money was 'in order to develop major centres of research', and as Ogg (1928: 156) notes:

> The single fact that, doubtless for good and sufficient reasons, foundations and other patrons and benefactors will rarely place money directly at the disposal of an individual, but will turn it to the support of a council or bureau or other continuing, responsible, co-operative organisation, would alone account for the emergence of many of our present research groups or bodies.

The 'good and sufficient reasons' mentioned by Ogg for foundation support of research centres rests on the imperative of foundations' own bureaucratic structure and the high value placed upon quantitative work – in particular 'the fact finding non-controversial areas of the social and humanistic sciences' (Hollis 1938: 289). To understand the attraction of the 'scientific' element associated with quantitative work, it must be remembered that the foundations' interest in serious research developed first in the natural and physical sciences, and their attitude towards the social sciences was to some extent coloured by that experience: it led easily to comparisons with the 'superior sciences'.[4] It is difficult, however, to separate such influences from the developing general pattern of American social science that fed into and gave support for such a comparison; nevertheless, the outcome tended to be an abstraction from the growing social sciences of that part which in the foundations' view most closely resembled the natural sciences, and which at the same time gelled with their own organisational ends and problem-solving approach to society. For example, Hollis (1938: 225) lodges a complaint against the foundations for having foisted natural science methods upon social science:

> The point to be established is that the social sciences are undergoing a profound and rapid development, and that more than any other supporting agency philanthropic foundations are pointing and guiding this phase of American higher education. . . . [They] have I fear been the chief offenders in forcing the techniques of research which developed in the natural sciences onto the social sciences and humanities.

Yet ten years later Donald Young (1948: 330), of the Russell Sage Foundation, noted: 'The appreciable measure of success which has attended the increasing concentration on making social science more scientific gives promise that further effort in this direction will be rewarding.'

A QUESTION OF CONFIDENCE AND DEFENSIVE TACTICS

As social problems became 'visible', and as a body of knowledge developed laying claim to an ability to generate solutions or ameliorative strategies, the foundations were impelled by their principles of 'improving man's welfare'[5] to engage the services of this knowledge to discharge their philanthropic duty. That was the developing paradox: in order to fulfil their philanthropic obligations, the larger foundations were obliged to engage in activity that required the help of social scientists, but to enter such a world was to enter the world of values and controversy at a level so direct that it exposed the weakness of their position. Once more suspicion of the motives and the rationale of the foundations bubbled to the surface and at times frothed over into outright hostility.

Nearly all foundations take the precaution of inserting statements of disengagement in published reports, either through an introductory note or else in a separate statement. But, even so, their practical effectiveness is not all that might be hoped for. As Emerson Andrews (1956: 164) points out, the findings 'will inevitably be attributed to the foundation itself'. A much more effective defence, and one that had major importance for the type of work that foundations were willing to support, was that of 'objectivity'. Clearly, one cannot raise the defence of objectivity in relation to the area of research chosen for support, but the defence of objectivity in the practice of such research has been adhered to very closely indeed. It is Alvin Gouldner's contention (1973: Ch. 3) that the insistence upon objectivity was one process by which sociology legitimised itself, but within the operating world of the foundations objectivity had the added advantage of being one of the few effective barriers that it could erect in defence of its bequests of money to the social sciences. This was revealed very clearly during conversations with several foundation officials, and is well expressed in the following conversational extract from an interview conducted with a senior figure at the Russell Sage Foundation:

> Where foundations have got into trouble is where they have done something political and not scientific. It is rare that a really good solid research project with good scientific methodology, which is supposed to produce objective results, is going to get criticised.

THE MOVEMENT OF HISTORY AND
ENQUIRIES INTO FOUNDATIONS

Foundations do not exist in a social vacuum, and thus the focus of suspicion has varied over time consequent on wider shifts in political–social mood. While the original criticism tended to cluster around fears that funds would be used to restrict social change, during the 1950s there was a *volte-face*, and criticism focused on fears that foundations were encouraging radical social change, or supporting groups that wished for radical social change.

Mention has already been made concerning suspicion of the intentions of the original donors, but it is also worth mentioning that the suspicion harboured towards the donors was translated into official enquiry in the form of hearings before the United States' Industrial Relations Commission in 1915. Turning to the Commission itself, one can clearly see concern over the purpose to which funds were being put, and the power of foundations to exert influence over recipients.[6] Thus, the Manly Report of US Senate's *Commission on Industrial Relations* (1916: 83) commented that 'the so-called investigation of industrial relations has not, as it is claimed, either a scientific or social base, but originated to promote the industrial interests of Mr Rockefeller'.

By the second decade of the century the Rockefeller Foundation began moving towards more direct operation of its own programmes, especially in the fields of health and medicine, and attempted to apply the same principles to the more volatile world of industrial relations. Unfortunately Rockefeller's own companies lacked an appreciation of the management of conflict that might have been learnt from the social sciences, preferring instead to use state militia to break strikes. Uproar resulted when one of the Rockefeller-controlled companies – the Colorado Fuel and Iron Company – in 1914 used state militia with incredible savagery to fire on strikers, resulting in what became know as the 'Ludlow Massacre'. As a result:

> The Rockefeller Trustees were given an uncomfortable lesson about the hazards of becoming involved in social and economic issues, especially if the foundation itself undertook to carry out the work. As a matter of policy they decided thereafter to restrict the foundation's direct operation to scientific areas such as public health, medicine and agriculture. If the foundation supported work in controversial social fields, it would do so through grants to other independent institutions.
>
> (Neilsen 1972: 53–54)

Entry into the social sciences was a lesson hard learnt. As a result, the Foundation did not move into support of the social sciences again until the 1920s. Between the 'unforgettable lesson' of the Ludlow Massacre and Rockefeller's second attempt at entry into social research, public opinion had changed considerably. Not only had the social sciences become more acceptable through their war service, but agencies such as the Department of Agriculture were engaged in more systematic research and in a more sustained utilisation of social science research.[7] This increased 'visibility' of the social sciences, and more particularly its growing acceptability, facilitated by the aforementioned 'war gift to industry', allied to the growing public toleration of trusts, both commercial and philanthropic, lessened the possibility of a repeat disaster. In the words of Fosdick, President of the Rockefeller Foundation, writing of the grand entry into the social sciences by the Laura Spelman Memorial: 'it must be admitted that for this activity the environment of 1922–23 was propitious' (Fosdick 1952: 215).

If the First World War eased the foundations' entry into the social sciences, a further impetus was provided by the employment of social scientists in the New Deal administration. The point here, however, is not so much the actual benefits that social scientists gave during the New Deal, but the recognition by the pragmatic Roosevelt administration of the social scientist as adviser, a role traditionally reserved for businessmen and lawyers. Even greater encouragement was given to the social sciences by the Second World War, but even so criticism was a constant reminder of foundations' unsettled acceptance. Thus, even though the social sciences may have received increased support from the foundations, particular areas within the social sciences remained dangerous places to venture. This is well illustrated by the Carnegie Foundation's trembling involvement in race relations.

Despite the increased confidence of foundations in supporting social science research due to the increased acceptance of the social sciences in general, the Foreword to Gunnar Myrdal's *An American Dilemma*, published in 1944, is full of worry and bated expectation of punitive criticism. The whole of the four-page Foreword is a justification for attempting such work, even to the extent of extolling the past work of the Carnegie Corporation and urging the reader 'that he makes every effort to read these statements intellectually and not emotionally'. Despite engaging in a search for a scholar from a country 'with no background or tradition of imperialism', Keppel (1944: v), President of the Carnegie Corporation, still felt it necessary to exonerate the foundation:

> Provided the foundation limits itself to its proper function, namely to make the facts available and let them speak for themselves, and does not undertake to instruct the public as to what to do about them, studies of this kind provide a wholly proper, as experience has shown, sometimes a highly important, use of their funds.

A DOWNTURN IN FORTUNES AND THE FORTUNES OF MEDIA RESEARCH

A defence resting upon adherence to 'scientific methodology' can have persuasive power only within a culture that regards this as the correct method. For what is considered correct procedure can change over time.

The atmosphere that allowed Myrdal's study began to ebb with the end of the Second World War and with the build-up of Cold War tensions, especially after the outbreak of the Korean War in 1950. The changed ethos produced a suspicion of foundations, a suspicion that was translated into two Congressional Enquiries – the Cox Commission of 1952, and the Reece Commission of 1953. The clouds which formed over the foundations, blown by winds of a more general uncertainty, resulted in accusations of communist infiltration and misfeasance over the allocating of grants to communists or to communist sympathisers. In discussions with officials in the Carnegie Corporation who had been in office in the 1950s the atmosphere was described as 'oppressive'. John Marshall, at the Rockefeller Foundation, recalled how

> from that time on we were virtually required to consider the kind of suspicion that the committee had manifested. I say *suspicion* because that is all it was. I don't think we were ever afraid of criticism but one had to be aware that suspicion of that kind could be handicapping to us.

In summary, Marshall considered the atmosphere within the Foundation to be more one of 'circumspection' than of fear. Be that as it may, the externals of the situation, so far as granting policies were concerned, were less circumspect and more direct. Hutchins (1956: 207), head of the Fund for the Republic, observed:

Congressman Reece was scoffed at. It was agreed that his investigation was a farce. I think he had good reason to be satisfied with himself. Without firing a single serious shot, without saying a single intelligent word, he accomplished his purpose, which was to harass the foundations and to subdue such stirrings of courage, or even of imagination, as could be found in them. As I have said, there were not many there when he came on the scene. Congressman Cox had been before him. If there was a foundation that was willing to be controversial, that was willing to take risks, it learned its lesson by the time Cox and Reece got through. Who will venture now?

Reading the Reece Report affords a glimpse into the workings of a true conspiratorial mind, ranging, as it does, from attacks on the Rockefeller, Carnegie and Russell Sage Foundations for initially sponsoring the *Encyclopaedia of the Social Sciences* to attacks on the 'dubious staff of the Ford Foundation' (Reece Report 1955: 36). One of the 'dubious staff' mentioned was Bernard Berelson.[8]

If we turn to the foundations, what is interesting in terms of the repercussions for communications research is that the Ford Foundation was singled out for particular criticism. According to Macdonald (1956: 25), the attacks on the Ford Foundation got under way in 1951, when the *Chicago Tribune* ran a story under the headline 'Leftist Slant Begins to Show in Ford'. This supposed Left slant was an allusion to the participation in various Ford programmes of individuals such as Paul Hoffman who, as head of the Marshall Plan, 'had given away 10 billion dollars to foreign countries'. This lead was taken up by Hearst columnists such as Westbrook Pegler, George Sokolsky and Fulton Lewis Jr. Hoffman was described by Pegler as 'a hoax without rival in the history of mankind', and the Marshall Plan as 'the fabulous Roosevelt– Truman over-seas squanderbund' (Reeves, 1969: 15). Attacks were also delivered from groups such as the right-wing Constitutional Educational League which distributed pamphlets against the Ford Motor Company, linking it with communism, the argument being that through ownership of a Ford motorcar one unwittingly gave support to communism, since the Ford Motor Company's profits were spent by the Leftist Ford Foundation. (MacDonald 1956: 27).

The singling-out of the Ford Foundation for attack was the result of two main factors. The first was the newly expanded programme of the Foundation, which included heavy support for the social sciences, both for their application to social problems and for their scientific development. In fact, Division Five of the Foundation, which was responsible for the establishment of the Centre for Advanced Studies in the Behavioural Sciences at Palo Alto, received special adverse comment in the Reece Report (Reece Report, 1955: 36) The reason why those who rallied to the banner of Cox and Reece objected to the social sciences was precisely the type of social science receiving support by the foundations, namely, fact gathering. What was demanded was not social enquiry to establish 'truths', but theoretical rumination to support the foundational truths of American values.

What we see is that although Marxists might take exception to the quantificatory side of sociology – its acceptance of facts – or, more precisely, the non-theoretical reflective treatment of social order, to see it as 'safe' activity and non-radical, the objection from the Right towards empirical sociology at this time was the reverse. Right-wingers viewed the collection of facts that might sit unfavourably with their own value assumptions, as tantamount to sedition. Yet the real wrath of those on the Right towards the Ford Foundation was due to the granting of $15 million for the establishment of the Fund for the Republic. This radical Foundation, whose purpose was the defence of civil liberties, and which sponsored such works as Stouffer's communism studies (1955) and Lazarsfeld and Thielen's *The Academic Mind*, a study into the effect of McCarthyism on intellectual life, time and again stung the foundations' critics to fury over its granting policies. Although the Fund was independent of the Ford Foundation, the Ford Foundation nevertheless was obliged to assume parental responsibility for its wayward child.

The attacks on the Ford Foundation left their mark, both at the personal level and at the level of granting policies. Macdonald (1956: 27) quotes Henry Ford as saying: 'The dealers send us in letters from customers accusing the foundation of being communist and warning that they'll never buy another Ford. But I don't bother much with that sort of mail. Why should I?' This statement by Ford is strictly for the 'official history' of the Foundation – reality was somewhat different. Ford *was* worried. In fact he showed some of his mail to his speech-writer and 'expressed deep concern'. (Reeves 1969: 15) Neither does Hoffman's view of Henry Ford lend support to this nonchalant statement concerning the letters of complaint.

> I told him [Ford] that I wanted to experiment . . . to change things and that change always means trouble. But every time we got a dozen letters objecting to something we had done . . . a radio show of an overseas program or what-not . . . I'd have to spend hours reassuring the board.
>
> (Reeves 1969: 15)

Henry Ford's behaviour under such pressure is also evidenced by his denunciation of the Fund for the Republic in 1955. This denunciation, circulated as it was in every major newspaper in the country, was an unexpected blow to the Fund (Reeves 1969: 177). Why had Ford done it? The reason would appear to be the amount and intensity of general criticism, plus criticism from dealers and customers. In an interview between Reeves and Elmo Roper, the pollster, Reeves (1969: 177) comments:

[Roper] knew that there had been heavy pressure from officials at the Ford Motor Company; Roper was given hints that his own business relations might be cut if he failed to resign from the Board, or to support the removal of the Fund's outspoken President. At one point, Ford himself had asked Roper to leave the Fund's Board.

If the pressure was too much for the Ford Foundation, it was too much also for the Fund for the Republic. Following a particularly blistering attack by Fulton Lewis Jr, based on his discovery that the Fund intended to study the American Legion, the members of the board meeting in September 1955 were extremely worried. The outcome was a decision to drop certain controversial programmes (Reeves 1969: 138).

The social-class background of both Foundation officers and trustees had not prepared them for the unsophisticated and libellous nature of the attacks that they received. Nor were the Henry Fords of the world accustomed to give accounts of themselves before a Congressional Enquiry, as Ford had been required to in the autumn of 1952. These attacks took their toll. The Foundation began to give large sums of money to 'safe' areas.

At their quarterly meeting in March 1955, the Ford trustees approved three big programmes on which they expected to spend $85 million, all, or most of it, within the next three years. This expenditure accounted for nearly half of the regular annual budget through until 1957 (MacDonald 1956: 166). In addition to the $20 million National Merit Scholarships, there was a $50 million programme to raise the salaries of college teachers, and a $15 million fund for research into mental illness. The attraction of these areas for the Foundation was precisely that they offered the maximum possibility for spending money with the minimum danger of getting into trouble. Commenting on this, MacDonald (1956: 170) offers the biting comment that 'even this program was not large enough for the well-Gaithersised [the President] foundation and at the end of 1955 another was announced that was even safer and a great deal bigger'. What MacDonald is referring to is a grant of half-a-billion dollars for privately supported institutions within America:

> The trouble probably was more lack of daring than of sophistication; those philanthropists at Ford are reasonable intelligent men, and it is unlikely that it did not occur to them that a more productive use could have been made of half a billion dollars than just giving it out pro-rata to everybody. They were scared or more accurately, Henry Ford, and Donald Young and other trustees were scared, and their fear communicated itself, through channels to the philanthropists who ran the foundations for them.
>
> (MacDonald 156: 170)

FOUNDATIONS AND COMMUNICATIONS RESEARCH

Berelson, writing in 1959 on the state of mass communications research, notes:

> The modern version of mass communication research began about twenty five years ago with the development of both academic and commercial interests . . . the former largely co-ordinated, if not stimulated by the Rockefeller Foundation Seminar of the late 1930s.
>
> (Berelson 1959: 1)

The seminars referred to were instigated by John Marshall, head of the Humanities Division of the Rockefeller Foundation, in order to have Paul Lazarsfeld clarify the conceptual progress made on the Princeton Radio Research Project which the Foundation had funded and had appointed Lazarsfeld as its director – the two other co-directors being Hadley Cantril of Princeton University and Frank Stanton, then in the research department of CBS (see Morrsion 1978 b).

Without wishing to become involved in any controversy over Lazarsfeld's style of research (see Mills 1959) from what has been said thus far it is easy to see that, from a foundation perspective, the fact-collecting empirical method of Lazarsfeld was ideologically attractive – its apparent objectivity could function as a defence against criticism. However, it must be said that the late 1930s and early 1940s was a period promoting confidence within the foundations to become involved in social research. Furthermore, John Marshall of the Rockefeller Foundation was an extremely self-assured and liberal individual. In addition, no objections were raised, from any quarter, concerning Rockefeller's entry into radio research. Even so, one witnesses, through close inspection of the Rockefeller archives, a certain nervousness in deviating from 'factual accounts' and entering into any kind of full social critique of the radio industry. This is exemplified by Theodor Adorno's experience while working with Lazarsfeld on the music study side of the Princeton Radio Research Project.

THE PROBLEM WITH ADORNO

Adorno's critical theory did not find ready acceptance within certain circles associated with the Foundation – it must be said that Adorno never helped his own case by the tortured and obscure style of his writing, (see Jameson 1967), much less by his arrogant manner in dealing with industry figures (see Morrison 1978a). Although Marshall, in overall charge of the Princeton Project on the Foundation side, was not impressed at being called 'a young ignoramus' by Adorno, he was impressed by Adorno's intellect. Even so, one finds, in response to an appeal by Lazarsfeld to extend Adorno's contract beyond the original agreed date, an inter-office memorandum from Marshall following his review of all Adorno's work since his start on the music study, that reads: 'much engaged by the originality of Adorno's approach . . . the real issue is the utility of the study, and that utility must be measured by the effect which can be anticipated for it in remedying the present deficiencies of broadcast music' (Inter-office memo from Marshall, December 1993, Rockefeller Archives [PRRP]). Basically, Adorno's work did not fit the Foundation's administrative demands.

The notion of 'remedy' may be undialectical, but Marshall's demand for Adorno's work to have some 'utility' was not an unreasonable one. What worried Adorno most was the 'danger of a methodological circle' – that in order to grasp the phenomena of cultural reification according to the prevalent norms of empirical sociology he would have to use reified methods (see Adorno 1969: 347). Nevertheless, faced with the opportunity to demonstrate the unity of theory and praxis within the cultural sphere, Adorno failed. This is not surprising. One of the failings in general of critical theory was its inability to handle praxis in any other than a theoretical manner. Marshall, and others on the Foundation side, felt that Adorno's work was destructively negative, not in the Hegelian sense of negation, but simply fault-finding to the point of bloody-mindedness.

Yet what is interesting about the employment of Adorno is the selection by Lazarsfeld, and the Foundation, of music as the one area of radio output for critical analysis. Although irritated at times by the Frankfurt School, and at times, as he told me, finding them 'irresponsible', Lazarsfeld did have a great deal of respect for its members and their work. Lazarsfeld wrote to the Foundation saying that it would be a great oversight not to study something as important as radio without 'looking into its setting in the whole framework of our culture'. Therefore, since he was aware that 'such an analysis might lead to somewhat controversial results, it seemed best to make the experiment in the field of music, which is least exposed to public distrust' (from Letter Lazarsfeld to Marshall, 27 December 1939, Rockefeller Archives [PRRP]). What this meant was that a 'social critique' of broadcasting was best attempted in the relatively safe area of music rather than any other form of output. Support is given to this by a letter that Hadley Cantril wrote to Marshall: 'The Directors, aware of their responsibilities (for reasons of tact as well as scientific integrity) have selected the field of music for the investigation of the influence of the social system upon today's broadcasting' (from Letter Cantril to Marshall, 7 March 1939, Rockefeller Archives [PRRP]).

Thus, although the Rockefeller Foundation entered media research with confidence in the favourable climate of the later 1930s and the early 1940s towards foundation support for the social sciences, a close weather-eye was kept on the possible repercussions that a critique of the social system might bring. Adorno's work was certainly not fact-finding but was, as he rightfully titled one of his papers, 'A social critique of radio music' (Adorno 1945). In such a case, had criticism followed, little shelter could have been taken behind the defence of 'scientific objectivity' on which foundations rested their support for the social sciences. However, by the 1950s even 'scientific objectivity' offered no defence against attack. Empirical enquiry was an anathema to the Reece Committee.

THE STILL-BIRTH OF TELEVISION RESEARCH

By the 1950s the Rockefeller Foundation, following the familiar path of foundations in general of supporting an area and then withdrawing upon achieving its goals, had already left the field of mass communication research. It could not, therefore, really have been expected to re-engage itself in mass communication research by examining the place of television within American life. Furthermore, its influence in supporting the social sciences had waned in face of the massive Ford Foundations' entry into the social sciences.

Given the emergence of television as a social issue it could readily have been expected that the Ford Foundation would have championed work on the medium in a manner similar to that in which the Rockefeller Foundation had earlier supported work on the medium of radio. The reason for the Ford Foundation's not entering television research might of course be explained had it had no intellectual interest in television research. That, however, was not the case. Indeed, what the Rockefeller Foundation was to radio research in the late 1930s and early 1940s the Ford Foundation was set to become for television research in the early 1950s.

During the winter of 1951–2 the Ford Foundation began to discuss the feasibility of studying the impact of television on American society. Several preliminary seminars and conferences were held to explore the possibilities of such work, and leading figures in the academic world and in the media were consulted. The outcome of this preliminary work was the establishment of an Advisory Committee on Television. The Committee met for the first time in New York on 21 and 22 August 1952, with Lazarsfeld as its Chairman. The Committee's brief was to develop proposals for something akin to a commission to study television and to make policy suggestions. Its report was finally submitted in the summer of 1953. Those involved in writing the report expected that the suggested proposals for research would be acted upon – they had been led to believe that action would be taken. In the event, however, nothing ever came of the Committee's recommendations.

A point of entry into the reasons surrounding the still-birth of the Commission is provided by a reading of the *Proceedings of the Kefauver Committee on Juvenile Delinquency*, published spring 1955. Lazarsfeld had been called before the Committee as an expert witness. As part of his testimony he discussed the lack of funds for research into television. He reported:

> Unfortunately the chances for such a turn of affairs [foundation support] are limited at this moment, because of the kind of criticism which has been levelled against the foundation in recent years. A Congressional Committee [Reece] has criticised the foundation boards for certain action in other areas. The boards are frequently cautious in making funds available for new areas of study. When radio appeared on the scene, the Rockefeller Foundation was still quite willing to finance large studies on the effects the medium might have on American life. Now that television is here, with presumably more intensive effect, no foundation has yet seen fit to sponsor the necessary research.
>
> (Kefauver 1955: 54)

In the report of the evidence given to the Committee, part of Lazarsfeld's original testimony was omitted. The missing part reads[9]

> Just as our Committee [refers to the Ford Advisory Committee on TV] submitted a detailed plan endorsed by industry as well as by critical reform groups, the attacks on foundations began and the sponsoring organisation [Ford] decided to drop the whole matter.

The reason for the omission of the above statement from the Kefauver report is that a high ranking official at the Ford Foundation wrote to Kefauver objecting to Lazarsfeld's interpretation of the reasons for 'dropping' the proposed project. Understandably, the suggestions put forward by Lazarsfeld did not make pleasant reading for the official. As a result, correspondence between Lazarsfeld and the official took place to 'clear the matter up'. However, far from 'clearing the matter up' the exchange of letters provides further evidence of the uncertainty surrounding the whole situation. The letters from the official indicate that he considered that it should have been obvious at the time why the project was never funded. If it was obvious to the Foundation, however, then it was certainly not obvious to Lazarsfeld, and for good reason. Lazarsfeld wrote to Vice-President McPeak:

> I am, of course, very eager to avoid any misunderstanding as to what happened with the Citizens' Committee on TV. Your letter came too late for changes to be made in the Congressional record. I am sure you realise where the difficulty lies. I have never had any communication from the foundation as to what disposition was made of our proposal. Whenever I was in New York some member of the Citizens' Group was likely to ask me about it. The most reasonable interpretation was

that the matter had got forgotten in the turnout created by the Reece Committee. This formulation saved me from embarrassment with my colleagues who had worked so hard on this assignment and I thought it also saved the foundation from the reproach of being discourteous to this distinguished group of men. Let me assure you that I will be equally co-operative in adjusting to your way of looking at the matter once you have explained it to me.

(Lazarsfeld letter to McPeak, 15.6.55
Ford Foundation Files, PA 53–15)

Considering the amount of work that Lazarsfeld had undertaken on behalf of the Foundation, the above is a remarkably restrained and polite letter, but it was shortly followed by another and somewhat sterner letter asking for clarification.

At the time I rendered my report every member of the group got a thank-you letter and was told that in due time we would learn of the disposition the foundation made of our recommendations. Since then, neither I nor any other member of the group as far as I know has heard from you. We of course took it for granted that the foundation had decided to drop the matter but because we were left without any information most of us developed the theory that the Reece episode accounted for all of it . . . including the silence. Therefore, there are two things I will want to clear up with you. One is laying the ghost of the old proposal which I think can be done in a few lines from you to me.

(Lazarsfeld letter to McPeak, 27.9.55, Ford Foundation Files)

This request by Lazarsfeld for an explanation as to why the proposal was refused funds did prompt a reply, but not an explanation. It was not even a case of receiving 'no adequate explanation'; there was simply no explanation at all, except to inform Lazarsfeld of what he already knew – that the project had been refused funds. Some insight into his understandable confusion over the whole situation is afforded by this extract from a conversation between Lazarsfeld and the author:

DM: In your evidence to the Kefauver Committee on Juvenile Delinquency you mention that the foundations were reluctant to support TV research because they were feeling the pressure of the times.

PL: Oh yes, the foundations – there was a Congressional Investigation of all the foundations.

DM: Well, there was Cox and Reece.

PL: Yes, that's right, they were badly affected – not financially – there was nothing you could do – the atmosphere was very unpleasant. This Reece was really just like McCarthy.

DM: I wanted to ask you about some information I discovered on the TV Commission while I was going through the Ford Foundation files.

PL: Oh yes, that I wanted to make you aware of – that is something we never touched on before because it never had the slightest consequence.

DM: Yes, that's exactly what I wanted to ask you about. I've got my own interpretations.

PL: So have I. Well, I have a definite theory about it, but I have no evidence really. There was one man on my Committee, or whatever you want to call it, who was very famous for many reasons but also completely erratic – that was Ruml. I think Ruml took a very definite dislike to me. I always had a theory that Ruml torpedoed the whole project and torpedoed it in the following way. There was a Vice-President who has since died – McPeak – who in my opinion was a very typical foundation bureaucrat, not in the least a John Marshall. And you know the reason. This Committee just disappeared and my theory was always that Ruml, who had a great influence on McPeak – and McPeak had no reason to like me either – I had hardly any contact with him – but between these two men it was killed. It's a very funny episode. One day, Hutchins asked me to take it over. I think he had asked [Frank] Stanton's advice and he suggested me. You know there were eight or ten monographs written around it. [Charles] Seipman and others and I worked. We worked endlessly and this was a very distinguished group. After all, these were top people on this board. I was very proud. One day, out of the blue, it was all ended.

(Lazarsfeld interview, 15.6.73)

From the position that Lazarsfeld occupied in the affair, the situation may well have appeared that way – and his supposition may well be correct with regard to the actual mechanics of the ending of the project. But the concern in the present context is more with the situation *within which* the mechanics operated – how it came to be that the project could be jettisoned.

Lazarsfeld and his colleagues had good reason to consider that the rug was being pulled from underneath the project. On 9 May 1952 the trade paper *Variety* ran as the front page headline: 'Ford Foundation Maps 1,000,000 Dollar Survey To Cure The Woes of TV'. No authorisation had been given for such a release; in fact, so far as can be gathered, it remained a mystery just who had leaked the information. The release caused consternation among those who were committed to the project since, in the early days of negotiations, such publicity was seen as detrimental. However, too much must not be read into the incident, except to note that it could have been responsible for Lazarsfeld's feeling that the project was being sabotaged. There is no evidence that the project was actually 'torpedoed', and it is reasonable to suppose that, because of the prestige of the individuals involved, plus the size of the enquiry and the Foundation's obvious commitment to it, any machinations powerful enough to sink the project would have become visible somewhere. This is not to discount behind-the-scenes manoeuvring, and it may well be that in the final demise of the project personal antagonisms did come into play – they were not, however, responsible for it. There is evidence available to account for its failure.

Hutchins was a moving force behind the whole project, but at the same time Henry Ford opposed the project on the grounds that it was too controversial. From the start Ford had insisted on the inclusion of the media industry in the project. His hope was that such inclusion would act as a buffer against criticism, despite early resolutions to exclude industry personnel on the grounds of 'vested interest'. While it is true that in the early days of the Committee certain sectors of the media industry were hostile to the idea of the proposed research, they were, however, placated by Lazarsfeld's diplomacy. As Lazarsfeld informed the President of the Foundation

> I am very eager indeed to talk with you about the progress of the preparatory committee on the TV Commission. We have made good progress intellectually as well as in our efforts to secure the support of the industry.
>
> (Lazarsfeld letter to McPeak, 15.6.53, Ford Foundation Files)

This point was underscored in conversation with Lazarsfeld:

DM: I know that Ford insisted that the project should only go ahead if there was representation from the media industry involved, and, if my reading of the Foundation's files is correct, the media people seemed quite responsive to the idea.

PL: Of course. Look, I had all sorts – I remember big station managers from the mid-west, and I was fairly skilled to reconcile them. The list of station managers is very impressive – the station representatives liked the idea. At least, they never created any trouble. It was one of the strangest episodes.

(Lazarsfeld interview, 15.6.73)

Unfortunately for the future of the project the support of the media personnel came too late. Henry Ford's uneasiness probably stemmed from the fact that he had phoned Frank Stanton of CBS, in the early days of setting up the Committee, to ask him to become a member. Stanton agreed, but was then criticised by the industry for doing so. This got back to Henry Ford, and made him unsure about the wisdom of such work. Further evidence of the existence of 'nervousness' in relation to the project is the insistence that an outside group approached the Foundation for support for the project when, in fact, the proposal had originated within the confines of the Foundation itself. A certain amount of subterfuge followed to cover this deception. What cannot be escaped, therefore, is the political nervousness existing within the Foundation over entering a potentially controversial area of research offered by television.

THE END COMES

The death-knell of the proposed Commission was sounded by two events – the first was the departure of Hutchings from the Foundation to help establish the Fund for the Republic; the second was the establishment by Reece of his Congressional Enquiry into foundations. Both of these events occurred in 1953, the year that Lazarsfeld submitted the proposal for the Television Commission. Hence, not only was the already tense atmosphere within the Foundation further reinforced by the proposed Reece Enquiry but, with Hutchins' departure, the project's principal supporter was removed. Once this lock-gate was opened, the waters of caution flooded in. However, the proposed Television Commission was submerged and not actually drowned, a fact that, to some extent, accounts for the absence of communication to Lazarsfeld regarding the Foundation's disposition towards his submitted report. Basically, the Foundation could not decide what to do with Lazarsfeld's report. It floated below the surface for some time in uncertainty, and even looked as if it might actually break surface, but finally excuses were given as to why it should not be supported. These excuses look very much like *post hoc* reasoning for dropping the proposal. They included the lack of financial support from the media industry and from citizens' groups, and the fact that the original release of money for Lazarsfeld's Advisory Committee had made no mention of guaranteeing support for any proposals made. All of these justifications can be discounted as serious reasons for ignoring the proposal. Alternative financial support had never been part of the committee's brief in the first place, and it is doubtful that the Ford Foundation actually needed the financial contributions that a citizens' group could make – unless, once more, it wished to spread responsibility for the Commission. In any case, such reasons were never communicated to Lazarsfeld. The statement that there was never any promise given to support research on television is disingenuous. Although it is true that the official release of the original money for the Advisory Committee contained no explicit promise of support for the proposals produced, there was nonetheless a definite if tacit understanding. Lazarsfeld and his colleagues were never in any doubt that their report would be accepted as a basis for funding a large programme of research. Lazarsfeld was adamant on this point, and re-affirmed his position to me during a later conversation than the above, at a meeting in Cambridge (28 March 1974).

Lazarsfeld's account for the absence of funds for television research to the Kefauver Committee was closer to the truth than perhaps even he realised. He had not mis-read the situation, far from it. Indeed, as Lazarsfeld stated: 'It was one of the strangest episodes.' In one sense the episode was strange, but in another sense not. The refusal of funds was reflective in many ways of the peculiarity of the times and the uncertainty existing within the foundations, but one must be careful in describing an epoch as 'strange'. It was real enough at the time, and the political situation leading to the questioning of intellectual questioning was real enough. Although perhaps a heightened case of political fear influencing research decisions, it serves to demonstrate that politics and research are inseparable twins no matter what the period. As stated at the very beginning of this chapter, money for research must come from somewhere, and that 'somewhere', no matter what the source, should provide it interest-free. Where there is money there are accountants. And one is called to account not simply financially.

NOTES

1   See Hollis (1938) for a brief but comprehensive history of foundations.
2   See Nielson (1972: 10–11) for description of donors.
3   See Hollis (1938: 240f.) for trends over time.
4   See Young (1948) in particular for an expression of this attitude.
5   See Bremner (1960) for factual evidence of the principle of 'improving man's welfare', particularly with reference to the commitment of Rockefeller and Harkness to this principle. Bremner (1960: 193–4) cites, for example, the Rockefeller Charter, which includes a commitment to promote the well-being of mankind throughout the world.
6   Criticism was also levied at the Carnegie Foundation over the reforms they made to higher education through the 'Carnegie Units' which institutionalised the PhD in American education, and the abandonment of sectarian affiliations by colleges to qualify for Carnegie money. See Horowitz (1972) for a scathing attack on the Carnegie Corporation and Jenks and Riesman (1968: 240–2) for the importance attached to PhDs even in areas where it was not strictly relevant.
7   Some progress had been made in the utilisation of social science in this direction prior to the First World War by, for example, the Progressive Movement in the rural mid-west using agricultural economists and rural sociologists – work that was to continue during the New Deal.
8   In conversation, Bereleson mentioned that Lazarsfeld out of generosity often had emigré Austrians 'hanging around the Bureau [of Applied Social Research] doing odd coding work and so on', and that one such individual out of 'patriotic duty' joined the informing industry to bother Berelson. Hans Zeisel – a colleague of Lazarsfeld from his days in Vienna and, as was Lazarsfeld, a member of the Austro-Marxist Social Democratic Party – one day sent Berelson a package. The package contained the 'informer's' Party membership card which Zeisel for some reason had kept from years earlier in Vienna. Berelson recounted with delight how pleased he was to 'now have the son of a bitch'.
9   The missing part of Lazarsfeld's testimony was discovered in the Ford Foundation's Files (File ref.: PA 53–15).

REFERENCES

Adorno, T. W. (1945) 'A social critique of radio music', reprinted in *Kenyon Review* VII (2) (1969).

—— (1969), '*Scientific experiences of a European scholar in America*', in Fleming, D. and B. Bailyn (eds) *The Intellectual Migration*, MA: Cambridge, Harvard University Press.

Andrews, J. E. (1956) *Philanthropic Foundations*, New York: Russell Sage Foundation.

Bereleson, B. (1959) 'The state of communication research', *Public Opinion Quarterley* 23 (1).

Bremner, R. H. (1960) *American Philanthropy*, Chicago: University of Chicago Press.

Fosdick, R. B. (1952) *The Story of the Rockefeller Foundation*, London: Vallentine & Mitchell.

Gouldner, A. W. (1973) *For Sociology: Renewal and Critique in Sociology Today*, London: Allen & Unwin.

Himmelweit, H. T., Vince and Oppenheim (1958) *Television and the Child*, London: Oxford University Press.

Hollis, F. V. (1938) *Philanthropic Foundations and Higher Education*, New York: Columbia University Press.

Horowitz, D. (1972) '*Billion dollar brains: how wealth puts knowledge in its pockets*', in M. Mankoff (ed.) *The Poverty of Progress: The Political Economy of American Social Problems*, New York: Holt, Rinehardt & Winston.

Hutchins, R. M. (1956) *Freedom, Education, and the Fund*, New York: Merdian Books.

Jameson, F. (1967) 'T. W. Adorno or historical tropes?', *Salmagundi* (Spring).

Jenks, C. and D. Riesman (1968) *The Academic Revolution*, New York: Doubleday.

Kefauver Committee (1955) Hearing before the Sub-Committe to US Senate Judiciary Committee (Kilgore): *The Sub-Committee to Investigate Juvinile Delinquency* (Kefauver). 83rd Congress, 2nd Session, Senate Resolution 89 (1954), catalogue no. 3151–4.

Keppel, F. L. (1944) 'Forward' to G. Mrydal, (1944) *An American Dilemma*.

Lazarsfeld, P. F. and W. Theilens (1958) *The Academic Mind: Social Scientists in a Time of Crisis*, Glencoe: Free Press.

Lindeman, E. C. (1936) *Wealth and Culture*, New York: Harcourt, Brace & Co.

Lyons, G. M. (1969) *The Uneasy Partnership: Social Science and the Federal Government in the Twentieth Century*, New York: Russell Sage Foundation.

MacDonald, D. (1956) *The Ford Foundation: The Men and the Millions*, New York: Reynal.

Manly Report (1916) *Commission on Industrial Relations*, Senate Document 415, 64th Congress, 1st Session, Congressional Document Serial no. 6929.

Mills, C. W. (1959) *The Sociological Imagination*, New York: Oxford University Press.

Morrison, D. E. (1978a) 'Kultur and culture: T. W. Adorno and P. F. Lazarsfeld', *Social Research* 45 (2).

—— (1978b) 'The beginning of modern mass communication research', *The European Journal of Sociology* X1X.

Myrdal, G. (1944) *An American Dilemma*, New York: Harper.

Nielsen, W. A. (1972) *The Big Foundations*, New York: Columbia University Press.

Oberschall, A. (ed.) (1972) *The Establishment of Empirical Sociology*, New York: Harper & Row.

Ogg, F. (1928) *Research in the Humanistic and Social Sciences*, New York: Century.

Reece Report (1955) *Report of Special Committee to Congress on Tax-Exempt Foundations and Comparable Organisation*, House Report 2681, 83rd Congress, House Resolution 217, 1954, Catalogue No. 396.

Reeves, T. C. (1969) *Freedom and the Foundation: The Fund for the Republic in the Era of McCarthyism*, New York: A. Knopf.

Schramm, W., Lyle and Parker (1961) *Television in the Lives of Our Children*, Oxford: Oxford University Press.

Stein, M. (1964) 'The Eclipse of Community: Some Glances at the Education of a Sociologist', in Vidich, A. J., J. Bensman and M. R. Stein (eds) *Reflections on Community Studies*, New York: Wiley & Sons.

Stouffer, S. A. (1955) *Communism, Conformity and Civil Liberties: A Cross Section of the Nation Speaks its Mind*, New York: Doubleday.

Wright, C. R. (1956) 'Sociology of mass communications 1945–1955, in H. L. Zetterberg, (ed.) *Sociology in the USA*, UNESCO.

Young, D. (1948) 'Limiting factors in the development of the social sciences', *Procedings of the American Philosophical Society* 92 (5).

—— (1969) 'Forward' to G. M. Lyons, *The Uneasy Partnership: Social Sciences and the Federal Government in the Twentieth Century*, New York: Russell Sage Foundation.

Part III

MEDIA MANAGEMENT

9

PRIME MINISTERS' AND PRESIDENTS' NEWS OPERATIONS

What effects on the job?

Colin Seymour-Ure

Media were integral to New Labour's rise to power. Tony Blair was an effective TV performer. Peter Mandelson worked magic as a communications strategist and media fixer. Philip Gould's market research popularised the term 'focus group'. Press secretary Alastair Campbell was a tough and skillful news manager. The technology was state-of-the-art magical, from the individual pagers keeping party workers on-message to the £300,000 Excalibur instant rebuttal database in the computers at the Party's Millbank headquarters. Magic was everywhere, if one believed much of the media hype. The policies of the Blair project may not have been clear, even after six weeks of electioneering, but its *style* positively shimmered. Political journalists seemed entranced by the operation – rabbits in headlamps. So they relished reporting New Labour's media methods as a key element in the larger New Labour enterprise.

This fascination with the mechanics and personalities of media management, and especially with the roles of Mandelson and Campbell, has continued since Blair has been in power. But what has been the impact on the nature of the prime minister's job? Not much attention seems to have been paid to that question. This chapter therefore sets out to explore it.

Not so long ago the question would have been barely researchable. Downing Street was impenetrable. Lobby journalists – some of them still writing anonymously in the early 1960s – would talk seriously only off the record. Even the Lobby membership list was confidential. The subject was best left to memoirs. Or so it seemed. Then Jeremy Tunstall published *The Westminster Lobby Correspondents* (Tunstall 1970), based on questionnaire and interview, and he showed it to be a researchable subject after all. Even so, his focus was firmly on the media side (which meant newspapers, as there were only two broadcast journalists in the Lobby at that time). The difficulty of saying anything useful about cabinet relations with media is illustrated by the thin or non-existent passages on the subject in the textbooks of the time (see e.g. Mackintosh 1968).

Across the Atlantic, the White House was more open to researchers – and there were more researchers. Wherever media were going, American media tended to get there first. Above all, media management was an essential tool for the president, certainly since Franklin Roosevelt turned the office into an engine of leadership. The American presidency was thus a natural point of reference for the British scholar inquisitive about executive–media relations, even though the presidency was constituted very differently from the premiership. What one could surmise about behaviour in the black hole in Downing Street was usefully considered in the brighter light of Pennsylvania Avenue.

Television had already started to effect a change in this situation at the time when Tunstall was writing. In the memorable phrase of Bill Deedes, TV likes to 'move the furniture around'. It became quickly clear in the 1960s that TV was transforming election campaigns; less clear, though, was how exactly it was changing the behaviour of the victors once in office. The latter was a question crystallised by the novel visibility of Mrs Thatcher's press secretary Bernard Ingham. His entrenchment and increasing prominence in her entourage, in a hitherto unremarkable job, along with the confusions about the propriety of his duties, made him controversial. But TV was not only an instrument that could be applied to the pursuit of a political goal: by the 1980s it was a principal factor in the entire conduct of politics, and a Bernard Ingham of some kind was therefore unavoidable. The contentiousness of his role simply confirmed that the constitutional conventions governing Downing Street news operations had not become settled in the way that they had, say, about the rights and obligations of Lobby correspondents or the rules for reporting parliamentary debates.

New Labour's media management, ratcheted up several notches from Mrs Thatcher's heyday, thus invites a question about its impact on the nature of the prime minister's job. But at the same time the growing use of media as an instrument of government invites comparison with their use by the American president – hence the incorporation of the president into this essay, despite its focus on the prime minister.

NATURE OF THE CHIEF EXECUTIVE'S JOB

Media management aims to influence public perceptions of the prime minister's or president's job. In the present context the job can thus be seen as a combination of *formal* and *informal* roles; *institutional* and *personal* roles; and *governing* and *non-governing* roles. Each pair is likely both to vary within itself and also to overlap with the others. The general effect of Downing Street and White House news operations, as they have developed in the 1990s, has arguably been to increase the range and flexibility of activity within each pair.

Formal and informal roles

Formal roles become so by acquiring constitutional or statutory definition. They are typically differentiated (especially clearly in the USA) as executive, legislative and judicial. In practice the human and organic nature of political behaviour supplements or even supplants them with informal roles. These latter are often implicit and/or they facilitate the formal roles.[1] Thus textbook models of the American presidency list, for instance, roles as head of state (formal), chief executive (formal), commander-in-chief (formal), legislative leader (formal and informal), party leader (informal), mobiliser of opinion (informal) – and a changing list of informal functional roles, depending on the writer's perspective and time of writing, such as moral leader and 'leader of the free world'. The familiar claim by Richard Neustadt that 'presidential power is the power to persuade' (Neustadt 1976: 78) lies chiefly in the constitutional principle of separation (or sharing) of powers. For media management is a key method of joining them up again, so that a president can achieve his goals.

In Britain, which lacks a single constitutional document, formal rules are less clearly defined and therefore less easily separated from the informal. The informal become formal, perhaps, when they are generally acknowledged as 'conventional' (for example, the convention that the prime minister must be a member of the House of Commons). The first statute which names the office of prime minister was an insignificant law in 1937 about ministerial salaries. The muddle is epitomised in the routine textbook claim that the prime minister is 'first among equals' – a self-contradiction – and can 'write his or her own job description' – an extremely vague formulation with little of the predictive quality likely to be found in a formal constitutional role. But we can say with confidence that the prime minister forms the government, in the sense that he chooses the cabinet (formal), is the legislative leader, with power to advise dissolution (formal), and is party leader (informal). The cabinet, too, has formal roles, such as having collective responsibility for its actions. But what this means informally is a matter of contention and employment among constitutional lawyers. It can thus be seen that the scope for media management affecting perceptions of the legitimate authority of the chief executive in Britain is immense; for the procedures and institutions with formal power to define it are confused.

Institutional and personal roles

This distinction separates the abstract and corporate from the personal and individual. In one sense the American president is corporate – 'the presidency':

153

a huge, formal, collective entity, of which the personal president is symbolic head, while wholly ignorant of detailed actions done publicly in his name. Even when limited, say, to White House staff, 'the president' is an institution of which the same can be said. But then there is the personal president – 'Mr President' – the human being who, with exceptions such as after Woodrow Wilson's stroke and on Reagan's off-days, knows exactly what he is doing. Finally there is 'Bill Clinton', not only a personal president but the incumbent.

Comparable distinctions can be drawn about the prime minister. They are not so sharp, because the president is formally a single chief executive, whereas the corporate premiership is mixed up with the collective cabinet. Nonetheless there *is* a corporate premiership, comprising the various offices attached to Downing Street. The press office is one of the larger, with a staff of about fifteen. Equally, though, the largest office in Downing Street (not in fact at Number 10) is the cabinet office, which serves the prime minister and cabinet collectively. But when a news reader says, 'The White House has decided' or 'Downing Street has announced', we know that the president or the prime minister has had something to do with it.

The point of making these distinctions between different versions of a prime minister or president is the potential for attaching one, but not another, to particular issues and events, through media management. During the Watergate scandal, Richard Nixon tried hard to present his deceptions and illegalities as a problem of the institutional presidency, not of himself personally (Dunn 1975: 292; Seymour-Ure 1982: Ch. 2). Over Monica Lewinsky's allegations, Clinton's initial strategy was to try to convince Americans that any relationship was informal and with 'Bill Clinton', and that it did not touch the formal or institutional president at all. Later, the same distinction underlay much of his defence against the possibility of impeachment. Tony Blair, in the earliest embarrassment of his administration, adopted a 'What, me?' pose of injured innocence, when the Labour Party was exposed as having accepted a donation of at least £1 million from the controllers of Formula One motor racing. These businessmen would have lost heavily if a planned ban on tobacco sponsorship, subsequently cancelled, had gone ahead. Blair gave a TV interview distancing himself from the affair, and he announced the return of the cheque. Prime ministers and presidents obviously do not have complete control over the version of themselves which the public perceives. But part of their media management is the continual exercise of choice about what to attach themselves to and in what version.

Governing and non-governing roles

The previous two distinctions have a bearing also on the balance of a chief executive's governing and non-governing roles. The point of the distinction, again, is the scope for mediating between the two by news management. Over a longish period of time (say a decade) it may be possible for incumbents to raise or lower public expectations about whether certain activities are part of the governing role at all. Mrs Thatcher, for instance, succeeded in reversing long held assumptions about the role of government, not least in ownership of such services as the electricity supply industry and the prison service.

More often, and in the short run, the flow of influence will be the other way and on a much smaller scale. That is, media management will be used to turn non-governing roles to advantage in the chief executive's governing roles. For instance, Reagan-as-patient, after being shot in Washington fairly early in his presidency, produced from the stretcher a series of one-liners, reported round the world, which underscored such desirable presidential characteristics as courage and unflappability.[2]

Spouse and parent can be important non-governing roles, with obvious potential links to governing capacities such as moral leadership. Kennedy's Camelot world – little kids, a beautiful wife, good taste, touch football – was an intrinsic (if sadly inauthentic) part of the Kennedy magic. It contrasted sharply with the Second World War aftertaste of the Eisenhower presidency. Hillary Clinton took on too explicit a governing role in relation to the Administration's healthcare programme, for her involvement caused some resentment, which may have contributed to its failure. Spouse and parent are perhaps more successful as symbolic roles. Children in Downing Street and the White House have been successfully protected from media exploitation, for it is the simple fact of their existence, plus the occasional photo opportunity, which can be turned to effect. The corollary is occasional inconvenience. The Blair government's schools' policy was awkwardly skewed, in the run-up to office, by his and his wife's much publicised decision to send their sons to a type of school which the Labour Party in general opposed.

Other non-governing roles that from time to time spill over into governing roles include religion and occupation. His religious beliefs are potentially an issue about Blair. Journalists noticed him privately attending mass by himself in the Roman Catholic Westminster Cathedral; his wife is Catholic and his sons go to a Catholic school. Catholicism, of course, was famously a political nettle that Kennedy had to grasp on his way to the White House. Occupational roles are routinely manipulated to show a chief executive's governing capabilities in the best light. Clinton had to moderate his former student role to combat allegations of draft-dodging and pot-smoking. Carter presented himself as a simple peanut farmer, not a corporate agri-businessman. Kennedy and Bush had wartime military roles to point up. Eisenhower and General Colin Powell were perceived as presidential material, on behalf of both major parties, purely on the strength of competence in a military role.

Lastly, one may mention the governing potential of non-governing facets connected in Britain with class – notably aristocracy and education. Historically, the old-school-tie sent out powerful messages of governing (in)competence. Journalists still routinely count the number of Old Etonians in a Conservative cabinet and the number of Oxbridge graduates in any cabinet. It is probably a help to Blair the public school–Oxford lawyer prime minister that his deputy, John Prescott, used to be a steward on transatlantic liners. Such differences affect, not least, the quality of relations prime ministers enjoy with journalists. Churchill, Eden, Macmillan and Douglas-Home were all happier with newspaper owners and diplomatic correspondents than with run-of-the-mill political reporters. Wilson, notably, took much more trouble with the reporters.

MEDIA MANAGEMENT: GENERAL EFFECTS

Before offering some tentative claims about the effects of their media management on the nature of the premiership and the presidency, two large (if obvious) points need stressing. The first is that *electronic technology has made the range of places from which chief executives can communicate with the public almost limitless*. Everything the chief executive does, and everywhere she or he does it, therefore has to take into account the *communication implications*. Historically, some political institutions were *for* public communication more than others. Representative assemblies and election campaigns were thus the first such institutions in modern times to adjust to the needs of media. The process of executive decision-making in cabinets and presidencies, by contrast, has been the most secretive.[3] There is no public gallery at Downing Street and the White House; indeed parts of each remain genuine 'private houses'. Much of the media's contact with the prime minister's press secretary still takes place at Westminster, not at Downing Street, and it is only in the last year or two that a briefing room has been constructed at Downing Street. Until then, the press secretary briefed journalists in his own office. Arrangements at the White House were correspondingly informal until well after the Second World War.

The second point to stress is the wholesale takeover by British politicians of modern techniques of marketing, such as sophisticated polling, focus groups, computer databases, junk mail and now the Internet – all summed up in the American literature as 'new media'. These helped to popularise the idea of 'the permanent campaign'. *They have brought the techniques of winning office into the activity of government itself*. As between Britain and the USA, the implications are greater and more recent for Britain. Once in government, party organisations have almost always had little to do with the prime minister's news operations. The orientation has been overwhelmingly towards the requirements of government – and thus of the civil service departments. Departmental press offices have been staffed by civil servants occupying a distinct information officer grade (with the general exception of the Treasury and the Foreign Office). Even if ministers have not been 'captured' by their civil servants, the communication machines of the parties have concentrated on local elections and by-elections, research, the annual party conference and preparing for the next general election, while departmental information offices have been studiously non-partisan. The Blair government's comprehensive and energetic media operations put this comfortable arrangement under strain. There were complaints about 'politicisation' of the government's information service and the supplanting of senior officers by partisan ministerial special advisers.[4] These provoked a disputatious inquiry by the House of Commons' Select Committee on Public Administration (1998). It is likely that the links between the Labour Party and Downing Street communications work are closer institutionally than under any previous government, and that there is greater seepage of partisanship into Whitehall than before.

The major effect of these developments – from the intrusion of TV to the media priorities of the Blair government – is that *prime ministers and presidents must, institutionally, spend progressively more resources and time on communications work*. This is confirmed by historical analysis, not only in Downing Street and Washington but in the 'Westminster' regimes of Ottawa and Canberra (Seymour-Ure 1991). The first stage in all these countries, at different times between the 1930s and 1950s, was the appointment of a general secretary to the president/prime minister, with functions that included primitive press relations (writing press releases, giving out advance copies of speeches). The communication role then gradually became *institutionalised, professionalised* and *diversified*. Separate press secretaries were appointed, followed by assistants, suites of offices, briefing rooms and mini-bureaucracies. As TV intruded and international summitry grew, the emphasis shifted and press secretaries were superseded by, or became subordinate to, 'communications directors'. These empires grew to include radio/TV grooming, news digests (now 'media monitoring'), media relations for the executive's spouse, out-of-town 'advance' work before the media hit a summit. After this came a wider political involvement, as politicians realised that increasingly the *substance* of a chief executive's work, such as the achievement of a particular policy initiative, was usually inextricable from its *presentation*. Chief executives began to think in terms of media *strategies*, perhaps with a ministerial colleague to have responsibility for them – and especially for co-ordination. Lastly, the wheel comes full circle, when and if chief executives feel their public communications are of such political priority that they themselves must take charge. It is thus no surprise to find that a list of the Clinton White House staff in 1997 included at least 107 people with communication tasks, linked to interest groups, parties, the media and citizens, with speech writers and the large logistical teams running the president's personal appearances. Hillary Clinton and the vice-president had their own staffs (*Capital Source* 1997). More communication specialists lurked in other White House offices, such as the National Security Council; and yet others, such as pollsters, were contracted from outside.

Prime ministers, then, have increasingly become managers and strategists in the field of media and communications. Tony Blair has gone beyond his predecessors. He is responsible for an operation involving at least the following parts. Central is the Downing Street press office, which strictly works for the cabinet as a whole and therefore shares the ambiguities of a prime minister's own position in the cabinet. The chief press secretary, Alastair Campbell, is spokesman, agent, manager and adviser to the prime minister. The prime minister's small private office becomes involved through a rule that ministerial policy statements must be cleared by it. A Blair innovation is the Strategic Communications Unit. This reports to Campbell and has a principal staff of six. Its job is 'pulling together and sharing with departments the Government's key policy themes and messages' (Select Committee 1998: xiii). Precisely what this means is unclear, and the Select Committee recommended that its tasks be explained in more detail. Another innovation, reflecting plainly the growth of radio and TV services, is the Media Monitoring Unit. This provides to departments and Downing Street a round-the-clock service, flagging up news stories as they develop. Backing these is a new computer information system, called AGENDA, which 'holds listings of forthcoming newsworthy events [e.g. ministerial interviews and visits], lines to take, key Departmental messages and themes, and Ministerial speeches' (Select Committee 1998: 107).

Life is meetings, as well as monitor screens. Campbell chairs a weekly meeting (established decades ago) of departmental information heads. This tends to be preoccupied with immediate problems of co-ordination, despite attempts to get it thinking strategically. More important is the daily early-morning meeting chaired first by Peter Mandelson and, after the July 1998 reshuffle, by Jack Cunningham, his successor as *de facto* minister for communication and media relations. This committee follows the model chaired by Michael Heseltine when deputy prime minister under John Major. It brings together 'key players' (the cabinet office's term) from Number 10 (including Campbell), the Treasury, FCO, deputy prime minister's office, the cabinet office and – crucially, the Labour Party and the chief whip's office (Select Committee 1998: 31). It thus links (which need not mean fusing) party and government personnel and priorities. Campbell himself, finally, continues the traditional twice-daily collective lobby briefings, to which he has made small but significant changes. First, he tapes them and circulates a transcript round Whitehall. Second, the briefings are on the record – which had more or less become the rule unofficially under John Major – and he permits himself to be identified as 'the prime minister's official spokesman'. He stopped firmly short, as a matter of principle, of agreeing to be named (Select Committee 1998: xvii).

Some of those developments, as has been indicated, were happening before New Labour came to office. The fact that two of the people most closely involved, Mandelson and Campbell, are Blair intimates, reflects their importance to the new government.[5] But the question thus far begged is to what extent Blair is himself directly involved. The more confidence reposed in his intimates, the less, one could argue, he himself need bother about communication strategy and management. For chief executives personally, as distinct from institutionally, the best hypothesis, then, may be that they *may* – but need not - spend *progressively more resources and time on communication work.*

In one way there is surely no doubt that chief executives *must* spend more time. Their third communication role is that of *performer,* and it is a truism to say that media performance has become a time-consuming activity of potentially crucial importance. One way of illustrating this, easily done for the president, is to differentiate specific communication activities, which would not have taken place otherwise (such as a press conference or TV interview), from activities that would have taken place but may well have been transformed by media coverage (such as a factory visit). Out of 436 cases of public communication by President Clinton recorded by the White House in 1993, only thirty-five (eight per cent) happened in places that were specifically *for* public communication, such as the White House briefing room. Even more surprisingly, a mere three took place in broadcasting studios. Yet all 436 were open to the TV cameras. Even when doing something 'private', the president is a public performer.[6] It is one facet of everywhere being a potential place of public communication. Much the same could be said for Tony Blair. The main institutional difference is that the prime minister has always performed in the legislature, and since 1989 he has done so in front of TV cameras.

Looked at in that way, some at least of the increased public performance is not an increase in absolute level but in performance geared to the media. It is to that extent a qualitative change – and it has required new skills, which an Eisenhower or a Churchill would have been reluctant to contemplate but which are now part of basic political equipment. It could be, therefore, that chief executives must spend more time *thinking about* public performance, but that they are not compelled by the needs of the job to spend relatively more time than, say, forty years ago actually doing it. It is striking that a journalist recalling Stephen Early, Roosevelt's press secretary in the 1930s, could comment: 'The whole administration was a public relations effort, and Early was right in the middle of it.' Such comments were made equally about the Nixon administration and, especially, that of Ronald Reagan.[7] One is reminded, again, of the fact that part of the prominence of press secretaries and spin doctors is that they are simply now so much more visible than in the past.

Adding all these things together, it seems fair to argue that prime ministers and presidents (distinct from their staff) are absolutely more active as public performers through routine exposure to TV; and that they may, if so inclined, give performance in and for media a higher priority than did their predecessors – but that the option remains for them not to do so. Blair, to take a particular example, has proved ready to attach his name quite frequently to ghost-written newspaper articles, but a successor might not do so. In general Blair gives performance a higher priority than did John Major – but Major probably gave it a lower priority than Mrs Thatcher. What seems less likely to go into reverse is the scale of machinery concerned with media relations. Work can be delegated, but the chief executive cannot escape responsibility for it, both in the administrative sense and in the sense that the consequences of malfunction may be more serious – ultimately in the ballot box – than in earlier times. Party management has long made the chief whip an occasional attender at cabinet meetings. Media management means that nowadays Alastair Campbell goes to cabinet too.[8]

MEDIA MANAGEMENT AND CHIEF EXECUTIVES' ROLES

The effects of media management can also be evaluated by reference to the three previously analysed chief executive roles. First, modern media management *changes the formal roles in relation to the informal*. Publicity about methods of cabinet decision making, for instance, modifies the formal claims of collective responsibility, demolishing the myths of collective ministerial participation and agreement. John Major first authorised the publication of the names and membership of the system of cabinet standing committees, which are the effective decision-takers for the majority of cabinet business. Blair's distinctive contribution, which is equally unlikely to be reversed, has been to blur the formal distinction between partisan and non-partisan roles in the central government machine. The change is exemplified in Campbell's own position. He is formally a 'special adviser', which denotes party-political status – yet he (and Blair's chief of staff, Jonathan Powell) is explicitly permitted by the legal instrument of an Order in Council to be in charge of permanent civil servants, so that he can carry out the management part of his job. The difficulties then of drawing the line between circumstances in which Campbell may and may not behave as a partisan were wonderfully illustrated in exchanges between the cabinet secretary Sir Richard Wilson and members of the Select Committee on Public Administration inquiring into the government information services. Wilson took refuge in metaphor (he talked about 'attacking the Opposition with bricks and bottles'), and he ducked and weaved in fine bureaucratic form (Select Committee 1998: 32–49). Changes introduced in order to modernise the government information services also look as though they may well make the informal maintenance of a clear distinction between partisan and non-partisan work more difficult than before.

Second, and along similar lines, media management *tends to personalise institutional roles*. Modern media exert a pressure to personalise. They have cracked apart civil service anonymity and have helped in the demolition of that old façade of the cabinet as a collective entity. Not only did the burly figure of Bernard Ingham become well known; he was criticised also for behaving like a minister – in other words, for using his intimacy with Mrs Thatcher to influence, intangibly, her thinking about people and policies. Alastair Campbell already enjoyed such intimacy when he took office, and he soon raised eyebrows for his treatment of certain ministers.[9]

Third, media management *tends to blur governing and non-governing roles.* Of the three types of change, this is perhaps of most practical concern to chief executives. It links so directly to their personal images – their very identity – and to the reality they seek to construct for electoral and governing purposes. Intrinsic to this, and indeed to the others, is a public–private dimension. While organised to protect an area of privacy around the chief executive, media management *tends to eliminate the distinction between public and private.*[10] An alternative formulation might be that media management *defines the private to fit a public image.* Holidays are a good example. Prime ministers in the 1990s must holiday in a fortress, protected by walls of stone or public unawareness. But the books they read, the games they play, the guests they entertain, are trumpeted beyond the walls – and pitched for public consumption. It is difficult to see how the public–private distinction can endure. In Washington its elimination became almost complete with the publication of the Starr Report on the conduct of President Clinton. The logic of the separation of powers, through the apparatus of a special prosecutor, not only reduces the president to the level of ordinary humanity but provides the rationale for exposing intimate details of his sex life.

A further effect of media management has probably been to *extend the potential of the 'symbolic premiership'.* Presidents, for example as heads of state, have symbolic roles built into their job description. Prime ministers do not. A distinction needs to be drawn between communicating *in* symbols and communicating *as* a symbol. Politicians have always communicated *in* symbols. If there is anything new about that in the electronic age, it is presumably the result of the greater scope that exists for visual symbols – the paraphernalia of clothes, hairstyle, body language and appropriately meaningful locations. But, with the exception of Winston Churchill in 1940, the British prime minister began routinely to communicate *as* a symbol perhaps with Mrs Thatcher – the 'Iron Lady'. The practice has several dimensions and links to the personalisation of the office, to the public–private distinction and to the prime minister as performer. It can also be offered, obviously, as one explanation for the development of 'spinning', which is about the deliberate attempt to give a preferred explicit meaning to ambiguous communications, of which symbols are one type.

Increased priority for media management also increases the seriousness for a chief executive of the fact that their news operations will tend *not to be in equilibrium with that of their media clientele.* The interests of chief executives and of media organisations are not identical, and their interaction is a product of the reactions of each side to changes in the other (executive incumbency and organisation; media ownership and technology, etc.). Hence the balance of control and satisfaction tips from one side to the other. Over a period of time, chief executives come to see themselves as the victims of irresponsible, ill-intentioned or incompetent media; while media see themselves bludgeoned and manipulated by cynical news managers. Memoirs on either side are full of hand-wringing and carpet-biting.[11]

It should in principle be possible to write the history of chief executives' news operations entirely in terms of these shifting balances, and to trace periods in which politicians have seized the initiative or fallen behind. The two years up to and the three since the 1997 British general election are an excellent contemporary example. John Major's last press secretary was a well liked professional civil service information officer who had previously served as the Downing Street deputy but was in the best sense purely a functionary. Political responsibility was given to the deputy prime minister Michael Heseltine, Major's opponent for the premiership. The government reeled from one public relations disaster to another. The Blair government took office on a wave of popularity and with the media management apparatus that has been outlined. The initiative was seized and held. But this did not in itself guarantee the government positive results, and no doubt the balance would eventually shift again.

Such a situation is normal for the American presidency. For the premiership, on the other hand, it is relatively new. Prime ministers have by definition commanded the House of Commons – historically a principal platform for public communication. Their command may have been weak, because of a slim majority or weak authority in their own party. The tradition of press partisanship gave newspapers a part in the party struggle – both between and within parties. So management of the press has been a strand in political leadership since the popular press developed more than 100 years ago. But in the last twenty-five years press partisanship has become more fickle. The difficulty of getting the prime ministerial agenda across, even if a paper supports it editorially, has increased, while detailed parliamentary reporting has simultaneously diminished. For this to happen at the same time as broadcasting entered the political arena has been a seriously destabilising factor for the premiership. Media management has become simultaneously more central to the prime minister's job and more difficult.

This last point brings the argument, finally, to the question of 'convergence'. Modern media management provides strong support for the proposition that *presidential and prime ministerial job descriptions are converging*. The claim is both about the parts of the job itself and about style – the way chief executives carry them out. Provided it is not made extravagantly, it is persuasive.[13] Techniques of electioneering highlight a prime minister more than his colleagues, so the 'permanent campaign' brings that pre-eminence into government. The

Downing Street press secretary formally serves the whole cabinet; yet the closer high-priority news operations bring him to the prime minister's core staff, the more he becomes the prime minister's own man. As the career of Bernard Ingham and the early anecdotes about Campbell showed, he inevitably becomes an instrument for managing cabinet colleagues so as to secure the prime minister's agenda. Under Blair, the entire communications machinery, old and new, is centralised in Downing Street to an unprecedented extent. (The head of the government information service, for instance, has been placed in the cabinet office.)

Again, the prime minister's increased scope for attaching and detaching himself to or from particular issues (Northern Ireland; economic policy, the odd smear of sleaze) is a presidential characteristic. 'Going public', to use Kernell's phrase about the rhetorical presidency (Kernell 1986), is a tactic familiar to prime ministers at least as far back as Gladstone in the nineteenth century (e.g. his Midlothian campaign). But modern communications have increased its scope and enable one plausibly to give the prime minister a role as 'mobiliser of opinion'. From time to time public performance even gives the prime minister a quasi-head-of-state role. Why else, for instance, did Blair read a lesson at Princess Diana's funeral, which was a uniquely difficult occasion for the Queen and royal family?

Modern media, lastly, tug the prime minister away from his base in the House of Commons and from other party-related activities that have traditionally been the source of his authority. One year into the Labour government, speaker Betty Boothroyd complained to the Commons about ministers' tendency to brief journalists before making announcements to MPs. 'If [the House of Commons] is to fulfil its function properly it must be the first to learn of important developments in government policy' (Hansard, 1998: 699). This has been an occasional bleat in the past; now its force is stronger. Parliament's first year under the Blair administration was generally listless. Blair took pains with the soundbite-laden weekly ritual of Question Time, but he was otherwise a poor attender in the Commons chamber.[13]

None of this changes the facts of political geography, culture and constitutional form, which put an ocean between the American presidency and the British premiership. Nor should convergence be seen as a steady trend and as necessarily irreversible. There will always be weak prime ministers for whom no amount of efficient media management will be successful in lifting them above their colleagues and crowning them with success.

That note is a good one on which to end. Media management in the Blair administration, to summarise, has seen changes of style and institutional innovation that amount to a further stage of professionalisation. The impact on the office of prime minister has been *qualitative* – an increased sensitivity to public communication as an instrument of government, party management and personal leadership. It has also been *quantitative*, although the administrative responsibilities have been delegated, with a correlative increase in the status of the ministers and 'special advisers' involved. Other prime ministers might manage the arrangements differently. Obvious though it is to say so, however, one must not forget that managing the *process* of public communication is no more a guarantee now of a successful outcome than it ever was. Chief executives are right to give a high priority to communication management, especially if the idea of politics as a kind of Socratic argument has given way to the psychological manipulation of images. But *management* remains obstinately different from *manipulation*. The paradox is that continual refinements of communication techniques will not necessarily achieve a chief executive's desired result more surely than if 'facts are left to speak for themselves' – which is what President Eisenhower, for one, wanted to do. The literature on the influence of media continues to show how difficult it is to change individuals' attitudes and behaviour in intended ways. Media management is an opportunity that must be seized. But it remains a great opportunity for failing.

NOTES

1 Good examples of formal institutions that have been supplanted informally are the monarch's Privy Council in Britain, from which the cabinet derives, and the electoral college for the president in the USA, which in fact still has the potential to produce a different result from the popular vote.
2 'Honey, I forgot to duck,' Reagan told his wife, when she rushed to his bedside. 'Please tell me you're Republicans,' he said to the doctors preparing him for surgery. White House spokesmen released a reassuring trickle of such quips (Cannon 1997).
3 There is still a corresponding contrast between the methodology typical of research about the American Congress and the necessarily anecdotal and less rigorous methodology of studies about the presidency.
4 A particular object of attention was Charlie Whelan, 'special adviser'/press secretary to Gordon Brown, who effectively sidelined the Treasury civil service head of information. See generally Select Committee (1998).
5 Mandelson resigned from the cabinet at the end of 1998, following public criticism of his failure to disclose a large loan from Geoffrey Robinson, a fellow minister. Mandelson was, however, reappointed ten months later, in October 1999, as secretary of state for Northern Ireland.
6 The transcripts from which these statistics are compiled were published on the 1993 version of the White House Internet site. For further analysis, see Seymour-Ure (1997).
7 The Early comment is by Richard Strout, quoted in Grossman and Kumar (1981: 23). A typical comment on the Reagan White House is by Les Janka, a deputy press secretary: 'The whole thing was PR. This was a PR outfit that became President and took over the country . . . [T]heir first, last and overarching activity was public relations' (quoted in Hertsgaard 1988: 6).
8 It is unclear from Campbell's evidence to the Select Committee on Public

Administration whether he attends as a matter of routine (Select Committee 1998: 49). His attendance, in any event, is as an observer.

9 In particular Campbell was teased for writing letters to Harriet Harman, social security minister, and Frank Field, one of her junior ministers, to rebuke them for briefing the press on welfare reform without clearance from Number 10 (Select Committee 1998: 53).

10 The point can also be made about royalty. Princess Diana is buried on an island in a lake in a park in deep countryside. But the effect, it seems, has simply been to destroy privacy locally.

11 A journalistic survey of prime ministers' relations with newspapers up to the late 1970s was subtitled 'The war between Fleet Street and Downing Street (Margach 1978). For prime ministers and television, see Michael Cockerell (1988).

12 A highly original discussion of presidential tendencies in the job of prime minister is Michael Foley (1993).

13 It is too early to make a comparison with Mrs Thatcher, but she proved the least 'parliamentary' of modern prime ministers, in terms of Commons' attendance (Dunleavy *et al.* 1990). Blair was reported in *The Spectator* (15 November 1997) to have voted in only two of the eighty-six divisions in the House of Commons between May and November 1997.

REFERENCES

Cannon, L. (1997) *Reagan*, New York: Perigree Books.

Capital Source (1997) Fall, Washington, DC: National Journal Group.

Cockerell, M. (1988) *Live from Number Ten*, London: Faber & Faber.

Dunleavy, P., G. W. Jones and B. O'Leary (1990) 'Prime ministers and the Commons: patterns of behaviour 1968–1987', *Public Administration* 68(1): 123–40.

Dunn, C. W. (ed.) (1975) *The Future of the Presidency*, Morristown, NJ: General Learning Press.

Foley, M. (1993) *The Rise of the British Presidency*, Manchester: Manchester University Press.

Hansard (1998) House of Commons *Official Report*, 298, 21 July, London: the Stationery Office.

Grossman, M. B. and M. J. Kumar (1981) *Portraying the President*, Baltimore, MD: Johns Hopkins University Press.

Hertsgaard, M. (1988) *On Bended Knee: The Press and the Reagan Presidency*, New York: Farrar Strauss Giroux.

Kernell, S. (1986) *Going Public*, Washington, DC: C.Q. Press.

Mackintosh, J. P. (1968) *The British Cabinet*, (2nd edition), London: Stevens.

Margach, J. (1978) *The Abuse of Power*, London: W. H. Allen.

Neustadt, R. E. (1976) *Presidential Power* (revised edition), New York: John Wiley.

Select Committee on Public Administration (1988) Sixth Report: *The Government Information and Communication Service*, HC770, London: the Stationery Office.

Seymour-Ure, C. (1982) *The American President: Power and Communication*, London: Macmillan.

—— (1991) 'The role of press secretaries on chief executive staffs in Anglo-American systems', in C. Campbell and M. Wyszomirski (eds), *Executive Leadership in Anglo-American Systems*, Pittsburgh: University of Pittsburgh Press.

—— (1997) 'Location, location, location', *Harvard International Journal of Press/Politics* 2(2): 27–46.

Tunstall, J. (1970) *The Westminster Lobby Correspondents*, London: Routledge & Kegan Paul.

10

POLITICAL ADVERTISING AT THE END OF THE TWENTIETH CENTURY

Winston Fletcher

Political parties in Britain, and indeed throughout the democratic world, now spend huge and increasing sums on media advertising in the run-up to important elections. Over £27,000,000 was spent in Britain, mostly on posters, by the parties contesting the 1997 general election. Little of this advertising is particularly informative: some of it is intended simply to be 'image building'; much of it is aggressively negative – deprecating and even maligning the competence and principles of the opponents. All of which raises a host of important questions. Is there any evidence the advertising is effective? If so, how does it work? Does the knocking copy bring the entire political process into disrepute, and contribute to the low esteem in which the majority of the public hold politicians? Is it worth the fortunes spent on it?

Political advertising dates back at least to Roman times (as indeed do many other forms of consumer advertising). The most direct evidence comes from Pompeii, preserved under a blanket of volcanic ash following the eruption of Vesuvius in 79 AD. There, among advertisements for traders and inn-keepers, prostitutes, sporting events and others, friends of political candidates recommended them as being worthy of office (Nevett 1982).

Both democracy and political advertising thereafter disappeared from western Europe – there being no call for the latter in the absence of the former – until the beginning of the nineteenth century. It would seem that the Reform Act of 1832, and the subsequent extension of the franchise, immediately spurred a growth in election advertising. In that year the Charles Barker Agency, which was founded in 1812 and is still trading, ran press campaigns for parliamentary candidates Sir Edward Knatchbull and Sir William Geary, each of whom spent more than £100 on their election advertising (Nevett 1982.) We know the exact sum because a complaint concerning Sir Edward's and Sir William's lavish expenditures was made in parliament by Sir Matthew Ridley. In reply to the complaint, it was explained that, in those days, newspapers charged political advertisers twice their normal rates. Politicians continued to use press, posters and handbills throughout the nineteenth century, though perhaps not surprisingly nothing is known about their effectiveness. In this respect political advertising was no different from other advertising of the period, though as we shall see this particular difference no longer pertains. The long ancestry of political advertising establishes that far from political advertisers copying baked beans and detergents, as the oft-repeated cliché has it, baked beans and detergents have copied political advertisers. This should not be surprising. Persuasive communication is the essence of politics, and has always been.

While political advertising is far from new, there have unquestionably been substantial changes in the ways politicians have used marketing communications over recent years. Television and market research, in particular, have come into existence only during this century; and both emerged as power players in politics, initially in the United States, almost immediately after the Second World War.

Earlier, in the 1936 US presidential election, Republican candidate Landon had, for the first time ever, used radio spots in his campaign against Franklin D. Roosevelt – unsuccessfully, as it turned out (Mayer 1958). The outbreak of the Second World War, and Roosevelt's continuing incumbency, meant that nothing much then happened until 1948 when the chairman of the Colgate Corporation, E. H. Little, generously offered the Republican Thomas Dewey a complete multi-media campaign created by Colgate's own advertising agency Ted Bates – then one of the 'hottest' agencies in New York (Mayer 1958). Political parties, certainly in recent times, have almost always employed the most fashionable advertising agencies of the time, presumably seeking fashion's reassurance in an arena they themselves know little about. (It is a nice irony that Ted Bates was later bought by Saatchi & Saatchi – at that time the UK Tory Party's agency, and certainly then one of the hottest shops in Britain!)

Thomas Dewey rejected E. H. Little's offer – and lost. These two facts may have been connected, or they may not. It was a risk Dwight D. Eisenhower's managers were unwilling to take. In the following presidential election in 1952 Eisenhower's spin doctors returned to the Ted Bates' Agency and got its chairman Rosser Reeves – then an advertising panjandrum who also captained the American chess team in Moscow – to devise their candidate's television commercials. That is when the political advertising shenanigans really got going. But like Dewey, Eisenhower did not relish becoming a geriatric electronic huckster. Between takes, he sat shaking his head despondently, and said: 'To think that an old soldier should come to this' (Bruce 1992). Reeves, however, was suitably eulogistic about his own work. 'If only Dewey had known these things', he boasted later about the techniques that had been used, 'he too would have been president' (Mayer 1958).

That was neither honest nor truthful. As knowledgeable commentators since have noted, Eisenhower was a cast-iron certainty, which was why the Republicans chose him. He would have won with or without Reeves' help. Equally, Dewey would almost certainly have lost. Politicians, however, have rarely been interested in such subtleties. They fell for Reeves' boast hook, line and pollster. Without advertising, Dewey bit the dust. With advertising, Eisenhower romped home. *Ergo*, advertising wins elections. The era of high-pressure, all

singing-and-dancing, political persuasion had arrived, especially in the USA, but on a lower key throughout the western democratic world. Harold Macmillan's general election triumph in 1959, followed by John F. Kennedy's in 1960, appeared finally to clinch the argument, if any sceptics still needed convincing.

Harold Macmillan's 1959 campaign, devised by the Colman Prentis and Varley Agency, again at that time one of the hottest shops in Britain, employed the memorable slogan 'Life's Better With The Conservatives. Don't Let Labour Ruin It'. This encapsulates the most common approach made by any party that is in power and is seeking to retain it: a positive claim followed by a negative threat – things are good, don't risk a change. The 1959 Tory slogan has repeatedly been copied, always more clumsily. In 1979 the Labour government proclaimed 'Keep Britain Labour And It Will Keep Getting Better', which was hardly positive, and lacked any threat. The voters were unconvinced.

In the run-up to the 1987 election, on 'Wobbly Thursday' (4 June), incumbent prime minister Margaret Thatcher – suffering with toothache – was shown an opinion poll that suggested the Tories were heading for defeat. The poll contradicted most other research findings at the time, and was almost certainly a 'rogue'. Nonetheless its findings wobbled Mrs Thatcher, and she is understood to have immediately called in one of her longest serving and most trusted marketing advisors, Tim Bell (now Lord Bell). She charged Bell with producing the kind of campaign which had served the Tories so well in the past. Bell went back to basics with the slogan 'Britain Is Great Again. Don't Let Labour Wreck It' (positive – threat) and Thatcher won a clear parliamentary majority (Butler and Kavanagh 1988).

This is not to suggest the campaign slogans were a principal cause of the Tory successes in 1959 and 1987. Election advertising, as we shall see, is not that important. But the phraseology in each case reflected the party's entire campaign stance. Tory campaigns have always been willing to attack ruthlessly, taking no prisoners and giving no quarter. In 1979, when they were out of office, the Tories famously employed their 'Labour Isn't Working' poster, which was a travesty of the truth. And in 1992 the Tory campaign, which probably helped them win that election against all the odds, was based on 'Labour's Tax Bombshell' and 'Labour's Double Whammy' posters – both of which powerfully clobbered Labour's taxation policies, forcing them on to the defensive. Although they have used negative themes, and indeed did so to some extent in 1997, Labour have always been uncomfortable about negative advertising. Labour politicians instinctively prefer, as many of them have said, to be positive about their policies rather than nasty about their opponents. Unfortunately, though it may sound depressingly negative, in political advertising the high ground is always captured by negative copy – for good positive reasons.

Not that negative campaigning is a new phenomenon in politics. Politicians, particularly in the USA, have always gone for each other's jugular. From the earliest days of the American republic, before political advertising itself was commonplace, politicians engaged in virulent personal attacks against their opponents. As G. S. Wood (1978) has put it: 'No accusation was too coarse or too vulgar to be made – from drunkenness and gambling to impotence and adultery.' To give just two nineteenth-century examples (from Johnson-Cartee and Copeland 1991), in 1842 supporters of candidate Clay chanted about his opponent: 'Do you know a traitor viler, viler – than Tyler?' (Songs and chants were the advertising jingles of their time.) And perhaps the dirtiest presidential campaign ever was in 1884, between Democratic presidential candidate Grover Cleveland and the Republican James G. Blaine. Cleveland had fathered a child out of wedlock, and the Blaine forces made much use of this well-soiled linen with the short chant: 'Ma! Ma! Where's my Pa?' Blaine himself then ran into accusations of financial corruption, leading to the Democratic response: 'Blaine! Blaine! Jay Gould Blaine! The Continental liar from the State of Maine!'

Things got still worse for Blaine after the Democrats discovered that he had himself become a father only three months after getting married. The Democrats naturally exploited this to the full, and after Grover Cleveland was elected his supporters marched through Washington chanting triumphantly: 'Ma! Ma! Where's my Pa? Gone to the White House – Ha! Ha! Ha!' Compared to this, even the nastiest of recent presidential campaign spats – between Nixon and McGovern, and between Bush and Dukakis, for example – were comparatively tame affairs.

But why, the question must be asked, is mudslinging relatively common in political campaigning, whereas it is almost unknown in the more humdrum world of competitive product advertising? The explanation usually proffered is that voters – particularly in the USA and Britain – now have such a poor opinion of politicians that they will believe only negative advertising. Only derogatory and pejorative words, it is argued, realistically reflect the public's present political perceptions. There may be some truth in that hypothesis, but it is not the whole truth.

There are half-a-dozen other reasons for negative advertising, all of which are contributory–cumulative factors:

1   In most advanced economies the chasm between the opposing parties is far from huge, hardly ideologically significant. All western democratic

parties now share much the same aims – economic growth, full employment, low inflation, less crime, better education, better health, sound defence and so on – and so the differences between parties are differences of means rather than of ends; and differences of means are difficult to dramatise.

2   This means that when a party tries to present its own virtues they sound like candyfloss. Their statements of aims are like 'motherhood and apple-pie' to the voters – warm and cosy, but widely shared and far from inspiring.

3   In those countries where the 'first past the post' electoral system pertains, particularly Britain and the USA, the main battle is usually between two parties (or two candidates). Negative copy can be effectively used only in bilateral, two-horse, races. If several parties or candidates are in with a strong chance, it is almost impossible for them all to sling mud effectively at each other. And in most commercial or product markets there are many more than two competitors. Interestingly, in the cola market, dominated by Coke and Pepsi, the latter has used knocking copy, to some degree.

4   Political advertising is almost always subject to less stringent controls than product advertising. The main reason for this is that those who are responsible for censoring product advertising would be accused of interfering in the democratic process if they started to try to control political campaigns. (A secondary reason is that political campaigns are generally over and done with before they can be properly investigated and brought to book. And it would be impossible to throw out a government, or a president, after winning the election, on the grounds that the electoral advertising employed might have been mendacious – which would, anyway, almost certainly be denied.)

5   Most political advertising, contrary to common belief, is *not* aimed at winning over voters from the other side. Most political advertising is intended to encourage existing followers, hold on to waverers, win back wobbly deserters – and to ensure that every possible supporter goes out and votes on the day. There is no better way of rallying one's own troops, as generals have always recognised, than whipping them up into passion by smearing the enemy. Negative campaigning is a lousy way of converting those who are against you, but an excellent way to enthuse your own fans.

6   Elections are held only every four or five years, and an awful lot rides on them. So those involved tend to grow fiercely passionate about winning, which can even lead to counter-productive sniping and dirty tricks. Product advertising is more or less continuous, and those who run it are, if only marginally, the more sanguine and analytic about the process.

Their inability to use negative advertising is one of the two principal reasons why centre parties find it so difficult to advertise effectively, as I gloomily discovered while working for the newly launched Social Democratic Party and the SDP–Liberal Alliance during the 1980s. (The other main reason is lack of money.) The essential advertising problem for a party in the centre of British politics is that it never knows about whom to be negative, who to attack. If it attacks Labour it looks as though it supports the Tories. If it attacks the Tories it looks like a wimpish version of Labour. To attack both simultaneously looks both feeble and confusing. (The 1983 SDP–Liberal Alliance election posters tried to do this. They were not an unqualified success.) So negative advertising cannot be done. And for the middle-of-the-road SDP, the communications problem was further aggravated by the carefully balanced, non-extremist, somewhat sanctimonious nature of its messages: competition with compassion on the one hand, toughness with tenderness on the other.

Does negative advertising work? It is indubitably increasingly pervasive, so the politicians and their advisors must believe it works. It is sometimes hard to define whether or not a particular advertisement or campaign is wholly negative – would the two Tory slogans mentioned above be accurately defined as negative? In America, however, things are clearer cut:

> Both academicians and consultants agree that negative ads make up a significant proportion of modern political advertising. Researchers estimate that between 30% and 50% of all political advertising produced can be described as negative.
>
> (Johnson-Cartee and Copeland 1991: 3)

In a moment I'll explore the fundamental difficulties involved in the evaluation of all political advertising campaigns. But it is worth noting that the public, when asked, certainly claim to dislike negative campaigns. A number of studies, particularly in the USA, have all shown that voters deplore mudslinging and personally abusive advertisements. G. M. Garramone (1984), for example, found that three-quarters of his survey respondents expressed disapproval in their assessment of negative political advertisements – a level of hostility which the author of this chapter has found to be broadly echoed in the UK, though reliable quantified data is unavailable here. And negative campaigning has been blamed for the dwindling turnout at American and British elections. If politicians portray each other as unprincipled shysters, the argument runs, this may engender – almost certainly does engender – a general level of cynicism that makes voters unwilling to vote at all. It is an hypothesis which has so far proved impossible to corroborate, but sounds far from unlikely. It suggests that it is not so much voters' low opinion of politicians that is the progenitor of negative political advertising, but negative political advertising that is, at least in part, the progenitor of voters' low opinion of politicians.

Other studies, however, have shown that negative political advertising is generally remembered better than positive advertising, and several psephologists have pointed out that voters' declared antipathy to negative advertising does not appear to be reflected in their behaviour at the ballot box, if they vote (see e.g. Devlin 1981). My own view is that insufficient attention has so far been paid to the fifth point listed above: much if not most political advertising is intended to bolster existing support – and that is an exceptionally difficult factor to measure.

Because politicians are, effectively, amateurs in the art of advertising – they get involved only sporadically, at elections, and even then it is not their highest priority, as so much else is happening – there are two problems that often mitigate against their maximising its effectiveness.

First, in planning and running fast-moving advertising campaigns a clearly defined and single-minded chain of command is essential. In politics, achieving this transparent necessity is rare. (In the SDP–Liberal Alliance, and for decades in the Labour Party, it was non-existent.) This is largely because politics and politicians normally operate by way of committees and meetings. Politicians imbibe the need to carry others along with them with their mothers' milk. They post-rationalise their predilections for committees, and claim them to be aspects of democracy at work. Well, maybe. But they are a lousy way to achieve effective advertising. It is perhaps unsurprising that Labour and Liberal Democrat campaigns have been continually bedevilled by committeeitis. But even the hierarchical Tories have not been immune. 'Wobbly Thursday' was a clear example of Mrs Thatcher interfering in the chain of command, and in the strategy that had previously been agreed.

Second, and contrary to present-day conventional wisdom, most politicians do not much like advertising and PR people. Margaret Thatcher was an exception, as maybe is Tony Blair. Michael Foot's refusal to be dressed up by image-makers, though extreme, was much more typical. To some degree the politicians' inclinations are admirable. They want to be natural, they want to be themselves, they do not want to be – they fear being – packaged and polished up into gleaming, gimmicky, glitzy glad-handers. From the moment they launch themselves into politics they learn how to win friends and influence people, how to earn people's confidence, how to cajole and persuade and convince, how to captivate a crowd and how to trounce an opponent. They feel no need to learn such things from callow soap salesmen who have never stood on a soapbox in their lives. So the relationship between politicians and their advertising advisers is far from easy-going. Dwight Eisenhower's distaste has been echoed many times, albeit often silently, in the subsequent decades. ('Do I have to do this?' John Major is reported to have groaned during photo-opportunities in 1992.) Richard Nixon quickly ditched his professional PR advisors. (McGinnis 1970.) President Clinton's attitude to his marketing advisors is reflected in this exchange, related in *Behind The Oval Office*, the sell-and-tell pot-boiler written by Clinton's ex-chief electoral strategist Dick Morris (1997):

'Can I golf?' Clinton asked the pollsters, his question dripping with sarcasm, 'maybe if I wear my baseball cap? . . . '
'No sir, go rafting.'

This snippet, however, reflects how important market research has become in politics even though politicians' attitudes to it are, like Clinton's, usually equivocal. Today politicians wallow in market research. It is market research, rather than advertising, that has most influenced the nature of political campaigning since 1945. It is noteworthy that immediately the ex-communist *bloc* nations threw off the shackles of the Berlin Wall their politicians began (and continue) to undertake opinion polls and political surveys.

Politicians of all hues pore over the floods of data which flow from the pollsters' computers; they read, mark, learn and inwardly digest the voters' views on everything from abortion to zebra crossings. Nobody – no business-man or marketeer, no sociologist or journalist – studies market research more assiduously than the modern politician. (Especially if the research happens to be about himself.) Despite his sarcasm, President Clinton was described by the *Wall Street Journal* as being, 'awash with market research data' – as had been his predecessors.

Back in the days of Sir Edward Knatchbull and Sir William Geary, the three ways in which politicians could learn the voters' views were via the local press, via their postbags and via political meetings. All three provide biased and shallow information. Doubtless Sir Edward and Sir William firmly believed they had their ears to the ground, and believed themselves to be in close touch with their constituents – just as MPs do to this day. In truth they only converse at any length with political activists, mostly their own supporters; only a tiny number of voters write to them; and the local press will have its own axes to grind. Market research changes all that.

The burgeoning of opinion polls over recent years has brought home to politicians, with a precision never before available, exactly how well (or how badly) the electorate understands them. Hence politicians have grown increasingly aware of the yawning gulf between their own, as they see them, sensible and defensible policies and the voters' lack of appreciation of their virtues. That is why the politicians have reluctantly turned, when they can afford it, to paid-for advertising to communicate their messages. And that is why commentators have come to believe that political advertising is powerfully influential. But is it? Does it achieve anything much, apart from goading the enemy?

Echoing Rosser Reeves' *bragadoccio*, advertising practitioners have always been quick to attribute to their own efforts any electoral success in which they have been even peripherally involved. British advertising mythology now claims, for example, that Saatchi & Saatchi effectively invented political advertising and that their campaign was instrumental in the Tories' 1979 triumph. Balderdash. The Tories were consistently well ahead, miles ahead, in the polls from 1976 onwards, long before Saatchis made any input. Indeed the Tories' popularity dipped slightly during the course of the campaign, from which you could deduce, if you so wished, that political advertising is counter-productive (Penniman 1981). Nor did Neil Kinnock's celebrated 'Kinnock' party political broadcast in 1987 achieve the impact with which it is widely credited. Neil Kinnock's own poll ratings improved a couple of points, but the Labour Party itself did not gain one iota (Butler and Kavanagh 1988). During the 1997 election the Labour and Tory shares of the poll held steady throughout the campaign, despite the £27,000,000 or so that was spent. Since 1959 the Tories have won six general elections, all employing agencies and heavy advertising. Labour, on the other hand, have won five elections without (until 1997) employing an agency or much advertising. Hardly convincing evidence, either way.

In the year following its launch the new Social Democratic Party captured one-third of its market, the electoral vote, with almost no advertising at all. At that time the advertising-less SDP was probably the fastest growing political party in British history. The welter of press and television publicity hugely exceeded the possible influence of any advertising the SDP could have afforded. And this *blitzkrieg* of political news and comment occurs at every general election, nearly drowning the advertising. (The same never applies to consumer goods.)

All this having been said, political advertising is not utterly ineffectual. It may not be as powerful in politics as its protagonists proclaim, but neither is it insignificant. Every SDP market survey, from 1982 onwards, consistently established that nowadays the electorate wants to be wooed. Voters today expect a party (particularly an infant party) to be seen to promote itself. The very act of advertising is almost as important as the message. It shows the party really means business. In my view the SDP venture was scuppered in 1987, by the narrowest of margins, at least partly because it failed to make marketing and advertising a priority. Having been launched with a flurry of marketing activity, it more or less gave up marketing entirely.

One of the fundamental differences between political and other advertising lies in its discontinuity. This makes measurement of its effects, if any, all but impossible. Commercial advertisers can and do test their advertising by desisting from it in regions of the country, for measured periods, but such experiments are not available to political parties. Even if a party were to carry out controlled experiments, during one election, by differentiating its campaigns regionally – and that would be a very brave, not to say foolhardy, course of action – who can say whether the results would still be applicable in utterly different circumstances five years later? The likelihood is that they would not.

So nobody knows, nobody can know, exactly what election advertising achieves. In Hilde Himmelweit *et al.*'s classic longitudinal study *How Voters Decide* (1985) the word 'advertising' is not used once. The only relevant test I have discovered was carried out in Illinois in 1972. Reporting this test, Lynda Lee Kaid begins her paper: 'No classic study of voting behaviour has found political advertising an important determinant of voter decisions.' The Illinois test to some extent contradicts this finding. On that occasion the results suggest that the newspaper advertisements swayed approximately 3 per cent of the voters from one candidate to the other. (There was no television advertising.) But it was a local election, the turnout was low, and Illinois isn't Britain (Kaid 1976).

The chances are, then, that advertising probably encourages a small percentage of voters to change sides. It undeniably activates the activists and supports the preconceptions of supporters. They are uplifted and galvanised into ever-greater exertions by seeing their side's slogans on hoardings as they wearily slog round the streets. And they love to see their side biffing the enemy. In an election like that of 1997, when the outcome was a landslide, the advertising was almost certainly irrelevant: a waste of money. But in a tightly fought election the influence of advertising would be significant. Every vote then counts. And in advance, who can ever tell whether the outcome will be a landslide or a close run thing?

REFERENCES

Bruce, B. (1992) *Images of Power*, London: Kogan Page.

Butler, D. and D. Kavanagh (1988) *The British General Election of 1987*, Basingstoke, Hampshire: Macmillan.

Devlin, L. P. (1981) 'Reagan's and Carter's ad men review the 1980 television campaigns', *Communication Quarterly* 30: 3–12.

Garramone, G. M. (1984) 'Voter responses to negative political ads', *Journalism Quarterly* 61: 250–9.

Himmelweit, H. T., P. Humphreys and M. Jaeger (1985) *How Voters Decide*, Milton Keynes: Open University Press.

Johnson-Cartee, K. S. and G. A. Copeland (1991) *Negative Political Advertising: Coming of Age*, Hillside, NJ: Lawrence Erlbaum Associates.

Kaid, L. L. (1976) 'Measures of political advertising', *Journal of Advertising Research* 16: 49–53.

Mayer, M. (1958) *Madison Avenue*, USA, Harmondsworth: Penguin.

McGinnis, J. (1970) *The Selling of the President*, Harmondsworth: Penguin.

Morris, Dick (1997) *Behind The Oval Office*, New York: Random House.

Nevett, T. R. (1982) *Advertising in Britain: A History*, London: William Heinemann and the History of Advertising Trust.

Penniman, H. R. (1981) *Britain At the Polls, 1979*, Washington, DC: American Enterprise Institute for Public Policy Research.

Sampson, H. (1874) *History of Advertising*, London: Chatto & Windus.

Turner, E. S. (1965) *The Shocking History of Advertising*, London: Michael Joseph.

Wood, G. S. (1978) 'The democratisation of mind in the American Revolution', in R. H. Horwitz (ed.) *The Moral Foundations of the American Republic*, Charlottesville: University Press of Virginia.

11

CULTURAL POLICING IN THE EARLY EIGHTEENTH CENTURY

Print, politics and the case of William Rayner

Michael Harris

Within the debates about the character of English society during the eighteenth century are embedded two questions that relate to the subject of this chapter. First, how and to what effect was power organised and applied by ruling elites at a time when many of the traditional structures of authority were being dismantled? Second, how far were the activities of these ruling elites challenged by individuals and groups whose interests were defined in alternative ways? In each case print has a key part to play in the analysis.

The force of print in all periods is related to its dual character as a commercial product and as a medium of communication. This interlocking combination appeared at its most dynamic in relation to serialisation, a publishing strategy introduced through the London trade in the early seventeenth century. Offering the irresistable combination of low cost and regularity, the printed serial became a means of organising the schedules of production as well as opening up and sustaining new readerships. With the newspaper as the primary product, circuits of communication began to be laid down along which flowed the shifting elements of news, information, advertising, correspondence and other components of the socially constructed forms of serial print (Harris 1997: 3-16).

It was the serial, in particular the news serial, that became the priority area for state intervention. The licensing system that operated sporadically through the seventeenth century provided a form of pre-publication censorship as well as a limitation on entry to the print trade. This impinged on the output of print at various points but its primary impact was on the publication of news. Manuscript newsletters continued to circulate widely but they had nothing like the potential for public access offered by serial print. Each time the licensing system broke down printed news and news-related serials flooded the market, and in 1695, when the supporting legislation was finally allowed to lapse, a similar process occurred (Nelson and Seccombe 1986: 2). It was the news serial that proliferated at this time, reflecting both the upswing in the number of printing businesses and the bouyancy of demand. The change was not a radical one, but the number and range of printed serials in London and in a widening circle of provincial towns locked this form of publication into the middling culture of eighteenth-century England.

The emergence of the newspaper as a pervasive and inescapable form was linked to the development of diverse overlapping structures, political, commercial and social, within which this form of print could be monitored and contained. The most direct response to the post-license build up in news serials was made through the medium of the state. Since the early seventeenth century the interests of national government had been served by the construction of information networks, consolidated in the secretaries of state's offices (Marshall 1994). Forms of clandestine and semi-public material had flowed through the circuits established by the secretaries and selected elements were redirected to the public sphere through the publication of news serials in print and manuscript. No government could supress the flow of news and information, and hence the series of official publications containing an approved narrative of events, of which the *London Gazette*, established in 1665, was the most durable – remaining tediously in print to this day.

The general shift in the character of English society, as well as politics, taking place at the end of the seventeenth century, was related to the emergence of *party* as the dominant organisational form. Starting in the closet politics of the court, party ideology soon became the medium of political expression for a burgeoning middle class whose engagement with the process was centred on the main lines of serial print. Public opinion was always a hazy concept, but its elements were most clearly defined in the debates and comments in the newspaper press (Harris 1984: 189–210). This development stimulated the interventions of successive administrations which, without the support of the ramshackle mechanisms of pre-publication censorship, devoted variable amounts of time and money to the dual strategy of publication and prosecution. Robert Harley and Robert Walpole were notably effective in policing the medium of print in each of these ways, producing large quantities of party propaganda as well as monitoring and attacking hostile publications (Downie 1979).

It is the second of these lines of action, leading to prosecution under the law, that is the concern of this chapter. The experience of state departments and officials in the general process of information gathering could easily be applied to the monitoring of print. Informers, more or less loosely linked to the secretaries' offices, were employed occasionally and regularly to report on the ebb and flow of publications and the identity of those responsible for writing, printing and publishing the material. Offers of information flowed in, sometimes answered in enigmatic newspaper advertisements, or were extorted from the humblest of print workers arrested and then turned to supply information to the government (Harris 1987: 144-6). This was a seedy and surreptitious business, but it was in line with the way in which the state operated in relation to its other main areas of interest. Most of the information targeted the printed serials.

During Queen Anne's reign Robert Harley at the Treasury became the sort of spy-master general who is more familiar in the context of Elizabethan government. Below the calm surface of eighteenth-century society the subterranean currents of intrigue and betrayal flowed on, driven by the insatiable demand in government for 'intelligence' of all kinds. The ministerial and state papers reveal something at least of the apparatus of this process. The printer Robert Clare provided Harley with a systematic account of the people writing and printing material with political overtones. His target was the lower end of the market where serials, pamphlets, ballads and songs were obscurely produced and circulated, carrying what could be seen as seditious messages into the lumpen mass of London's population (Snyder 1967). When Clare was identified by his fellow workmen as a government informer he became unemployable in the trade and had to be found a job on the *London Gazette*.

The question of why a stamp tax was introduced by the Tory administration in 1712 has been the subject of much indecisive speculation. Was it purely a revenue measure or was the tax applied to price the news serial out of reach of a sector of potential readers? Elements of each may have been in play (Downie 1981). However, it is possible that another idea lay behind the imposition of the tax, a measure that would bring news publications into a normative framework. The application of the law meant that the line between legitimate and illegitimate publications could be clearly identified and that output was monitored title by title in a consistently visible way. The presence among Harley's papers of stamp figures for all the London serials fitted with his general interest in what might be called *policing* (Snyder 1968 and 1976).

Harley's system remained more or less intact over the subsequent decades of political upheaval, but its elements were brought into a more active conjunction under the administration of Robert Walpole. His spending on printed propaganda was notorious, though it was allied to what appears to have been a close supervision of opposition material focused in the *Craftsman* but extending through all forms of serial. Nicholas Paxton, Treasury solicitor and Walpole's co-ordinator of journalists, became in 1722 the salaried overseer of all printed papers and pamphlets published in the British Isles (Harris 1987: 136). Paxton received materials from the Messenger of the Press and the Comptroller of the Post Office indicating to the secretaries items that appeared to merit prosecution. Paxton was one of Walpole's hatchet-men and his malign presence was a matter of public comment through the 1730s and up to the time of his arrest following the prime minister's resignation in 1742 (Thompson 1990: 213).

The formal checks on material were supplemented by the casual interventions of members of the ruling elite. Items from newspapers and pamphlets were referred to the secretaries by individuals, bishops, lords and MPs, among others who felt that material overstepped the bounds of legitimate comment. Within the secretaries' offices a small group of individuals followed up the complaint, taking action initiated under specific and general warrants, interviewing suspects and taking depositions. The undersecretary Charles Delafaye, who had been involved in news gathering and supply at least since Queen Anne's reign, was still active in the 1730s, as was Samuel Buckley whose position as gazetteer (compiler of the *London Gazette*) gave him a consistent link to the general area of serial print (Harris 1975; 1987: 117). At ground level the King's messengers acted as the executive arm of political authority. They purchased items liable to prosecution, marking it up as proof of publication for use during legal proceedings, and made sweeps through sectors of the trade arresting and holding anyone loosely associated with the production process. The messengers could, by the use of brute force and the wholesale seizure of records, completely dislocate the operation of a printing office (Harris 1987: 142-3).

Prosecution was a potentially serious threat to both health and business. Its application was erratic. It was almost impossible to get at the principals – the politicians and writers responsible for constructing the barrage of criticism of the Walpole administration that appeared in print. It could be effective against the under-funded fringe members of the print trade who often acted as authors and publishers as well as printers. In other respects the notoriety of the action was generally counter-productive. Even so, the policing of political materials served to define the boundaries of what was acceptable. With suppression off the agenda, the authorities patrolled the frontiers of party politics picking off extremists, mainly individuals and publications with Jacobite sympathies, and crushing those commercial speculators who were spreading political comment through the popular sectors of the market. However, the activities of the state were only part of a more generalised network of interventions meshing with political interests but extending far beyond them. To some extent, the struggle by parliament to prevent public access to its debates and to the decision-making process reflected a general sense of embattled self-interest located elsewhere.

In the book trades the collapse of the licensing system seemed to indicate the end of formal controls organised through the Stationer's Company which until 1695 had also provided a focus for state intervention. In fact, the company remained a less formal but still effective mechanism in controlling access to the trades through apprenticeship and, to a lesser extent, in monitoring output through registration which became involved in the struggle over literary property. This issue of copyright had already begun to give informal shape to the trade outside the company. Groups of shareholders in such valuable properties as the works of Milton and Shakespeare began to construct a secondary level of organisation through the cartels known as the *congers* (Mandelbrote 1997). They served partly as defensive alliances against commercial speculators, attempting independent and often cut-price publication of material claimed by the trade, who by the early eighteenth century were referred to under the generic title of *pirates* (How 1709).

The sense of challenge and response is clear enough. Print was the commercial basis for this conflict but it was also the medium through which the members of the book trade sought to exercise a degree of control over the expanding market. By becoming shareholding proprietors of all the legitimately stamped daily and tri-weekly newspapers published in London, the groups of respectable booksellers were able to establish a collective dominance over the structures of publication (Harris 1989). The pamphlet sellers, coffee houses, Post Office clerks and other primary distributors of newspapers became the *de facto* clients of the respectable booksellers who through these publications also controlled the primary medium of advertising. This enabled them to squeeze the interlopers, outsiders or pirates into vulnerable areas of activity. With low cost and sensation as their primary appeal, the fringe trade, which became increasingly involved in publishing politically sensitive material and unstamped newspapers, fell within the grasp of the law and the state.

Within the broader setting of London's complex urban environment the notion of cultural policing becomes more diffuse. Even so, the lines of containment are visible within the expanding framework of middling society. From the seventeenth century structures were evolving in support of what has been described as the formation of a public sphere (Habermas 1989). This concept has been challenged and modified over a long period, but the core idea of the emergence of a specific form of social, cultural and political interest centred on a commercially active middling sector is still useful. In London the coffee houses, theatres and party groupings formed part of a system that to a great extent was both defined and held together by print, in particular serial print. The pervasive presence of daily and other newspapers simultaneously available in a wide variety of public spaces provided the basis for conversation as well as for the formation of opinion and a guide to action and behaviour. The interactive nature of the newspapers at a variety of levels meant that their content was held in place by the interest of the producers, readers and others making commercial or political use of the circuits running through society. At the same time, their content was subject to forms of detailed scrutiny that might be categorised as a line of cultural policing.

At an individual level this could mean checking out the different kinds of personal reference that were scattered through the news and advertising sections of the London newspapers. The number and range of private actions taken under the laws of libel and slander are uncertain. However, the depositions, informations and indictments, and all the paraphanalia of the process, fill an unknown number of bundles and sacks stored with the other records of the Court of King's Bench (Public Record Office). None of the newspaper producers could have been in any doubt that his position was vulnerable, and all requests for material carried in the papers themselves clearly indicate that any personal controversy would be closely vetted, and usually refused.

The open-ended public skirmishing represented by these actions had a more formal manifestation. During the first half of the eighteenth century the Grand Jury remained a mechanism by which elements of anti-social or criminal behaviour could be identified and brought into the courts. To some extent this form of policing, which had strong moral components, represented an extension of the activities carried out by such socially engaged interest groups as the Society for the Reformation of Manners, which flourished into the 1730s (Shoemaker 1992). The Middlesex Grand Jury was clearly an arm of the establishment. Its members were Justices of the Peace, or men of equivalent status, and their concerns tended to chime with those of the political administration. Even so, they can also be identified with the culture of the middling sector, acting to support a shared ideology. Print was a target, and again the Grand Jury patrolled the frontiers of the acceptable, falling on political extremism, blasphemy and pornography, presenting the material and those responsible for it for action by the courts. At street level the local Justices organised erratic but effective drives against the hawkers of printed material identified through any form of prosecution.

How did this interlocking network of constraint work in practice? The elements came into clear conjunction in relation to actions launched in the early 1730s against William Rayner and others. Rayner remains a shadowy and rather obscure figure, though his cultural positioning gives him a particular interest. He was apprenticed in 1714 to a printer through the Stationer's Company though he did not take up his freedom until the late 1730s (Harris 1987: 91). By the late 1720s he was described as both printer and pamphlet seller, and was running a shop with his wife E.(Elizabeth?) Rayner 'next door to the George Tavern' (*Memoirs* 1732). There he probably engaged in both the production and the publication of material, and the names of both Rayners were displayed on imprints stating 'printed for' and 'printed by' appearing on pamphlets of all kinds. E. Rayner was associated most consistently with what might be described as romantic fiction, but this was far from an exclusive arrangement.

William Rayner gives the impression of lining up with other hyperactive entrepreneurs of the early eighteenth century who, like Charles Povey,[1] moved in and out of the print business. The name is a common one, so it is not always possible to separate out the William Rayners moving through the commercial and cultural sectors of London.[2] Even so, Rayner's interests embraced an unusually wide range of materials including text, pictures, music and most of the forms of material that were in demand across the market for print.

His inclination to follow where the market led was reflected in two elements of his nominal output. First, pirated items: Rayner's publications were shot through with material claimed or owned by others. The ambiguities of copyright and the difficulties of exerting control provided Rayner with a set of commercial opportunities that he exerted to the full. He even engaged in some semi-legitimate skirmishing with Edmond Curll, and it was in advertisements for Henry Fielding's play *The Welsh Opera* that he was described as a 'notorious Paper Pyrate' (*Daily Post* 3674, Monday 28 June 1731).

Second, he published material that contained variably inflamatory attacks on the Walpole administration and on Walpole himself. By 1730 Rayner and his associate the printer–publisher Robert Walker were notorious also for publishing this material. In 1731 the author of the *Daily Courant*, in listing the forces of the opposition, referred to the 'Infinite Number of *Banditti* and *Marauders*, sent forth from the fruitful presses of Messieurs *Walker* and *Rainer*' (*Daily Courant* 8271, Tuesday 27 July 1731).

The flagship of the opposition to Walpole in terms of serial print was the weekly newspaper the *Country Journal; or, the Craftsman*. This drew the main fire of the administration during the late 1720s as actions were launched again and again against its putative author Nicholas Amhurst and its publisher and printer Richard Francklin. The Special Juries, constructed from a panel nominated by the authorities were devised to offset the anti-Walpole feeling that led to high profile not-guilty verdicts. The force of the *Craftsman* as a medium of propaganda extended well beyond its existence as a news serial. The leading essays it contained were being continuously recycled, sometimes geared to specific issues such as the excise crisis or else reissued in total in an alternative form.[3] The latter was the case in June 1731, when the entire sequence of leading essays was republished in seven small (12mo) volumes, each with an allegorical frontispiece reflecting on the Walpole administration.[4]

It was at this point that Rayner and his associates became involved. The precise timing and the nature of the events that followed is not easy to reconstruct, but the evident notoriety of the pictorial content of the volumes persuaded Rayner and others to try to cash in on the public interest. Two pamphlets appeared, one published by C. Davies and the other by William Rayner, deconstructing the rather elaborate meaning of each of the pictures. Rayner's pamphlet was entitled *State Hieroglyphycks: Or, Caleb Decypher'd*.[5] The authors' stated intention was to interpret the new edition,

> as its seven Volumes, render its Price too great to be every Body's Money; so the enigmatical Frontispieces before each, set it above an ordinary Reader's understanding.[6]

The Davies pamphlet seems to have had its own frontispiece composed of the seven pictures, with verses below which did not appear in the volumes, on a single sheet and with the title *Robin's Game, or Seven's the Main*. *Robin* was a conventional allusion to Walpole, while *seven's the main* was a reference to a randomly selected losing throw in the dice game of 'Hazard'. The sheet may have been issued separately, and a version may have been issued by Rayner. A second version beginning *Robin's Reign* was clearly in circulation, and neither had any attribution. At Rayner's trial the rolling-press printer George Kitchin deposed that Rayner had brought him a copper plate with the *Robin's Reign* title and that

> by his Direction he wrought off 150 Copies thereof, and that at the Request of the Defendant he altered the Title from *Robin's Reign*, to *Robin's Game*, for which the said *Rayner* paid this Witness one Shilling.
>
> (*Tryal* 1733: 19)

This fails to clarify anything.

All this material was probably in circulation by July 1731, when the Middlesex Grand Jury, apparently alarmed at the volume of anti-administration print, presented a string of publications for prosecution to the Court of King's Bench. These included both *Robin* sheets, a ballad called *The Chelsea Monarch; or, Money Rules All*, as well as specific issues of the *Craftsman* and another leading opposition weekly *Fog's Journal.*[7] Prompt action followed. A journeyman printer named Collins was arrested and presumably coerced into naming his principals in the production of the collective frontispieces. At the same time, the messengers John Wiggs, Edward Hopcroft and John Ibbot began a sweep through the pamphlet shops at Charing Cross and the Strand purchasing the *Robin's Reign* sheets for use as evidence of publication (British Museum 1873: 684; *Tryal* 1733: 17-19).

About a week after the arrest of Collins, a string of further arrests was made: Robert Walker, printer, William Rayner and Samuel Slow, publishers, and the pamphlet sellers Lynn and Cricheley. All were bailed, Walker, Rayner and Slow at either £100 or £200, though one report claimed that as Walker could not find the money he was committed to Newgate (*Grub Street Journal* 81, Thursday 15 July 1731). There the matter seems to have rested for over a year. In November 1732 Rayner, described in the *London Evening Post* as 'A person at Charing Cross', received notice of trial to be held at the Court of King's Bench on Wednesday 15 November (*London Evening Post* 772, Saturday 11 November 1732).

The prosecution of Rayner was set against a background of multiple actions taken against individuals involved in other publications, mainly serials, carrying political material adjudged to be on the edge of acceptability. In January 1732 a Special Jury convicted Richard Francklin of seditious libel in publishing the notorious 'Hague letter' in the *Craftsman* revealing secrets of British diplomacy. He was fined £100, sentenced to a year's imprisonment and ordered to find two sureties in £500 each to guarantee his future good behaviour (*Political State of Great Britain* 43 (1732): 211-12). Francklin was in prison in November, though the *Craftsman* continued to be produced by his employee Henry Haines, at the printing office as before. In March a series of arrests was made of those involved in printing and publishing *Fog's Journal* while, almost as a counterpoint to the trial of Rayner, the newspapers reported a series of actions focusing on the weekly *Royal Oak Journal*.

This was a low-key publication which carried an explicit appeal to Jacobite sympathisers in its title. The paper contained personal attacks on Walpole and the King, and on 11 November 1732, the same day that Rayner's notice of trial was reported, the *London Evening Post* stated:

> On Thursday Night last Mr. Matthias Earbery, a Nonjuring Clergyman, was seized by three of his Majesty's Messengers, in Ship-yard near Temple-Bar whither a Person had decoy'd him under Pretence of employing him to write a Weekly Journal.
> (*London Evening Post* 772, Saturday 11 November 1732)

Earbery, as writer of the *Royal Oak Journal*, was still receiving notice of trial six years later, and as part of a personal protest about this treatment he held a one-man street demonstration with a copy of Magna Carta hung round his neck (Harris 1987: 141). A few days after Earbery's arrest Robert Walker and the pamphlet-seller John Dormer were taken up, while in January 1733 JPs from different parts of London were reported to be rounding up numbers of hawkers who were selling the journal and other political items.[8]

William Rayner's trial received extensive coverage in the London newspapers and a full report of the hearing appeared in a separate pamphlet.[9] A Special Jury was empanelled including two of those who were also on the list for membership of the Middlesex Grand Jury. One had been involved in the original presentment of the *Robin* items, and was set aside. The other was allowed to remain (*Tryal* 1733; *London Evening Post* 774, Thursday 16 November 1732). The case was heard before Lord Chief Justice Raymond, and it is clear that Rayner was identified as an important target. In the indictment he was conventionally described as 'a malicious and seditious Man, and of depraved Mind, and wicked and Diabolical Disposition' (*Tryal* 1733: 12). In the charge of printing and publishing *Robin's Reign*, the main emphasis was put on the verses appearing below the frontispiece to volume 4:

> See R—t O—'s L—'s & B—'s buy
> Speak then Spectator, — is Corruption high.
> Mark well the Visage of each slavish Tool,
> The Blockhead, Hypocrite, & gawdy Fool,
> 'Tis these Great Men, who give our Wealth away,
> Borrow in P—n—'s, but in V—'s they Pay,

Like Judas thus, for Gold betray the State
His Crimes they share, & may they share his Fate!
(British Museum 1873: 689)

As well as the evidence of publication from the pamphlet-sellers, taking a dozen or so copies each and accounting with Rayner, his wife or the shop girl, the defence attempted to prove that Rayner's shop was in fact owned by Mrs Elizabeth Blackbourne who was called in evidence, but whose statements lacked conviction. Much of the case was taken up with arguments over the meaning of the blanks. The crown made the straightforward case for *Orators, Lords, Bishops, Pensions* and *Votes*. The defence, in an heroic struggle to deny these implications, even suggested that P—n—'s could be filled out using either *Pins* or *Puns*. (*Tryal* 1733: 23-4.)

Rayner was found guilty, but before sentencing he absconded and it was not until February that he either gave himself up or else was apprehended (*Daily Courant* 5257, Tuesday 13 February 1733; *Craftsman* 346, Saturday 17 February 1733). Either way, he was committed to the King's Bench Prison until 1 June. In spite of the pleas by his counsel that 'he was not worth Five Pounds in the whole World, if all his Debts were paid, and his Wearing-Apparel excepted', and that he had already been confined for four months, he was fined £50, sentenced to two years in prison and ordered to find security for good behaviour for seven years. This was a harsher sentence than Francklin had received, and the question arises of why such an apparently modest individual received such close attention from the authorities for merely recycling the sort of material that was already in circulation?

The answer seems to relate to the general issue of cultural policing, as identified in the first part of this analysis. Rayner was in some sense a populariser. His publications amplified the material directed at Walpole through more respectable forms of print, and its more general appeal, particularly in the use (as here) of pictures, became part of an undertow of criticism in which elements of Jacobitism were represented. Rayner was also a person who was not protected by the conventional structures of a respectable trade. His piratical activities left him, as a commercial outsider, exposed to whatever forms of prosecution the state chose to apply. The involvement of the Grand Jury seems to reflect a general social concern about the promiscuous spread of political criticism and debate among groups not identified as part of the political process. This was in some ways allied to ideas about respectability and decency. Low-key publishers like William Rayner and Samuel Slow had interests that extended to the outer areas of publication. During 1732, for example, Slow published *Dirty Dogs for Dirty Puddings. Or, Memoirs of the Luscious Amours of the several Persons of both Sexes of Quality and Distinction*. This sort of dubious material formed part of the environment of political pamphleteering, and probably served to stimulate direct action.

Rayner was committed to the King's Bench Prison in Southwark, where he remained until the early 1740s. He obtained the Rules which enabled him to work in the vicinity and opened a printing office in Falcon Court. Here, he continued to flout the law, publishing numbers of unstamped newspapers and pirating other people's titles and projects, as before. However, he was quite literally contained. Rayner's motives were apparently always commercial, and when he was enabled to join the ranks of the respectable through a fortunate marriage he immediately did so. In some ways he was a harbinger of those who, later in the century, were to challenge the underlying structures of society through radical politics circulated through low-cost printed serials. In others he indicated, through his own unfortunate experiences, the force with which interest groups in English society were able to defend their position through forms of cultural policing.

NOTES

1 Povey was a long-term speculator who during Queen Anne's reign published a newspaper entitled the *General Remark on Trade* which he ran as an adjunct to a general brokerage business. During the 1730s he advertised a range of entertainments centred on Belsize House in north London.
2 An actor named William Rayner, who performed at Bartholomew Fair during the 1720s, is a case in point.
3 Advertisement for *An Argument against Excises, in several Essays; first published in the Craftsman and now collected together*, in the *Craftsman* 340 Saturday 6 January 1733.
4 Advertisement for the seven volumes in the *Grub Street Journal* 74 Thursday 3 June 1731. A further eight volumes of leading essays were published in 1737 (British Museum 1873: 683-93).
5 Imprint: Printed for E. Rayner, next to George Tavern, Charing-Cross, and sold by the Booksellers of London and Westminster. 1731. (Price Six-pence.)'
6 Ibid.: 3.
7 The presentment of this material appeared in the news summary published in the *Grub Street Journal* 80, Thursday 15 July 1731.
8 As well as the *Royal Oak Journal*, arrests were also made for the ballad *Britanniae Excisa* (*Daily Courant* 5226, Monday 8 January 1733; 5230, Friday 12 January 1733).
9 As well as the account in the *Tryal* a full description was also published in the *London Evening Post* 774, Thursday 16 November 1732.

REFERENCES

British Museum (1873) *Catalogue of Prints and Drawings in the British Museum*, Division 1, *Political and Personal Satires, 2 June 1689 to 1733*, London: British Museum.

Downie, A. (1979) *Robert Harley and the Press*, Cambridge: Cambridge University Press.

—— (1981) 'The growth of government tolerance of the press to 1790', in R. Myers and M.Harris (eds) *The Development of the English Book Trade*, Oxford: Oxford Polytechnic Press.

Habermas, J. (1989) *The Structural Transformation of the Publick Sphere: an Inquiry into a Category of Bourgeois Society*, trans. T. Burger, Cambridge: Polity Press.

Harris, M. (1975) 'Newspaper distribution during Queen Anne's reign', in *Studies in the Book Trade*, Oxford: Oxford Bibliographical Society.

—— (1984) 'Print and politics in the age of Walpole', in J. Black (ed.) *Britain in the Age of Walpole*, London: Macmillan.

—— (1987) *London Newspapers in the Age of Walpole*, London and Toronto: Associated University Presses.

—— (1989) 'Paper pirates: the alternative book trade in mid-eighteenth century London', in R. Myers and M. Harris (eds) *Fakes and Frauds: Varieties of Deception in Print and Manuscript*, Winchester and Detroit: St Paul's Bibliographies and Omnigraphics Inc.

—— (1997) 'Locating the serial; some ideas about the position of the serial in relation to the eighteenth-century print culture', *Studies in Newspaper and Periodical History* 2: 3-16.

How, J. (1709) *Some Thoughts on the Present State of Printing and Bookselling*, London.

Mandelbrote, G. (1997) 'Richard Bentley's copies: the ownership of copyrights in the late 17th century', in A. Hunt, G. Mandelbrote and A. Shell (eds) *The Book Trade and its Customers 1450-1900*, Winchester and Newcastle, Delaware: St Paul's Bibliographies and Oak Knoll Press.

Marshall, A. (1994) *Intelligence and Espionage in the Reign of Charles II, 1660-1685*, Cambridge: Cambridge University Press.

Memoirs of the Life of Robert Wilks, Esq. (1732), London.

Nelson, C. and M. Seccombe (1986) *Periodical Publication 1641-1700*, London: Bibliographical Society.

Shoemaker, R. B. (1992) 'Reforming the city: the reformation of manners' campaign in London, 1690-1738', in L. Davison, T. Hitchcock, T. Keirn and R. B. Shoemaker (eds) *Stilling the Grumbling Hive: The Response to Social and Economic Problems in England, 1689-1750*, Stroud and New York: Allan Sutton and St Martin's Press.

Snyder, H. L. (1967) 'The reports of a press spy for Robert Harley: new bibliographical data for the reign of Queen Anne', *Library* (5th series) 22.

—— (1968) 'The circulation of newspapers in the reign of Queen Anne', *Library* (5th series) 23: 206-35.

—— (1976) 'A further note on the circulation of newspapers in the reign of Queen Anne', *Library* (5th series) 31.

Thompson, E. P. (1990) *Whigs and Hunters*, Harmondsworth: Penguin.

The Tryal of William Rayner for Printing and Publishing a Libel, Intitled, Robin's Reign; or, Seven's the Main (1733), London.

12

CONFLICTS IN THE NEWS

Publicity interests, public images and political impacts

Rodney Tiffen

Conflict pervades society, and the news gravitates to conflict. News coverage of conflicts commonly generates its own contentiousness, with partisans typically accusing the media of bias against their side. Despite the frequency with which the topic arises, the relationship between news reporting and socio-political conflicts has received surprisingly little systematic analysis either in media studies or in conflict studies.

In the most comprehensive, although now somewhat dated, review of conflict research, Gurr (1980) listed over 1,250 works, and not one of their titles mentioned the media. Several referred to communication or perception as factors in conflicts, but there seemed no attempt to include media institutions and practices as integral to those problems. It is perhaps sobering for media scholars to learn how rarely researchers in other fields include the media as a serious part of their analysis.

The common-sense and dominant mode of analysis within media studies, even more dominant in critical commentaries on the media, has been a simple 'bias' model, which concentrates on exposing media content. These studies of course vary in quality and value. Some – in the line of defence most commonly adopted by media practitioners – simply betray the biases of their authors rather than exposing those of the media. Some impose unreal expectations in their harsh evaluations of media performance, not paying sufficient attention to audience considerations and the influence of news values, to questions of cost, or giving due regard to the limited knowledge which journalists possessed at the time of publication and the difficulties they were confronting. But, as often as not, studies in this tradition mount telling and persuasive critiques of media coverage, exposing distortions, lack of proportion and double standards. The criticisms directed against the studies can often be addressed – the points of substance debated, fairer tests of media performance agreed upon, and the methods and standards of the studies hopefully thus progressed.

The more basic problem with simple bias studies lies not in their critiques of content but in their (usually implicit) models of cause and effect. Explanation is in terms of editorial attitudes. The most immediate problem is how rarely they take seriously the news media as institutions with their own routines, constraints, incentives, and traditions. Even in the more ideological critiques, while the analytical trappings typically stress structure (the role of capitalism, etc.), the accompanying morality play is pure agency. The implication is that the news media could and should behave differently simply by an act of will, a change in editorial attitude, and that if they wanted to they would.

If the bias approach fails to adopt a properly institutional perspective, it is not surprising that it also fails to pay serious attention to environmental factors. Each conflict has different types of relationship between the contenders, different stakes and different modes of resolution for allocating the outcomes. Consequently the media figure differently as arenas, more central in some conflicts than in others, and the contenders have differing publicity interests and strategies. The evidence and analysis in bias studies are neither internalist nor externalist, in Schlesinger and Tumber's terms (1994: 26–7), but rather are limited to disembodied textual critiques.

Equally, the implicit model of media effects in these studies has had a 'democratic bias', casting the media's role in terms of its impact upon public opinion. This has been true even in left-wing analyses stressing the media's role in maintaining hegemony. This has had some unfortunate side-effects. It creates a methodological problem, because there is a vacuum of unobservable data at the centre of any consideration of media impacts. It also tends to equate effects with content, but it is not necessarily the case that news coverage has most impact when it is most biased. The fundamental substantive point, however, is that only in elections and referenda is public opinion directly decisive: while it is not necessarily irrelevant to the outcome of other conflicts, neither is it necessarily 'determining'.

In this chapter I explore in turn six types of conflict in the news, grouped according to their participants and the stakes involved. The formulations presented here result primarily from reflections on Australian media and politics, but an attempt has been made to state the key relationships so that their relevance to other liberal democracies will be apparent. Naturally the conflicts considered are not exhaustive of types, but they include some of the most consequential and common. The procedure is simply to state the central characteristics of each of the six types of conflict, and then to consider the publicity interests and strategies of the contenders, the characteristics of each conflict which are likely to affect its coverage in the news, and how that coverage may impact upon its pursuit and outcome. The usefulness of this procedure is always threatened because the idiosyncrasies of examples within each type seem too numerous to allow meaningful comparisons between generic classes of conflict. Although the danger of generalisation is ever-present, the types of conflict considered here provide sufficient contrasts to illustrate how important it is to include the nature of the conflict and the varying roles of the media as an arena when analysing news coverage.

INTER-PARTY CONFLICT

In a two-sided party system, as exists (with important qualifications) in Australia, the UK and USA, the electoral contest to form the next government is a zero-sum winner-take-all game, decided by public opinion.

There is a recurring institutionalised dynamic to inter-party conflict based on the inevitable and constantly replayed competition for the indivisible prize of control of government. There cannot be a win–win solution. It cannot be that both sides' prospects are improving simultaneously. One prospers electorally only at the expense of the other. This irreconcilable conflict exists irrespective of what other differences (e.g. over policies and ideologies, or as representatives of competing social groups) the contest may embody at some particular moment. Resolutions – the electoral defeat of one side by the other – are landmarks in an ongoing conflict that will always be renewed as long as the party system continues.

A zero-sum winner-take-all game is conducive to the most ruthless of tactics, where winning by whatever means is preferable to losing nobly. Over recent decades the major parties have pursued the essential logic of the game with a spiralling cynicism and toughness. Both parties have increasingly viewed policy debates primarily through the prism of gaining partisan advantage. Each has adopted the view that it is easier to persuade swinging voters of the other's defects rather than its own virtues, and that such voters' decisions are guided more by who they want to vote against rather than who they want to vote for. The result is the production of constantly negative claims by each about the other.

More than in almost any other conflict, inter-party politics encourages the exaggeration of difference. The constant search for publicity and for partisan point's scoring lends itself to posturing and shadow play. Pursuing the conflict in this way generates a peculiar picture of public policy and social causality. The opposition seeks to portray the government as the primary cause for whatever problems currently confront the electorate. In turn, the government seeks to claim credit for all positive developments while deflecting the responsibility for all negative ones.

The competition for publicity is most dynamic when the news organisations' audiences are of mixed partisanship. Depending upon media structures, an open embrace of one party against the other is commercially hazardous if a significant segment of the audience would be offended. Because the audience tends to be evenly split, and because figures from both parties are valued as good sources (although government much more than opposition), there is commonly an emphasis on balance in reporting inter-party conflicts, especially during election campaigns.

Inter-party conflicts are the most intensively covered in the news. The constant and heavy news attention is produced by a strong concentration of elite reporters, centered upon an institution – parliament – which is the most prolific generator of newsworthy information in society. But the reporting of inter-party conflicts has many unique features, which makes it impossible to extrapolate to other kinds of conflict. In almost no other conflicts is the logic always and inevitably zero-sum, negating the possibility of reconciliation or compromise. They are the only conflicts where public opinion is directly the arbiter, so that securing publicity through news is prerequisite to success. The incentive towards public posturing, and the magnification of differences, the wish to cast their opponents in a negative light, are ever-present features.

INTRAPARTY CONFLICT

In contrast to inter-party politics, intraparty conflicts are between ostensible allies. 'Conflicts tend to interfere with each other' (Schattschneider 1960: 67), and electoral strategists certainly believe that internal 'disunity is death' is the external party competition. So intraparty conflict threatens to undermine the party's larger purpose. Its public appearance must therefore be controlled and subordinated to the inter-party electoral competition. The immediate forum for the resolution of intraparty conflict is not the public but the party's internal organs. Even though in electorally pragmatic parties, internal operations must be carried through in ways acceptable to the public, the weight of opinion within the party is often distributed very differently from the weight of opinion outside.

The resulting publicity interests and strategies are obviously very different from those of inter-party conflicts. Rather than generating public perceptions that magnify the contrasts, there is an incentive to minimise them. However, the optimal strategy is not always simply to avoid all coverage. Because news surveillance of party politics is so intense, some coverage, whether wanted or not, is likely, so participants must have strategies for dealing with it. But beyond coping with inescapable coverage, publicity may serve a positive purpose for contenders in their internal aims. Faction leaders may seek publicity to signal to their own constituencies that they are indeed pursuing the course that their followers would want, or to signal more publicly their dominance over factional rivals. Or they may try to use publicity to convince waverers by shaping in a self-fulfilling manner the perceptions of the balance of forces within the party. Or challengers may seek to shift support by using publicity, provoking incidents to de-stabilise existing patterns. As always, the use of publicity by one side tends to escalate, inviting further responses from the other side.

193

In public statements, there is often the attempt to achieve differentiation without disloyalty or open dissent. Disagreement is normally expressed obliquely, with a difference of emphasis rather than direct rebuttal, and without personal criticism. Even more importantly, however, intraparty publicity strategies are more likely to use covert manoeuvres, leaks and background briefings, where the name of the source is not publicly revealed. These allow much greater latitude than do the constraints of party loyalty in public statements. In one – typically less than subtle – example, a challenger to Victorian Labor leader John Cain gave a series of 'correct' answers during an interview with a press reporter. As she was leaving he called out after her: 'It's funny the things you're prepared to say on the record, and those you're willing to say off the record.'

The prevalence of covert manoeuvres, especially in a leadership struggle, where clear evidence of the state of party sentiment typically does not exist, has important consequences for the quality of media reporting. It allows more scope for competitive 'scoops', but also carries more risks of public disavowals. Often, however, it means that unsourced news reports have a more substantial basis than the public, especially the partisans of the affected party, realise.

The pressure to maintain the appearance of unity is strong and, in a disciplined party, is likely to prevail in all but the most extreme conflicts. In terms of policy difference or the allocation of internal positions and patronage, the benefits of unity produce strong incentives towards finding and publicly displaying common ground. In the face of persistent policy differences, there is often a studied ambiguity, or even a willingness to bow to the leader for the sake of unity. However, in some areas, such as party leadership contests, given the unshakable ambitions of each contender, such compromise is not possible.

Media coverage has frequently been centrally implicated in the development of leadership challenges. One reason why such challenges have been so frequent in Australia in recent decades (Tiffen 1989 lists twenty-three challenges between 1968 and 1989; since then there have been around another fifteen) is the perceived importance of media coverage of leaders in affecting a party's electoral fortunes. Moreover, the process by which leaders are challenged mid-term is not institutionalised and regular but rather is problematic, and relatively uncharted. As a result news reports have often become flash-points, major steps of escalation, sometimes even catalysts in forcing a showdown.

The impact of publicity in intraparty conflicts is often explosive because, more than in any of the other conflicts considered, the contenders have a complex relationship through which they are allies as well as antagonists. They have a direct personal relationship, but one that is also refracted through the news media. News reports are biased to highlight the most dramatic aspects, in this case the degree of conflict between the leaders. This is often expressed with a hardness and sharpness quite different from the rhythms and fluidity of actual personal encounters. The participants frequently accord more political currency to the public news reports than to their actual private interactions. Especially when there are unfavourable news reports based on covert sources, they can directly affect issues of trust and workable personal relations.

BUREAUCRATIC CONFLICT

Conflict within the bureaucracy is a vital aspect of the exercise of power and the direction of government policy. Yet this type is the least newsworthy of the six here considered, and the media are typically of least relevance in its pursuit and resolution.

Sometimes bureaucratic conflict is intense, sometimes enduring because of the clashing orientations of the departments involved. Sometimes the conflict is overlaid by, and gains extra force from, strong personal rivalries and antipathies. However, the essential characteristics of bureaucratic conflict are that it is highly rule-governed, instrumental and concerned with well-defined finite stakes. The contenders inhabit the same social world, sharing many career goals and social understandings, and have a direct and continuing relationship with one another. Especially in a Westminster-style career public service, most contenders have an incentive to adopt a longer term perspective, in which the immediate conflict is not allowed to escalate to become something more disruptive and threatening.

In terms of observability and newsworthiness bureaucratic conflicts do not lend themselves to coverage. They are conducted in closed forums, by publicly anonymous personalities who do not seek to publicise their activities. The stakes are often subject to disaggregation, to incremental resolution and compromise, where any threat of dramatic show-down is deliberately defused and delayed. Although the stakes are very often tangible ones concerning resources and administrative power, they are typically couched in technical language, remote from the experience of the public, and buried in sub-clauses which only the most determined can penetrate. Moreover, the outcome may become clear only after implementation, at which stage the evidence is dispersed in time and space.

Until recently, and even now within strict limits, most public servants have lacked the right to an independent public voice. So the most frequent source of important publicity about bureaucratic conflict is from covert manoeuvres. Leaks are primarily a weapon of disaffection, a tactic for vetoing rather than advancing bureaucratic moves. They are most likely to occur when official actions are running against proclaimed policy with at least some insiders thus aggrieved. As always, the mystery surrounding the identity of the leaker can itself be part of the impact.

Publicity can impact upon bureaucratic conflicts by elevating the political temperature, and bringing the involvement of other groups. However, the weight of power inside the bureaucracy may be very different from public opinion or the volume of voices outside. Sometimes the altered political equations that publicity brings can change the outcome. On other occasions it only produces the appearance of a revision, influencing the timing or presentation rather than the substance of what's done. A review is called, public attention fades and, after a delay, the original plan is substantially achieved.

The traditional situation affecting coverage of bureaucratic politics in the news is clear. In contrast to the regular and intense news coverage of party politics, bureaucratic politics, despite its importance in policy making, receives the least news coverage of the various conflicts considered. Official regulations, media considerations of observability and newsworthiness, and bureaucratic tradition and prudence have all conspired in the same direction.

Nevertheless many straws of change are in the wind. Not only has freedom of information legislation been introduced and official regulations about secrecy substantially liberalised, but these have induced a more far-reaching cultural change with greater official dissemination of information about departmental activities and achievements and more pro-active attitudes to publicity. Several political factors have led in the same direction. It is probably not coincidental that the *Yes, Minister* humour of bureaucratic mandarins, immune from the power of mere elected politicians, gained currency in popular culture just as it was in fact becoming less true. The greater intensity of party conflicts has been accompanied by an increasing ascendancy of politicians over bureaucrats and an orientation towards achieving results over the traditional pre-eminence of due process. Increasingly, the idea of bureaucratic impartiality has been diminished, as senior appointments have been influenced by changes in the party in power and the growth in number of ministerial advisers has offered an alternative, and more politically attuned, source of advice. Moreover, the notion of a long-term career service has been eroded not only by the increasing partisanship of senior appointments and the emphasis upon outcomes over process, but by the variety of routes towards accelerated promotion. All these factors mean that the traditional long-term perspective may give way more to short-term considerations, making victory in immediate conflicts more important. A more politicised, *results*-oriented, bureaucracy, with *market*-influenced career patterns, is likely to further break down conventional constraints. In turn, these changes will increase the visibility of bureaucratic conflicts in the news.

INDUSTRIAL CONFLICT

The most recurrent of industrial conflicts, over wages and conditions for a particular union's members, are typically focused on well-defined material stakes. They are decided by bargaining strength and by the calculation by the contenders of their interests and possibilities. Negotiations between the groups are highly institutionalised, and although the representatives of the employers and the unions typically belong to rather different social worlds, the crucial arenas in the conflict's resolution involve direct, if limited and stylised, interactions between them. The news media are clearly a secondary battlefield.

Presentation of industrial conflict has been one of the most criticised areas of news coverage (perhaps most famously by the Glasgow University Media Group 1976 and 1980, cf Tunstall 1977 and 1981). The most common critical themes are that it is the consequences of strikes rather than the causes that are reported, that unions are only newsworthy when they are undertaking publicly disruptive activities, and that disputes are described in a language that always conveys greater legitimacy to the employers' views. It is also the area where complaints by reporters were most common about the editorial treatment of their work (e.g. Tiffen 1989: 46–9). Industrial relations reporters' criticism of the editorial treatment of their coverage partly reflects that this is the area of greatest conflict between news values and the outlook of major sources. Their most common sources are trades union leaders, but editorial judgements of newsworthiness and audience interest commonly run in an anti-union direction (cf Tunstall 1971: 124, 268).

However, problems in news coverage of industrial conflict reflect not only editorial weakness, willful or inadvertent, but stem from genuine difficulties of reporting occasioned partly by the publicity strategies of the contenders. Both sides are comprised of professional negotiators and experienced deal makers. They generally seek to maximise their flexibility, which too much accountability in process can inhibit. The public statements of both are marked by a high degree of bluff. Typically between ambit claims for far more and a refusal to countenance anything different from what exists, there is incremental movement toward a mutually acceptable compromise. Equally typically, the straight reporting of the antagonists' public statements en route would have conveyed a very misleading impression of the actual state of nego-tiations and the eventual outcome. The situation is ripe for public rhetoric to give the appearance of intransigence while hiding strategic suppleness in practice.

The impact of news coverage on the outcome of industrial conflicts, especially those focused on salary demands of a specific group of workers, is rarely substantial. To the extent that such reporting affects the evolution of a conflict, overwhelmingly it is through a hardening of attitudes, and so a prolongation of the dispute. As in intraparty conflicts, the contenders are often dealing with each other both directly and as refracted through the media, and if what they see in the news contradicts understandings reached in private those understandings can be destroyed. Nevertheless, the two sides are in search not of spiritual harmony but simply a mutually workable material outcome. Nor is the outcome dependent upon some amorphous public opinion. So, between professional negotiators focused upon well-defined stakes, publicity may have less of an impact here than in many other conflicts.

The other important way in which publicity can inflame an industrial conflict is to provoke intervention by third parties, most often the government. Political parties and other pressure groups, business and union, may seek to use particular industrial conflicts for their own broader purposes. The involvement of other parties will typically widen and deepen the original conflict, raising and re-defining the stakes.

As with bureaucratic politics, the nature of industrial conflict has been changing radically in the last two decades. The frequency of strikes has (in several countries, perhaps for contrasting reasons) declined sharply. When industrial conflict is conducted under a centralised wage-fixing system, with industry-wide occupational trades unions, as traditionally it has been in Australia, it is more visible in the news, especially insofar as it was conducted and resolved via public hearings in the Industrial Commission. When the emphasis moves towards a more decentralised company-based system of enterprise bargaining, there is much less visibility in the news, unless one side wants to publicly highlight a dispute, normally by making it a 'test case'. As the pattern of industrial conflict has changed, so has the nature of news coverage.

PRESSURE GROUP AND SOCIAL MOVEMENT CONFLICTS

The range of conflicts included under this rubric is even more diverse than elsewhere. Both pressure groups and social movements vary in their aims, their resources, their sophistication and their ideological trappings, even more than do the organisations already considered. Despite this almost infinite variety, three main publicity interests are generally applicable:

- to maintain, mobilise and extend their constituency;
- to influence the public agenda; and
- to affect government policy.

The last of these aims is the most finite and focused. The crucial consideration here is that a group's inclination to seek publicity is in inverse proportion to the likelihood of its achieving its aims. Especially with sectional interest groups seeking resource advantages for their own constituencies, insofar as a pressure group is likely to gain what it wants from government without a vocal public stance, it is likely to remain quiet. If the government is receptive to the group's viewpoint, it is more likely to negotiate quietly with the bureaucracy and the ministers than to voice its demands in public. Moreover, as with all conflict participants, public stances are marked by special pleading and selective emphasis, highlighting their handicaps and omitting their privileges, proclaiming their unfulfilled demands while keeping silent on the concessions and benefits they have already achieved.

In the larger, more diffuse, battles to influence the public agenda and increase their support, pressure groups and social movements often perceive themselves as in conflict with those of opposing views. But their relationship is quite different from most other conflicts. Often there is little or no direct contact between them, and there is no reason why they need to reach any reconciliation or accommodation. In this typically remote and unfocused conflict, the media can play a peculiar role, because the contending pressure groups often gain their knowledge of each other to a considerable degree from news coverage. The reported actions of one group trigger responses from its opponents, and so the media themselves are often catalysts in how controversies develop. Indeed one side is often energised by what it sees as the outrageous demands and claims of the other, resulting in a greater intensity of activity and a greater prominence of the issue in the news agenda.

Nevertheless, while media prominence plays a role in mobilising constituencies, it can also escalate internal tensions. It may intensify competition between groups trying to represent the same cause. It may increase jealousies between leadership rivals, if one is accorded the higher status in the media (Gitlin 1980: 128–9). 'Leaders' of these organisations do not necessarily have the same authority, and the groups do not necessarily have the same internal discipline, as the groups considered in the preceding conflicts. The tensions between building cadres and pursuing electorally acceptable outcomes may be intense. Nor is there any necessarily compelling reason for them to capture some middle ground of public opinion, because maintaining solidarity and enlarging their constituencies by reiterating ideological certainties may be more internally rewarding.

Pressure groups figure frequently in the news, but not commonly under conditions of their own choosing. They more often appear in a reactive than a pro-active way. Their capacity to achieve publicity may depend on their skill in reacting to stories currently on the news agenda, in acting as sources in running controversies, providing either viewpoints or information in a timely and newsworthy way. This partly explains the apparent paradox that pressure groups are often in the news, but their members often feel frustrated by their inability to achieve coverage.

In terms of initiating news coverage, their campaigns are often ignored. Most often their news-initiating potential is a negative one, either in their ability to make credible threats or to stage events that become spot news, but typically then framed as disruptions or curiosities rather than dissent. In staging such campaigns their capacity to generate attention may depend not on how mainstream they are but on how deviant and outrageous.

The ability of interest groups to provide reactions to running stories is most basically a matter of resources. The variable capacities of pressure groups for publicity can be extremely pronounced. A professional organisation whose primary purpose is to monitor and react to public debates, to challenge contrary views, to gather and disseminate newsworthy information has a news generating and hence lobbying potential which others lack.

In judging the relevance and newsworthiness of a pressure group, there is often more than the usual room for editorial discretion, for news judgements to be affected by editorial sympathies and partisanship (see e.g. Goldenberg 1975). The ability of pressure groups to make news is more inherently problematic than for political party leaders, who have both the legitimacy of leading representative constituencies and the ability to take indisputably consequential political actions. Such judgements are sometimes simply a matter of individual attitudes, but often they reflect tendencies in the wider political environment to which news coverage is sensitive. Whereas two decades ago, it was almost impossible for environmental groups to achieve prominent coverage, now they are routinely part of the news agenda.

More than in the previously discussed conflicts, the news coverage of pressure groups and social movements generates apparent paradoxes, propositions that run against immediate expectations: Their visibility and 'vocalness' have no relation to their likely immediate impact on government policy; the prominence accorded to their opponents may also benefit themselves by stimulating the issue area; yet success in achieving prominence may increase internal tensions; and pressure groups do figure prominently in the news but largely in a reactive, and only occasionally in an initiating, way.

In conclusion, a final difference can be noted: in some senses, especially for social movements, news coverage may be an end in itself, rather than just a means towards some other political or policy end. The stakes for social movements often have a symbolic as well as a material dimension. Battles over status politics – gaining official endorsement of their world view, or recognition of the importance of their viewpoint, or acceptance of themselves as legitimate representatives – are often a major pre-occupation of social movements. So the nature of news coverage generated, of publicity, of how it is framed, may itself be one measure of success. While this represents significant success of a kind, it often generates rhetoric, which will bear at best an uncertain relationship to any changing allocation of material resources.

INTERNATIONAL CONFLICT

News coverage of international conflicts differs from all the domestic conflicts considered above in two fundamental ways:

1   The news audience falls entirely on one side of the political division.
2   The news sources are drawn overwhelmingly, perhaps entirely, from one side of the conflict.

As a result, there has traditionally been much less emphasis on balance, and much more partiality in news reports. As in issues involving social deviance, the political rewards for in-group conformity are pronounced, while questioning orthodoxy can be politically dangerous. As conflict escalates, and the domestic political temperature rises, this tendency becomes even more pronounced.

News coverage of international conflicts has typically been marked by ethnocentrism, as is international news generally. The more unfamiliar or remote the country, the more familiar and dramatic tend to be the themes in the stories selected, whether or not these priorities actually capture the orientations and priorities of the participants. There is also a search for 'home town' angles, especially among the more popularly-oriented media: during the pivotal month of August 1990, when Iraq invaded Kuwait, Sydney's *Daily Telegraph* featured the crisis on its front page on twenty-three occasions, and sixteen of these focused on Australia or Australians (Tiffen 1992). International coverage is often an extension of domestic political controversies and agendas, often in ways which allow government interests and outlooks to dominate. This can allow markedly different priorities and themes to dominate in different countries. My favourite example comes from the 1960s when the United Nations used to regularly criticise Australia for its colonial policies in Papua New Guinea, which used to anger (and embarrass) the government and especially its minister for territories, Charles Barnes. On one occasion the pro-government Melbourne *Herald* covered this story under the headline 'Barnes Rebukes United Nations' – although it carried no information as to how stung the rest of the world was by this rebuke.

In terms of its impact on conflicts, news coverage is rarely a factor in their actual international dimensions. One country may have its perceptions of the other fashioned by what is in the former's media, but most of the time governments thankfully have much more substantial sources of information. Any such media influence is probably infrequent and marginal.

In fact, the media's major impact is likely to be in fashioning governments' perceptions of the domestic political possibilities, the costs and benefits of certain actions. It should be remembered that every international conflict has a *domestic* dimension. How a leader is perceived to handle an international conflict will impact upon his or her domestic political standing. Most leaders are acutely aware of this. Even when the world was hovering on the brink of nuclear war during the Cuban missile crisis in 1962, still prominent in President Kennedy's thinking were the possible ramifications on the upcoming congressional elections.

In the build-up of tensions, the media is more likely to be a force for escalating than for reducing tensions. In those very intense conflicts that can lead up to war, the news coverage is especially prone to emphasising righteous indignation rather than canvassing precise estimates of the likelihood of success, the costs of conflict and the relative military power of the opposing sides. Although it would be rare for this to be a decisive factor in any outbreak of international violence, in situations of heightened tension it is more common for the news media to give succour to the war party than to the forces for peace.

However, the news media have fewer constraints to enforce consistency of viewpoint than almost any other social institution. While the tenor of their coverage is more likely to favour hawkish viewpoints, there are many tensions between the presence of the media, even an editorially supportive media, and the military conduct of a war. Media's demands for immediate disclosure, their exaggeration of the most recent trends (both positive and negative), their (erratic) focus on the sufferings occasioned by the war, and their highlighting of divisions within allied ranks all make their role more problematic and diverse.

Moreover, the dominant pattern of insularity and ignorance of the other side in international conflicts has been significantly qualified by the rise of globalisation. Especially in the less-intense conflicts, where 'patriotic funda-mentalism' is not aroused, there is now more diversity in the views presented, although this is usually far short of parity. National boundaries have become more porous. All types of international exchange – trade, tourism, culture, etc. – have increased enormously. Some parts of the media themselves are now more internationally structured and much more mobile than they used to be – both technologically, where instant communication between most areas of the globe is now possible, and economically. The weight of the markets for international news agencies, for example, has changed enormously, so that emphasis now falls on the breadth of an agency's clientele – to the extent that the mid-1970s' criticisms made by UNESCO and others probably need qualification. The trend has profound implications for the reporting of international conflicts. During the Gulf War, for the first time in history there was instantaneous reporting via satellite from both sides of the military divide. The media's mobility, and its ability to broadcast in real time, make effective censorship far more difficult than ever before, although news management and other control mechanisms are still strong.

CONCLUSION

News coverage of socio-political conflicts does not conform to a single pattern. Nor do the media play a consistent role in the various conflicts here considered. However, neither are the variations random nor inexplicable. This analysis suggests that the nature of a given conflict influences the publicity interests and strategies of contenders, the capacity and desire of the news media to cover that conflict, and whether and how news coverage impacts upon its conduct and resolution. Table 12.1 outlines what the foregoing discussion has suggested are the central questions about conflicts and their news coverage. From these and other considerations a more extensive discussion

Table 12.1 Central questions about conflicts and their news coverage

Conflict characteristics

Are the overt stakes in the conflict but one part of a larger relationship, in which both parties have some interest in mutual accommodation and workable relations? Is there a direct personal working relationship between the contenders?

How amenable is the conflict to compromise? Do the stakes lend themselves to disaggregation and/or incremental resolutions?

Has either of the participants an ulterior interest in escalating the conflict over and above the overt stakes?

How rule-governed, institutionalised and instrumental is the pursuit of the conflict?

In what forum, how and by whom is the immediate conflict resolved?

How institutionalised are the two sides pursuing the conflict, how internally disciplined and united? How representative and authoritative are the spokespersons?

New Coverage

How do media audiences overlap with the political constituencies involved?

How do regular news sources relate to the lines of conflict?

What sorts of easily observable and newsworthy occasions does the conflict generate?

How important is publicity to the successful pursuit of the conflict? Is publicity intrinsic, helpful, irrelevant or counter-productive?

To what extent does the conflict generate opportunities for shadow play? What bonuses, if any, do the contenders get from public pursuit of the conflict?

How regular and intense is news coverage?

could be generated of hypotheses about the quality and direction of coverage and the degree of media impact upon its intensity and/or the direction of its outcome.

As an institution, the news media are geared primarily towards their audiences and sources. Where, as in inter-party conflicts these have a rough parity, the reporting is more balanced. Where viewpoints are not strongly represented in either sources or audience, there is more often overt partiality and less cross-testing of views. The dominant pattern of partial and one-sided coverage of international conflicts, for example, should not be surprising, although to remind ourselves of it is still important.

News organisations are geared towards regular output. Conflicts vary in the types of occasion and showdown they generate, and hence in how easily observable they are for news organisations. While some are pursued in public forums and occasionally generate spot news, perhaps the most prolific source is in the public stances and posturings of the contenders. A basic variable is, then, whether the nature of the conflict makes publicity an intrinsic and/or desirable part of its pursuit, and in particular whether the public escalation of differences is politically rewarding? The answer is a clear yes in inter-party conflict, often yes in international and industrial conflicts, and usually no in intraparty and bureaucratic conflicts. It is in these latter, where the political costs of posturing are most substantial, that covert manoeuvres – leaks and briefings – are most likely to be used. In those conflicts where there are ulterior rewards for magnifying the differences news coverage is likely to be both more extensive and more strident in tone than some 'objective' measure of the conflict's intensity would provide, while the converse also holds: in those conflicts where neither side seeks to posture, conflicts can be more intense and important than ever appears in the news.

While the quality of news coverage is to a considerable extent affected by the interplay of publicity interests, typically in nearly all conflicts, the capacities for publicity of the contenders are unequal and asymmetrical. They are most nearly balanced in inter-party conflict, but even here there is always a substantial difference between government and opposition in news generating capacities. The publicity interests of any contender coincides only erratically with complete accuracy and extensive disclosure. Without countervailing mechanisms of accountability from opponents and/or journalists, they are likely to have adverse implications for the reliability and balance of news coverage.

The media's role in affecting the outcome of disputes should not be exaggerated. These conflicts are determined most of the time by the balance of forces surrounding the issue at stake. Nevertheless, given that the frame for most news coverage of conflicts is to accentuate the sharpness of the antagonism it is likely that, to the extent that the antagonists' views of each other are refracted through the media, the impact on their attitudes will be towards rigidification and escalation rather than towards compromise and conciliation. Moreover, when the media act as sources of fresh information about the intentions and actions of the other side, news coverage can provide the flashpoint or catalyst in the further development of the conflict, sometimes dramatically so.

The time when news coverage is likely to have the most substantial impact on the outcome of a conflict is when publicity changes the political equations by moving the conflict from a closed arena to a more open and public one. This changes the weight of political considerations, e.g. from bureaucratic considerations to more general political and electoral factors. Sometimes the media impact may be in terms of how the coverage changed public attitudes – and sometimes as a result of biased coverage – but this will constitute at best only one small strand in any comprehensive consideration of the media's role in socio-political conflicts.

REFERENCES

Gitlin, T. (1980) *The Whole World is Watching: Mass Media in the Making and the Unmaking of the New Left*, Berkeley, Los Angeles and London: University of California Press.

Glasgow University Media Group (1976) *Bad News*, London: Routledge & Kegan Paul.

—— (1980) *More Bad News*, London: Routledge & Kegan Paul.

Goldenberg, E. (1975) *Making the Papers*, London, Lexington.

Gurr, E. R. (ed.) (1980) *Handbook of Political Conflict: Theory and Research*, New York: Free Press.

Schattschneider, E. E. (1960) *The Semi-Sovereign People*, New York: Holt, Rinehart & Winston.

Schlesinger, P. and H. Tumber (1994) *Reporting Crime: The Media Politics of Criminal Justice*, Oxford: Clarendon Press.

Tiffen, R. (1989) *News and Power*, Sydney: Allen & Unwin.

—— (1992) 'News coverage', in M. Goot and R. Tiffen (eds) *Australia's Gulf War*, Melbourne: Melbourne University Press.

Tunstall, J. (1971) *Journalists At Work*, London: Constable.

—— (1981) 'No news is bad news', *Encounter* (May).

—— (1977) 'The problem of industrial relations news in the press', in Oliver Boyd-Barrett, Colin Seymour-Ure and Jeremy Tunstall (eds) *Studies on the Press*, London: HMSO.

Part IV

MEDIA PROFESSIONALS

13

CONFLICTS OF INTEREST

Newsworkers, Media, and Patronage Journalism[1]

Hanno Hardt

The emergence of 'public' journalism in the United States coincides with significant changes in the newsroom culture of the press. Both mark the latest cultural transformation of American newspapers and confirm the lack of professional freedom among newsworkers in the face of an increasingly competitive and centralised media industry characterised by 'concentration, conglomeration, and hypercommercialism' (McChesney 1998: 96).

The decline of journalistic authority in the United States remains a serious social and cultural issue – too often dismissed as only the erosion of an elitist notion whose public credibility vanished long ago; it is replaced by public opinion as a favorite argument to capture the attention of the media with promises of change if not salvation. Similarly, assertions of the ignorance of the masses have been superceded by expressions of hope for the wisdom of the public and its desire for enlightenment.

At the same time, technological change and economic necessity have pushed the practice of journalism beyond traditional expectations. As a result, the prevailing commercial interests of the media, in an increasingly competitive environment, have begun to transform the status and the skills of the workforce, and to undermine its authority, while mass audiences have moved beyond the reach of a traditional press and are replaced by a prospective affluent middle-class clientele with specific information needs.

This chapter addresses the role of newsworkers in an era when the decline of capitalism and socialism as the dominant utopias of the twentieth century is accompanied by a collapse of their respective ideological constructions of communication, participation, and democracy. It is also a reminder of an historical process that reveals the subordination of journalism as a cultural practice to the economic rationale of marketing and new information technologies. Over the course of the last century, the utopian vision of journalism as an independent fourth estate – based on the collective accomplishments of journalists rather than on the institutional claims of the press – has been replaced by an aggressively commercial solution, the economic consequences of which have trivialised traditional, social and cultural co-determinants of journalism, including the role of journalists, the nature of newswork, and the pursuit of public interests.

In fact, the idea of journalism as a cultural practice has undergone significant definitional change related to shifting notions of work, technological advancement in the workplace, and the predicaments of a volatile market economy, as media interests have merged with the politics of mass society. The press has rarely been a facilitator of intellectual labor, free from a business-oriented paternalism that directed journalists in their work. The social and political consequences of a hegemonic approach to professionalism are the demise of traditional notions of journalistic practice and the rise of corporate power and control over the contemporary role and function of journalists, the manner of 'mass' communication, and the social and political purposes of media in general.

A crusade for responsive journalism – supported by the financial resources of several foundations – has united academics and press management to change the ways of local news coverage with the help of the public. At the center of these activities are the Project on Public Life and the Press, funded by the John S. and James L. Knight Foundation (together with the Kettering Foundation, the American Press Institute, and the New York University Department of Journalism), and the Pew Center for Civic Journalism, funded by the Pew Charitable Trusts (together with the Poynter Institute for Media Studies). In the most recent effort to turn around the fortunes of American journalism the former focuses on the making of 'public' journalists and 'public' journalism, while the latter advocates 'civic' journalism. Their collective judgement calls for public participation in a joint-endeavor to restore proximity and relevance to the press and its reporting practices.

Such developments have serious consequences not only for the profession – including professional education – but for society and the relationship of information, knowledge, and democracy. They not only suggest a new system of gathering and distributing information but, more fundamentally, a new authority for defining the nature and type of information that provides the foundation of social and political decision making and a new partisanship that embraces the patrons of commerce and industry; in this sense, it offers a new understanding of democracy as private enterprise rather than public commitment, when extent and quality of information – including its specificity and accessibility – depend more on the social, economic, or political needs of commerce and industry than on the requirements of an informed public. A recent documentary, *Fear and Favor in the Newsroom*, tells about the double standard developed by news organisations and its effect on journalists (Sanders and Baker 1998: 165–74).

At stake are the definition of journalism and its role in contemporary society, the nature of professional work, and the future of journalists. Ultimately, the campaign for 'public' or 'civic' journalism demonstrates the institutional power of media foundations to shape press policies; their arrangement of a new *raison d'être* for the American press as a commercial concern should be reason enough for journalism faculties to feel uneasy about the industrialisation of higher education and the potential impact of specific media interests on the location, size, and content of journalism education in the United States.

In the face of major institutional changes that have redefined notions of *the public* and of the *work* of *journalists*, the proponents of 'public' or 'civic' journalism promote a new definition of journalism to respond to the demands of the public and the desires of the industry with positively endowed notions of *the public* and of *journalism* to project the scope of their undertaking. After all, journalism has always been considered *public*, in the *public interest*, or *for* the *public good*, while journalists have always been defined as members of a fourth estate, privately employed and *protected* by the First Amendment. Yet, there are limitations to the new definitions, which do not encourage the pursuit of public interest journalism under new forms of ownership and public participation or a new understanding of professionalism that frees journalists from editorial controls and acknowledges their professional independence.

In fact, the accounts of 'public' or 'civic' journalism are reminiscent of progressive ideas about the need for change in an effort to improve the conditions for democracy. Unfortunately, however, those conditions seem to have worsened, and it turns out that the problems of journalism are the problems of society. Thus, disillusionment among journalists and their reported cynicism are symptoms of widespread alienation and cynicism, while dissatisfaction with work (and pay) in the face of shifting requirements concerning the type and quality of intellectual labor in the media industries are signs of fundamental social and economic changes in society and their effects on the workplace.

The myth of a strong and impartial press operating in the interest of society has prevailed throughout this period, strengthened, no doubt, by self-promotion, including the writing of a celebratory history of journalism, and occasional journalistic accomplishments that had more to do with indulging the unfettered activities of individual enterprising journalists than with collective corporate action based on the social consciousness of press ownership. Such an image of the press includes the labor of journalists whose role has been successfully contained within the organisational media structure through a ritual of appropriating not only journalists but audiences themselves, the obvious accomplices of journalists in their search for societal truths. *Appropriation* describes the historical process of the incorporation of journalists into the system of information gathering and news production while dominating the conditions of employment and the definition of work, including the determination of content. It involves the reinforcement of traditional myths representing notions of institutional power and expert communities, and suggests the active involvement of journalists in the activities of the fourth estate and its professional practices; it is a process that confers status and – combined with the promise of upward mobility – reflects effective social and cultural incentives for individuals in their quest for personal recognition and success.

However, the drive for 'public' journalism fails to examine the prerequisites of journalistic practice – e.g. the nature of newswork and ownership of the means of production, and the consequences of changing conditions of labor for the future of newsworkers – when it seems appropriate (and necessary) to question the practices of those in control of the means of communication. Instead, the advocates of 'public' journalism appeal to the civic conscience of individual journalists or, with management support, ask for compliance with their new rules of civic engagement. Their arguments replace earlier discussions surrounding the emergence of a fourth-estate model of the press which have focused on the institutional representation of such estate, while the position of journalists as members of the estate and their relations with the owners of the means of communication have not been problematised; even critics of this model have disregarded issues of intellectual production (journalistic practices) as a separate problematic. By dealing with the press as an inclusive notion, considerations of intellectual labor become neutralized and serve the anti-labor interests of the media rather than the interests of working journalists and their particular concerns, as they relate to the conditions of labor, freedom of expression, and the means of production.

The conditions of journalism in modernity are shaped by an inevitable shift to an information society which has made different demands on journalists and their relations to each other and to their institutions; it also affects the notion of *work* itself when information and knowledge rather than property constitute social and political power (and divide society into classes). Consequently, 'work comes to be less and less defined as a personal contribution and more as a role within a system of communications and social relations,' according to Alain Touraine (1995: 188), who also observes (ibid.) that

> the one who controls exerts influence on the systems of social relations in the name of their needs; the one who is controlled constantly affirms his existence, not as a member of any organization, element of the production process, or subject of a State, but as an autonomous unit whose personality does not coincide with any of his roles.

The result is not only an increasing sense of alienation but a changing perception of what constitutes journalism and, therefore, *public interest* and *social responsibility* at the dawn of the twenty-first century.

And yet, in the past, the celebration of technological progress obscured or concealed the fate of journalistic labor, particularly in historical accounts that shaped the understanding of journalism in society. Thus, mainstream narratives of American journalism – specifically Mott (1942), Jones (1947), Hohenberg (1973), Emery (1978), and Emery and Emery (1988) – remain oblivious to the impact of technology on newsworkers, but agree that media technologies are essential elements in the trend towards specialisation among newsroom labor without elaborating on the conditions of newsworkers who have been forced repeatedly to reinvent their professional existence in light of encroaching technologies (Hardt 1990: 351).

Standard journalism history texts support and reinforce popular beliefs – and a crude form of capitalism – that media technology is an assertion of inevitable progress; they are produced in a spirit that endorses an institutional history of the press which refuses to problematise the rise of media technologies and totally neglects the human dimension of labor – like the impact of technology on the work environment, on the definition of work, on freedom of choice, and ultimately on the professional status of individual newsworkers.

However, the loss of control over definitions of work and professional identity among newsworkers appears in more recent observations by media historians. When news evolved as a central value of American journalism during the 1870s, according to Dicken-Garcia (1989: 60), it resulted in a shift from 'news persons to news selling, and an editor-centered, personal structure gave way to corporatism, focused on advances in technology, increased competition, large circulations, diversification, and advertising as a means to profit.' Similarly, Carey observed some time ago (1969: 32) how the rise of objective reporting demanded technical instead of intellectual skills and resulted in a 'conversion downward' for journalists. However, the subsequent introduction of new communication technologies – ranging from telegraph and telephone to computers – not only strengthened control but increased the anonymity of the work process and reduced the expectations of journalists of recognition for their unique intellectual or creative contributions to the profession. In fact, the contributions of newsworkers since the late nineteenth century have been 'increasingly bordered, and in turn valued, by their technological place in the production process of gathering, writing, and producing news,' according to Salcetti (1995: 49). Douglas Birkhead (1982: 20) observed that, historically, 'the journalist as professional seemed to extend the rationality and efficiency of technology into the newsroom,' while Charles Derber (1983: 327) warns that 'technicalization' of professionals will lead to 'ideological proletarianization.' Finally, Im (1990: 112), has acknowledged a decisive change in the status of journalists when he concluded that 'reporters, as a newly created breed of newsworkers, still carried the old label of journalists, but without as much individual voice and discretion . . . as journalists of the earlier days of personal journalism.'

The 'downward conversion' reflects commercial considerations of the marketplace that focus on the technical expertise required for information retrieval rather than on the competence of critical analysis; the latter has been shifted to (educated) consumers or left to experts whose ideological perspectives, even if oppositional, seem most agreeable to media management; after all, authorised dissent helps legitimise the dominant power structure. Hence, intellectual requirements among contemporary journalists are replaced by technical knowledge in compliance with corporate media goals. The latter divide the workplace and fragment the reportorial process, destabilise the professional worth of journalists, and alienate them from their own labor. All the while, decisions regarding the definition and treatment of news are centralised in a media bureaucracy that is dominated by specific management concerns. Under these circumstances, it has been noticed that 'professionally trained journalists . . . could become increasingly less necessary to the process of gathering and distributing information' (Burnham 1996).

In other words, contemporary journalists encounter increasingly routinised work situations and an understanding of professional autonomy that is 'bordered' by technical aspects of news production and dissemination which constitute their concrete experience of the labor process. This understanding of work has prevailed in American journalism for some time – certainly long enough to have created an atmosphere of diminished expectation among journalists and despite institutional efforts by the press to counter-produce a positive empowering image of professional standing and social responsibility by identifying with journalism as a public service and appropriating journalists as executors of the public will. Journalists, on the other hand, have grown less committed to their choice and place of work, and remain autonomous in their personal life and in their attitudes towards a specific engagement in the public cause of journalism. As William Solomon (1995: 31) observes, 'like their counterparts of more than a century ago, today's newsroom workers increasingly are coming to view their work as combining a sacred public trust with a temporary job.'

Despite the undisputed theoretical or historical importance of the role of journalists in the democratic process, there has never been a sustained public debate in the United States about safeguarding their professional practice for the sake of a free and independent flow of ideas – regardless of proprietary economic or political interests that represent the ownership of the press. Thus, when the activities of the media occupy the public imagination because of their perceived effects on society, journalists are frequently viewed collectively by society as members of the media establishment. Consequently, as long as they are identified or identify with the institution of the press, journalists will be defined in terms of private rather than public interests. In fact, corporate media authority treats journalists as newsworkers rather than as free-floating intellectuals by appropriating their professional aura and obstructing or blocking opportunities for forging professional alliances among journalists

214

or with their readers in defense of journalism as an intellectual contribution to the discourse of society. As a result, journalists have for a long time experienced subjugation by those in control of the means of communication, who have used the idea of professionalism to validate their own commercial purposes and/or enhance public perceptions of the press as an institution.

The notion of professionalisation became a major ideological weapon of press management in the separation of newsworkers from fellow employees and the public. The former were regarded as sufficiently different in their practices while the public was constructed as an objectified source and/or destination of information rather than as a cultural context of subjective experiences and participation. Indeed, the evolution of professionalisation as a strategy for separating shared labor interests of printers and editorial workers – by providing promises of social status and professional independence – remains a major source of explanation for the diffusion of the editorial labor process and the continuous domination of twentieth century journalism by management. The organisation of labor interests among journalists as a potential weapon in a fight for independence was successfully quelled when professional status came to be recognised as a myth that was carefully constructed by press ownership to isolate and defeat union activities in the wake of mounting pressures from organized labor. Herman recently observed that 'professionalism was not an antagonistic movement by the workers against the press owners, but was actively encouraged by the latter' (1996: 120). He characterises it as a 'badge of legitimacy to journalism' which divided the varied interests of labor in media industries; but it also offers an appropriate example of how professionalism in modern society evolved into an ideology which, according to Meiksins (1986: 115), more generally 'exercised a power-ful hold over significant portions of the workforce and placed formidable barriers between those occupations which define themselves as 'professions' and other types of wage-labour.'

But the question of professionalisation is ultimately tied to the changing notion of work; while intellectual labor originally constituted an autonomous personal contribution to the advancement of knowledge – or the spread of information, for instance – its contemporary version of editorial work under the control of media management becomes a technical requirement within an information system designed to serve an elitist clientele rather than the public. In this context, journalists seem to lack the power of a professional class whose policies and practices should matter enough to warrant First Amendment protection of intellectual autonomy against the influence of media organisations, for instance, on editorial decision making. Private business interests prevail over potential public concerns regarding the need for professional independence and occupational integrity, resulting in the defense of institutional rather than individual welfare.

In addition, the creation of *public* or *civic* journalism anticipates a commu-nity capable of responding to its own desire for information or to institutional

215

propositions articulating collective interests. After all, the presence of 'civic capital' depends on a socially and politically active, culturally aware, and economically stable public and describes the activities of the middle class. Since *public* journalism refers mainly to the constituents of a political culture, there is not much room in these discussions for a notion of culture as a way of life in which issues of communication and participation become crucial elements of a complex social existence. Consequently, it may make sense to think in terms of aligning the middle-class concerns of audiences with the commercial intent of the media to better represent those class interests; but it remains questionable whether an alienated and fractured middle-class public can be restored to its ideal function by changing the practices of journalism. What is lost in these grand schemes to improve journalism for the benefit of society is an opportunity to broaden the spectrum of public communication by empowering journalists as intellectual workers and privileging the concerns of the underprivileged.

The changing definition of news has become a major issue in ongoing debates among journalists and in a literature that deals with the consequences for the press of particular business philosophies and management styles. More recently, for instance, Underwood has provided a detailed analysis of how a marketing approach to journalism is reshaping contemporary media. Although highly critical of these trends, the author suggests (1993: 181) that the (daily) press still has an opportunity to present an independent, analytical, and in-depth alternative to television; unwilling to give up on the press, he pleads with press ownership to adjust profit margins, reject the formation of media conglomerates, and embrace the 'traditional values of public service and the principles of public trust that are the bedrock of the profession.' It seems highly unlikely that the owner of the press will follow his advice; on the contrary, with a labor market saturated with inexperienced journalism (and other university) graduates as sources of cheap labor – or unemployed journalists with expert standing – media management will continue to dictate conditions of labor and extend its reach into new media markets, especially with the increasingly competitive pressure from new media, such as computers and information services like the Internet. As a result, there is a growing need to seek maximum profits in the attempt to absorb competitors or to reinforce their current hold on their own market. This is particularly the case with newspapers in light of the circulation losses that continue to plague the industry (Fitzgerald 1995).

The process of newsgathering has typically been informed by an under-standing of existing social and economic inequalities in society; however, the rapidly shifting imbalance between accumulations of wealth and the growth of poverty accommodates representations of political and economic strength and prescribes considerations of class, gender, or race as economic categories of consumption that redefine the adversarial function of the press and result in a friendly alliance with the interests of business and industry. Indeed, the key to understanding the dilemma of contemporary journalism lies in its definition by the owners of the press; such definition, however, is always self-imposed and more often than not serves its immediate political and economic interests.

As Milton Friedman observed over 25 years ago (1970), businesses are responsible only for making profits and obeying laws. Consequently, the commodification of news – that is, news as an industrial product – remains immune to traditional demands for socially responsible content; it is guided, instead, by market requirements and the standard legal restrictions governing defamation or invasion of privacy. In this sense, the manufacture of news no longer demands professional involvement, but can be accomplished by a cheap-labor force which is computer-literate and more attuned to packaging information than to exercising analytical skills.

In fact, the process of *deskilling* – a term introduced by Harry Braverman (1974) as an explanation of how technology (or scientific rationality) has transformed the status and the skills of the modern work force – continues to affect contemporary labor; it also threatens journalism, and ultimately devalues journalistic labor power. As an historical phenomenon, the process of deskilling moved from the creativity of personal journalism to the routines of objective reporting, when events rather than ideas began to direct professional practice. Im (1990) examines Braverman's deskilling thesis in the context of arguing for a labor process approach as a conceptual framework for a labor history of journalism which would address issues of work and class. Most recently, however, the reproduction of information has overshadowed earlier developments and determines the nature of journalistic labor. This shifting notion of *skill* raises questions about the nature of professionalism at a time when the threat of unionisation has been diminished, if not actually eliminated, and large-scale replacements with cheap labor have become a real alternative under changing definitions of newswork. The process of deskilling as a managerial practice confronts individual journalists everywhere and yields responses ranging from attempts to preserve or redefine skills – in an effort to satisfy the demands for a new type of journalism – to active resistance and, finally, resignation from the profession altogether.

In fact, journalists have never challenged the organization of media power directly and collectively. This is partly because their ideological position – a shared belief in the virtues of capitalism and the subordination of subjective notions of professional practice to technological demands – has always been maintained with organizational consent, if not urging, and partly because journalists have traditionally relied on constructing labor problems in terms of individual and local conditions rather than systemic, class-related, issues. They also compensated in other ways – ranging from a short-term commitment to journalism, or physical mobility, to engaging in unrelated external activities.

In the long run, dissatisfaction among the dependable and loyal, if critical, rank and file may become particularly troublesome for management. The

217

published findings of a national survey by the Human Resources Committee of the American Society of Newspaper Editors (Stinnett 1989) provides a good example of this quandary. Its discussion of the newsroom – including a characterization of newsworkers – reflects the expectations of management, but cannot hide the discontent among journalists. What emerges is an individual who 'feels involved in the community, professes the religious values of the whole society, and maintains a deep love and respect for journalism. Many are willing to make personal sacrifices, if necessary, to stay in the newspaper business,' according to Stinnett (1989: 27). Although professional aspirations concern the opportunity to write rather than to occupy an intellectual role that would include 'having an impact on society' (ibid.: 31), the accompanying wish-list of important tasks is led by analysis and interpretation of complex problems, investigative work, and fast dissemination of information to the public (ibid.: 67). These ideals are severely affected by low pay, lack of recognition and low job satisfaction and the feeling that the press is 'adequate, but not outstanding' in its pursuit of community issues. Also, journalists have a weak sense of longevity when it comes to their positions, despite the education and job preparation they have gained through journalism education. In a nationwide 'newspaper departure' study it was suggested that over 60 percent of employees who leave newspapers also leave the industry, and do so for lack of 'fairness in promotions; involvement in decision-making; opportunities for advancement; supervisor concern for employees' personal success; fairness in pay; equitable treatment; and contributions in value' (*Editor & Publisher* 1995: 23).

Some time ago, authors like Breed (1955), Sigal (1973), Gans (1980), and Gitlin (1980) commented on the practices of journalists and their position in newsrooms; together with other more recent observations or laments they seem to substantiate current findings (e.g. Weaver and Wilhoit 1996) that newsworkers are caught unhappily in a work situation that leaves little room to maneuver.

Emerging from the practices of contemporary advertising and public relations efforts is a journalism of a new type which promotes the construction of corporate realities at the expense of a common-sense desire for a fair and truthful representation of everyday life. Its ideological role resembles the political task of a Soviet-style press with its specific goals of organising and propagandising the masses for the purposes of maximising socialisation in an effort to centralise political power through participation in the commercialisation of social differences to form a *consumer* culture. In this process, freedom of expression is reconstituted as an institutional element of freedom of the press with claims about representing individual interests that sound not unlike earlier claims of centralised political systems – such as those in eastern Europe under Soviet rule – to speak collectively for society. It is one of the dangers of the anticipated or realised business mentality of the media that content – which represents an expression of freedom – will be defined by those who seek to serve the public as consumers rather than by society as participant and source of democratic power.

In its ideal version the press, as a vehicle of journalism and business, fulfills public duties and pursues private goals; its investment in the social and political life of society – uniquely protected by a constitutional amendment – constitutes a significant contribution to the working of democratic principles regarding the pursuit of knowledge and the need to be informed. In reality, however, the commercial impulse of the press – supported by law and barely controlled by the ethical considerations of its owners – also guides journalistic practices, while the desirable balance between responsible journalism and profitable business is rarely accomplished. In fact, contemporary economic and political developments – summarised most appropriately by the notion of deregulation and introduced and practiced since the Reagan administration – have resulted in the privatisation of public property – like the recent FCC auction of public airwaves – and prepared the stage for the demise of public broadcasting. However, more fundamentally, ideas of responding to public concerns and representing a public trust are being absorbed or replaced by the strength of private interests, signaling the end of government intervention and public control of excessive commercial power. This process confirms an era of privatisation – pitched at home and abroad, and particularly in the newly established democracies of eastern Europe, as the key to a free market system – flawed by an utter disregard for the public good, including the protection of workers, among them journalists. Media organisations in many parts of the world are heavily affected by these developments in the United States, whence a CNN version of journalism has conquered the global airwaves and makes its endless rounds as media everywhere seem to reconceptualise traditional understandings of news and public responsibility in light of increasing commercialisation while mistaking private enterprise for democratic practice.

Pressure from advertisers, long recognised as a hazard to aggressive journalism, has now turned into a regular succession of requests that more often than not leads to co-operation and collaboration as a community service. In other words, while none of these occurrences is new – newspapers have dealt with them before – they are now widely received in the form of guided opportunities to help promote business and improve the standing of the press in its community. Such a community, however, is limited to the community of affluent readers and businesses, both major clients of the information industry. Moreover, in a world in which work is disappearing rapidly, according to William Julius Wilson (1996: 133–4), media are being used by corporations to exclude the poor from sharing information about a shrinking workplace by, for instance, not advertising in black neighborhoods, thus effectively isolating people from jobs and information about them.

Indeed, the press has joined the electronic media, and particularly television, and incorporated older practices of the magazine press which were aimed at providing business with a reliable, credible, and effective forum for the dissemination of commercial information. Additional downsizing of media corporations, mega-mergers, and a dwindling number of competitors will strengthen these developments and assure their continuation into the twenty-first century. The losers will be not only those newsworkers – those who refuse to co-operate or retire from the press – but the public itself, which will be robbed of the professional skills of newsworkers to undertake the surveillance of business and politics as a matter of public interest.

Left to make their own decisions about how to manage the future of the press, owners have made a series of decisive moves in the attempt to remain competitive in the media market and to comply with the demands of their major customers – affluent readers and advertisers. As a result, investigative reporting, analytical writing on social, economic, and political issues, and confrontational stances have been largely replaced by a notoriously placid – if not socially and politically irrelevant – coverage of events. David Burnham (1996: 11) suggests that American news organisations

> tend to be passive and unreflective. Although independent-minded investigative reporting often is celebrated by journalists, it is in fact a rare phenomenon. Despite the self-congratulatory rhetoric, the basically acquiescent nature of daily journalism is a problem that has long been observed by a handful of astute observers.

In addition, there is no review of media practices – together with a lack of historical consciousness – nor a return to self-criticism and public scrutiny of press performances.

These are the conditions of late capitalism under which the press intends to advance, for its own benefit and that of its customers, after definitions of the role of journalism in American society have been finally rewritten by the public relations practices of the press. The fourth-estate model of the press has never been more outdated than it is in the current era of political and economic dependence among major institutions in society, when a technology-driven information and entertainment culture has converted the labor process into a limited and highly controlled activity, leading to the homogenisation and degradation of labor including the media, newswork, and journalists, respectively.

Also, the demise of journalism as independent intellectual labor may be related to the ignoring of class positions and the embraced assurances of social status, since class and class relations remain significant issues in contemporary considerations of public communication, including journalism (Hardt 1996). Initially journalists shared both proletarian and bourgeois characteristics, and expressed expectations of middleclass status. But among celebrations of robust individualism in the liberal–pluralist atmosphere of 1920s' America, the struggle over recognising the collective interests of newsworkers was lost to the efforts of media organisations to redefine their work force in terms of professionalism, isolating it successfully from other, non-editorial, workers while supporting and reinforcing the denial of economically expressed working-class conditions of newsworkers. In the 1990s, finally, the drawn-out struggle over maintaining the status quo of professionals – including the quasi-independence of editorial work – failed with the adoption of a patronage model of the press; the latter understands journalistic labor in terms of routinised technical tasks responding to specific commercial interests, such as the production of non-idea, non-event-centered, narratives. The latter cater to the entertainment interests of consumers, thereby satisfying the demands of advertisers for non-controversial contextual material to help maximise the impact of commercial messages.

Alternative solutions will not be offered by the commercial marketplace; they will, at best, be introduced by a new type of media practice through periodicals – or, more likely, electronic publications rather than daily news-papers – with the kind of determination and direction that mark ideologically committed journalism capable of providing a point of view for an enlightened readership. It may very well constitute the only viable journalistic alternative based on the quality of information, its sources, and objectives that decide questions of public service and social responsibility. Such a solution, however, also relies on the growing desire of a critical general public for more comprehensive information and analysis, suggesting that the success of journalists depends on the cultural and economic competences of a democratic society to support its rising need for journalism; it suggests also that an alliance between journalists and their respective publics is necessary for the sake of reclaiming the pivotal role of journalism in the making of democracy.

Jürgen Habermas (1996) promotes the idea of a deliberative democracy – based on the centrality of communication – that embraces equality of opportunity, participation, and the process of forming autonomous opinions as a desirable alternative to existing (and applied) conceptions of democracy. It represents a procedural ideal that promotes an ideal speech situation, the core of his theory of communicative action. Similarly, it could be argued that the inadequacy of existing media theories resides in a failure to rethink relations between media and democracy in terms of the potential of communication as a social process that privileges participation and exchange and the autonomy of journalists; in the latter instance, journalism emerges as a responsive cultural practice, administered in a professional manner that is successfully insulated from the control of media management and sensitive to the need for public participation in constituting social knowledge.

On the other hand, by becoming their own agents commercial and govern-ment institutions will continue to produce information packages that serve their specific purposes, with increasing opportunities for direct access to consumers and citizens, and bypassing traditional systems of news processing while challenging alternative sources of information and analysis. In fact, this is the dawn of a new partisanship of the traditional media, the result of a larger political process of bargaining and compromise to promote and protect selfish interests rather than public participation; it will shift the balance between private interest and public responsibility towards a patronage system that considers information a privilege rather than a right, as it replaces the specter of a nineteenth-century partisan press. Consequently, a professional vision of journalism ends at a time when American society needs a critical reportorial force; instead, a new journalism emerges in the form of 'mass' communication that will benefit commerce and legitimise the function of advertising in the 'commercialization of culture,' as Matthew McAllister (1995) suggests.

Finally, the demise of the fourth estate has been long in coming, when one recalls the impressive literature of press criticism that has accompanied the economic and technological developments of the press during the last century. But while market forces shaped and strengthened the media as a cultural, political, and economic institution in the United States, journalists – whose intellectual labor has lent professional credibility to the process of public enlightenment – have been exchanged for wage labor in the evolution of the information society. Michael Schudson (1995) once declared that news is culture and, as such, is apt to change, although he did not know how. The political and economic developments of the last decade, in particular, suggest that news will fit the requirements of a patronage system, in which journalists serve the interests of an affluent and educated commercial class, consisting of businesses and their clienteles, as a new type of partisanship and a new understanding of public interest begin to dominate the public sphere.

NOTE

1 This chapter is based on two earlier essays: 'The quest for public journalism,' *Journal of Communication* (1997) 47(3): 102–9; and 'The end of journalism. Media and newswork in the United States,' *Javnost/The Public* (1996) 3(3): 21–41.

REFERENCES

Birkhead, D. (1982) 'Presenting the press: journalism and the professional project.' unpublished dissertation, Iowa: University of Iowa.

Braverman, H. (1974) *Labor and Monopoly Capital. The Degradation of Work in the Twentieth Century*, New York: Monthly Review Press.

Breed, W. (1955) 'Social control in the newsroom: a functional analysis,' *Social Forces* 33 (May): 326–35.

Burnham, D. (1996) 'The lens of democracy,' *News in the Next Century. Digital Debate: Covering Government and Politics in a New Media Environment*, Chicago: RTND Foundation, 11–15.

Carey, J. (1969) 'The communication revolution and the professional communicator,' in P. Halmos (ed.) *The Sociological Review Monographs*, No. 13: 23–38.

Derber, C. (1983) 'Managing professionals: ideological proletarianization and post-industrial labor,' *Theory and Society* 12(3): 309–341.

Dicken-Garcia, H. (1989) *Journalistic Standards in Nineteenth-Century America*, Madison: University of Wisconsin Press.

Editor & Publisher (1995) 'Preliminary results issued in newspaper departure study,' (May 6): 23.

Emery, E. (1978) *The Press and America*, Englewood Cliffs, NJ: Prentice-Hall.

Emery, M. and E. Emery (1988) *The Press and America*, Englewood Cliffs, NJ: Prentice-Hall.

Fitzgerald, M. (1995) 'Newspaper circulation report,' *Editor & Publisher* (May 6): 12–13.

Friedman, M. (1970) 'The social responsibility of business is to increase its profits,' *New York Times Magazine* (13 September): 32–3, 122–6.

Gans, H. (1980) *Deciding What's News: A Study of CBS Evening News, NBC Nightly News, Newsweek and Time*, New York: Vintage.

Gitlin, T. (1980). *The Whole World Is Watching. Mass Media in the Making and Unmaking of the New Left*, Berkeley, CA: University of California Press.

Habermas, J. (1996) *Between Facts and Norms. Contributions to a Discourse Theory of Law and Democracy*, Cambridge, MA: MIT Press.

Hardt, H. (1990) 'Newsworkers, technology, and journalism history,' *Critical Studies in Mass Communication* 7(4): 346–65.

—— (1996) 'The making of the public sphere: industrialization, media and participation in the United States,' *Javnost/The Public* 3(1): 7–23.

—— (1998) 'Looking for the working class: class relations in communication studies,' *Interactions. Critical Studies in Communication, Media, and Journalism*, Boulder, CO: Rowman & Littelfield, 41–62.

Herman, E. S. (1996) 'The propaganda model revisited,' *Monthly Review* 48(3): 115–28.

Hohenberg, J. (1973) *Free Press, Free People*, New York: Free Press.

Im, Y.-Ho (1990) 'Class, culture, and newsworkers: theories of the labor process and the labor history of the newspaper,' unpublished dissertation, Iowa: University of Iowa.

Jones, R. W. (1947) *Journalism in the United States*, New York: E. P. Dutton.

McAllister, M. P. (1995) *The Commercialization of American Culture*, Thousand Oaks, CA: Sage.

McChesney, R. W. (1998) 'This communication revolution is brought to you by US media at the dawn of the 21st century,' in Peter Philips and Project Censored (eds) *Censored 1998. The News that Didn't Make the News*, New York: Seven Stories Press, 95–108.

Meiksins, P. (1986) 'Beyond the boundary question,' *New Left Review*, 157 (May/June): 101–20.

Mott, F. L. (1942) *American Journalism*, New York: Macmillan.

Salcetti, M. (1995) 'The emergence of the reporter: mechanization and the devaluation of editorial workers,' in H. Hardt and B. Brennen (eds) *Newsworkers. Towards a History of the Rank and File*, Minneapolis: University of Minnesota Press, 48–74.

Sanders, B. and R. Baker (1998) 'Fear and favor in the newsroom,' in Peter Philips and Project Censored (eds) *Censored 1998. The News that Didn't Make the News*, New York: Seven Stories Press, 165–74.

223

Schudson, M. (1995) 'How news becomes news,' *Forbes Media Critic* 2(4): 76–85.

Sigal, L. V. (1973) *Reporters and Officials. The Organization and Politics of Newsmaking*, Lexington, MA: Heath.

Stinnett, L. (1989) *The Changing Face of the Newsroom. A Human Resources Report*, Washington, DC: ASNE.

Solomon, W. S. (1995) 'The site of newsroom labor: the division of editorial practices,' in H. Hardt and B. Brennen (eds) *Newsworkers. Towards a History of the Rank and File*, Minneapolis: University of Minnesota Press, 110–34.

Touraine, A. (1995) 'Post-industrial classes,' in James D. Faubion *Rethinking the Subject. An Anthology of Contemporary European Social Thought*, Boulder, CO: Westview Press.

Underwood, D. (1993) *When MBAs Rule the Newsroom. How the Marketers and Managers are Reshaping Today's Media*, New York: Columbia University Press.

Weaver, D. H. and G. C. Wilhoit (1996) *The American Journalist in the 1990s*, Mahwah, NJ: Lawrence Erlbaum.

Wilson, W. J. (1996) *When Work Disappears*, New York: Alfred A. Knopf.

14

THE WASHINGTON
REPORTERS REDUX,
1978–98

Stephen Hess

At the beginning of 1972 I joined the Brookings Institution, the Washington think-tank, as its resident presidentialist. Five years later, having said all I wanted to say at that time about the presidency, I looked around for another public policy institution to explore and settled on the press with a particular interest in news from Washington. My problem was that I had never been a journalist or trained as a scholar in that field. Moreover, neither American journalists nor American scholars were of much help. Most of the books by Washington journalists, although often entertaining, could have been titled *Presidents Who Have Known Me*, and the last scholarly book on Washington journalists had been published in 1937 (Rosten, 1937). It was at this point that a British reporter told me he had once been interviewed by a sociologist called Jeremy Tunstall for a book he had written about the Westminster lobby correspondents. I tracked down this book (1970) and then the grander book *Journalists At Work* (1971) of which it was a part, poring over the questions Tunstall asked, considering why he asked them, how he asked them, and the answers. Although I had not then met Jeremy, he became my teacher.

My own book was published in 1981, based largely on surveys and interviews I conducted in 1978. It strikes me therefore as most appropriate in honoring Jeremy Tunstall on his university retirement to return to that work to see if it is possible to discover what has happened to news from Washington after a gap of twenty years.

This chapter is a scaled-down replication of 'Stories,' Chapter 5 in *The Washington Reporters*, which examined the three television networks' evening news programs and a passel of daily newspapers during a typical week in April 1978. In updating this effort I was aided by the impressions of sixteen of the journalists I had interviewed at that time who still practice their craft in the capital.[1]

The media landscape is now radically different, of course. Two years after my survey Ted Turner created the Cable News Network (CNN), derisively called Chicken Noodle Network by 'serious' journalists. But by 1998 Americans were as apt to watch news on the multitude of cable channels as on the broadcast networks. An average home in Washington (mine!), without 'premium' service and paying about $30 a month, receives fifty-seven channels, including two CNN stations, one for headline news; two CNN clones, one owned by Rupert Murdoch, the other co-owned by Bill Gates; two stations called C-SPAN, providing gavel-to-gavel coverage of the US House of Representatives and the Senate; two channels that show city council meetings and other activities of the District of Columbia government; five PBS or public broadcasting channels, often offering the same programs but at different times; a 24-hour regional news channel, two sports channels, a business news channel, a legal channel, and a weather channel. (Cable penetration in the US is 63 percent of TV-owning households.) The broadcast network news divisions, at the same time, placed a new emphasis on hour-long magazine shows in prime-time, featuring celebrity interviews and gotcha investigations. Although they had to compete with entertainment programming, their productions were considerably less expensive to put on than the drama or comedy competition, and were owned by the networks rather than leased from outside companies. Newspapers also looked different. A new national paper *USA Today* taught editors how to splash color on the front and back pages, and otherwise improve graphic design. Unable to be first with breaking news, the dailies turned more and more to analysis and interpretation. Still, newspapers had lost ground: readership was down about 10 percent of the adult population over the two decades. Talk radio, on the other hand, came of age: stations adopting this format tripled to over 1,000 between 1990 and 1995 (Egan 1995). And, most recently, the Internet as an instrument for obtaining news had begun to grow at an astonishing rate. According to the Pew Research Center (1998), Americans claiming to get news from the Internet at least once a week climbed from 4 percent in 1995 to 20 percent in 1998.

Yet a re-examination of network evening news and daily newspapers is not an exercise in nostalgia. The three supper-time TV programs, anchored by Peter Jennings (ABC), Tom Brokaw (NBC), and Dan Rather (CBS), still have a concentration of viewers that far exceed anything the splintered cable universe can deliver (except at unique moments, such as the US bombing of Baghdad in 1991) and daily newspapers still are the medium of choice for consumers who are most apt to provide community example and leadership.

In choosing April 9–15, 1978, the 'trick' was to make sure that nothing exceptional happened, no overriding event that might send Washington's journalists rushing off to the same fire. In finding a comparable seven days in 1998 I picked April 21–7 to avoid Easter week and to have Congress in session. (*Tyndall Weekly Report*, which charts network news, wrote: 'Flaccid is the only word to describe this week.' It was the week Pfizer released the anti-impotence drug Viagra.) Besides the three networks, the survey followed Washington news in five newspapers: *Atlanta Journal-Constitution*, *Boston Globe*, *Dallas Morning News*, *New York Times*, and *San Diego Union-Tribune*.[2]

The first conclusion of my 1978 study had been: 'What is most immediately apparent is that news of Washington dominates the media's attention [throughout the United States].' This is no longer true. Whereas the newspapers surveyed in 1978 averaged twelve Washington stories a day (including those by reporters traveling with the president or secretary of state whose datelines were other than Washington), the number was cut in half – six stories a day – in 1998. Every other indicator shows declining interest in Washington, especially on network TV where lead stories from Washington went from twelve of fifteen in 1978 to seven of fifteen in 1998. A clue to the relative weight that newspaper editors now give to Washington stories can be found by looking at the Sunday papers. Sunday is the day on which papers have the most pages, the most readers, and stories that have the greatest journalistic cachet. In 1978 Sunday was the big day for Washington stories: half the papers in my sample ran more Washington stories on Sunday than on any other day. But Sunday was the nadir for Washington stories in 1998. There were even more Washington datelines on Monday, and the number kept increasing until it reached its apex, on Thursday.

The media trend line was away from Washington and toward local news. Local TV news programs – an amalgam of crime stories, weather, sports, and 'news you can use' – have become the most popular source of information in the United States. When a Harris poll in 1996 asked Americans to list their single most important source of news, 34 percent said local TV, followed by network TV at 17 percent, newspapers 15 percent, radio 8 percent (Smith, Lichter, and Louis Harris & Associates 1997). The reversal in emphasis can be seen in Table 14.1, which shows what the editors of the papers surveyed chose as their front-page leads (excluding the internationalist-minded *New York Times*).

Part of the lack of interest in the nation's capital can be traced to the end of the Cold War. Foreign policy had been the Number 1 ranked subject of Washington TV and newspaper stories in 1978. Also, as *Newsweek*

Table 14.1 Editorial front-page selections of sampled Monday–Sunday newspapers

Datelines	Front-page lead stories %	
	1978	*1998*
Washington	45	36
Local (city/state)	37	54
International	11	7
Another state	7	4

contributing editor Eleanor Clift put it, there was now 'the conventional wisdom that people don't care about politics.' Politics had been another popular subject in 1978 (1978 and 1998 were comparable congressional election years).

Some operations, such as Thomson Newspapers, shrank their Washington bureaux; others actually increased staff. According to Robert Rankin of Knight Ridder Newspapers, which include the *Philadelphia Inquirer* and the *Miami Herald*

> As the 1990s evolved, our papers showed less and less interest in any news from Washington. In response we changed our beat structure. In addition to traditional beats such as the White House and Congress, we added theme specialties such as science and technology, religion and ethics, and consumer affairs beats. . . . As time went on we shifted our mission to be less a Washington bureau and more a national bureau.

When Newhouse Newspapers' bureau chief Deborah Howell, whose papers include the *Times Picayune* in New Orleans and the *Star-Ledger* in Newark, arrived in Washington in the early 1990s she, too, promptly revamped the beat structure she inherited, moving one-third of her national staff to assignments with labels like 'social trends' and 'race' (Robinson 1992).

These organisations were at the high end of change. The more common way to deal with the public's loss of appetite for Washington news was to downplay what one reporter called 'turn of the screw daily developments' and another called 'he said, she said daily stories.' Newspaper reportage from Congress in 1978 very much mirrored the classic textbook treatment of how a bill works its way through the legislative process, rightly giving special attention to the key committee stage. Not so in 1998, as Table 14.2 indicates, when the emphasis was overwhelmingly on final-floor action rather than the complicated hand-in-glove work that preceded it.

These stories reflect also the regional nature of newspaper reporting from Washington. The *Boston Globe* was covering the introduction of a congressional

Table 14.2 Newspaper reportage from Congress, 1978 and 1998

	Newspaper stories %	
Legislative stage in story	1978	1998
Introduction of legislation	3	8
Subcommittees	20	12
Committees	37	16
Floor action	35	60
Conference committees	5	4

bill because it was being introduced by a senator from Massachusetts, an event that did not interest the other papers in the survey. The *Atlanta Journal-Constitution* gave the most space to a major education bill because its sponsor was a senator from Georgia. The San Diego paper, being located on the Mexican border, created a beat in its Washington bureau to report stories on immigration, drug trafficking, and cross-border pollution problems. While all bureaus, as in 1978, pay lip service to regional news – 'the issues and people closest to our readership' – the record continues to be spotty at large enterprises like the *New York Times*. Smaller Washington offices are more focused. At the *Cleveland Plain Dealer*, a five-person bureau in mid-1998, bureau chief Tom Brazaitis reviewed his resources:

> We have one reporter assigned to cover the Senate, another to cover the House. We monitor the Supreme Court for cases originating or of special interest in Ohio. We do not cover the White House full time and rarely travel with the president anymore, even to Ohio, except during the campaigns. It's too expensive. More importantly, it's redundant.

My book described Washington news gathering in 1978 as a 'procedural pluralism' in which each bureau did its own thing, meaning that many organizations covered the same stories at the same locations, producing roughly the same copy. A gaggle of journalists in 1998 were still waiting for Kenneth Starr's next witness to emerge from the court house, but, as Brazaitis suggests, on less overheated Washington happenings the bureaux now do a better job fighting redundancy. (It is demanded of them by their front offices.)

Newspaper editors also do a more creative job of mix-and-match when choosing from the torrent of words that flows in from their own people in Washington, the wire services, and the supplemental news services.[3] The *New York Times* is almost entirely staff-written (51 of 54 articles); the other papers, however, look to their own reporters for articles tailored to their needs, to the wire services (Associated Press and Reuters) for relatively routine news, and to the supplementals they subscribe to for investigative pieces and special features. The change of direction can be seen from Table 14.3, which excludes the *New York Times*.

In the week under study, for example, the *Boston Globe* ran two long articles from its eleven-member Washington bureau on the sums New England lobbyists spend to influence Congress and a dispute between the Pentagon and the White House over a proposal to protect a breed of whale that makes its home off Massachusetts, various stories about campaign finance legislation proposed by a congressman from the region, and other Washington stories from AP, Reuters, *Washington Post*, *Baltimore Sun*, *Los Angeles Times*, Knight Ridder, and States News Service. While Washington reporters still cherish a

Table 14.3 Washington stories, 1978 and 1998

Type of byline	Washington stories % 1978	1998
Staff	29	25
Wire	57	45
Supplemental	12	31
Freelance	2	0

good scandal – 15 percent of the 1998 stories related to President Clinton's involvements with Paula Jones or Monica Lewinsky – the consumer-friendly direction of many bureaux has redirected reporters in search of information. Government agencies such as the Food and Drug Administration and the National Institutes of Health are more likely now than twenty years ago to produce news, as are non-governmental organisations that monitor health or environmental issues. Quotable 'experts' now are more regularly found in the universities, think-tanks, and advocacy groups.

Likewise within the political government there have been notable changes in sourcing since 1978. Twenty years ago both chambers of Congress were controlled by Democrats; few reporters in Washington could remember when the House of Representatives was not controlled by the Democrats, and most probably expected it to be ever thus. While the presidency was in the hands of a Democrat, Jimmy Carter, both parties could expect regular turns in the White House. The Senate, home of astronauts, sports heroes, billionaires, and future presidents, received greater press notice than did the House, and my 1978 finding that Democrats in Congress received 10 percent more attention than did Republicans was not surprising. Some had assumed this reflected the liberal leaning of the Washington press corps. Rather, I thought, this repre-sented a 'bonus' for the press awards to the majority party because it controls the agenda. Then in the 1994 elections Republican House candidates, led by Newt Gingrich, unexpectedly won a majority of the seats and continued to retain narrow control in 1996, even as Democrat Bill Clinton was being re-elected president.

Would the press bonus now swing over to the congressional Republicans? And what would be the effect on House and Senate coverage?

The answers were of seismic proportions. Republicans now received greater notice than Democrats, and the House of Representatives greater notice than the Senate. House Republicans (doubly disadvantaged in 1978) had the greatest notice of all. Counting names in newspapers (there were not enough TV stories about Congress to be coded in this way) does not indicate that the attention is favorable or unfavorable, merely that the person mentioned or quoted is considered newsworthy. One week's worth of Congress-watching in the leading papers of Atlanta, Boston, Dallas, and San Diego produced twice as many statements by Republican legislators as by Democrats. Of all the names counted (228), 88 were House Republicans, 62 were Republican senators, 40 were Democratic senators, and 38 were House Democrats. What happened was that the press had framed the capital's basic political–governmental story as Newt Gingrich (and his troops) versus Bill Clinton. A not unusual lead paragraph in the *Boston Globe* reads: 'Prospects for a major tobacco law grow dimmer daily, even though everyone from President Clinton to House Speaker Newt Gingrich says he wants one.' Gingrich's legislative counterpart Richard Gephardt, the Democratic leader of the House, was virtually the forgotten man and even the august US Senate was often excluded from the main tent unless the issues were those over which that body had special constitutional responsibility, such as confirming presidential appointments and approving treaties.

The 1978 study, in keeping with previous investigations, had affirmed TV as the medium of presidents. By comparison, Congress was too splintered and varied of interest. In 1998 the differences were even more pronounced. Bill Clinton – young, handsome, virile, by presidential standards – seemed to be designed for TV. Jimmy Carter had been judged boring by the White House press corps (Hess 1978). Table 14.4 makes this point, but unfortunately I could only code thirteen 1998 stories.

The judiciary, the Constitution's third branch of government, produced possibly the most stunning changes in press attention. Twenty years ago I had paid scant attention to court and law reporting in Washington. Law was a specialised beat in a profession dominated by generalists, covering the courts was rarely how people got ahead in journalism. But in 1998 the Supreme Court reporter for the *New York Times* won the coveted Pulitzer prize and the US appeared to be drowning in law-suits and trials that were of immense public interest. Nor, in Washington, were all the legal matters of April related to President Clinton's problems. On Tuesday the *Atlanta Journal-Constitution* reported that the Supreme Court would rule on an anti-loitering ordinance 'intended to control the expanding cancer of urban gangs.' Wednesday's *Boston Globe* reported: 'The Supreme Court heard arguments yesterday on whether federal law supersedes a Massachusetts statute that permits some felons to own firearms.' On Thursday the *Dallas Morning News* reported: 'The Supreme Court said Wednesday that the out-of-wedlock daughter of a Texas man and a Filipino woman is not entitled to American citizenship.' On Friday, according to the *San*

Table 14.4 Television reportage of political stories, 1978 and 1998

Subject of story	TV stories % 1978	1998
President	59	79
Congress	41	21

Diego Union-Tribune, '[p]rompted by judges' decisions that were unpopular in California and elsewhere, the House yesterday approved a Republican attempt to restrict the power of federal judges nationwide.'

When observing Washington journalists twenty years ago I was fascinated by how news had a rhythm set by reporters for the leading newspapers that then traveled a circuitous route back into the political government and out again to the rest of the country via the electronic media. This, too, has been reversed by time and technology. 'Everyone in Washington watches CNN and so do the editors in every news organization around the country,' notes Washington bureau chief Carl Leubsdorf of the *Dallas Morning News*. 'Its pervasiveness has reduced the amount of control each news organization can exercise over what gets into its paper or TV station; once a story has been live on CNN, it's much harder to argue that it shouldn't be in the paper, even if it has a questionable basis in fact.'

The broadcast networks' evening news programs of April 1998, however, had their own designs, which were not determined by either CNN or the insiders of Washington journalism. If the newspapers of 1998 were marginally different, but still recognisable, the Jennings–Brokaw–Rather programs bore little resemblance to the 1978 model. Compare, for instance, the story packages of the *CBS Evening News* on the two Tuesdays, twenty years apart, in my surveys, shown in Table 14.5.

CBS, is actually considered to have the most traditional of news values. The 'life-style' trend began at NBC, a subsidiary of General Electric, and is

Table 14.5 CBS Evening News' stories on two Tuesdays, two decades apart

Tuesday April 11, 1978	Tuesday April 21, 1998
(Washington) President Carter's speech, anti-inflation proposals	*(Washington)* Government rules on juice products that can make you sick
(Washington, Kansas) Reactions to proposals; energy bill in Congress	*(Los Angeles)* Government sues Microsoft; introduction of Windows 98
(Washington) Top USSR UN official Shevchenko disappears	*(Washington)* Auto engineers try to find ways to make sports' utility vehicles safer
(South Lebanon) Israeli plans for partial withdrawal	*(New York)* Viagra produces record profit for drug company
(North Carolina) Profile of 103-year-old woman	*(Washington)* Accusation of shoddy work at FBI crime lab
	(Boston) Strange tale of man who abducted his daughters
	(Florida) Concludes two-part series on dangerous drivers

credited with moving that network's evening news into the top-rated slot. Because the three network programs are now less committed to breaking news than in 1978, their daily menu of stories is more variegated. Defining and defending ABC's product at a meeting of television critics in July 1998, David Westin, its news division president, said his operation was pursuing 'deep' rather than 'hard' reporting. 'In a world of too much information, there is too little explanation,' he said. 'You can do hard news shallow and you can do soft news in depth . . . ' (Waxman 1998).

Deep or shallow reportage may be a matter of opinion, but there is no doubt that the networks and the national newsmagazines have been choosing soft over hard and are therefore using Washington correspondents in ways different from their 1978 usage. Washington newsmagazine covering stories of the modern era resemble 'Turning Fifty,' with a photograph of Hillary Clinton (*Time*), and 'The Young Kennedys: A Dynasty in Decline' (*Newsweek*). Soft is not synonymous with frivolous, but it can be dangerously close if journalists relax their guard.

In a moment of general prosperity, such as the United States is presently experiencing, it is easy for news organisations to ignore most of what Washington does and is expected to do, dismissing the grunt work of government as of interest only to unblooded academics. When the rates of inflation and unemployment rise again perhaps the media's attention will snap back to the purposes of governance. But there can be no excuse for America's mainstream media's ignoring the rest of the world. This declining attention is reaching the level of 'Stop the World, I Want to Get Off.' For instance, the percentage of space devoted to international news at the three newsmagazines was cut almost in half between 1985 and 1995. As Neil Hickey, editor at large of *Columbia Journalism Review*, concludes: 'The public is being drastically shortchanged in its capacity to learn what's going on in the world outside the US's borders' (Hickey 1998).

Veteran Washington journalists, when comparing then and now, almost always made observations about the changed technology of their craft:

- 'The wordprocessor makes articles practically write themselves, well, maybe not quite' (Rochelle Stanfield, *National Journal*);
- 'I get many of my story ideas from websites and do a large degree of reporting via email' (Marlene Cimons, *Los Angeles Times*);
- 'Everything of mine is edited on a laptop, I mean the actual sound waves, not just the words, and transmitted through the computer' (Pye Chamberlayne, UPI Radio).

Enthusiasm was sometimes tempered by the implications of the speeded up process. 'Here's an example,' says Carl Leubsdorf. 'In September 1978 I covered the Camp David Summit; it ended on a Sunday night. For Monday, I wrote a story about the end of the Summit and the outcome; for Tuesday,

I wrote a reaction story; for Wednesday, I wrote a political analysis. Today, we'd do all three in the first day's cycle.' AP's Walter Mears noted: 'There's not much time to think.' For those relieved of the dailiness of journalism, however, advances in technology were perceived as liberating. 'I don't miss the good old days of typewriters, paste pots and click-clacking teletypes,' muses Finlay Lewis of the Copley News Service.

More troubling is what some see as a changed attitude among Washington journalists. Martin Tolchin, a former *New York Times* reporter who now publishes *The Hill*, a weekly newspaper, expresses this concern:

> Pre-Watergate, pre-Vietnam, journalists basically assumed that public officials and others in authority were honest, competent, trustworthy, and cared about the interests of their constituents. Since then, in a change that continues to gather momentum, the basic journalistic assumption is the opposite: that public officials and those in authority are *per se* dishonest, incompetent, untrustworthy, and more interested in their own careers than in the problems of their constituents. . . . Of course, both approaches are wrong. They relieve journalists of having to do the necessary reporting to determine the quality of those they are covering.

Adds Tom Brazaitis: 'Why are we surprised when surveys show most Americans are cynical about politics? Hell, we're the cheerleaders of cynicism.'

Whatever the faults of the press corps, as seen by Washington veterans, they do not tend to place the blame on those who have come after them: 'The younger reporters are very much like our generation: eager, ambitious and perhaps as contemptuous of their older peers as we were,' says Lance Gay of Scripps Howard Newspapers. 'They are much more in tune with technology, but a little less experienced in the rookie street work we all used to have to go through, working police beats. . . . They are much better educated than we were, and more come into the business with journalism degrees. . . . I haven't done any scientific survey, but have the impression the younger generation is drawn from middle-class backgrounds, and fewer from the lower classes than in the past.'

The final word on how the reporters of two decades ago view those who will be their replacements belongs to Walter Mears, a former executive editor of the Associated Press: 'They certainly aren't funnier . . . and [are] less likely to be found sharing war stories in the bar after the day and night's work is done. Our humor was not lubricated with Perrier.'

NOTES

1 My original 1978 survey was of 396 Washington journalists, 65 of whom were still active in Washington journalism twenty years later. I wrote to the 'hardy survivors,' asking for their thoughts on how Washington journalism has changed, and my special thanks go to the sixteen who responded, with often detailed letters: Tom Brazaitis, Pye Chamberlayne, Marlene Cimons, Eleanor Clift, Ann Compton, Alan Emory, Lance Gay, George Gedda, Frank Greve, Monroe Karmin, Carl Leubsdorf, Finlay Lewis, Walter R. Mears, Robert Rankin, Rochelle Stanfield, and Martin Tolchin. Two of these journalists, inspired by my request for information, wrote newspaper columns as well: see Brazaitis, T. (1998) 'Reporting is better now – really,' *Cleveland Plain Dealer* (28 June): 2D; and Emory, A. (1998) 'Technology and news: changes in Washington,' *Watertown (New York) Times* (10 May): 2.

2 I wish to thank two interns for gathering and coding this material: Matthew Segal (Brandeis University) and Afshin Mohamadi (University of Michigan).

3 This differs markedly from how American newspapers choose news from other countries, which overwhelmingly comes from AP, regardless of the amount of excellent reportage they pay for from the *New York Times* News Service, the *Los Angeles Times–Washington Post* News Service, and other supplementals. See Hess, S. (1996) *International News & Foreign Correspondents*, Washington: Brookings.

REFERENCES

Egan, T. (1995) 'Triumph leaves no targets for conservative talk shows,' *New York Times* (January 1).

Hess, S. (1978) 'President and press: the boredom factor,' *Washington Post* (May 13).

—— (1981) *The Washington Reporters*, Washington, DC: Brookings Institution.

Hickey, N. (1998) 'Money lust,' *Columbia Journalism Review* (July/August): 32.

Robinson, T. S. (1992) 'A new direction at Newhouse,' *Quill* (April): 20–3

Rosten, L. C. (1937) *The Washington Correspondents*, reprinted 1974, Arno Press.

Pew Research Center (1998), News release, Washington, DC (June 8).

Smith T. J., S. R. Lichter and Louis Harris & Associates (1997) *What the People Want from the Press*, Washington, DC: Center for Media and Public Affairs.

Tunstall, J. (1970) *The Westminister Lobby Correspondents*, London: Routledge & Kegan Paul.

—— (1971) *Journalists At Work*, Beverly Hills, CA: Sage.

Tyndall Weekly Report (1998) New York (April 26).

Waxman, S. (1998) 'ABC News heralds shift in coverage,' *Washington Post* (July 17): 7.

15

NEWSPAPER POWER:
A PRACTITIONER'S
ACCOUNT

David Walker

This paper is offered in celebration by a practising journalist, a friend, collaborator (Tunstall 1977: 7; Tunstall and Walker 1981) and admirer of Jeremy Tunstall. Yet it falls to me to register failure. In his research career – productive even by the exacting latter-day standards of higher education's army of number-fixated auditors – Jeremy Tunstall must have interviewed many hundreds of journalists, in the electronic as well as print media, at home and abroad. Books such as *Journalists At Work* (1971) and *Television Producers* (1993) bespeak a detailed engagement with the work of media professionals and offer at least the beginnings of a critical conversation between two groups, journalists and social scientists, with much in common and much to learn from one another. If journalism is a kind of ethnography, all the more reason why its practitioners should warm to a student of their work, habitats and power structures.

There are strong reasons why journalists need the self-knowledge that comes from external norm and criterion referencing: as carriers and makers of 'culture', their truest accountability (see below) stems from their willingness to speak about their assumptions and values to the society that is the subject and object of their work. (A similar point could be made about social scientists: their performance as disseminators tells of their exercise of responsibility for and to the society they purport to study. The growing diminishing audibility and visibility of academic work as it retreats into the never-never land of peer-reviewed journals and esoteric monographs signals a sad retreat from that responsibility.)

Suffice it to say here that the conversation Jeremy Tunstall's work might have inaugurated never got going. Producers and editors opened their doors to him but the analyses he afterwards made they rarely chose to read let alone absorb in a bid to inform themselves about themselves. The academic literature of sociology, media studies or cognate disciplines nowadays goes almost entirely unread by journalists; meanwhile the exigencies of the modern academic and research career drive the two groups even further apart. 'Social knowledge', once blithely assumed to be a unity (Crawford and Perry 1976: 26), becomes a divided terrain which calls for the torches and compasses of a new kind of intermediary-guide (Haslam and Bryman 1994: 12).

Such 'crossover' literature as there is, for example the *British Journalism Review*, struggles for audience and impact: it is rarely on view in the newsrooms where I have worked. I – this is not an exercise in confession, merely an illustration – went with the flow to write editorials contemptuous of media studies (*Independent* 1996). Journalistic self-appraisal takes place – some might say to an excessive degree – but inside the pages of newspaper media sections or BBC review committees where critical self-reference is tightly controlled. The old principle of dog not eating dog (the name of a rubric above an anodyne column in the periodical *UK Press Gazette*) still largely holds. If there are more signs these days of criticism of one newspaper by another it is usually anonymised, citing proprietors rather than the editors and writers who carry out their bidding (with, in my experience, the minimum of hesitation or debate). The regular fare of media pages in the broadsheet newspapers where they appear is celebratory.

The exercise of 'investigative journalism' rarely extends to the relationships of journalists with each other, with politicians or proprietors. When 'Drapergate' broke in the summer of 1998 (*Observer* 5 July 1998) coverage of the suspicious dealings of lobbyists and politicians was sharp and voluminous; but the related ethical position of journalists in their dealings with politicians, special advisers and the corporate sector escaped attention. The irony of 'lobbying' alongside the existence of an institution called the Lobby (the association of newspapers and other media political specialists based at Westminster) was missed, and not for the first time (Cockerell, Hennessy and Walker 1984).

The absence of critical dialogue between journalists and students of their behaviour matters is because the nature of journalistic work has been changing, along with its norms and values (as of course have the nature and the values of British academic work), yet rarely have the tensions and losses of that course of change been registered in exchanges outside journalists' ranks. A group of people whose business is communication hardly ever communicate about themselves, at least, not in any disciplined and critical fashion. They certainly have no audience or interlocutors among those who make a professional study of media; they have become as unselfreflexive as the academics.

That is my cue for offering, here, the paradoxical observation that the 'power' of British metropolitan newspapers has held stable or even grown, while that of the journalists who produce them has declined, and that the (inarticulate) awareness of this dissonance can help explain the increasingly febrile and excitable tone of newspapers, thus allowing some access to the phenomenon of 'dumbing down' extensively written about in the United

States (Washburn and Thornton 1997), but in Britain the subject so far only of allusion and anecdote. It is, incidentally, also to take issue with the Golding and Elliot aphorism that 'news changes very little when the individuals that produce it are changed' (quoted in Curran and Seaton 1997: 277).

A brief biographical account may put these observations in context. I joined the *Times Higher Education Supplement* in 1973 (then owned by Thomson) and, after a Harkness Fellowship to the United States and two years at the *Economist*, was recruited to *The Times* in 1981 just after its takeover by Rupert Murdoch, to join a short-lived entity created by then editor Harold Evans and directed by his friend Bernard Donoughue, now Lord Donoughue of Roade. It was jocularly called 'the think-tank' – at a reception, new proprietor Murdoch's response, on being introduced to myself and colleague Peter Hennessy, was 'Do I pay you buggers to think?' In practice, it functioned as a features' 'hit squad', with Bernard Donoughue, who was also writing leaders, identifying gaps in coverage and organising writers to fill them. One project was a series of full-page profiles of Whitehall departments, Bernard sitting in on interviews with officials, some of whom he had worked with during his own years in the government machine with Prime Minister Harold Wilson and James Callaghan. With the departure of Harry Evans, the 'unit' folded (the tale of Evans' dismissal has become a classic; see Evans 1983). I survived to become local government correspondent and leader writer under the editorship of Charles Douglas-Home and, after his death in 1985, of Charles Wilson (for whom, against the odds, I became leader writer at the *Independent* some eleven years later). I contributed to the news pages under the by-line of social policy correspondent, later public administration correspondent, and following the departure of Peter Hennessy picked up his mantle as writer of a regular column, 'Whitehall brief'.

In 1986 *The Times* moved to Wapping in traumatic circumstances. I left the paper in the summer of 1986 to become, briefly, education correspondent of the *Daily Telegraph* then, in January 1987, chief leader writer of Robert Maxwell's short-lived venture in the capital's media market, the *London Daily News*. On its demise I returned to *The Times* and stayed there until being dismissed by Simon Jenkins, Charles Wilson's successor as editor, after writing an article critical of the way changes in the paper's editorial line had been handled (Walker 1990: 12). Later I contributed occasionally to the paper and edited its 'Public Management Page'. In 1996 I made a – surprise – return to *The Times*' features page as a bit-part player in a marital drama. *The Times* reprinted from the *Daily Mail* a diatribe from an aggrieved ex-wife about the other woman in her ex-husband's life. It was not the kind of article on which the historical reputation of the newspaper was founded; nor did the decision to run it exhibit any of those traditional editorial characteristics lovingly chronicled by *The Times*' latest official historian (Grigg 1993), as if newspaper identity were some sort of entelechy, managing to wing its way from one London location to another. After working on contract at the BBC as presenter of Radio 4's *Analysis* programme and as (bi-medial) urban affairs correspondent, and freelancing, I joined the *Independent* as leader writer (working for three different editors and two proprietorial regimes in just over two years) before moving, in 1998, to become editor of the 'Analysis Page' and leader writer at the *Guardian*. It is a chequered history which leads me to wonder whether 'journalistic career' is oxymoronic; it does, however, leave me with a good amount of participant-observational data on which to base the generalisations in this chapter.

In anticipation of my main argument, I offer these observations. The recent history of the British press could be written as a meditation on the influence on newspapers of two phenomena: television and Rupert Murdoch. Newspaper production has become a dialectic with what is reported on television (the category of reportage having been extended to include documentary, the 'cognitive' elements in soap opera and public affairs' discussions in chat shows); and the processes of influence from the one medium to the other are complicated, in Britain, by the growing cultural dependence of broadsheets on tabloids as guides to 'what people think', and so to tabloid response to television. What Castronovo and Tranfaglia say about Italy applies here when they talk about television's conquest of the imagination driving

> a large part of dailies and magazines not only to dedicate an ever greater attention . . . to television personalities and programmes, but also to seek to imitate the structure of relationship with readers and advertising typical of television, going so far as studying ways of combining or synergy between the printed page and television's rubrics.
>
> (Castronovo and Tranfaglia 1994: v)

Of course the relationship is two-way. British broadcasting, and not just at the BBC, is parasitical upon the newspaper press. Stories (in my experience as a correspondent) often do not exist for BBC newsdesks unless they have first appeared, and so been validated, in print; this is especially true of political reports. Television and radio talk is often cued by tabloid opinionating. Celebrity in television depends critically on newspaper reaction.

Murdoch is the other key, especially since his takeover of *The Times* in 1981. The lines of influence are both direct and indirect – directly through his personal command of the opinions expressed in a large segment of the metropolitan press, and indirectly through the copying of Murdoch styles of management and editorial decision making in competing newspapers. The conduct of David Montgomery, chief executive of Mirror Group Newspapers (and part owners of the *Independent* until 1998) owed much, in my judgement, to what he had learnt both as a Murdoch employee and his desire to emulate the tycoon. One manifestation was harshness and crudity in personnel decisions, coupled with pecuniary generosity, which had the effect of silencing criticism. Why has an excellent and clear-seeing columnist such as Andrew Marr drawn such a tight veil over his experience as the *Independent*'s editor under Mr Montgomery or (another fascinated copier of Murdochian style) Tony O'Reilly – experience which might be thought germane to Mr Marr's continuing commentaries on the state of British culture and politics? For a contemporary historian (which is what good journalists surely aspire to be) it might be considered a pressing obligation to add to the literature spawned by the launch of the *Independent* amid such high hopes (Garland 1990; Glover 1994) – not for sake of vanity or self-justification but to offer the public, in a spirit of reciprocity, access to the processes of journalistic production, the values and conduct of journalistic organisations. Mr Marr like his predecessor Ian Hargreaves, now a recruit to academe as a professor at the University of Wales at Cardiff, evidently consider discretion to be the better part of valour. But that choice of silence may leave the public under-informed in ways that no sociological investigation from outside, however assiduous, can fully supply.

True accountability relies on self-knowledge, and cognition in turn rests on a principle of difference: to tell a convincing tale about yourself to an external interlocutor is to start to give account. If Day and Klein are right, that accountability presupposes agreement about the language of justification to be used by actors in defending their conduct (Day and Klein 1987: 5), then the accountability of those whose business is the daily use and reshaping of the language itself becomes critical. Yet self-exculpation by journalists is rare, their memoirs more often taking the form of self-congratulation (Jameson 1989) than of institutional analysis or even disclosure. The memoirs of Murdoch offered by Andrew Neill (Neill 1996) are remarkable, not just in being produced so soon after Mr Neill's departure from the editorship of the *Sunday Times* but in being produced at all. Neill's account shows, in detail, the way Murdoch's worldview colours and shapes his newspapers; his contempt for British institutions and personalities, especially the journalists he employs. To produce widgets for a company the owner of which despises his workers might sound like a banal description of everyday capitalist economic organisation. But when the 'widgets' are judgements, facts, values and the voicing of 'public opinion', the situation looks more ominous.

What kind of culture informs the work of a journalist working for a proprietor who despises his journalists; what sort of resentments or deformations seep into the writing or editing process? A full chronicle of Murdoch's influence on the London press has yet to be written; the several tales of the 'remarkable rise of the best-selling soaraway *Sun*' are not it (Lamb 1989). Such an account would, of course, include the treatment of Murdoch's satellite television and sporting interests in his newspapers and the knock-on effects of *The Times*' pricing policy, as well as the much-discussed triangular relationship between Murdoch, successive British prime ministers and Murdoch's editors. If there is a 'professional crisis' among metropolitan journalists, their collective loss of cultural nerve stems in no small measure from Murdoch's political and commercial success, which in turn has as much to do with his fortuituous cultivation of Margaret Thatcher and the Tories as his insight into the taste of the newspaper-reading public (see Tunstall 1998: 7).

Jeremy Tunstall, with a scholar's cautiousness, hints that in general journalists are rarely willing to tell the 'whole story' about their work relationships (Tunstall 1996: 422). This 'tight-lipped British silence' is of course not confined to journalists. The professional practice of, for instance, academics is a closed book when it comes to the procedures adopted in marking student scripts or refereeing colleagues' work for grants or publication; it is noteworthy how, despite the efforts of Chelly Halsey, the sociology of academe remains underdeveloped (Halsey 1992: vi; 1996: 228). But the silence of journalists is all the more remarkable because of Murdoch's evident leverage in the politics of a country that considers itself a democracy and frowns on lobbying and other exercises of corporate persuasion on elected governments: here is a cadre of journalists, ostensibly wedded to truth-seeking and the policing of power, colluding in the manipulation of democratic politicians by a foreign potentate. It is not, of course, that Murdoch is immune to press criticism. At the *Independent* I spilled much ink in editorials savaging his power and pricing strategy. But such criticism is vitiated by a lack of honesty about one's own organisation. How many *Independent* journalists, myself included, ever wrote in their own newspaper about the effects of ownership by Mirror Group Newspapers? In the moral economy of modern British metropolitan newspapers a little transparency would go a very long way.

Two further and related observations are called for. Embourgeoisement did not detach Luton car workers from their collective organisations (Goldthorpe, Lockwood, Bechhofer and Platt 1968) but in newspapers material improvements do appear to have been purchased on a rising tide of individuality and declining collective identity. Dispersal from Fleet Street after the destruction of printing syndicalism in the 1980s has been the occasion for the widespread introduction of individual contracts and a readier self-identification by journalists of themselves as middle-class proponents of 'economic modernism' (i.e. the propositions that 'you cannot buck the markets', that income inequality is functional for the working of private enterprise, that direct taxation should be minimised). Newspaper management has grown in its capacity to command and control but – *pace* the cliches of antediluvian Marxism – the relative rewards of middle-ranking and senior journalists have also risen (especially *vis-à-vis* academics). Anecdotal evidence has senior journalists owning shares, company cars and second homes and educating their children in private schools with – it must be assumed – concomitant effects on their attitudinising. I became particularly aware of this on *The Times* in the later 1980s when privatisation was a big issue of public policy. Journalists started making exact calculations of their personal gains from share ownership, which was hardly likely to diminish the enthusiasm with which they wrote about privatisation (though given the predilections of Rupert Murdoch, their enthusiasm was guaranteed anyway). Declining membership of the National Union of Journalists is associated with growing uncertainty of employment and a nakedly authoritarian occupational culture.

Having worked until recently for a commercially precarious newspaper (is that tempting fate now I am at the *Guardian*?), I must beware of generalising, but it is a fair proposition that the daily working conditions of most metropolitan journalists have become 'tighter' in the sense that what they do and how they do it have become subject to closer inspection and alteration, also that their standing in their workplace has diminished. Editors come and go; departmental heads mill about – consultation and staff involvement is minimal. This is true not just in relation to personnel and resources. The 'authoritarian' nature of the editor's function seems to have grown. Even (perhaps that should be especially) on liberal-minded newspapers not only is the editor's word final but editorial whims go unchallenged. (The BBC offers a specific narrative of changes in power relationships between staff and management, at least during the tenure of Sir John Birt as director-general since 1992 and his prosecution of internal reorganisation on a 'rational' template. There, too, the growth of managerial prerogatives is paralleled by increasing editorial authoritarianism, though decisions at the BBC – it being still a classic bureaucratic structure – are rarely clear-cut.)

One result of recent change I would like to capture is the growing sense of alienation, even a refusal to acknowledge the common editorial project on a newspaper. *Alienation* is at one and the same time desperately imprecise as a description of psychological states and all too definite, given its Marxist provenance; there is, moreover, a tradition of citing alienation as a breeding ground for literary creativity, which might suggest that journalism gets better the more journalists consider themselves dispossessed. What I want to get at is the homology between the personal detachment of journalists from their newspapers as moral or cultural entities with a defining ethos (which I believe has grown) and the increase in their 'irresponsibility' – their cavalier criticism of persons and institutions, their refusal to see that public writing has consequences for individuals and collectivities, and the abandonment of self-reinforcing standards of grammar or factual accuracy. The claim '*The Times* has a special responsibility to maintain the standards of a philologically correct, unslovenly, and accurate English' (*The Times* 1953: Foreword) has a normative and cultural import – it says *The Times* knew itself in relation to its society and took upon itself the role of rule-setter. Such a claim could not nowadays be made with any plausibility, because *The Times* is so normatively compromised by Murdoch ownership. But the reason has also to do with the loss by its journalists of intellectual and moral capacity to attempt to order the society in which they live, because they no longer have any capacity to order their immediate environment as the despised employees of News International.

Recent years have seen the growth of 'internal segmentation' in newspapers with growing numbers of sections, edited separately. For example, the *Guardian* of Saturday 29 August 1998 counts as well as its news pages' separate section labelled Travel, Saturday, Jobs, Sports, Guide to Entertainments, Weekend and a synoptic presentation of other newspapers' coverage (called *The Editor*). Such a compendium cannot be edited in the traditional sense. The editor's role has become one of attending mostly to a limited number of pages, usually the 'front of the book'. This could appear to be something of a reaffirmation of traditional journalistic autonomy – section heads and their writers and process editors being left to get on with it. But this can, in my experience, increase the sense of non-commitment, non-belonging, of distance from the ostensible central values of the newspaper. The result is normative incoherence, noticeable especially in those newspapers which espouse a strong political line, such as the *Daily Mail*. The paper's views on gender relations, the sanctity of the family and the iniquity of popular entertainments are not upheld in its sections addressing women, young people, etc. There is, to be sure, nothing new about internal competition within newspapers for space, editorial patronage or budgets. Newspaper management never was an exact science; it is noteworthy how 'under-theorised' newspaper management remains compared with editorial direction at the BBC. What may be new is the detachment of the journalists from their newspaper as a unified enterprise, thanks to the individualisation of their contracts of employment. The result is the growth of a culture of editorial irresponsibility.

'Newspaper power' can in theory be caught in a number of dimensions, on politics, public opinion, culture, consumption and, as Paul Mosley (1984) showed, on business and economic policy, too. Yet practical demonstrations of that power are few, perhaps as Jeremy Tunstall notes (1996: 422) because of the secretive way in which, for example, the press–politics relationship is conducted. The passage of time helps. Peter Hennessy usefully turned the phenomenon on its head by citing a series of 1940s' examples of what the press never said (Hennessy 1985) and Richard Cockett studied the conduct of one newspaper during the Suez crisis (1991: 9). Suffice it to say here that any narrative of contemporary British history that neglected the influence of newspapers on political destiny would be seriously adrift. It would be uncontroversial to say the media are powerful, in terms, say, of newspapers' influence on the agenda of public policy debates, the tone of political discourse, the shaping of collective decision making. But my argument rests on the specific proposition that the 'power' of newspapers has grown or, at its weakest, has remained strong in a context of institutional delegitimation or self-questioning. If politics and the professions are, to put it bluntly, up for grabs in an iconoclastic age, why not journalism? The answer is what Pierre Bourdieu (1996: 25) pejoratively calls the capacity of journalists to enforce 'closure . . . mental banging-up', preventing the media becoming a subject of critical discussion in the same way as, say, schools, hospitals, corporate boardrooms or the cabinet. Whatever the opinion polls say about journalists' standing in the scales ranking various jobs, cultural prestige continues to attach to metropolitan journalism – albeit prestige generated by self-same metropolitan journalists commanding the means of conversation. Perhaps the attractiveness of media studies courses (whatever newspapers may say about them) rests in part on the perception of young people that journalism and its cognates in public relations and advertising is invulnerable – the arrogance of the practitioners to whom they are exposed on television and in print is inviting.

But my argument is that this perceived autonomy is diminishing. Individual journalists have less discretion as they write for or produce national newspapers. (And this is in spite of the plethora of columnists. Columnists' freedom is constrained by their pigeonholing. Their expression of opinion is predictable. *The Times* did not recruit Melanie Phillips in 1998 to laud the teaching profession; Janet Daley in the *Daily Telegraph* knows her employability correlates with her reactionary prejudices.) For newspaper journalists at large the mid-1980s was the watershed. Andrew Neill's account of his takeover of the *Sunday Times* in 1983 (Neill 1996: 49) captures the new dispensation. He has his managing editor count column inches produced – an anticipation, academics might observe, of their own research assessment exercises. The commodification of journalism has been aided and abetted by the introduction of information technology (though, as in all complex systems, the enlisting of computers to strengthen management depends on the cleverness of controllers, and cleverness in newspaper management is a quality in short supply).

The importance of the cash nexus grows. Loyalty to title diminishes. This is important when titles continue to be distinguished by their political leanings: if journalists start to move on freely upon the production a chequebook, what does that imply about their capacity to adapt personal political preferences to the prevailing climate? One result is a growing sameness in British metropolitan journalism, not just the same stories and opinions but the same kinds of treatment and language. Bourdieu asserts that there is a structural tendency in journalism towards homogenization (1996: 23); it has grown in Britain over the past two decades, partly as a result of London journalism's changing sociology. Yet it's a raucous sameness. Newspapers have always shouted, at least since the Edwardian revolution in style associated with Northcliffe. But lately it's not so much volume as tone that has coarsened. Tabloid habits – the perennial sneer, the rush to judgement, the substitution of reaction for reflection – have become noticeable in the broadsheets.

Two linked processes seem to be operating. As they lose self-confidence within their organisations, so journalists compensate by (figuratively) shouting louder. This is partly 'look at me' journalism, a message addressed to potential alternative employers. It is also a bid at self-reaffirmation, hoping that a bludgeoned reader can be a source of psychological–occupational validation.

This loss of confidence has to do with the way metropolitan journalism has during the past two decades 'lost touch' with its societal and cultural moorings: to do, perhaps, with their embourgeoisement, with growing cultural 'distance' between London and the rest of Britain, with alterations in the map of political geography summarised by the rise, first, of Thatcherism, then by the triumph of Blair, journalists are bereft.

Much has been made of how the newspapers were 'caught short' by the public response to the death of Diana, Princess of Wales, in 1997, how they desperately rushed to catch up with a public opinion over which they had no control nor even a means of ascertainment (which is certainly how it felt on the *Independent* in the week following the death). The same, however, could have been said in less colourful terms about the way the national newspaper press misconceived the political circumstances which carried Tony Blair to power in May 1997: it was not only the rightward bias of the press that robbed them of perspicuity. The advent of focus groups and the strenuous attempts to consult existing and potential readers have not, it seems, been a ready substitute for the taken-for-granted relationship that once seemed to obtain (though, if it did, it did not stop national newspapers declining in circulation). The upshot is that metropolitan journalism is at sea. It has lost a sense of its readership's, hopes and prejudices – and this is true even on the *Daily Mail* which, during 1998, improved its circulation without pricing gimmicks.

Is it going too far to label this a 'professional crisis'? Yes, since national newspaper journalists do not constitute a profession in the sense of controlling entry or maintaining disciplined norms of conduct. But something is amiss. It shows both in the coarsening of tone mentioned above and also in the retreat from intellectual or cultural standards. No longer even pretending to know their readers – this point applies especially to the broadsheets – journalists pander. The very idea of authority enforcing objective standards of language use or professional practice speaks its anachronism: squeezed by commercial and editorial authority within the newspaper organisation, it is as if journalists yearn for (vindictive) anarchy in their work. Their power, newspaper power, gets wielded insensitively, arrogantly. A Freudian might draw an analogy between the behaviour of a child who, oppressed at home, misbehaves outside (and there remains something juvenile, if not actually childlike, about the journalistic temperament). But that analogy falls down because the misbehaving child knows right from wrong. In the 'professional crisis' of modern British newspapers, the means of affirming norms of good conduct have long been decaying. External 'ethical' conversation of the kind offered over the past thirty or so years by students of journalism such as Jeremy Tunstall, which might have helped build up self-awareness as a building block of self-policing standards, has been rejected.

REFERENCES

Bourdieu, P. (1996) *Sur la télévision*, Paris: Liber.

Castronovo, V. and N. Tranfaglia (eds) (1994) *La Stampa Italiana nell'età della TV 1975–1994*, Bari: Editoria Laterza.

Cockerell, M., P. Hennessy and D. Walker (1984) *Sources Close to the Prime Minister*, London: Macmillan.

Cockett, R. (1991) 'The *Observer* and the Suez crisis', *Contemporary Record* 5 (1).

Crawford, E. and N. Perry (eds) (1976) *Demands for Social Knowledge*, London and Beverly Hills: Sage.

Curran, J. and J. Seaton (1997) *Power Without Responsibility*, London and New York: Routledge.

Day, P. and R. Klein (1987) *Accountabilities*, London and New York: Tavistock.

Evans, H. (1983) *Good Times, Bad Times*, London: Weidenfeld & Nicolson.

Garland, N. (1990) *Not Many Dead*, London: Hutchinson.

Glover, S. (1994) *Paper Dreams*, London: Penguin.

Goldthorpe, J. H., D. Lockwood, F. Bechhofer and J. Platt (1968) *The Affluent Worker: Industrial Attitudes and Behaviour*, Cambridge: Cambridge University Press.

Grigg, J. (1993) *The History of* The Times. *The Thomson Years 1966–81*, London: Times Books.

Halsey, A. H. (1992) *Decline of Donnish Dominion*, Clarendon Press: Oxford.

—— (1996) *No Discouragement*, Basingstoke and London: Macmillan.

Haslam, C. and A. Bryman (eds) (1994) *Social Scientists Meet the Media*, London and New York: Routledge.

Hennessy, P. (1985) *What the Papers Never Said*, London: Portcullis Press.

Independent (1996) 'How not to be a journalist' (31 October).

Jameson, D. (1989) *Touched by Angels*, London: Penguin.

Lamb, L. (1989) *Sunrise*, London: Macmillan.

Mosley, P. (1984) *The Making of Economic Policy*, Brighton: Harvester.

Neill, A. (1996) *Full Disclosure*, London: Macmillan.

The Times (1953) *Style Book*, London: The Times.

Tunstall, J. (1971) *Journalists at Work*, London: Constable.

—— (1977) *The Media are American*, London: Constable.

—— (1993) *Television Producers*, London: Routledge.

—— (1996) *Newspaper Power*, Oxford: Clarendon Press.

—— (1998) 'The prime minister–media mogul policy connection', unpublished paper for International Association for Media and Communication Research, Political Communication Section, University of Strathclyde.

—— and D. Walker (1981) *Media Made in California*, New York: Oxford University Press.

Walker, D. (1990) 'Follow my leader', *The Listener*, 123 (3158).

Washburn, K. and J. Thornton (eds) (1997) *Dumbing Down. Essays in the Strip Mining of American Culture*, New York and London: W.W. Norton & Co.

16

THE PRINT JOURNALIST, UK AND AFRICA

Rex Winsbury

FLEET STREET

Jeremy Tunstall was and doubtless still is fascinated by journalists, what they do and how they do it, without seeking to impose some sociological theory on what he discovered about this amorphous trade at whose workbench I have slaved (I use the term advisedly – see below) most of my life. In my time in Fleet Street – at a time when it *was* Fleet Street – I used to try to enlighten him about the quaint Spanish customs by which journalists went about their secretive business, at least in my branch of what some call a profession, but which I still doubt qualifies for that name.

Jeremy used then, as a good researcher, to try to check my allegations with other journalists in the same branch (industrial journalism, a typical Fleet Street euphemism for trades union reporting, in a now-forgotten era when trade unions were front page news). Mostly, they denied all knowledge of such practices, for fear that their trade secrets would leak out and their livelihood be threatened. So Jeremy often could not put those practices into print in his several excellent and, at the time, ground-breaking books about journalists. Those practices may have vanished with the people who practised them (or perhaps not, I don't know). But if you agree that journalism, whether print or electronic, sets some sort of social agenda, then *how* that agenda is set, matters.

One typical example was the way that the hard core of industrial specialists from different newspapers used to club together in groups, and within each group of say, two or three newspapers they would share out the often boring chore of phoning up trades union officials in the early evening and then pool the results in time for their stories in the first edition. Then, when the first editions were published, the very first copies off the press immediately circulated by courier to all the other national newspaper offices (mostly only yards away, of course), there to be scrutinised and where necessary used as feedstock for catch-up stories if there was something you had missed. Thus was the news *homogenised* as the evening wore on, so that by the time that the all-important London editions were printed (the first edition usually vanished to Scotland or abroad, which didn't really count), there was a remarkable unanimity in what the papers presented as having been yesterday's events.

The essential point was not that this was necessarily a true account, or the sole possible account, or necessarily a complete account, let alone a fair one. No, the key was that all the newspapers should say more or less the same thing. The one exception to this informal rule was that if you had a really good scoop, you were allowed to reserve it for your later editions, when it was too late for others to copy it – it was dignified with the name 'follow-up' – without ruining your co-operative arrangements with the newspapers with which you were supposed, in newspaper theory, to be in competition.

This practice was not exactly conspiracy theory at work. It was essentially defensive in purpose. If your story was attacked or challenged from outside (say, by the subject of your story daring to deny your version) and you had to justify it to your editor or proprietor (see below), you could at least defend yourself by saying 'Well, all the other papers had the same', so there must be something in it, mustn't there?

The converse of this was that the key test of a story was not whether it was true, but whether it could be disproved. It was a negative test. You searched your first draft of a story for facts or figures or statements that might make you vulnerable to a come-back. How bullet-proof was the story? Many were the semi-fictitious sources or 'experts' conjured up to give apparent authority to statements or opinions that you believed to be true but from which you wished to distance yourself, just in case. . . . Yet on the other hand, as any good researcher like Jeremy Tunstall knows, truth is an elusive quarry, if indeed it exists at all, and perhaps it was the best that could be done. These memories come to me on the still-frequent occasions when my work takes me down Fleet Street, now truly a 'Street of Shame', whose derelict or city-fied offices are in morose contrast to the heady days when, as a final-year student, I first trod the hallowed paving stones of 'The Street' and swore that, one day, I too would enter this nirvana of print and prestige.

I have often paused outside what we called 'The Black Lubyanka', a reference to the once–notorious KGB prison and interrogation centre in Moscow (now renamed). We meant, of course, that gleaming but sinister black between-the-wars glass monster that housed the Beaverbrook empire, notably the Daily Express and its Sunday stable-mate, once the archetype of brilliantly reactionary journalism and autocratic proprietorship, complete with Crusader and Sword, more recently a sad abandoned hulk awaiting demolition, covered in half-torn flyposters and traffic grime. The shattered visage of Ozymandias, indeed.

But what *was* it all about? What did we stand for in the great days of Fleet Street, once the biggest centre of newspaper activity on earth, exemplar to the world of a so-called free press? Standing and staring at the abandoned fortress of a now forgotten Fleet Street barony, I reflect that I too worked, not for one, but for two of the world's newspaper barons, in widely different places and at widely different times: one in Fleet Street, the other in Africa. In certain key respects, the experiences were much the same, and in those respects, they were not very impressive evidence for the theory of a free press. In other respects, they were profoundly different, and in those respects, they pointed up the enabling role of a vigorous press (and, where and when appropriate, television) in sustaining or creating a pluralistic society, whether in industrialised or emerging economies, and the benefit of having press proprietors with enough financial muscle to stand apart from government. This is a deliberately modest claim – an 'enabling role' is not a phrase that theories of democracy generally use, and newspaper barons are often portrayed as villains. But the role is an important role, to be ranked alongside of (but not superior to) elimination of poverty, education, good health and justice, as hallmarks of a society in which centres of power are more or less accountable to the general population. Quite why the players of this enabling role are to this day often autocratic and idiosyncratic individuals rather than, say, journalistic co-operatives, is still to me something of a mystery. But I have concluded, most particularly on the basis of my time in Africa, which I describe below, that in an imperfect world where the balance of domestic power is the key issue, it is far better that they play it, than that it is not played at all. But then, I would say that, wouldn't I, having worked for two of them?

Let me begin with two anecdotes that may both amuse and illuminate the quandary. Each concerns one of the two newspaper barons for whom I worked.

Anecdote 1

I joined the *Daily Telegraph* in London as a junior industrial reporter, still starry-eyed, after a two years' apprenticeship at the *Financial Times* (to which I later thankfully returned). It was an astonishing experience, not just because of the dust that lay thickly over piles of yellowing files, not just because the deputy news editor took me aside after my third week there and taught me how to fabricate my expenses claims (so as 'not to let the side down, you understand'), and not because after two years we parted company by mutual (dis)agreement. Rather, it was the shock of working inside an unadulterated autocracy.

Every morning (it was the 1960s) the grand proprietor, Lord Hartwell, otherwise known as 'Mr Michael' (i.e. Michael Berry), would summon the editor into his presence, and go through that morning's paper in fine detail, comparing it to the other papers, criticising and demanding follow-ups, new stories, elaborations or whatever. The editor, hardly the august figure that theory demands, took all this down in short-hand, and it was later transcribed onto an endless roll of paper rather like a white lavatory–roll. This was then snipped up by the news editor, item by item, into small slivers of paper, on which he wrote the name of the journalist who should deal with each item. Each sliver of paper was then put into a small dirty brown envelope, and arrived on the desk of the luckless journalist as he reported for work in the morning, around 10.30 a.m.

There was no challenging the instructions on these slips of paper. They were the word of god, and no amount of protest to the editor or the news editor would do any good. Useless to say 'Done it before' or 'There's no story there'. The response was: 'Sorry, old chap, the boss wants it.'

It kept us on our toes. We lived in dread of these missives. The *Telegraph* was and is justly famous for the breadth of its news. No doubting the effectiveness (then anyway) of this autocratic approach to news management, not dissimilar to Lord Beaverbrook's next door at the 'Black Lubyanka', except that Beaverbrook used the telephone, mostly, rather than shards of paper. My one direct encounter (or rather, near-miss) with the god upstairs came when I had a phonecall summoning me instantly to the top floor from which Hartwell ruled his fiefdom. Having survived the uniformed commissionaire who, Cerberus-like, guarded the foyer to his master's lair, I was shown into an empty room, a bag of nerves. No sign of anyone, let alone His Lordship. I fidgeted.

Then a pair of double doors opened, and there appeared one of the smallest men I have ever seen in Europe, outside of the old feudal estates of southern Italy, dressed in black trousers and a frock coat. He was evidently the butler. He said: 'Mr Michael would like to know . . .'. I forget exactly what it was, but it doesn't matter, I gave the answer, and the little man retreated back behind the double doors. After a short time, he reappeared and said 'Mr Michael would also like to know . . .'. Again I gave the answer. He again retreated, only to reappear a third time and say: 'Thank you, that will be all', and I was dismissed. I didn't see Mr Michael, not then or ever.

Anecdote 2

The other autocrat I worked for, this time in Africa, I saw often, and in the eyes of some, he really was a god, not just a man behaving like one. He was the Aga Khan, the country was Kenya and the newspaper was *The Nation*. I was there in the 1980s. To the devout Ismaelis who worked for him, the Aga Khan, whatever his mortal and colourful parentage, was some sort of a deity, repository of both the central beliefs and the central finances of the Ismaeli community. He was an active, urbane and thoughtful man (if man he was), whose ideals and ambitions I admired and still admire. Otherwise, I would not have worked for him.

He was also a major owner of racehorses – some 450 when I was a lowly employee of his – and no one ever dared to dispute his wishes. Perhaps churlishly, I found it hard to address him as 'Your Highness' as everyone else did, and resorted to the good old English 'Sir', which may or may not have contributed to the fact that, after four years or so, I parted company with this employer also. Or maybe it is that, however hard I try. I can't work for autocrats indefinitely.

One of my major tasks in Kenya was to try to get a new building constructed to accommodate The Nation Group (for more about that, see below). To get it built and financed meant dealing with several financial institutions in Kenya that, unlike *The Nation*, were purely Ismaeli – managed and run by shrewd but strict followers of the faith. So when a fax or telegram would arrive from the Aga Khan's headquarters, at Aiglemont outside of Paris (next to a major racecourse, of course), the wording was pored over, debated, interpreted but never questioned, as if it were (as it was to them) an edict from god, treated with much the same reverence as were Lord Hartwell's bits of paper twenty-odd years before.

I felt fairly certain that the messages were drafted by a secretary or, at best, by one of the several non-Ismaeli lieutenants who manned the headquarters: so hardly the word of deity. But my view was without weight. He had spoken, and it was for us to obey. And obey they did, with great ingenuity.

In the case of the new building, they were required to do two things that could have been mutually contradictory. One was to build a grand prestige building that would win international acclaim for its design (the Aga Khan, apart from racehorses, is keen on architecture). The other was to maintain a strict business plan that over time yielded a clear financial pay-back on the project: it is an Ismaeli axiom that business is business.

What struck me very forcibly was that every time some new embellishment or other cost (e.g. marble facing) was added to the building, they would never challenge it as endangering the pay-back, but would re-do the business plan with new and larger numbers and still show a respectable pay-back. This repeated itself many times. I cannot say whether the spreadsheets were right or wrong: I do not know. But it reminded me that figures are more elastic than statisticians would have us believe.

All that is by way of a preface, though I hope an informative one, to the serious question of what the Kenyan newspaper was for, at that time in that country in Africa, and whether it bore any relation to western theories of the press.

THE PRESS IN KENYA

Unusually at that time, the mid-1980s, Kenya had three competing national newspapers, of which two were independent of the government. Unusual, because the normal situation in post-colonial post-independence Africa, where one-party states and one-man rule were the norm, was that there was only one national newspaper, owned and published by the government, just as the local radio and TV station was government-owned and operated. In other words, the media were one arm and the mouthpiece of the ruling (and only legal) political party. The theory behind this, if there was any theory other than the dynamic of absolute power, was that the overriding cause of national development and nation building did not permit a plural, critical and potentially divisive press, but instead demanded that the press play its part in mobilising the people's efforts behind the nationalist government.

Kenya was, however, different, for reasons embedded in its history and industrial structure. There were three daily titles on sale. First, there was *The Standard*. Founded in the 1920s, this had been the newspaper of the white (mainly British, but also South African) settlers in pre-independence days, and was for long the only newspaper in Kenya. By the 1980s, however, it was owned by the multinational company Lonrho, and Lonrho had extensive business interests in Kenya and all over Africa, in hotels, the motor trade, agriculture, mining and elsewhere, under its charismatic and controversial founder and boss 'Tiny' Rowland who, just like an African chief, ran the company as a personal fiefdom. Lonrho clearly had plenty of non-newspaper commercial interests to protect – interests that, in their turn, served to protect the newspaper. The content of *The Standard* in the 1980s still reflected a predominantly white readership.

Then there was the *Kenya Times*. This had started as a private venture in the hands of, probably, Kenya's best-known journalist, Hilary N'gweno, a Kenyan, but had not prospered. So it was taken over by Kanu, the ruling and sole political party, and became in the 1980s a mouthpiece for both party and government. Like many other such publications, it veered a bit uneasily between its official role and the need to compete in a three-cornered fight for readers, and so Kanu searched around for a solution to this difficulty, of which more below.

Third, there was *The Nation*, for which I worked for some four years. This had been founded by the Aga Khan (leader of the Ismaeli community) in the 1960s, around the time of Kenya's independence but initially with a mainly white staff recruited from Britain, as a gift to the newly independent Kenya, to give the newly enfranchised African population its own voice, and as a contribution to the country's political and social development. The Aga Khan had and has extensive other interests in Kenya, such as hotels, manufacturing enterprises, hospitals, schools, banking and insurance. The founding of *The Nation* was also said by many – and I have no reason either to believe or disbelieve this – to have been a shrewd move to protect these interests and the interests of the substantial Ismaeli community in Kenya, by demonstrating its commitment to the country and to its progress. But *The Nation* was not in any other sense an Ismaeli institution. Over the years, the initially white staff trained and gave way to a predominantly Kenyan African staff, so that by the mid-1980s there were only half-a-dozen white faces still to be seen.

So each of the three daily titles published from Nairobi had a distinctive, colourful and still potent history. The obvious common feature of all three was that they were published in the English language. The language situation in Kenya was complex. The official national language was Swahili, as also in neighbouring Tanzania, for example. This was because, after the bitter struggle for independence, the Kenyan African nationalists could not stomach the idea of retaining English as the official language (although India had done). But Swahili was really a coastal language, not widely spoken in the interior; it was regarded as a 'kitchen language' and also as the language of populist political discourse. All commercial and official business was conducted in English, and of course Kenyans needed English to communicate and do business with the outer world. On top of that, all Kenyan Africans spoke their local tribal language – Kikuyu, Luo, etc. – since like most African countries many different tribes lived within and across its (British-made) borders.

This meant that, on the one hand, all Kenyans of any status had to speak three languages before they even left the country and, on the other hand, there was a drive to acquire and speak English because of the status it implied, and English was inevitably the common language of people who could read and wanted to follow events. As a result, there were Swahili-language newspapers, two of them, but they were poor relations of the English-language press, with many fewer pages, yesterday's news (being translations from English), and were seen mainly 'in the kitchen'.

What was the press for?

Thus the English language press had at least four roles to play in Kenyan society, deriving from this unusual historical background. First, it kept alive the idea of a press that was independent of government, in a continent where that was very unusual. Second, it demonstrated (or tried to) the virtues of a plural, and so competitive, press as a mechanism for arriving at something like the truth. Third, in a country where the rate of illiteracy at that time was still high, it tried to sustain and improve the standard of English-language usage, and to sustain the drive towards literacy generally, even though the journalists' grasp of English at that time was far from perfect. Even for many of the literate classes, reading a newspaper would be the only reading done after leaving school or college. Fourth – but this was a hidden agenda at that period – it was itself in the business of survival, against the day when multi-party politics would be restored to Kenya and a free press could play its full part in a new and more democratic dispensation (a day which, at the time of writing, is nearer but has hardly arrived).

The total circulation of the English-language press was not large compared to the population of the country – perhaps 400,000 copies a day, for a country of nearly 20 million people. But copies were passed from hand to hand, and read out to groups in shops, bars and private houses. The 'reach' was much greater than circulation might indicate. And, of the three papers *The Nation* was by a wide margin the biggest selling, at around 200,000 copies a day. As market leader, it had special responsibility, both commercially and politically. The party-owned *Kenya Times* trailed behind the other two.

It is to be noted here that in the privatisation and democratisation programme that has sputtered through Africa during the 1990s, mainly but not only at the behest of the World Bank and the other major international donors of aid and support funds, the hiving off of the press and TV away from government control has been one of the key objectives. It has not been exactly a universal success, but technology, in the form of satellite delivery of trans-border TV signals, may gradually be succeeding where political pressure has only partially succeeded. Nevertheless, it has long been recognised that in a country with a poorly developed political life, with a dominant political party that retains a near-monopoly of power, and with few other strong institutions to counter-balance the power of the executive, a strong newspaper may be the best, indeed only, effective opposition to the party in power.

In principle, the media infrastructure for a more democratic polity was already there, in Kenya, at least in the press, and it was our job in the 1980s to preserve it. It is an irony that we could do so only because we were owned and supported (for wider reasons than just the independence of the press) by two international businessmen-turned-press-barons. Even so, it was not an easy task, not least because of the unexpected intervention of yet a third international press baron.

The Maxwell factor

Not long after my arrival in Kenya in 1986, there was a political rally in the main football stadium in Nairobi, at which President Daniel arap Moi spoke in Swahili, as he always did, being more at home in that language. The official English-language version of his remarks (often at odds with what he actually said) contained nothing untoward. But the photographers remarked that there was an unknown Englishman sitting next to him. Only on the day after did we ask his name, and see the photos. Our blood froze. It was – surely it couldn't be, but yes, it was – Robert Maxwell. What on earth was he doing there?

Maxwell had formed a commercial alliance with the *Kenya Times*, under which he undertook to revive its still ailing fortunes and promote it as a (the?) leading publication in Kenya. Why did he do that? It has remained a mystery – but, then, so much of what Robert Maxwell did was a mystery. The best guess was that he hoped to pick up lucrative state printing contracts, for example, for school books. But the most obvious sign of the Maxwell intervention was the arrival, some months later, of a reconditioned offset printing press at the *Kenya Times* (said to have been surplus to requirements in Mexico) and of various ex-*Daily Mirror* staff, reconditioned or otherwise, to help run and write the newspaper.

So the fight was on, between three famous non-Kenyan international media barons, for supremacy of a tiny but prestigious newspaper market, each of them with other parallel agendas.

In the circumstances, President Daniel arap Moi saw little reason to make life easy for the rest of the press, and he did not. Periodically, in his public speeches, he would depart from his official script to deliver an attack (in Swahili) either on 'the foreign-owned press' for its 'interference' in Kenyan's internal affairs, or he would particularly single out *The Nation*, as market leader, for special criticism. This was not just routine politicking. Control of the press can be done by means other than official censorship.

The Achilles' heel of *The Nation*, as of the other papers, was import licences. Everything that the newspaper needed in order to publish – reasonable quality newsprint, since the local stuff was poor and kept breaking; ink; spares for existing presses and other machinery; new machinery – had to be imported, and that meant import licences, to be obtained from the relevant government department, where our demand for import licences competed with other licence applications for scant foreign currency.

A hostile speech by the president was the perfect excuse for civil servants to relegate our licence applications to the bottom of the in-tray. As a result, we alternated between boom and bust in our newsprint store. When we could, we built up a large supply of newsprint in the warehouse, perhaps three months' worth, a far larger tying-up of company funds than a western newspaper company would tolerate. On the other hand, we were often down to a few days' supply, when licences, and so imports, had failed to materialise in time, and faced not being able to publish at all.

But it must also be recorded that we never failed to publish. In short, the regime played cat and mouse with us. This was apparent in other ways. Journalists, photographers and distributors were sometimes arrested by the police, and Kenyan prisons were very unpleasant places. But this did not happen frequently. Less easy to quantify was the virtual hot-line that existed between the editor and the president or his entourage.

That the president did personally telephone the editor, and if not the president, then a close associate of his, was not doubted. What we did not know was how often, or what was said, or what influence this had on the content of the newspaper. The editor said this was a private matter – and with some reason, for he was between a rock and a hard place. On the one hand, he was supposed to produce a newspaper that answered to western criteria of independent news reporting and freedom of the press. On the other hand, he had to ensure that the newspaper stayed out of serious trouble, not least because it was generally assumed (though I never heard this from the Aga Khan himself) that the boss did not want trouble at *The Nation* to rub off onto his other interests in Kenya.

In the context of a virtual political dictatorship, this was an impossible task and, hardly surprisingly, the occupant of the editor's chair changed every so often. But then what's so new about that? As if all this were not enough, there was a further threat to the survival of the press in the form of the capacity of *The Nation* to print itself, and that is where I came in.

The technology trap

I should make it clear that I had no editorial function. Indeed, I was specifically warned to stay away from editorial matters. For one thing, the time for expat white journalists to be writing for a black readership was long past. There was a white training editor who attempted to improve standards of English and of reporting, and a white adviser to the editor; one was Australian, the other Irish, so I suppose they were more politically acceptable, as fellow ex-colonials.

For another thing, it was alleged that a recent predecessor of mine had been forced by the government to leave the country at short notice, after he had 'interfered' in editorial matters. I say *alleged* because rumour was more prevalent than fact in Kenya at that time, one more product of curtailed media. My role was both more mundane and more fundamental: it was to plan, and at least begin, a total overhaul of the company's physical assets. When *The Nation* was founded in the 1960s, it brought in what was then the latest and best newspaper technology. But that was twenty years or more earlier than my time and little had been done in the meantime to keep up with the technological revolution that overtook the newspaper industry worldwide in the 1970s and 1980s.

As a result, *The Nation*, like many newspapers in Africa, was in perpetual production crisis. The once-innovative but now obsolete paper tape-driven photo-typesetting system was continually breaking down. The film and plates for offset printing were messy and the equipment old. The presses needed constant attention, aggravating the problems of using (as we often had to) locally made poor quality newsprint. Spare parts were hard to get, and might not even be made any more. The whole enterprise was housed in a converted bakery with a tin roof. And there was no capacity to expand circulation, let alone introduce colour. In short, the whole enterprise needed a total overhaul of its physical infrastructure if the newspaper was to go on publishing – and that in a context of severe external difficulties.

One of the key facts about renewing newspaper plant is that you cannot just shut down for a week or a month, as most other industries can, while the new gear is wheeled in and tested. The newspaper would lose too much money (and too much circulation to rivals) by not appearing every day. So production must be uninterrupted.

There was another, less tangible, factor but one that frequently confronts investors in developing countries. What level of technology do you bring in? In many but not all such countries, if you bring in the very latest, leading-edge stuff there is unlikely to be the skilled staff and specialist supplies needed to maintain and upgrade it. But there is little point in laying out good money for obviously obsolete equipment, and local pride will not allow you to do it. So, in a fast-moving industry, you need proven robust equipment that is demonstrably modern but needs little upkeep.

And you have to pay for it, in scant foreign currency. Here we were fortunate to find USAID (the foreign-aid arm of the US government) prepared to lend $1 million dollars on a back-to-back arrangement, whereby (in effect) USAID paid for the equipment in hard currency and the equivalent sum in (non-convertible) local currency was made available for local aid projects. It meant that we had to buy American, which in an ex-British colony was a pity, but it got us a new computerised typesetting system as the first stage in an almost total overhaul of the basic assets that then extended to cameras, platemaking, new units for the press and a brand new European-designed building that now graces the streets of Nairobi. All this took time, and was not completed until well after I left Kenya, four years after my arrival there.

A verdict

Was it all worth it? Ten years on, President Daniel arap Moi is still in office as president of Kenya. As I write, he is intriguing with his former political enemies to stay in power into the foreseeable future. He is a wily and wealthy politician. Now there are legal opposition parties, which there were not in the 1980s, and political debate is much freer. But Kenya can hardly be said to be a democracy yet, with the same party still in power since its independence. But it could be getting there. The economy is not in a good state, and like most of the rest of Africa Kenya has to contend with the HIV/AIDS epidemic which is knocking out people in the productive age-groups.

On the other hand, apart from the short-lived *coup d'etat* in the early 1980s, it has so far avoided the bloody tribal civil wars that have devastated some other African countries, and its record on political detainees is not as awful as it was. In the new climate, *The Nation* has become much more outspoken than it used to be. It is not the fault of the press that the new opposition parties in Kenya are so fragmented that they have been unable to unite to oust President Moi.

I believe that the plural and independent press which somehow survived in Kenya through the difficult years, however circumscribed it may have been, played an important part in gradually loosening up the political structure of the country and enabling it to move gradually, perhaps fitfully, towards a more open and democratic way of life, while avoiding (fingers crossed) the bloodshed seen in Uganda, Rwanda, Somalia, Ethiopia, Mozambique, Zaire and many parts of West Africa.

In the nature of things, this is hard to prove. But if it is accepted, then making sure that the leading newspaper group had the basic technical means to carry on publishing was an important contribution to the political evolution of the country, and perhaps of Africa. There is much talk these days of an 'African renaissance'. Equally, there are the pessimists who say that only the new South Africa can act as an engine of economic growth in sub-Saharan Africa, and are doubtful that its early promise in this direction is being carried through. So a final verdict is still some way off, and perhaps will never come. What remains unique is that situation, of a three-cornered fight for readers between newspapers owned by three famous, powerful and autocratic men, in a small country of which none of them was a native, under the watchful and distrustful eye of a fourth powerful and autocratic man, the president. Robert Maxwell, 'Tiny' Rowland, the Aga Khan and President Moi – what an extraordinary collection of magnates to be active in one place at the same time. But I doubt whether, under any other dispensation, the semblance of a plural independent press would have survived in Kenya.

Just this once, let us praise newspaper tycoons – as long as they do not hold a monopoly.

17

THE INTERVIEW IN MANAGEMENT RESEARCH

A cautionary tale for journalists[1]

Stuart Macdonald and Bo Hellgren

INTRODUCTION

The interview is a primary means by which journalists gather information. Time and effort are spent in training journalists in the technique, and in educating them in the advantages and limitations of its use. The interview is also an important research tool for many academic researchers, who receive rather less, if any, such training. This is not to say that there are too few manuals on how to interview but rather that the implications of using the technique in academic research are rarely explored. This paper attempts to rectify this deficiency by examining these implications in relation to management research, an area relevant to the interests of many journalists.

The days are long gone when the active journalist might pick up a story from a passive academic. If there ever was an ivory tower, it has long since been demolished, a victim of the requirement that academic research be not only useful but seen to be useful. Media coverage does much to satisfy this requirement, and academics are expected to be proactive (a term which says rather more than it means) in securing it. Thus it is that the Economic and Social Research Council (ESRC), the UK government funding body for academic research in the social sciences, runs workshops for researchers on how to use the media to disseminate their research findings. Academics have joined the politicians and senior managers, in both private and public sectors, trained in how to present their endeavours and themselves in interviews. As one ESRC official, on a media training course for academics, expressed it: 'The agenda which you have is to get publicity.'

Academics are no longer – if they ever were – dispassionate objective observers, and journalists should be as wary of information derived from academic research as they are of information from any other source. Academic research these days serves the needs of users. Research proposals must identify users and are judged in terms of the benefits the users can expect from the research. Whatever value academic research has as a public good is a judgement made largely in terms of the value of that research as a private good. Moreover, users are to be involved in the research itself. The result is that what emerges from academic research in the social sciences is not a product of academics standing back and studying, but of an alliance between academics and users. Given that the latter determine the funding of the former, it is not an alliance of equals.

It would be dangerous to assume that academic researchers use the interview in much the same way as journalists, and therefore that what comes out of academic research based on interviews is particularly appropriate for media consumption. Commonality of approach might suggest commonality of purpose, but the suggestion is misleading. The journalist uses the interview to gain information for a story; wittingly or unwittingly, the academic uses the interview for much more than research data. It seems important for journalists to appreciate this, even if academics themselves are not always aware of the constraints under which they operate when they embark on interviews for their research.

THE RESEARCH CONTEXT OF FIELDWORK

Fieldwork is not merely a technical exercise, a rational response to an obvious research problem (Pettigrew 1985: 222). Fieldwork is also a social process, a matter which is often neglected by those who teach research techniques (see Hyman 1967). While fieldwork itself is acknowledged to be complex, the reasons presented for undertaking it are commonly simple. Fieldwork is supposed to capture reality (Sciberras 1986), and to be an especially useful means of studying the dynamic reality of change. Fieldwork, and particularly interviewing, are the 'going and seeing' which both balance and complement the 'sitting and thinking' (Emmet 1991: 14).

Just how important to management research is fieldwork in general and interviewing in particular? We will argue that the importance lies not so much in the gathering of information as in altogether different functions. One of these is the need to satisfy the requirements of those who fund research. Private funding bodies generally expect fieldwork to be carried out; public funding bodies generally insist. Such are the demands on academic resources these days, especially in the UK, that extensive empirical research cannot be undertaken without discrete funding. Having accepted that private benefit is a reliable indicator of the merit of academic research, public funding bodies regard fieldwork as a sign that the researcher is also aware of the importance of this indicator. Fieldwork is evidence of contact with an important market for research, and is thus a sign that public research funds are being well spent.

The ESRC has a corporate mission statement which declares its intention to promote research:

> placing special emphasis on meeting the needs of the users of its research and training output, thereby enhancing the United Kingdom's industrial competitiveness and quality of life.
>
> (Department of Trade and Industry 1993: 29)

Even when research is undertaken without direct funding, there is still an expectation that it will include fieldwork whenever possible. Fieldwork is the preferred way to discover what is really going on, and theory should be supported by empirical results, so that the more fieldwork the better the research. The result may be that information is sought on the cheap, a trawling process that might net something which can be used somewhere:

> As one of our first research projects, we are carrying out research into the importance of company philosophy and mission as a tool of management. . . . Can you help? Can you send us any statement that your company has made about its purpose, objectives, values or philosophy?
>
> (Circular letter from management researchers to CEOs)

In an ideal world, empirical and theoretical research advance together. Management studies, however, has not developed its disciplinary characteristics to the point where theory can be rigorously tested by empirical observation. In fact, there seems to be more interest in *accepting* theory than in *testing* it. There are those who would protest that the field is not suited to scientific experiment and consequently to the testing of theory, that nothing can be repeated because every case is different. Perhaps, but this is no excuse for failure to scrutinise theory all the more carefully. The simplification of theory should explain rather than hide the complexity of reality.

> The reasons given for many of these things, looking back, are totally spurious. So many of these things are bizarre, driven by opportunities, by individuals.
>
> (Interview with senior manager)

If management studies is a discipline at all, it has yet to mature (Commission on Management Research 1994: 5). Hence, its practitioners might be forgiven their determination to amass a body of theory as soon as possible. One recent publication presents sixty-four citations to supporting theories in its first two paragraphs alone (Hatch 1993). There is always room in management studies for yet more theories and little stomach for testing existing ones (Hubbard and Armstrong 1994). Much academic publishing in the field is bland, unchallenging and often unchallenged in as much as peer review is considered to be a process by which that which is exceptional is excised. Indeed, there is even some evidence of an inverse correlation between intellectual curiosity and the propensity to publish research results in management studies (Hancock, Ray, Lane and Glennon 1992). The ESRC recently organised an inquiry into the quality of management research, so serious did it perceive the problem to be. Its report, to which we will refer again, identified fundamental problems:

> Much management research has lacked the rigour and critical reflection more common in other social science disciplines. Studies have tended to be atheoretical and non-comparative. Case study research has predominated with inadequate emphasis on developing long-term and cross-sectional data.
>
> (Commission on Management Research 1994: 16)

THE INTERVIEW IN THEORY

Sometimes, perhaps often, the interview is the only means by which the management researcher can secure certain information about the organisation under study. Without the interview, some research topics simply could not be studied. More typically, the interview itself, and the contact with the organisation it necessitates, offer the potential for the addition of realism to the study. The detail to which the interview exposes the management researcher, and the familiarity with the organisation it makes possible, help differentiate research in management studies from that in, say, industrial economics (see Davies 1994). The interviewer may actually become more knowledgeable about some of the organisation's activities than the interviewee:

> You are probably privileged more than myself to know what the strategy is. . . . I am not absolutely sure what the rationale was.
>
> (Middle manager in interview)

The interview also allows interaction between the researcher and interviewee. The research takes place in real time, permitting the continuous re-appraisal of both answers and questions. The more open-ended and unplanned the interview structure, the greater the chance that new lines of enquiry will become apparent, even that the original hypothesis will be revised (Moore 1983: 27). Issues that were not perceived from a vantage point outside the organisation become visible within, allowing amplification or diversion of the research along promising lines. Fieldwork and interviews are also essential for full-blown interactive research, whereby any change induced by the research can itself be studied.

The feedback provided to the organisation, whether overtly or tacitly, is an almost inevitable part of fieldwork, and one that can make the research more enjoyable and rewarding for both parties.

> I think this is the most difficult area – how to get organised. That was the area I would be interested to talk to you about.
>
> (Senior manager in interview)

Management research is expected to supply its findings to the wider community of practising managers. As journalists know full well, quotation derived from interviews can be a powerful means of conveying information to such an audience.

> The key here is to let the views of the manager be heard in a way that other managers can recognise. This works most directly when the text is written in managers' own words through the use of suitably chosen quotes. It is a powerful means of reforming experiences in ways that other managers recognise and so 'see' the issue in a new way.
>
> (Hammond 1993: 2)

But, considerable though the advantages of the interview are, its importance for management researchers is not explained entirely by the research information it provides, nor by the assistance it offers in the dissemination of results.

THE INTERVIEW IN PRACTICE

Those management researchers who do interview are commonly keen to talk to the most senior people in the organisation, and are commonly triumphant when they succeed. They reason that the more senior the individual, the more knowledge that individual will have about the organisation. The organisational hierarchy is taken to be an information hierarchy. This empirical practice is in conflict with a great deal of experience and theory indicating that top management may not have the closest knowledge of what is going on in the organisation, that middle management is likely to be better informed, and that junior managers may be the most knowledgeable about specific matters (Johansson and Mattsson 1988 and 1992). It may be that researchers prefer interviewing senior managers because their research is more concerned with the making of decisions than with the operations of the organisation; or perhaps that researchers are less interested in the acquisition of information than in the acquisition of an authority for their findings that would not be bestowed by more junior managers. It is not unknown for management researchers to measure the success of an interview in terms not of the information procured, but of the organisational importance of the individual interviewed and the time he or she has spared.

Management researchers are not always specific about whether their empirical findings emanate from very few interviews or from very many. The assumption must be that findings are sometimes based on very few interviews (Kumar, Stern and Anderson 1993), simply because those researchers who conduct many interviews take pains to make this quite clear. The greater the amount of information, the more numerous the problems in the handling of information – the very information overload that senior managers seek to avoid. As interviewing is extremely resource intensive for both the researcher and the organisation (Mintzberg, Raisinghani and Theoret 1976), it is important to learn to appreciate just when the returns begin to diminish. Yet this is not an obvious concern of management researchers: their attitude – perhaps derived from survey methodology – seems to be that the more numerous the interviews conducted the better the research (see Marcus 1988; Ghoshal and Westney 1991; Simsons 1991).

> In excess of 359 recorded interviews, conducted at all levels of the firm and sector involved over a three-year period, indicate the scale and intensity of the research.
>
> (Pettigrew and Whipp 1991: 36)

> We interviewed 236 managers in the nine companies, both at their corporate headquarters and in a number of national subsidiaries.
>
> (Bartlett and Ghoshal 1989: 217)

It is always naïve to assume that the value of information is unrelated to its source, but in management research value may also be related to the means by which information is acquired. While theoretical information gains in authority the more it has been used – the more second hand it is – just the opposite seems to hold for empirical information. Value attaches to empirical information not having been disclosed before, to its virginal status. Just why should empirical information that is second hand be considered second rate? It may be that the information is valued less for its meaning than as proof that the researcher has first-hand knowledge of the organisation and therefore knows what he is talking about.

Despite the heavy reliance of management researchers on interviews, researchers are not totally comfortable with the methodology (Miller and Friesen 1977). This may be because they are anxious not to be confused with others who might explore issues in management and who rely heavily on interviews, specifically journalists. Consequently, the academic must be seen to be interviewing, but not to be dependent on the information obtained from interviews. This is really the nub of the problem: the interview may well provide a wealth of first-hand information about what is really going on in the organisation, but it also imposes constraints, constraints that are seldom acknowledged.

CONTROL

Where the organisation being studied is also funding the research, doubts may be raised about the objectivity of the findings. But even where there is no direct funding, and the organisation attaches no conditions to the nature of the findings or to the form and timing of their presentation, or the audience to which they will be released, there may still be an expectation that nothing will be said of which the organisation would disapprove. Implicit expectation, because it is boundless, can be more inhibiting than explicit restriction. Good research practice is to define before the empirical work begins precisely what control the organisation will have over results. These agreements are redolent with a tacit 'no surprises' understanding, the product of a situation in which neither side can know in advance precisely what results the research will produce. They cannot, however, be dynamic and much may change in the organisation during the years between the beginning of empirical work and academic publication.

All empirical research gives the organisation under investigation a degree of influence over the results of the research. When an organisation completes a survey form or gives access to documents, it can obviously control its input to research. But controlling the information given by individuals in interview is not so easy. Consequently, the organisation may insist on scrutinising output. Sometimes the researcher may find this a helpful exercise, sometimes less helpful. The interview may open up the organisation for the inspection of the researcher, but – much more than any other form of fieldwork – it allows the findings to be laid bare for dissection by the organisation. Objections to the revelation of even minor details can often preclude the use of more significant information, and can undermine major arguments. In consequence, the researcher has some considerable incentive to avoid detail, or at least to avoid making any substantial use of it.

> The factual information given by (the author) about (the company) has no obvious errors. I have not had the chance to check the accuracy of the scores of references. . . . (The author) expresses a number of unsubstantiated and potentially damaging opinions. . . . (The author) liberally laces the document with quotations, many of which are injurious, many of which are unattributed. A continually damaging theme is thereby built, without enabling the reader to judge the reliability of that theme.
>
> (Senior manager commenting on draft paper)

ACCESS

Interviewing requires access to the organisation under study. Even where the organisation is not directly funding the research, it is contributing resources in terms of expensive managerial time, and access may not be granted lightly. In practice, the need for access may make the researcher more subject to organisational constraints than would any direct funding. It is possible, of course, to talk to a few individuals within the organisation without official sanction; but it is not possible to interview large numbers of senior managers without the organisation's formal approval. A research project with such an interviewing base must be a project deemed important by organisational criteria.

Most management researchers who interview in organisations crave access to the executive suite. Only a few gain entrance (Greiner 1985: 251). How do they achieve this? Pettigrew describes the process as networking, insinuation into an organisation so that access to one individual leads on to access to another.

> (In) Britain the game that's played is essentially a networking game. They allow access in a small node or corner of the network, and then you get tested out on that node. And if you are deemed acceptable on whatever criteria, then you pass on to the next part of the node and then the next part.
>
> (Pettigrew 1985: 264)

What, though, are the criteria by which acceptability is judged? It is conceivable, though only just, that the researcher gains acceptance through impressing senior managers with the value of a radical viewpoint. It may be rather easier to gain acceptance by displaying willingness to adapt to the values of managers, by sharing their views of reality (Hultman and Klasson 1994).

THE HOSTAGE SYNDROME

If the hostage, no matter how badly he is treated, begins to identify with his captors, it is hardly surprising that the empirical researcher can begin to identify with the organisation he or she is studying. The organisation's interests become the researcher's interests. Researchers who resort to interview, because they are thrust into personal contact with managers, would seem to be especially susceptible to the syndrome. The risks are increased because most academics have themselves never been in anything but the most minor of management positions: interviewing puts them into direct contact with those responsible for decisions which affect thousands, with those who allocate vast resources, with those who are powerful in another world altogether and who exercise skills utterly different from their own. Moreover, unlike the academic, who has only his or her title and reputation, senior managers are surrounded by the structure and trappings of power. Nearly always, these are the surroundings in which interviews take place, and in which objectivity can easily turn to deference, impartiality to common cause. It is interesting to speculate whether the information garnered from interviews, and for that matter the questions asked, would have been very different had the interviews been conducted in universities or on neutral ground. We might speculate also about the extent to which the cult of the chief executive as organisational hero is associated with experiencing him holding court in full regalia (see Hellgren, Melin and Pettersson 1993). Would academic promotion of the cult be quite so strong were these chief executives interviewed while digging the garden?

Moreover, just as the hostage's fortunes are in the hands of his captors, so the academic may well calculate that his or her fortunes lie with senior managers in the organisation he is studying. The academic must satisfy powerful people in order to ensure continued access. The more interviews the researcher completes, the greater the investment and the greater the dependence on the organisation for permission to continue the research. We have already considered how the satisfaction of certain powerful people in the organisation can open up for the researcher access to other powerful people, but on this same satisfaction also depend access to other organisations, and – to some, often considerable, extent – offers of consultancy work and appointments to advisory positions, prospects of further funding and hopes of academic advancement. All these considerations are, of course, quite irrelevant to the immediate purpose of the interview, and would certainly be beyond the purview of any text on empirical research, but it is not inconceivable that they can influence the manner in which the interview is conducted. It is just possible that they will also influence research findings.

> We have co-operated with you in the past in what we believe has been a constructive relationship but this latest paper is both inaccurate and wholly unacceptable and will undoubtedly destroy that relationship . . .
>
> (Senior manager commenting on draft paper)

CULTURAL CHASM

Fieldwork places the researcher within the environment of the organisation. Much can be learned by walking into a factory, without necessarily talking to anyone. Interviewing is much more intimate. The more involved the academic becomes in the environment of the organisation being studied, the greater the risk to the academic of being overwhelmed.

Business culture is radically different from academic culture. The former is fundamentally hierarchical and tightly structured, especially in large organisations: the latter – at least traditionally – is just about the opposite, and especially in research, where the findings of the famous may be publicly challenged by the unknown. For the academic researcher, peer review and membership of a community of scholars are important. Senior managers may find difficulty appreciating this importance.

> They tell me you academics write two or three papers a year. How many thousand words is that? I must write that much in a week.
>
> (Senior manager in interview)

The researcher may find herself forced to defend her values, to preserve her culture, in a hostile environment. This can be difficult: it is no easy matter to question closely a manager who normally would not tolerate being questioned at all. It is much easier for the researcher simply to accept what is said, to accede to the culture of the organisation. It is easier still, and much more conducive to reaping the benefits that flow from the satisfaction of those interviewed, to ask the questions managers wish to answer, and to ask them in ways managers will find immediately acceptable. Thus, for example, a question on the role the manager has played in corporate success is much more acceptable than a question about his role in corporate failure. In management studies, there is remarkably little fieldwork-based research on failure (see Major and Zucker 1989), though it could be that there is more to be learnt from failure than from success.

Because managers are unfamiliar with academic culture, and find that what they do recognise is sometimes inimical to their own, problems can arise in using information gained from interviews. Managers may not be sympathetic to the demands of academic rigour: for example, the need to check what they say against information from other sources. Managers may be unsympathetic towards the interpretation needed when accounts are at variance, towards integration with information they have not supplied, and towards aggregation that diminishes the prominence of their own views. Good research practice demands that those who are interviewed approve the use of their information in the context in which the researcher has placed it. The difficulties many managers experience of distinguishing between confirming their meaning and accepting organisational responsibility for its application result in this convention not always being observed in management studies. Even complying with agreements to ensure that information published is accurate and not confidential can pose problems. Individual managers do not relish this responsibility, and there is no obvious institutional office to accept it. That part of the organisation that deals with public relations may well be left to handle the task – with predictable results.

You asked various of my colleagues to comment on your draft. . . .
Some confusion has arisen because it is our normal – and preferred –
practice to have drafts of this kind sent to the Department of Public
Affairs . . .

(Letter from the director of public affairs)

The first paragraph of page 20, which may be an accurate quotation,
is not something we would wish to have included within a published
document.

(Letter from the director of human resources)

The latter observation is quite unexceptional, but in this case the objection
was to a statement made by a manager in another company altogether.
Similarly, one Swedish company demanded not only that its managers'
answers be changed in the draft paper it was sent, but also that the questions
be altered (Melin 1977). From the perspective of the company's public affairs
department, publication about the company should be publication which will
make a favourable impression on the public.

There was a time when managers were less guarded than they are now
over what they said to academics and what academics would make of it. That
was when almost the only outlet for academic publication was academic
management journals, largely unread by managers themselves. But the same
pressures that have forced academic research to become more obviously useful
(and more empirical) have also encouraged academics to disseminate their
findings more widely, especially through the media. What is said about the
firm by the media concerns managers greatly, especially in the UK, where
much effort is made to discourage the publication of information that may
have an adverse effect on share prices. The point is a small one, but it encapsulates nicely many of the problems of the interview as a means of acquiring
information in management studies. It is incontrovertible that the interview
can provide invaluable information about the organisation, but the greater the
attempts to exploit this wealth of information, the greater the difficulties
encountered (Miles 1979). In practice, there is every incentive for researchers
to claim that their research has benefited from interview information, while
avoiding the problems that arise from using this information.

We are told that over 400 people were interviewed to secure a variety
of perspectives; few make their appearances in these pages and we
learn little directly of what they had to say.

(Mangham 1993: 27)

AGGREGATION AND INTEGRATION OF INFORMATION

Interviews yield such a quantity of diverse information that even simple aggregation presents problems. Contradictory information is often the rule rather than the exception. Consider the problems posed by a single sentence from one senior manager, interspersed with comments (in parentheses) from other senior managers' interviews in the same organisation.

> [The] non-executive directors recognised that there was the need for another leader to come and cause change to happen in the company,
>
>> [That's why he was brought in: he was brought in by the non-executive directors of the company to make a radical change, but this is definitely not for attribution]
>
> and one of the great things that the new CEO has brought to the company is not only the creation of the mission statement,
>
>> [Our strategy mission statement here is motherhood]
>
> but the rigidity with which we have applied it to our businesses since.
>
>> [Does there have to be synergy? . . . I know that the main board have often thought of becoming a holding company. . . . I mean that might bring into question then the CEO's quest for the sort of company that since I have known him he has started to say less about looking for. He has just expressed frustration that it didn't happen]

The survey approach – where '77 per cent of managers think that . . . ' – overcomes these difficulties, but at the unacceptable cost of masking the variety and individuality of interpretation that interviews reveal. Conveying these elements is never easy. Sometimes managers will insist that the most interesting information is not to be used.

> I think at the present time it's the Minister that opposes it. As I understand – and I hope you fillet out this part – he is extremely paranoid about it.
>
> (Senior manager in interview)

Sometimes the most important arguments are expressed with an emotion that is difficult to capture in academic prose, and which is quite unsuitable for quotation:

270

The parent company can go to bloody hell. They make zilch contribution here. . . . I look upon the parent company as a bank. It provides no more than finance.

Managerially and in social terms, the manager was a buffoon. He's got no political savvy at all, and has behaved in a way which is frequently very insensitive to the rest of his colleagues.

I'm fascinated by someone who is so incompetent, as far as I can see, in understanding any kind of management theory, and doesn't seem to have any insight into where this business is going, but can nevertheless manage to make money in private industry. If anything has convinced me that it must be a bloody pushover out there, it's watching (the manager) in action.

(Senior managers in interview)

Specific examples and quotation from interviews capture some of this intensity and variety, but they are inevitably selective, reflecting the perspective of the researcher as much as that of the manager:

It is from this mix of opinion and fact, of detailed descriptions and broad impressions, that we have developed our conclusions. . . . Our hundreds of pages of interview notes are full of stories, anecdotes and quotes.

(Goold and Campbell 1987: 7)

Empirical work – and especially interviewing – is guaranteed to provide a mass of detail, but the insight required to make good use of this detail must come from the academic. In practice, the academic encounters real incentives to deny the complexity of reality that interviews can expose.

It is a collection of thoughts and public statements made by executives in various firms. . . . I do not see a systematic thought emerging from this collection of statements (which is considered as empirical evidence by the author – I don't think that is a correct claim).

I still have doubts about the included quotes. Can we learn anything from such anecdotes? How do we know that these quotes are representative or were merely selected to fit the points that the author wants to make?

(Referees' comments on papers based on interviews)

The interview is far from being the only means available to the empirical researcher of gaining information about the organisation. Much information may be in the public domain and can be obtained without the consent of the organisation. For instance, there are the organisation's own publications, unpublished archives in public collections, articles in the media, academic publications directly concerned with the organisation (such as case studies), publications from other organisations (such as government departments and trade associations), and a whole host of peripheral publications (such as trade magazines; see Chen, Farh and Macmillan 1993).

The researcher encounters major problems integrating information gained from interviews with other information about the organisation. Among these is the problem of reconciling the manager's view of reality with other views, particularly those from outside the organisation. It is not that academics are unaware that views of reality will differ; almost the opposite, in fact (Myrdal 1970). Managers, and the organisation as a whole, are simply less appreciative of views from outside the organisation that are in conflict with their own. The problem becomes acute when the mixing of public information with that from interviews reveals more – often much more – than managers intended. Because the mix may not satisfy the organisation, the academic can be faced with a very practical choice of using either interview information or other information, but not both. For example, the use of public information, properly cited, will generally reveal the identity of a company promised anonymity by the researcher. Because of the huge resource investment in interviews, the researcher may prefer to sacrifice other information in preference to interview material. Consider the following information, which, because it was given in confidence, severely restricted the use that could be made of public information about the event:

> In a nutshell, there was a cabal, almost a secret society within the subsidiary, of a few individuals – not that many. We were trying to collect debts, we were sending in the heavies, sending in the heavies to take back property in lieu of debt, all that type of thing. I'm not too sure whether money was actually being laundered. Certain of the individuals are going to be, and are being, prosecuted. . . . The director responsible did not know what was going on at all.
>
> (Senior manager in interview)

Interviews confront the academic with a variety of managerial views that he must somehow exploit. The academic is hard-pressed to handle in a similar way the much greater diversity of opinion and belief available in the outside world. Consequently, he is tempted to simplify these external views, to unify, so that the focus of attention remains on the empirical information he has unearthed. Resources being finite, and interviews exceedingly resource consuming, there may be few to spare to treat external views as exhaustively as the internal. So, the researcher may find himself prisoner of his or her own methodology, condemned to look inwards, deprived of the context that external views of reality provide (see Mangham 1993: 27).

No academic study can rely on empirical information alone, no matter how rich that information. Empirical information must be integrated with theory, and this is often no easy task (see Flanders 1965: 9). It is particularly difficult to integrate interview information with theory. Unless they are unacceptably led by the interviewer, managers cannot be expected to provide their information in a form that is compatible with theory. This, of course, is where the researcher's skill should be brought into play, but the skills required to extract information are not necessarily the skills required for integration. There may be evidence of this in the tendency of academic publications in management studies for empirical information to be presented quite separately from theoretical information. This makes starkly evident that fieldwork has been done while minimising the problems of integration.

CONCLUDING THOUGHTS

What, then, might be done to solve these seemingly intractable problems? At several points we have stated that a shortage of resources is a basic problem. Empirical research is extremely resource intensive, and an extensive interviewing programme particularly so. This may mean that insufficient resources are available not so much for interviewing, for that need is obvious, but for the gathering of other information, and then for processing all the information acquired. The more interviews conducted, the greater – not the fewer – resources are required for non-interview research. Neither inadequate funding nor further dependence on the organisations being studied is conducive to reputable research. But resources are always limited, and the mere provision of more would not overcome the fundamental dependence we have been at pains to identify. The solution – if one is to be had – lies in greater appreciation of where the balance should lie in the allocation of research resources.

The dogma of the times, particularly in the UK, is that academic research must be useful. It is hard to quarrel with this, but useful to whom? Little of the academic research that is undertaken can even aspire to be useful to everybody, and none can be equally useful to all. So, academic research is expected to find its market. For management studies, this is seen to consist of organisations themselves, those who make policy that will affect those organisations, and others who study organisations. Of the three, it is the organisations themselves that are reckoned the most important segment of the market, the reasoning being that their use of the research not only satisfies one market but actually validates the research for other markets. A crude legitimation process has been set in place.

But is it satisfactory for organisations to be regarded as the primary customers of research in management studies? Two assumptions would seem to be critical. The first is that organisations know what research will be of most use to them – in the long and the medium term, as well as the short term. The second assumption is that the research which is of most use to organisations is consequently research which is of most use to the economy and to society as a whole. Neither assumption is justifiable.

It is open to question that managers have ever learnt much from academic publication, or ever will. Senior managers do not typically keep up with the latest academic literature in management studies. They are much more aware of what the management gurus are saying. The popularity of the folksy analogies and simplistic prescriptions of the gurus is an exemplar to those academics who value successful dissemination, and perhaps the rewards of dissemination, more than successful research. Interviews often make the resulting confusion all too evident:

> The more modern thinking about empowerment as autonomy actually fits this company very, very well. . . . I mean, you just can't manage that matrix other than at the local level. The principle by which we try to manage our business was the notion of global localisation. Or was it local globalisation?
>
> (Senior manager in interview)

This does not mean that managers cannot learn from academic research, but perhaps they can learn more indirectly than they can learn directly. It is quite disingenuous to insist that research on the organisation, research in the organisation, even research for the organisation, should have a direct impact on that organisation. Such insistence assumes that no research findings can reach the organisation from suppliers, competitors or customers, from government departments or from industry and trade associations, or from consultants, or from the personal contacts and networks of individual managers – or from the media (see von Hippel 1988).

Why does management studies give credence to the notion that academic research is good academic research only if its product is primarily a private good? Perhaps the chief reason is that such research is easier – much easier – to evaluate than is research whose product is intended to be a public good. The user can express his satisfaction, most tangibly by funding, or by supporting the funding of, more such research. There is no equivalent means by which the general public, a whole economy or an entire society can express its approval of certain research and so encourage more. Thus it is that less and less research is performed as a public good, publicly funded; and more and more research is directed towards satisfying the immediate demands of specific users. Consequently, there is every incentive for the academic to undertake the sort of research that the organisation adjudges appropriate to its interests. Equally, there is every incentive to adopt a methodology which demonstrates how central to the research are the views of the organisation's managers. Fieldwork in general, and the interview in particular, have thus become increasingly important components of research in management studies. As we have seen, it may be that the costs of this sort of research sometimes exceed the benefits.

There are major obstacles to change, which certainly include those who provide the resources for research in management studies. But perhaps the greatest obstacle of all is the academic community itself. It has been quick to seize the advantages that fieldwork and interviewing offer research in management studies, and slow to acknowledge the disadvantages. There is a role for the journalist here, at least for the critical journalist. It is not to present management research to the public as if it were a public good, the role in which the management researcher would have the journalist cast. It is to screen and report on those findings of management research that have genuine public value. This, of course, requires that journalists possess considerable knowledge of the field and particularly that they appreciate the constraints under which management research is conducted.

This chapter has explored some of the implications of reliance on the interview in order to expose some of the issues of which journalists should be aware. It closes with the hope that journalists will be more critical in their approach and more thoughtful than the members of the ESRC Commission into the quality of management research. Their report (CMR 1994: 27) concludes with an observation that says much more than was ever intended about the problems faced by management research.

> Research can and does contribute to today's problems, but it has a greater contribution to make: it should also contribute to tomorrow's problems.

NOTE

1 An early version of this chapter was published electronically in 1998 as 'The interview in management research', *Iconoclastic Papers* 1(2). It is available online at: www.solent.ac.uk/sbs/iconolastic/index.htm.

The authors are grateful to a number of colleagues who have been generous in sharing their experiences of fieldwork, and especially to Chris Bennett. They are grateful also to the many managers who, over the years, have permitted the authors to interview them.

REFERENCES

Bartlett, C. and S. Ghoshal (1989) *Managing Across Borders. The Transnational Solution*, Boston: Harvard Business School Press.

Chen, M.-J., J.-L. Farh and I. Macmillan (1993) 'An exploration of the expertness of outside informants', *Academy of Management Journal* 36(6): 1614–32.

Commission on Management Research (1994) *Building Partnerships. Enhancing the Quality of Management Research*, Swindon: Economic and Social Research Council.

Davies, S. (1994) 'Empirical research: the future', *Journal of the Economics of Business* 1(1): 19–21.

Department of Trade and Industry (1993) *Realising Our Potential. A Strategy for Science, Engineering and Technology*, Cm 2250, London: HMSO.

Emmet, E. (1991) *Learning to Philosophise*, London: Penguin.

Flanders, A. (1965) *Industrial Relations: What Is Wrong with the System?*, London: Faber & Faber.

Ghoshal, S. and D. E. Westney (1991) 'Organizing competitor analysis systems', *Strategic Management Journal* 12: 17–31.

Goold, M. and A. Campbell (1987) *Strategies and Styles. The Role of the Centre in Managing Diversified Corporations*, Oxford: Blackwell.

Greiner, L. (1985) 'Response and commentary', in E. Lawler III, A. M. Morhman Jr., S. A. Morhman, G. E. Ledford, T. G. Cummings and Associates (eds), *Doing Research that Is Useful for Theory and Practice*, San Francisco: Jossey-Bass.

Hammond, V. (1993) 'Communicating research results effectively to managers: writing to influence', paper presented to the *British Academy of Management Annual Conference*, Milton Keynes, September.

Hancock, T., J. Lane, R. Ray and D. Glennon (1992) 'The Ombudsman: factors influencing academic research productivity; a survey of management scientists', *Interfaces* 22(5): 26–38.

Hatch, M. (1993) 'The dynamics of organizational culture', *Academy of Management Review* 18(4): 657–93.

Hellgren, B., L. Melin and A. Pettersson (1993) 'Structure and change: the industrial field approach', *Advances in International Marketing* 5: 87–106.

Hubbard, R. and J. S. Armstrong (1994) 'Replications and extensions in marketing: rarely published but quite contrary', *International Journal of Research in Marketing* 11: 233–48.

Hultman, G. and A. Klasson (1994) 'Learning from change? A note on interactive action research', paper presented to the *Conference on Learning and Research in Working Life*, Lund, June.

Hyman, H. (1967) *Interviewing in Social Research*, Chicago: University of Chicago Press.

Johansson, J. and L.-G. Mattsson (1988) 'Internationalization in industrial systems', in N. Hood and J.-E. Vahlne (eds) *Strategies in Global Competition*, London: Croom Helm.

—— (1992) 'Network positions and strategic action – an analytical framework', in B. Axelsson and G. Easton (eds) *Industrial Networks*, London: Routledge.

Kumar, N., L. Stern and J. Anderson (1993) 'Conducting interorganizational research using key informants', *Academy of Management Journal* 36(6): 1633–51.

Major, M. and L. Zucker (1989) *Permanently Failing Organizations*, London: Sage.

Mangham, I. (1993) 'Judgement and book covers', Review of A. Pettigrew, E. Ferlie and L. McKee, *Shaping Strategic Change: Making Change in Large Organisations: The Case of the National Health Service, Times Higher Education Supplement*, 26 November, p.27.

Marcus, A. A. (1988) 'Responses to externally induced innovations: their effects on organizational performance', *Strategic Management Journal* 9: 387–402.

Melin, L. (1977) *Olika Strategier, Olika Organisationsformer och Olika Vardesystem*,

Research Report 72, Department of Management and Economics, Linkoping University.

Miles, M. (1979) 'Qualitative data as an attractive nuisance: the problem of analysis', *Administrative Science Quarterly* 24: 590–601.

Miller, D. and P. Friesen (1977) 'Strategy-making in context: ten empirical archetypes', *Journal of Management Studies* 14: 253–80.

Mintzberg, H., D. Raisinghani and A. Theoret (1976) 'The structure of "unstructured" decision processes', *Administrative Science Quarterly* 21: 246–75.

Moore, N. (1983) *How to Do Research*, London: Library Association.

Myrdal, G. (1970) *Objectivity in Social Research*, London: Gerald Duckworth.

Pettigrew, A. (1985) 'Contextualist research: a natural way to link theory and practice', in E. Lawler III, A. M. Morhman Jr., S. A. Morhman, G. E. Ledford, T. G. Cummings and Associates (eds) *Doing Research that Is Useful for Theory and Practice*, San Francisco: Jossey-Bass.

Pettigrew, A. and R. Whipp (1991) *Managing Change for Competitive Success*, Oxford: Blackwell.

Sciberras, E. (1986) 'Indicators of technical intensity and international competitiveness: a case for supplementing quantitative data with qualitative studies in research', *R&D Management* 16(1): 1–14.

Simsons, R. (1991) 'Strategic orientation and top management attention to control systems', *Strategic Management Journal* 12: 49–62.

von Hippel, E. (1988) *The Sources of Innovation*, New York: Oxford University Press.

Part V

INTERNATIONAL MEDIA
AND GLOBAL IDENTITY

Part V
INTERNATIONAL MEDIA
AND GLOBAL IDENTITY

18

THE HISTORIAN AND THE NEWS AGENCY

Present thoughts on past performance

Michael Palmer

Historians and news professionals observe 'events' and formulate, construct and produce 'copy' from different vantage-points: they operate under different constraints of time and space. Both, however, have a similar premiss or concern – they wish, first, to establish an accurate record of what happened; they strive to elucidate the facts, ascertaining who or what did or said what to whom or to what, where and when; they may, subsequently, move on to examining how and why. Both, in short, are concerned with establishing a report or record, and constructing a text or account, that answers the questions that Quintilian, in ancient Rome, presented as the essential points to which an orator should address himself: '*Quis, quid, ubi, quando, quibus auxiliis, quomodo, cur.*'[1] This set of questions, in many respects, seems more meaningful than the 'holy of holies' of the Lasswellian litany: 'who says what in which channel to whom with what effect':[2] the set of 'Qs', rather than the '5 Ws', highlights the congruence of questions posed by (certain) historians and (many) journalists; they include the issue of presentation, the mode or manner – *quomodo* – of relating the message; and they stress the link between the modes of address of rhetoricians and of news and editorial style guides or manuals, across the ages.[3]

That said, the attitude of the historian and the journalist – as they assemble information and prepare to produce their 'copy' – differs in many ways. Several of these are obvious. Here, I wish to examine how the *historian of news agencies* approaches the various logics that fashion the production, transmission and distribution of 'copy' by news agency journalists. The historian of international news agencies is well aware that several of today's leading news organisations have existed for decades, if not for centuries:

- France: Havas, 1835; AFP (Paris), 1944
- Britain: Reuters 1851, (London)

- Germany: Wolff 1849, (Berlin) / DPA (Hamburg) 1949
- USA: AP (New York), 1848.

Often, the historian requires the authorisation and co-operation of the existing news agencies (whatever their status – media co-operatives, companies quoted on the Stock Exchange, multinational corporations or public sector actors, or a hybrid of public and private – AFP, for example, has a legal status described as *sui generis*), so as to gain access to archives and personnel that together 'inform' his or her research. Furthermore, he or she may frequent the offices and personnel of today's organisations; knowledge of how they work *today* influences the questions the historian asks of their *past*. And, of course, many accounts of news agency history were produced by journalists, including people who later became historians.

Several news agency historians have both explored the corporate records of news organisations and consulted the *news product*, as preserved in public and private archives – such as collections of the *Correspondance Havas*, in the Bibliothèque (Nationale) de France (département des périodiques). Here, I wish to list certain questions that arise from juxtaposing information accessible in archives containing material concerning the history of the news agencies with issues that arose during a month-long observer-participation study of AFP, based in its Paris headquarters in May 1997. The premiss or starting-point is that ongoing concerns about the writing of the *history of news agencies* and of the news flow are influenced by the *present environment* in which news media operate – however careful historians may be to guard against *anachronism*.

In listing these questions, I draw also on experience gleaned while working in the corporate archives of Reuters Holdings plc (a 'public' company – floated on the stock exchange in 1984), and from talks with Reuters journalists and executives, over many years. Two issues or case studies underpin these remarks: one has to do with *quality control mechanisms* and *impact studies* conducted (with different resources and aims) by Reuters and AFP; other centres on *international news agency coverage of Russia* – tsarist, Soviet and post-Soviet. A third issue – news film and television – is raised in conclusion.

The very diversity of the material, issues and perspectives suggested hitherto indicates one of the difficulties facing news agency historians: what is the central issue that they address? To list but some of the many possible answers:

- The writing of a company history?
- The logistics and output that fashion or reflect news-agency coverage of a given event, a theme, an 'actor' or a world region?
- The relation between the news product, the state, the media, technology, finance and commerce?
- The competitive environment in which news agencies operate?

- Ownership structures and market conditions?
- The training, performance, career pattern and professional norms of the journalist and non-journalist personnel employed by news agencies?

There is, of course, a preliminary question: is the generic term 'news agency' applicable both to the same organisation at all times – the Reuters of 1851 and the Reuters of 1999 – and to the leading international news agencies, collectively, in the 1850s and the 1990s?[4] Obviously, these are only some of the concerns common to news-agency historians. It is likely, however, that they share these, just as much as the 'more traditional' issue of the perceived tension between, on the one hand, journalistic independence *vis-à-vis* the government and other political, economic or socio-cultural actors that seek to influence output, . . . and, on the other, the economic viability (and survival) of the organisation for which the agency personnel work. Some agencies (and agency personnel) refer to a public service tradition in which news and information are a public good.[5] By this reasoning, in the final analysis, news agencies serve citizens, nations and peoples, and not the state, capitalism or the media that together – in response to different, but at times overlapping, logics – contribute to the commodification of news. Others, however, stress that they walk the narrow path between the Scylla of financial dependence on state funding (subsidies, etc.) and the Charybdis of dependence on Mammon: i.e. they serve markets, including many non-media actors whose information demands relate to oiling the wheels (and conducting the transactions) of the international *real-time* marketplace. They add that, as seasoned professionals, they strive also to maintain their 'balance', by diversifying the sources of their information.

News agency journalists and historians are concerned with time and space: but their perspectives differ markedly. 'News', as is well known, comprises several elements: *informare* includes the 'account' or 'report' of 'new things' ('new–s'), as well as both the nature of that which is reported and the perception of the significance of the event related for the public thus informed. News executives and journalists plan the coverage logistics of many of the stories that are anticipated or expected to figure high on the news agenda, weeks, months and sometime years hence;[6] yet they prefer the unanticipated breaking story (for all the additional work it may entail) to the foreseen or 'pre-ordained' event. Journalists are concerned with preparing the logistics of coverage; once a story is produced, and even before its 'shelf-life' has expired, many of them are primarily concerned with preparing coverage and copy of the next story. Their *service de production* or news bureau, organises its resources, calling if need be on colleagues from other production centres; thus, in AFP, to cover the French parliamentary elections of May–June 1997, the *service politique* of AFP called at times on the *info(rmations)s géné(rale)s* and on the 'social' and 'economic' news departments; the news-editorial *rédaction en chef centrale* overviewed both the logistics of coverage and the news output. In some ways, a story once covered is as soon forgotten; in this respect, the attitudes of the journalist and of the historian are totally at odds. Historians operate less under the pressures of time and space; yet, as professionals, however far they travel, however long they take in assessing an abundance of evidence (factual information; oral testimony; visual representations, cultural perceptions, etc.) from a range of sources, they too have to produce within – admittedly different – constraints of time and space. Historians might add that they are more concerned with distinguishing between data, news, information and *sense*, *relevance* or *significance*; they are tempted, perhaps, to echo the words of the poet:

> Where is the Life we have lost in living?
> Where is the wisdom we have lost in knowledge?
> Where is the knowledge we have lost in information?
> (T. S. Eliot, *The Rock*)

But news agency history and poetic philosophy make for odd bedfellows.

Journalists, an AFP (non-journalist) executive observes, are 'creatures obsessed by the instant'. For many agency journalists, a story has a shelf-life of a half-day, at most. Quality-control mechanisms or units – such as exist in Reuters and AFP – assess performance and impact across the world's time-zones during 'the past twenty-four hours':

- How did we do on a given story compared to other news-media?
- How much was our copy used, compared to that of the competition?
- Were we minutes ahead, or behind?
- Who used which angle, which type of material?

For example, AFP issues 'impact sheets', two to three times a day based on reports filed by bureaux worldwide; these monitor coverage of the 'dominant' stories of the international news agenda of the previous twenty-four hours. Thus, in May 1997, from a monitoring of assessments made by bureaux worldwide of the Zaire–Mobuti story,[7] the 9 May impact report showed that AFP-Mexico reported more use of AFP material than of EFE and Reuter's material – 'Mobutu lego a Gabon'; but AFP-Quito classified use of agency copy thus: 'EFE/AFP/ANSA: 'Mobutu viajo y los rebeldes avanzan'.[8]

The news agency historian has somehow to take these perceptions and pressures into account: news is a commodity that grows stale as soon as it is formulated, processed and released – *mise en forme et diffusée*. Journalists are concerned with the various forms and ways of *assembling* the news-product; once ready, 'desked' and validated for transmission and issued on one or several 'wires', the output interests them only insofar as lessons can be learned from studying the impact of the copy and the performance of other agencies and news organisations. On the other hand, the news agency historian has to be attentive to the different forms of both the packaging of the news-product, and the ways in which the news is *angled*. This packaging has nothing to do with distortion or manipulation; it has to do with presentational techniques, so as to provide different clients with the angle and variety of copy required for instant or longer term use, for a range of vectors and purposes (press, TV, multimedia, online internet sites, data banks; and also banks and other non-media clients, including governments and international governmental and non-governmental organisations). The news product is presented in different forms. These have to do with:

- the nature of the text – such as the 'lead', whose opening sentence is to convey in a maximum of thirty words the succinct answer to the '5 Ws' listed above, but also, for example, a 'news analysis', a 'side-bar' or a 'wrap-up';
- the language in which the story is produced (Arabic, English – be it British English, American English or 'international English', French, German, Portugese, Spanish; for agencies such as Reuters up to a total of twenty-five languages);
- the relation between words, digits and other communication symbols or icons;
- the relation between 'the text' and the various print, audiovisual, electronic and other media and non-media, clients, subscribers and 'end-users' for whom the output, copy or material is intended.

The selection process has to do not only with which story to cover in which form and for which service, but involves choosing the priority to be given to the transmission of a story, and the degree of urgency – P1, P2, P3 or P4 (in AFP newspeak) – to be given to different stories that compete for a place in the copy-flow of different services; news-editors desking the stories have priorities that differ according to the world region or thematic interest of the service in question. Much agency energy is spent on ensuring that computer storage and retrieval systems and transmission systems are so devised that clients know beforehand what is (up)coming, and have the tools and filters that enable them to access what they want when they want it. Hierarchy and order are the name of the game: just as the copy-flow has increased – with Reuters speaking of producing four million words a day, and AFP two million – so has the capacity for clients to access what they want, when they want, and fashion 'à la carte' services from a general news service output.

News agency historians note that while the output has increased, and the speed of collecting, processing and distributing the output has accelerated, concerns with reconciling accuracy, speed and client satisfaction were voiced by agency executives in the 1880s just as in the 1990s. However, whereas in the nineteenth century agencies tended to adopt a low profile, ministering as wholesalers to the news needs of governments, financiers and the commercial media, Reuters, AP and AFP in the 1990s tend to be more up-front and concerned with their corporate image as news vendors serving a host of marketplaces. In the rhetoric of real-time, globalisation and multi-media multinationals, these three long-established actors stress that they have a century-long tradition of expertise in harnessing information and communication technologies to the news demands of media and non-media markets worldwide. They also have had, periodically, to 'reinvent themselves', and adapt to changing market conditions in both their home-base country, and to changing geopolitical and market conditions worldwide. It would be possible to argue that Reuters was helped, rather than hindered, by being the one international agency that did not have to give paramount concern to the needs of the media and non-media markets of the home-base country: the Press Association, formed in 1868, was the British domestic news agency (with which Reuters had news exchange agreements), whereas AP and Havas-AFP acted as domestic news agencies, whose international network was established so as to serve (primarily) the demands of domestic media and/or non-media markets. In the past twenty years (at least) AFP, and – seemingly to a lesser extent – AP have reorganised themselves so as to better serve world regions; but AFP's success in serving English-language clients in Asia (a region served from Hong Kong, and stretching from Afghanistan to Australia) is little understood by French provincial newspapers (some of whose representatives sit on the AFP board), worried by the abundance (and cost) of coverage of international news for which they themselves have little use in their columns.

THE NEWS FROM RUSSIA: 1904 AND 1991

The news agency historian therefore has to look at one and the same time at agency output, company strategies and market conditions, and note that, while there are 'constants', there are many variables in time and across space. On many occasions, issues of availability and accessibility, of sourcing and accuracy, appear paramount. Consider the European news agencies in tsarist Russia in 1904: wanting to improve their all-too-modest coverage (centered in Saint Petersburg), Reuters, Havas, and Wolff (and, through the news-agency alliance, ring or cartel, of which these three were the architects, the AP), in 1904, admitted a newly founded (official) agency, the Saint Petersburg Telegraph Agency, to the alliance. They rapidly found its coverage poor, when the Russo-Japanese war and the 1905–6 riots and strikes across Russia made events in Russia a dominant *leitmotif* of the international news agenda: faced by competition from rival news agencies and news media, Reuters and Havas sent their own correspondents to Saint Petersburg, Moscow and elsewhere to make up for the unsatisfactory coverage of news from non-official sources, that the SPTA provided late, insufficiently, or not at all. At the same time, the Reuters and Havas correspondents operated under constraints fixed by their employers, in which straight factual reporting was an important, but not necessarily the sole, consideration: tsarist Russia was an ally (the sole major ally) of republican France; one French family in six (by 1914) had invested in Russian government bonds and loans or in companies involved in the industrialisation or modernisation of Russia; Havas executives and editors in Paris were under pressure both from the French government not to alarm the French public and from Paris newspapers that published dramatic eyewitness accounts by their correspondents in Russia; as for Reuters, its news managers explained to the SPTA that it wished to carry news on developments from a range of sources, both favourable and unfavourable (to the government), and that its own correspondents abroad (such as Guy Beringer, sent in 1904 to Saint Petersburg), were to report news as seen 'through British spectacles'.[9]

Eighty-five years later, in the years of *glasnost* and *perestroika* in Soviet Russia, Reuters and AFP correspondents based in Moscow operated in the heady atmosphere that followed decades of controls and restrictions on western correspondents; yet, at the same time, there were voices raised within both organisations, questioning whether western news media did not at times 'go over the top' in relating developments connected to the *leitmotif* of the dominant international story of the time – the implosion of the Soviet *bloc*, from Berlin (November 1989) to Moscow (the abortive coup of August 1991). Thus, reflecting on agency production at the time, a Reuters journalist based in ('far-off') Beijing, asked (rhetorically): 'Are we truly a 'world' agency, if we report events through', what might be termed, the prism or lens of 'western' spectacles?[10] Agencies cover events by referring to hard, straight, factual reporting, but fully aware that they must provide copy angled to market needs and expectations; other, competing, news organisations do the same, thereby increasing the pressure.

Furthermore, wheareas all journalists revel in breaking news of events whose implications are momentous, the premium placed on speed is linked to the awareness that 'news moves markets'. For instance, in the early morning (GMT) of 19 August 1991, Reuters news services reported at 03.27: 'Soviet U. P. Yanayev takes over as president due to Gorbachev health'; at 04.04, they reported: 'Dollar rises two-and-a-half pfennigs on Gorbachev news.' Market-sensitive news in a world of real-time data flows and interconnections increases the burdens or onus on agency operatives. Reuters is the bench-mark: in the early 1990s, some of its quality controllers – known in-house as 'quacks' – stressed that while accuracy and speed were of the essence, the version of a story for 'econ.' screen-based clients took precedence over the version of the story for 'media clients'; they added that it should not take more than three to five minutes to 'turn around' and put out the story for the second client-category, based on the report for the first. In AFP, where economic and financial services developed substantially in the 1990s (the Paris-based economic news service had forty-eight staff in 1997), there was recognition that Reuters remains the leader in the provision of both the news and the delivery systems that interconnect to enable informed decision-making, resulting, at speed, in the conclusion of transactions; but there was also a determination that the agency could and did exploit the information flows stemming from France's position as a leading economy of the developed world; there was also, in AFP as elsewhere, awareness that a relative newcomer, Bloomberg (1981), competed hard against Reuters in some of the most financially market-sensitive data–information–news markets: indeed, AFP ventured into real-time television news by providing feeds to Bloomberg Television.

Market-sensitive news increases the pressure on delivering news quickly, and increases the risk of mistakes. Unintended errors – often due to institutions (even as respected as the German Bundesbank) – are not infrequent; and speculators can sometimes take agencies for a ride, for a matter of minutes, but time enough to make a killing. News-agency historians may point out how agency lore or mythology nurtures various skeletons in the cupboard or the memory of past affairs. Havas and AFP executives used to recall how agency executives in the past were in the position of insiders, enjoying privileged access to, and prior knowledge of, information that was market-sensitive; Léon Pognon, who a century ago was first an 'ace reporter' and later a senior news executive of the Havas news agency, had contacts in the French foreign ministry and with Russian diplomats: it was long rumoured within the Havas agency that he had used, for personal gain, prior knowledge of developments during the turmoil affecting French investments in Russia in the 1900s.[11] Today's news agencies and news vendors have had, for a long time, guidelines ensuring that employees do not compromise the company's reputation for integrity and ethical conduct. For example, the entry on 'insider trading' in the Reuters *Styleguide* (1995) includes the following:

> [We] must avoid not only impropriety but also any appearance of impropriety. . . . Insider trading and tipping . . . are grounds for dismissal. . . . Put simply, you would be guilty of insider trading or tipping if, while possessing information about a company that is not in the public domain, you bought or sold securities or gave to a third party information on the basis of which they bought, sold, or retained securities. . . . Information is considered non-public until it has been publicly disclosed (in a major news publication or wire-service, in a public filing made to a regulatory agency or in materials sent to shareholders) and the market has had enough time to absorb and react to the information. It should be assumed that information obtained in the course of employment by Reuters is non-public.

How much time is 'enough' is of course a moot question, but one that seasoned professionals know how to answer. On the other hand, competitive pressures in an age of real-time data flows, 'electronic conversations' conducted via screens and terminals served by systems run by news vendors (Bloomberg,

Reuters, AP-Dow Jones, etc.), accentuate the danger that speculators may succeed in briefly circumventing the safeguards agencies put in place. In August 1995, for a few brief minutes, the fail-safe system of checks and counter-checks observed by AFP proved inoperative: a speculator, in the guise of a 'Monsieur Bordereau', succeeded in passing himself off as a spokesman of Eurotunnel, a company whose stock was highly volatile; the 'error' was discovered within minutes – after Reuters had flashed what AFP was reporting. AFP quickly issued a 'kill' – as have other agencies on similar occasions.

In 1996, CNN executives observed that 'all agencies make mistakes (especially in the era of real-time and market-moving news)'. So, of course, do CNN, the BBC and other reputable news organisations: in late May 1997, reporting on a NATO meeting attended by Russia's Boris Yeltsin and Britain's Tony Blair, a BBC service flashed 'Yeltsin invites Blair to Britain . . .'. Historians of leading news agencies and other news media might stress not only that *errare humanum est*, but that it is remarkable that so few factual errors are committed. No less important is the analysis of the presentation and packaging of news and information – according to the perceived or expressed requirements of target markets. This is not necessarily an issue with which historians are familiar: many of them were first trained in how to establish the veracity of the accounts that are available. Yet in adjudicating between different accounts of the same event – the 'life of Jesus' according to the four gospels, for instance – they scrutinise presentational and representational techniques.[12] News-agency historians have to do likewise. Difficulties arise because news agencies are peopled both by journalists striving to establish accurate information quickly, and by staff fully aware of the commercial and competitive environment in which news vendors operate. Even to ascertain the number of company employees, and the breakdown between journalist and non-journalist (full-time and part-time) personnel, can prove time-consuming: definitions vary over time and according to the agency.

There is a further issue that it seems relevant to raise here: rhetoric about 'globalisation', 'the information society/economy', 'real-time data flows' and other buzzwords of 1990s' tele-com(p)unications 'convergence' are part-and-parcel of news personnel *modus operandi* and media ecologies. To a certain degree, these are merely 'up-dates' of past rhetoric: 'a deadline every minute' (of the 1930s) or 'follow the cable' (the slogan encapsulating the go-getting electro-magnetic telegraph-hunting business attitude of Paul Julius Reuter [1816–99]). In 1999–2000, seasoned newsmen may have little time for such rhetoric: sales and business managers, technicians and engineers, however, sometimes recognize that there are indirect benefits in being seen as part of an enterprise at the 'cutting edge of state-of-the-art technology'. To work in a news agency archive, however, is to glimpse the occasional tension between the different strands of a corporate culture. Historians likewise glimpse these, but they may concentrate on rather different aspects. Socio-economic and cultural concerns are pinpointed by the excellently entitled study of Carolyn

Marvin; *When Old Technologies Were New*,[13] which reviews nineteenth-century technologies that 'harnessed' electricity. Some histories of news agencies survey the relationship between electric telegraphy, the news flow and the implications for the debate about the commodification of news.[14] Others explore public and private archives to illuminate institutional histories of news agencies.[15] Sometimes, corporate archives of news organisations echo the contemporary rhetoric concerning the 'image' agencies project to their own personnel and to customers, while containing material that makes it possible to explore the history of a theme or issue about the company's strategy or development that is currently in the news. I shall close by touching on one such instance: the news film/television strategy of Reuters.

CONCLUSION: MICRO/MACRO AND 'MEDIA UP-DATE' VERSIONS OF NEWS AGENCY HISTORY

An article in the December 1997 issue of a Reuters in-house journal argued thus:

> [The] entire concept of RFTV [Reuters Financial Television] or news-on-demand would have been utterly alien and incomprehensible to the people who first established the forerunner of Reuters Television in 1957. Their aim was to ensure there was a non-American television news agency source of material for broadcasters worldwide so that coverage of the British Commonwealth and one or two other corners of the globe would not be neglected.[16]

The same article noted: 'Reuters television has been through difficult times since the Associated Press launched a TV service three years ago, entering a market which was already congested and generating low margins.'

Rhetoric in 1997–8 was all the more likely to fashion perceptions of past developments in that, in June 1998, the three major agency players in the provision of international news film were reduced to two: AP outbid Reuters to acquire the third global television news agency, Worldwide Television News.[17] Against this, the media/agency historian might argue that however valid the underlying logic – i.e. competition at news/editorial, technical and commercial levels between news organisations striving to equate professional and financial criteria – an exploration of the minutiae of material in agency archives, and the news output itself, informs an understanding of the variety of contexts and pressures under which news professionals operated and operate. I write this in the knowledge that working over the years with Jeremy Tunstall has both sensitised me to how 'media sociology' has helped identify issues that historians have long ignored; and in the belief that the historian of the international news flow, and of news as a commodity, has both to read and to 'meet' news professionals of today and of the past. For instance, the quotation preceding this paragraph is illuminated by the words of a past chairman of Visnews' trustees, recorded in a text in the Reuters corporate archive:

> Visnews was inaugurated in February 1957. . . . The project had taken shape in the previous year when Sir Ian Jacob, Director-general of the BBC, had resolved to break the American monopoly of sources of international newsfilm, and had conceived the hope (as he reported to the BBC Governors) of setting up 'a British agency which would hold in the newsfilm world the same position that Reuters does in the world of words'.[18]

But the historian knows that this statement is not enough: he must further explore the Visnews records, and indeed, those of the BBC, etc; he should likewise call on oral history.

There is here a difficulty, which lies in the different *modus operandi* or mindsets of media historians and of professional newsmen. Both, in the main, are concerned first with accurately ascertaining 'the facts'. News – as the product of both a profession and an industry – is itself the result of a process of commodification: this was pointed out by, among others, Harold Innis in the twentieth century; the dramatist Ben Jonson did so (satirically) in the early seventeenth century. Historians, however, are sometimes ill at ease with both the ephemeral and the commodity aspects of news output, which is suggested by the belief in some agencies that a given report has a shelf-life of about twelve hours, at the most. Agency output – updates and all – must appear 'seamless': a recurrent metaphor. It reflects a series of logics, pressures, constraints. These are not just those imposed by the orderly (if sometimes discordant) operations of newsmen, commercial staff and technicians, for they reflect also the perceptions implicit in client (media or non-media) expectations. The greater the variety of client, the greater the amount of news product (in an ever-growing number of languages and formats), the greater the attention paid to measuring customer satisfaction and assessing the impact of an agency's product, and of its performance, compared to these of competitors.[19] This pressure intensifies, but was already present over a century ago – when, for example, existing relationships based on the growing worldwide use of electric telegraphy were questioned anew with the advent of telephony and 'wireless' radio.

Historians may feel uneasy about the sheer scale, speed and rapid obsolescence of news output. Following Raymond Williams[20], we may monitor the use of certain terms: 'news-value' (Julian Ralph, Columbia University, New York, 1892) – for instance; or, again, the relationships within and between agencies, or those between agencies and their sources, or with their markets.

Some historians strive to monitor how the agencies themselves developed their classifications or taxonomies of 'news categories'.[21] Agencies *per se* exist for at least 160 years – if one accepts the conventional agency lore that Havas, established around the same time that Paul Julius Reuter was 'setting up shop' in Germany and the Low Countries, is the 'oldest' of the world's major agencies.[22]

Positioned, in today's rhetoric, at 'the cutting edge of technology', agencies have often – and understandably – stressed their media-centred news values and editorial reputation ('accuracy and impartiality at speed'), when technological, financial and other non-media constraints were also contributory factors. For the historian of international news-flows and of the relationships between exchange, information, decision-taking and the circulation of news as a commodity, there are several fair-to-excellent news-agency company histories, invaluable archival material (in public and private registries/records), and, finally – in leading established agencies – a relatively favourable approach to academic study, which was not always the case a generation ago. Historians, faced with the rhetoric of 'breaking news' and of 'market-moving news', can introduce a measure of 'distanciation': in the past, speed, networks and the wish to overcome the barriers of time and space, appeared as imperative to 'news-mongers' as they do to today's news professionals. I would argue that Jeremy Tunstall, from *The Westminster Lobby Correspondents, The Media Are American* and *Media Sociology* onward, has embarked on a similar life-long odyssey of explaining contexts, documenting what was little known and questioning conventional wisdom or assumptions.[23]

NOTES

1 *Institutio oratoria*, published about 95 AD.
2 Christopher Simpson writes that it's as if the formula was carved in stone over the portals of most communications departments on university campuses across the US. See Simpson, C. (1993) 'US mass communications research, counterinsurgency, and scientific 'reality', in W. Solomon and R. McChesney (eds) *Ruthless Criticism*, Minneapolis and London: University of Minnesota Press, 318.
3 Compare, for example, Reuters, AP, AFP and UPI style books.
4 Reuters executives, in the 1990s, for example, are not particularly fond of the term 'international news agency' or 'organisation': it does not accurately reflect the media and non-media activities, interests, clients and technologies of the corporation, and suggests a 'comparability' with other organisations that is considered inappropriate. Similarly, the company does not like being referred to as 'London' or 'British'-based: this minimises the organisation's plurinational personnel and transnational character.
5 Paul-Louis Bret, formerly a London bureau chief of Havas and chief executive of

AFP, 1947–50, argued thus: 'ideally, news should be made available to the nation "free", as is public education'; see Bret, Report to the Joxe Commission (on the status of AFP), 7 May 1947, quoted in Boyd-Barret, O. and M. Palmer (1982) *Le trafic des nouvelles: les agences mondiales d'information*, Paris: Alain Moreau, 123, and 679–97; also Tunstall, J. and M. Palmer (1991) *Media Moguls*, London: Routledge.

6 In London, in spring 1997, I met a Reuters computer-graphics executive, recently returned from Sydney, Australia, and preparations for the Olympic games of 2000.

7 As the forces of Laurent-Désiré Kabila advanced, the regime of 'marshall–president' Mobutu, at the head of one of Africa's largest countries, collapsed.

8 Efe, the Spanish agency; ANSA, the Italian agency. Source: AFP impact reports, 9 May 1997.

9 See Palmer, M. (1997) 'Quand les agences rapportent l'événement: 'l'actualité' russe, 1904–1906', in F. d'Alméida (ed.) *La question médiatique*, Paris: Seli Arslan, 205–19; and (1998), in Boyd-Barrett, O. and T. Rantanen, *The Globalization of News*, London: Sage.

10 Dinmore, G. (1990) 'Devil's advocate', *Highlights* (Reuters in-house editorial news magazine) (April).

11 The word 'pognon' is slang for money.

12 A Reuters quality controller once quoted Saint Luke 1: 56; 'Mary stayed with Elisabeth about three months and went home', and added: 'had Mary had a press secretary, the account of the event would have filled 400 words'.

13 New York: Oxford University Press.

14 See, for example, Blondheim, M. (1994) *News Over the Wires*, Cambridge, MA: Harvard University Press.

15 These include Read, D. ([1992] 1999) *The Power of News*, Oxford: Oxford University Press; Schwarzlose, R. A. (1989–90) *The Nation's Newsbrokers*, Evanston, Ill: Northwestern University Press, 2 vols.

16 'The future is video', *Reuters World*, 24–5.

17 ABC News sells WTN to Associated Press', *Financial Times*, 3 June 1998.

18 Crawley, J. (March 1977) 'The history of Visnews: notes for the first chapters', Reuters archive.

19 See Palmer, M. (1996) 'L'information agencée, fin de siècle: visions du monde et discours en fragments', *Réseaux* 75 (January–February): 87–111; 'Agences de presse: urgence et concurrence', in 'Les médias dans le conflit yougoslave', *Mots* 47 (June 1996): 73–88.

20 Williams, R. (1976) *Keywords*, London: Fontana and Croom Helm.

21 Reuters (London) and Havas (Paris) in the 1880s, both urged other agency contributors of news to follow their own news categories and priorities. See Palmer, M. (1983) *Des petits journaux aux grandes agences*, Paris: and Read (1999), cited in note 15.

22 Or rather, was. Charles Louis Havas (1783–1858) opened a modest translation bureau in Paris in about 1832 or 1833; this led to the creation of an agency in 1835. The news-division/operation of Havas ended in 1940. Founded in 1944, AFP has, on occasion, summoned up the ghost of its Havas predecessor. The Havas name persists, even when, in 1998, the Havas media–advertising–

tourism–communications conglomerate was acquired, by the CGE group, which itself was rebaptised Vivendi.

23 I remember the surprise of David Wood, *The Times'* political editor, when Jeremy published the 'in-house' (or in-Palace) regulations of Westminster Lobby correspondents.

19

HOW AMERICANS VIEW THE WORLD

Media images and public knowledge[1]

Kurt Lang and Gladys Engel Lang

Since in international relations we do not act personally, as we do with our baker, but through a complicated chain of representatives and agents, we never have a chance to test or revise our image, as we would our image of the baker if we discovered that transactions based on that image were frequently unsuccessful.

(Buchanan and Cantril 1953: 96)

The issues and participants in foreign affairs are remote. Members of the public – and, importantly, journalists – are unlikely to have any direct experience with them. . . . With our geographic isolation and limited language skills, Americans are not equipped – by inclination or ability – to deal with the world on equal terms.

(Manheim 1991: 129)

The United States is, by any measure, an information-rich society. Television ownership has become just about universal, and electronic gadgets may soon follow. By 1996, there was a modem in 1 out of 4 American households, roughly half of which were used daily to 'go online.' (Princeton Survey Research Associates 1996: x, xi; RTNDF 1996: 73). The various print media, still prospering, are filling the gaps by adapting their practices to the instant and open world made possible by electronic communication.

The images of other nations that people carry in their heads depend largely on what is conveyed in the almost unavoidable stream of messages facilitated by new technologies. In view of their unprecedented capacity for transmitting more information ever more rapidly and with greater verisimilitude to more people and at a lower cost, these media are shaping the perspective from which the American public views the rest of the world. As shown on maps of the world, this places America in the center bounded by two oceans. The large land mass of Eurasia is cut in two. What was once the Far East has become the Pacific Rim and moved closer to the US, if not geographically then certainly cognitively, strategically and, to some extent, even culturally and politically.

Still more graphic, and certainly more vivid, than two-dimensional maps are the various video images. They have the power to overwhelm and even erase the traditional, often exotic, ideas of other countries derived from lore, literature, and remembered history. Implicitly or explicitly, they define proximity or distance along dimensions other than that of physical space. Accordingly, people are prone to view countries not so much as nearby or faraway but as important or unimportant, friendly or hostile, co-operative or obstructive, democratic or authoritarian, advanced or undeveloped, and so forth.

Nevertheless, most Americans most of the time do not feel directly touched by the issues and conflicts that constitute foreign affairs. Is this, as the epigraphs that introduce this chapter imply, the inevitable result of the geographical distance and limited language skills of Americans? Or are the media remiss in providing the information that audiences need to be able, as Manheim (1991: 129) puts it, to 'deal with the world on more equal terms'? Keeping these questions in mind, we take a schematic look at how the production, dissemination, and utilization of foreign news has been refracting how the world appears to Americans.

THE PRODUCTION OF INFORMATION

The world is full of fascinating happenings. No one will ever know what transpired unless someone is there to tell about it in a way that people can understand. With the advent of radio and especially television, the collection of information about events has come to be dominated by the Anglo-American media (Tunstall 1977). This dominance was not built solely or even primarily on technology. Entrepreneurship, a pool of talent, and a language understood in many parts of the world were at least equally important. The investments required by changing technology have encouraged the formation of media conglomerates which, with their many links and resources, control most of the information that makes it into international channels.

The glamorous foreign correspondents, who followed every revolution and disaster and fascinated the pre-television world with accounts of their derring-do, are being replaced by teams beholden to corporate management. Today only a few major American newspapers maintain their own correspondents abroad. The rest depend on wholesalers, like the Associated Press (AP), as their major channel of news from abroad. In fact, most newspapers nowadays get their news-agency copy directly from satellite feeds into newsroom computers,[2] which puts hard copy releases from other sources at a disadvantage if they must be retyped (Giffard 1989: 272f.). Meanwhile, journalists have tended to use the electronic news libraries available to them more for preparation and finding the sources for local stories than for foreign reporting (Garrison 1995).

On television, where the distribution of newstape is also largely in the hands of such corporations as World Wide Television News (WTN), the foreign correspondent is also on the way to becoming an 'endangered species.' The financial burden of his/her maintenance is only one factor in this threatened demise. Garrick Utley attributes their increasing rarity on the network newscasts, where most people would see them, to producers and network executives who 'believe the mass audience's interest in daily events beyond their nations borders is declining, so little such news is offered – which exacerbates the high cost/low return (or low visibility) nature of international coverage' (Utley 1997: 2).

Furthermore, the resources for news gathering are not evenly distributed throughout the globe. The news departments of even the largest media organisations maintain news bureaux in only a few capital cities, which then become the places from which the most 'newsworthy' information emanates. Highly efficient transmission capabilities combined with the mobility afforded by jet travel now make it possible to keep tabs on developments in a number of countries without a far-flung network of correspondents. The resources for on-the-scene coverage can be deployed quickly wherever needed. Such operations remain costly. The major American networks have therefore cut down on the number of news teams headed by experienced correspondents with area knowledge and the appropriate language skills. In their place, they like to shuttle their own highly visible anchors around the world for live reports directly from what is presumed to be the scene of action.

Reporters become 'firemen' flying from one international conflagration to the next. A 'quiet news period,' as one reporter recalls, was when he covered 3 stories in 3 countries on 2 continents in 5 days (Utley 1997: 4f.). More important is that the jet travel that makes this kind of reporting possible and the satellite communication that encourages it leave reporters little time for developing expertise in any one country. As a consequence, they come to depend heavily on local sources for facts and, to the extent that they have access, on information from databases to fill in the background and context of the 'facts' they report. The less their contact and familiarity with the country on which they report, the greater such dependence.

Some locations are served by stringers, mostly part-time reporters and camera crews, on whom headquarters can call in case of unexpected developments in out-of-the-way places. Many are natives of the countries from which they report. But their input is to some extent neutralised by editors at the main office who fit what is sent to them into a framework suited to gain the attention of an American audience.

The problem takes another form in reporting on a society that practices censorship. Here, as Larson (1984: 55, 59) documented with regard to the

Soviet Union, news about that country more often than not came from external sources. On newscasts by the three major American networks between 1972 and 1981, the Soviet Union was a subject (i.e. mentioned) in 1 out of every 6 international stories on major news programs, but only 3.8 percent of these reports originated in the USSR – and this despite the fact that all three had permanent news bureaux there. Still more closed to American reporters was Iraq, where they had little to go on except what officials wanted them to know. In the months before American troops opened their attack to drive Iraqi forces out of Kuwait, 55 percent of the news stories emanated from the United States and only 8 percent from Baghdad, where media organisations had few representatives (Cook 1994: 112). Because of similar obstacles to the coverage of North Korea, at least until the death of Kim Il Sung and the start of negotiations over food shipments, the severe famine building in the late nineties had gone essentially unreported. No pictures or film or videotapes of its starving people had made it into the extensive archives that major news agencies, like WTN, had developed over the years. Such holdings, now computer indexed for rapid retrieval, allow networks to meet the demand for picture documentation when crises occur in more open societies.

When all is said and done, the most important sources for foreign news are the agencies of the American government, in particular the White House, the State Department, and the Pentagon. Each has its own view on the countries about which the media are likely to report and an interest in having that view disseminated. An international crisis adds to their ability to manage the news flow about foreign countries. Attention is focused on them. Everybody wants to know how the government will react. At the same time, these officials are privy to much information from diplomatic channels, intelligence activities, satellite surveillance, and so forth not available to anyone else. They can withhold information, as they have done at times, on such matters as human rights violations, when, in their opinion, its release could adversely affect public support for administration policies. Other privileged information – for example, on terrorist activity – is sometimes released selectively to a small coterie of outsiders, who can then use this 'inside' knowledge to appear onscreen as experts on the subject, though their comments all too often do no more than echo the views prevalent within some part of the government.

Threats emanate not only from foreign militarists and terrorists; administrations have themselves found it useful to highlight certain dangers, real or imagined, to advance their own agenda. John F. Kennedy, during his 1960 campaign for the presidency, proclaimed a missile gap, where none existed, and Lyndon B. Johnson converted a rather minor incident in the Gulf of Tonkin into a daring attack on American forces. The 'crisis' each provoked for his own political purpose resulted in serious public misperceptions of the capabilities and intent of countries with which Americans did indeed have serious differences. Other, more recent, examples are the media depictions of

Columbia, Panama, Mexico and/or Cuba as chief suppliers of the illegal drugs flowing into American cities. They divert attention from the evident failure of domestic policy to curb this scourge, a failure for which no politician wants to take responsibility.

Foreign governments are not that far behind the United States in the public relations techniques they employ. The very practices pioneered in America are now being used to influence its views of foreign countries. By 1986, so Manheim informs us, the number of American firms representing foreign clients had reached 824 and was still growing. Mostly these firms were lobbying for commercial interests and/or promoting tourism but some were also providing political services, helping to train foreign embassy personnel in news management and giving advice on 'the workings and news values of American news organizations. The heaviest users of such political services, in descending order, were Japan, Israel, Canada, Saudi Arabia, Indonesia, China, South Korea, France, Australia, Angola, South Africa, and Taiwan' (Manheim 1994: 9, 21, 130).

Government agencies and representatives have not been alone in vying for favorable media attention. Such human rights organisations as Amnesty International and America Watch have also tried to influence the reporting on other countries. While hardly novices at the public relations game, their input into the news flow has, however, rarely matched that from official sources. Their best chance to grab public attention comes when publicity about atrocities or other outrages fits government policy or when that policy is facing a serious challenge on Capital Hill.

In order to supplement and enliven their news reports about developments in other countries, media organizations will on their own turn to individuals unconnected to organised constituencies – to scholars for their expert knowledge, to travelers for personal accounts of events they may have witnessed, to refugees and victims for accounts of tribulations they have experienced. Normally, such persons are not autonomous news makers; they are brought in only as journalists seek them out. These same journalists can also create news merely by their presence. Pointing a camera aimed at demonstrators has encouraged behavior that elevates an otherwise trivial incident into a newsworthy media event with potentially serious political consequences. What would the significance of students surrounding the American embassy in Iran have been without the presence of television? We will never know.

To summarize: most foreign news available to Americans has become essentially a home-grown product put together by the mainstream media with a content more or less in line with the policy needs of their government. Not that dissenting or divergent views are not represented. They are, but as a rule only to the extent that they conform to the interest of some other significant group with the ability to make itself heard. And the media, by selecting the information about foreign countries that enters the news stream, play a crucial gatekeeper role in the process through which policies are accepted, modified, changed, and sometimes discarded.

THE DISTRIBUTION OF INFORMATION

No more than a tiny fraction of all the information about foreign countries from any source, whether in print or electronically encoded, ever enters the news flow. Some of it is proprietary and, hence, unlikely to be released unless or until this is in the owner's interest. Beyond that, even information sent out as a press release has to compete for scant space and time as well as for the attention of the ultimate consumer.

In terms of the proportion of space or time devoted to foreign events, American networks have given them significantly more attention than has the press. Especially after NBC and CBS expanded their nightly newscasts to 30 minutes in 1963, these two networks began to build their foreign coverage. During the ten-year period from 1972 to 1981, such items (including those on ABC) averaged 40 percent of the telecast time. In absolute terms, this amounted to a mere ten minutes of program time (Larson 1984: 41). But foreign news received even less time on unaffiliated stations, which had to depend entirely on satellite connections of their own, on barter dealers, and on independent suppliers of news film.

Yet the years covered in Larson's 1984 content analysis, when the Cold War was still on everybody's minds and American troops not yet extricated from Vietnam, may have marked the zenith of foreign news coverage by American media. According to a later but less detailed study, the time that the networks devoted to news from abroad had fallen from 45 percent of program time in 1970 to an emphatically tiny 13.5 percent in 1995 (Moisy 1996). The space in newspapers given to foreign news had similarly declined over roughly the same period. In 1971, it filled 10.2 percent of the newshole; in 1982, this was down to 6 percent (NAB, cited in Hoge 1997). Seven years later, another content analysis found only 2.6 percent of the non-advertising space in ten leading American newspapers carrying news from abroad (Emery 1989). News magazines have exhibited the same downward trend. Between 1985 and 1995, the space devoted to international news declined from 24 to 14 percent in *Time*, from 22 to 12 percent in *Newsweek* and from 20 to 14 percent in *US News & World Report* (magazine editorial reports, cited in Hoge 1997).

One also encounters within this general downward trend some peaks and troughs. They reveal the effect of the ebb and flow of events on what becomes 'foreign news.' Thus foreign coverage was stepped up significantly during the Vietnam War, literally soared with the Iranian hostage crisis and, after a drop, increased again during the Gulf War. Television news, even more than newspapers, has generally been driven by crisis, conflicts, and disaster (see Gans 1975), a pattern also manifest in the news that comes from abroad. From

Larson (1984) once again we learn that, during the period he covered, approximately 27 percent of such items in networks news dealt with civil unrest, war, terrorism, coups, assassinations, disasters, and similarly adverse events.

Foreign news is also skewed geographically. Some countries have been consistently more newsworthy than others: from 1972 to 1981 the Soviet Union was the most frequent subject of reports while western Europe and the Middle East accounted for about two-thirds of all foreign reports on the networks. The fewest came from Africa but Latin America was not very far ahead (Larson 1984: 147). But a serious confrontation commanding international attention will induce network news to refocus, and quickly, even on countries at the periphery, as happened in 1978–9 when Americans were held hostage in their own embassy in Teheran. During the first six months of the controversy, which lasted a full 444 days, air time devoted to Iran on nightly network news actually surpassed the earlier coverage of Vietnam (Adams and Heyl 1981), leaving little time in the nominal thirty-minute newscast for news from any other country.

Spectacles like the Olympic Games or an international conference attended by heads of state are planned with the media in mind. By sending an unusual number of personnel to the country that hosts them, media organisations turn into news events there that they would otherwise overlook. Thus the travels of the president, or even his surrogate, draw media coverage, as did Hillary and Chelsea Clinton's trip to Africa.

These tendencies are aggravated by an underlying uniformity in the way the American media cover the news. It is not unusual for network newscasts to lead with the same story on any given night and, over a longer period, the frequency with which countries are covered follows a nearly identical rank-order. By and large, national newspapers, like the *New York Times*, the *Washington Post*, and the *Wall Street Journal* set the news agenda for local media, whose editors will take their cues from them (Whitney and Becker 1982: 62). Only specialised journals with a small readership are free to chart their own course.

Using item counts in the *Media Monitor* for the ten big stories for five of the years 1991–7 on US network news, we made some small calculations of our own (see Table 19.1). In 1991 the Gulf War, which ended in March of that year, accounted for 18 percent of all items in newscasts. The disintegration of the former Soviet Union, hastened by a failed coup, was the second most reported story. It averaged eight stories per week. Iraq was fourth, with a focus on the Kurdish refugee crisis and coverage of weapons of mass destruction an important secondary component. Also important were two other stories about the Near East – American efforts for an Arab–Israeli peace settlement and the long-awaited homecoming of western hostages held by pro-Iranian kidnappers in Lebanon. When items dealing with these two stories are added to items bearing on Iraq, the coverage of the Near East that year, *excluding items about the Gulf War*, actually exceeded coverage of the USSR.

Table 19.1 The ten biggest stories on US network news for five of the years 1991–7

1991 (n = 13,847)		1993 (n = 13,474)		1994 (n = 13,632)		1996 (n = 13,201)		1997 (n = 12,547)	
Gulf War	17.8	Crime	12.6	Crime	14.3	Campaign '96	14.1	Crime	12.9
USSR	9.2	Economy	10.8	Health issues	9.0	Crime	9.3	Health issues	6.9
Business/economy	6.8	Health issues	8.1	Economy	8.7	Health issues	6.1	Business/economy	6.3
Iraq	5.0	Yugoslavia	6.7	Former Yugoslavia	4.8	Business/economy	4.5	Accidents	4.5
Health issues/AIDS	4.8	Natural disasters	4.1	Middle east	4.8	Aviation accidents	4.3	Weather	3.7
Crime	4.2	Russia	3.5	Haiti	4.2	Russia	4.2	Military/defense	2.9
Arab–Israeli peace	3.2	Middle east	2.9	Russia	2.9	Bosnia	3.0	Civil litigation	2.9
Lebanon hostages	2.1	Somalia	2.1	Midterm election	2.8	Weather	3.0	Space	2.7
Environment	1.6	US military issues	1.6	Disasters	2.2	White House scandal	2.9	Clinton scandals	2.5
Thomas Nomination Hrgs	1.6	Entertainment	1.9	Clinton scandals	1.9	Israel	2.2	China	1.9

Source: Media Monitor (1991–97)

Two years later in 1993, with the crises in these two regions past history, the Soviet Union and the Near East had both been downgraded. The focus had shifted to Yugoslavia, while Russia and the Middle East were being overshadowed by Somalia, at least for a while. So much less newsworthy had Russia become that, by 1994, events in the tiny Caribbean nation of Haiti, to which hardly anyone ever paid much attention, attracted more coverage by the networks, then sank again within two years into near-oblivion. In these two instances, as in the Iranian hostage crisis, coverage was as much determined by American involvement as by the location and nature of the event. By 1997, the top *foreign* news story was China, which barely made it into the top ten.

Beyond that, news about foreign countries, regardless of how or from where it originates, tends to become domesticated as it makes its way through American news channels (Gans 1975). Direct satellite pick-ups also enable each station, whenever so inclined, to put its own local spin on events from afar. The result is achieved partly by selection but also by how events are contextualised.

To illustrate the domestication by selection: after the seizure of the American embassy in Iran, the coverage focused on the hostages as victims and on the deposed Shah while a file of films continued to feature crowds of anti-American demonstrators, even as most Iranians were going about their usual day-to-day business (Altheide 1981). Contextualisation was documented by Wallis and Baran (1990: 175), whose systematic coding of foreign news items on CBS-TV and CNN revealed that nearly half of them were coupled with information on the American relationship to one or more other nations. Such coupling may be mandated by time constraints but their frequency points to the injection of a distinctly national perspective into the reporting of news from abroad.

What is more, the selection of news, even in the elite press, is usually, though by no means always, in accord with US policy interests. According to Gerbner, the *New York Times* was about five times as likely to mention martial law when it was imposed by a Soviet ally, or to write about Soviet dissidents, than to carry news about similar situations in a country friendly to the United States (Gerbner 1991: 32). Manheim suggests that the reportage in the *Washington Post* during the late 1980s was preparing its readers to view events in Asia and eastern Europe, but not in Latin America or Africa, as movement along the road to democratic progress. Much of the contemporaneous struggle between the government and the drug lords in Columbia, he avers, 'could readily have been characterized as a struggle for the survival of democratic institutions (1994: 96f.), but that conception did not fit the then predominant concerns driving American foreign policy.

Furthermore, in covering international conferences, American media usually concentrate disproportionately on issues raised by their own emissaries. And when it comes to the reporting of terrorism, that term has been virtually appropriated by mainstream media and spokespersons to signify atrocities *against* the West, even though by literal definition of terrorism, argues George, 'the United States and its friends are the major supporters, sponsors, and perpetrators of terrorist incidents in the world today' (1991: 1). Setting the record straight is difficult. Many such incidents, including Third World conflicts, had been cast into an East–West news frame. With the Cold War winding down, some changes have emerged. From 1985 to 1989 coverage of the Soviet Union was shifting away from military matters toward internal and foreign policy matters as well as becoming more positive (Richter 1991: 92).

How do such policy-related perspectives insinuate themselves into a nominally free media system? As already indicated, major suppliers of television footage and of news over the wire usually turn first to government sources, with which they have an established working relationship and whose views they can ill-afford to ignore. These same sources typically get lead billing ahead of the alternative views needed for a 'fair' balance. Then, as a dispatch moves down the line from international and national media to local outlets, the original text, usually at the end, is often truncated in order to fit the available space or time, thereby magnifying any initial bias.

AUDIENCES FOR FOREIGN NEWS

For two generations of Americans, television has been the most frequently used source of world news and will remain so despite the wealth of other available material. Newspaper reading has been eroding, particularly among the young, and news magazines have not exactly filled the niche. Online services have more than tripled between 1995 and 1998. According to surveys by the Pew Center Research Center, in 1995 just 4 percent of Americans went online for news and current events at least once a week; by 1998, it was anywhere from 15 to 26 percent. Nevertheless, these surveys provide no evidence that the Internet has become a significant diversion from mainstream news consumption. Internet news consumption functions primarily as a supplement for conventional news. Those who go online to take advantage of the accessibility, convenience, and breadth of available information, continue to favor the web-sites of conventional news outlets, like newspapers, televison networks, and news magazines, which cover a lot besides foreign news. In the most recent survey, the weather drew the largest audience (64 percent of online news consumers), followed closely by news about technology, entertainment, and business. (Pew Research Center 1999; see also Smith and Lichter 1997; Robinson and Godbey 1997; Princeton Survey Research Associates 1996, 72 and 74). And while penetration of computers and modems for all demographic groups soared between 1994 and 1998, households with incomes over $75,000 are 20 times more likely to have access to the Internet than those in the lowest income category and more than 9 times to have a computer at home. The digital divide along lines of income and education between information 'haves' and 'have nots' has actually grown rather than diminished (Census Bureau 1998).

Pictorial reports do have an authenticity that these other sources lack. 'Despite the stereotypical and brief appearances of most pictorial images' on TV news, notes Doris Graber (1990: 134), 'viewers' recall of TV news stories [is] enhanced by visuals, especially those that are personalized through unusual sites and human figures.' That TV has a dominant place in the time budget does not mean, however, that it is the richest source of information. News viewers who rely on television are actually less well informed than nonviewers while 'exposure to print media is generally associated with higher levels of news comprehension' (Robinson and Levy 1986: 232f., 1996; Graber 1988; Neuman *et al*. 1992). The generalisation applies more strongly today in view of the movement of viewers away from national network TV toward local news broadcasts (Nielsen ratings, cited in Mattlin 1997), whose foreign affairs content remains minimal. Nor is it changed by recent increases in the number of documentaries: they have too much soft news packaged as entertainment. Much viewing is casual, a function of living with the set turned on.

Only 'big stories' with saturation coverage on television still command attention. Nearly two-thirds of Americans were following *international* news only when 'something major' was happening, and most people still count on television, though less on the networks than the newer cable channels, to inform them most quickly of developments abroad. By 1998, 40 percent were regularly tuning in on CNN. This is where they first turned in order to learn about any kind of breaking story (Pew Research Center 1998).

There is, of course, more than one pattern of media use. Audiences are stratified not only in terms both of access and use but also in terms of communicative competence. No more than about 12 percent of the public, according to the Pew Research Center (1998), make up the 'serious news audience with a relatively high interest in politics, international affairs and science technology.' Being more educated, they look beyond news to information from national public radio, major newspapers, periodicals, and the astounding variety of specialised journals, newsletters, and books on foreign affairs that roll off the presses every year and most recently on the Internet. They are also more male, more Republican, and more interested in following the ups and downs of the global marketplace.

Persons involved in foreign trade obviously have a special need to keep up to date with developments in other parts of the world. An oft-cited but dated survey of such chief executives showed them to be 'consumers of an extensive but quite uniform set of communication media . . . [with] an overwhelming reliance on domestic as opposed to foreign material for information' on world economic matters. The overwhelming majority of these Americans were reached by the *New York Times*, the *Herald Tribune*, and the *Wall Street Journal*, as well as by news weeklies and general business magazines, supplemented through travel and conversation. Even this elite stratum read very 'few high-brow or foreign publications' (Bauer *et al*. 1967: 163). Some things have no doubt changed since the late 1950s when the study was conducted. For one thing, printing over the wire has made foreign subscriptions easier to obtain; and, for another, the *Tribune* has long since disappeared from the American scene. But constraints on time and poor language skills, still prevalent, make it unlikely that the dominance of domestic sources has been diminished by the arrival of new media, except perhaps for information directly relevant to the conduct of their business, which is being supplied at an ever more rapid rate through highly specialised channels. A replication of the earlier study would be useful.

The relationship of the makers of foreign policy to the media, like that of other policy elites, is complicated by their need to anticipate the reactions by a public many of whose members are poorly informed. For this reason, the working day of most people in Washington used to, and still does, begin with at least a glance at the front pages of key newspapers (Cohen 1973). Television has added a new element. It assumes overriding importance during a foreign policy crisis. A majority of senior foreign policy makers interviewed by O'Heffernan could recall a number of situations where the media were the only or the most rapid source of information, while Robert McNamara, Kennedy's Secretary of Defence, does not recall turning to television even once during the two weeks of the Cuban missile crisis (US Congress 1994: 28). Today, when the media are widely perceived as playing an active role in setting policy agendas, in defining the information environment in which policy is made, and sometimes even providing a front channel of communication outside of routine diplomacy, such disregard would be most unlikely for anyone so critically positioned in the making of foreign policy (O'Heffernan 1994: 236). Where formerly a government might release a statement it could later deny so as to test the likely response of a foreign country or even of its own population, today television coverage has achieved an immediacy and density that has supplemented conventional diplomacy with direct communication between the principals via live video as, for example, between US spokespersons and Saddam Hussein during the Gulf War, or most recently in the televised exchanges of the Chinese and American leaders during Clinton's official visit in June 1998. Whenever an exchange of this sort is taking place, policy makers must also keep a close eye on the polled responses of their own public. A media strategy is a component of foreign policy.

THE REFRACTION OF IMAGES

The American public has no deep knowledge base from which to view the rest of the world. Most people are aware only vaguely of geography beyond the countries and oceans that border the United States. The average respondent was able to locate 8.9 out of 16 countries they were asked about on a world map without place names. Correct placement was lower again for the locales of two recent conflicts once prominent in the news: 32 percent for Vietnam and 25 percent for the Persian Gulf (Gallup April/May 1988).

Second, the American public expresses less interest in news about 'other countries' than it does in local, regional, and national news. Interest in a foreign country rises when its involvement with the United States is concerned (Wanta 1993; Gallup 1994), particularly if this involves the presence of a significant number of American troops. In October 1990, 66 percent of a national sample said they were following '*very* closely . . . Iraq's occupation of Kuwait and the deployment of US forces to Saudi Arabia,' a degree of interest largely but not fully attributable to a rise in news coverage. It stayed close to this level throughout the Gulf War. Attentiveness to news about other involvements of American troops in operation abroad also rose, though not quite so dramatically. Comparable figures are: for the invasion of Panama in January 1990, 60 percent; US air strikes against Libya in October 1986, 58 percent. Both were also aimed against perceived enemies of America. The intervention in Haiti in October 1994 and the deployment of US troops in Bosnia as part of the NATO peace-keeping still attracted a good deal of attention from the public, but the landing in August 1990 of US marines in Liberia, which received much less coverage and must have seemed remote, had been very closely followed by only 27 percent. As a rule, the more sensational stories about space explorations and disasters are those most closely followed by the public (Pew Research Center 1988–98).

Third, perceptions outweighed geographical proximity when it came to identifying countries in which the United States had 'a vital interest . . . for political, economic or security reasons.' Mentioned by three-fourths or more were Japan, Russia, Mexico, and Saudi Arabia; at least three-fifths also acknowledged 'a vital interest' in such countries as Canada, Great Britain, Germany, China, South Korea, and Israel (Gallup 1994). Bosnia, though then in the focus of attention, was perceived as vital by only 44 percent, placing it between Egypt (45 percent) and France (39 percent). At the time of the survey (October 1994), Rwanda, along with Poland and India, was among those perceived to be least vital to American interests.

Fourth, the public has limited staying power. Attention to Somalia waned quickly once American troops pulled out. For example, the number paying 'very close' attention in March 1993 was 28 percent, down from 52 the previous January. The public has exhibited a similar volatility in relation to other events.

Fifth, although interest and attention stimulated by coverage creates familiarity, a focus on the American role can leave an inaccurate impression. Among Americans highly attentive to news about US forces in Bosnia, 3 out of 5 had a distinct misperception about the extent of American participation in the NATO peacekeeping force thinking that their troops would make up about half or more of the force and only 21 percent understood that they would constitute a minority (Pew Research Center poll 1/11–14/96).

Sixth, images of other countries derive equally from feelings of cultural or political affinity that take time to develop but also contribute to their stability. As far back as 1939, before they became partners in the Second World War, Americans were found to 'feel most friendly' by far both to the British people and to their government (Buchanan and Cantril 1953: 117). After the war ended, they continued to hold top rank: the four adjectives most frequently used to describe them were *intelligent, hardworking, brave*, and *peace-loving* in that order (Buchanan and Cantril 1953: 51, 216); and in 1989 their country still was ranked highest among eight that the General Social Survey asked respondents to rate. More recently, Gallup respondents thought that Britain was the least likely of eight governments to make use of spies against the US government; also, their overall opinion was predominantly favorable and they gave Britain top rating among the countries in terms of its citizens' individual freedom (NORC 1990).

The converse holds as well. With the onset of the Cold War, the Russians, long viewed with some suspicion, quickly displaced the Germans and Japanese as the 'least friendly' (Buchanan and Cantril 1953: 117, 216). And during the Cold War years Russia came to be perceived, with good reason, as the country most likely to send spies while the two former enemy nations came to be seen as culturally and politically more congenial than this American ally in the Second World War (Roper Starch 1993).

Seventh, the lower the level of knowledge about another nation, the more easily does its imagery change. Americans, who readily admit to both a low level of knowledge about the Soviet Union and a heavy reliance on television for information, are therefore more prone to influence from news events. Their views were not so much 'ideologically founded' as based on the international behavior of the Soviet Union and thus readily revised in response to changes in the Soviet stance, even before there had been any change in its system of government (Hinckley 1989: 248). Polls between 1951 and 1990 record significant movement on whether 'it is possible for the United States and Russia to reach agreements to help keep the peace.' The Soviet invasion of Czechoslovakia caused a sharp decline of nearly one-third in the number of optimistic responses, from 49 percent in June 1968 to 34 percent in August. In 1973, with the developing détente, optimism rose back to 60 percent but then, after the Yom Kippur War, slid again to 45 percent before rising once more in the 1980s and 1990s during the gradual wind-down of the Cold War (Holsti 1996: 66f.).

Eighth, more volatile yet are the images of countries less prominent in the news. Their leaders, when they enter the limelight, are lifted from obscurity. Saddam is the prime example of someone elevated to world villain almost overnight. In 1980, the year he had secured power by murdering every potential rival, only 17 percent of the respondents presented with a list of fifteen countries that 'could be a threat to the security of the United States' selected Iraq, putting it far behind the Soviet Union (84 percent), Iran (56 percent), and China (41 percent) and, interestingly enough, just ahead of Saudi Arabia (14 percent). Years later, during its conflict with Iran (September 1987), 43 percent were still siding with Iraq, as against 8 percent for Iran, in the war between the two countries; a near-majority had no opinion or simply did not care (Lang and Lang 1994). A bare week after the foray into Kuwait, 60 percent of the American public agreed with President Bush, who had likened Saddam to Hitler (Dorman and Livingston 1994: 72).

A final point bears on differences between the mass public and those who make up the more educated and better informed segment of Americans. The perceptions of the latter, especially the experts, are more complex, more differentiated, better grounded in factual detail, logically more coherent, and more conducive to liberal views on foreign policy issues. Nevertheless, all were found by Richman (1972: 246–9) to respond to the same media environment in much the same way. Differences in the direction of movement among educational levels are quite small but the increase in attention during periods of rising international tension narrows the gap in the proportions with 'no opinion,' typically higher among those with less education.

Even expert opinion shares some blind spots with the public at large. There is a considerable trade of information between journalists and academic and government experts (see Tunstall 1971), who also, to considerable extent, feed on the same sources and look upon the world from the same peculiarly American perspective. An event like the overthrow of the Shah of Iran seems to have caught everyone by surprise. Few of the experts writing in *Foreign Affairs*, the *Middle East Journal*, and *Foreign Policy* between 1970 and summer 1978 had detected or predicted the revolution. To be sure, 'many articles did describe problems, some minor and some major. Even these articles, however, missed the mark as far as reporting the grass roots anti-shah sentiment or detecting the popular revolution boiling right beneath the surface' (Mowlana 1984: 77). Their perceptions of threat, including that of the CIA, so far as one can tell, centered on the pro-Moscow Tudeh Party.

One of this chapter's authors had a similar experience in 1992, when he asked a panel of Soviet experts at a small conference why they had failed to predict the collapse of the Soviet Union. They assured him that there was no dearth of knowledge about the inefficiencies and cracks in the system. Most experts, he was told, more or less 'knew' that this could happen some time but, given the dominant consensus to the contrary, none was about to go out on a limb.

THE KNOWLEDGE DEFICIT

Americans appear neither much interested in following political developments in far-off countries nor particularly well informed about them. As noted in the epigraphs that preface this discussion, they are 'not equipped – by inclination or ability – to deal with the world on equal terms.' Foreign affairs are simply too remote, culturally as well as geographically. The images that all but the most widely traveled Americans carry in their heads remain highly dependent on the information that reaches them through the various news media.

Surely these media have expanded people's horizons. Just about everyone has ready access to more vivid images, but not necessarily the time, skill, or inclination to make use of the full range of information potentially available in a variety of sources. There is a real knowledge deficit. Why does it continue to exist in a highly developed information society?

We addressed this question, but only obliquely, in our admittedly sketchy overview of the flow of information through four levels: the organised activities involved in the production of world news, the selective distribution of the products that constitute world news, their utilisation by various consumers, and the process through which they are constructed into the images Americans have of other countries, images whose building blocks are little more than 'scratches on our minds,' as Isaacs (1958) once put it.

No one sees but a small part of the world. This is how it has to be – first, because the media coverage is highly selective and, second, because people in protecting themselves from information overload are disinclined, unless literally inundated by information, to pay much attention to that which does not fit their personal interests and requirements. These limits to the acquisition of new knowledge allow any number of misperceptions to survive. On the other hand, the less people know about a country, the more easily is the image changed by the saturation coverage given to certain events that enter the awareness of nearly everyone. The problem is that the new information can lead to more misperceptions or feed into existing stereotypes.

That news, especially on video, tends toward the 'episodic,' a format of quick-moving events with relatively little context and historical perspective (see Iyengar 1991), confronts us with still another problem: namely, who within this information-rich society will take responsibility for increasing public knowledge about an increasingly interdependent world? Technology by itself is no solution. Its rapidly shifting focus on a variety of distant events needs to be complemented with a strategy to promote understanding. This is a task for the educational community, ideally in co-operation with the media managers and professionals active in the expanding communication complex, most of whom, however, prefer to think of themselves as journalists, not educators, and so, despite all declarations to the contrary, have been hesitant to pay more than lip-service to any such effort.

NOTES

1 The authors express their gratitude to Alan Richman, USIA Office of Research and Media Reaction, for invaluable assistance and guidance to relevant public opinion data.
2 Local copy is the only thing their own staffs keyboard.

REFERENCES

Adams, William C. and Phillip Heyl (1981) 'From Cairo to Kabul with the networks, 1972–1980,' in William C. Adams (ed.) *Television Coverage of the Middle East*, Norwood, NJ: Ablex, 1–39.

Altheide, David L. (1981) 'Iran vs. US TV news: the hostage story out of context,' in William C. Adams (ed.) *Television Coverage of the Middle East*, Norwood, New Jersey: Ablex, 126–57.

Bauer, Raymond A., Ithiel de Sola Pool, and Lewis A. Dexter ([1963] 1967) *American Business and Public Policy: The Politics of Foreign Trade*, New York: Atherton Press.

Buchanan, William and Hadley Cantril (1953) *How Nations See Each Other: A Study of Public Opinion*, Urbana: University of Illinois Press.

Census Bureau (1998) *Current Population Survey* (December), Washington DC: US Department of Commerce.

Cohen, Bernard (1973) *The Press and Foreign Policy*, Boston: Little, Brown.

Cook, Timothy E. (1994) 'Domesticating a crisis: Washington newsbeats and network news after the Iraqi invasion of Kuwait,' in W. Lance Bennett and David L. Paletz (eds) *Taken by Storm: The Media, Public Opinion, and US Foreign Policy in the Gulf War*, Chicago: University of Chicago Press, 105–30.

Dorman, William A. and Steven Livingston (1994) 'News and historical content: the establishing phase of the Persian Gulf policy debate,' in W. Lance Bennett and David L. Paletz (eds) *Taken by Storm: The Media, Public Opinion, and US Foreign Policy in the Gulf War*, Chicago: University of Chicago Press, 63–81.

Emery, Michael (1989) 'A declining species: the international news hole,' *Gannett Center Journal* 3(fall): 151–64.

Gallup (1988) Unpublished report of survey sponsored by *National Geographic*, Princeton, NJ: (April/May).

—— (1994) Unpublished report of survey sponsored by the Chicago Council on Foreign Relations, Princeton, NJ (October).

Gans, Herbert (1975) *Deciding What's News*, New York: Panthéon.

Garrison, Bruce (1995) 'On-line services as reporting tools: daily newspaper use of commercial databases in 1994,' *Newspaper Research Journal* 16(4): 74–86.

George, Alexander (1991) 'Introduction,' in Alexander George (ed.) *Western State Terrorism*, Cambridge: Polity Press.

Gerbner, George (1991) 'The image of Russians in American media and the "new epoch",' in Everette E. Dennis, George Gerbner, and Yassen N. Zassoursky (eds) *Beyond the Cold War: Soviet and American Media Images*, Newbury Park: Sage, 31–5.

Giffard, C. Anthony (1989) *UNESCO and the Media*, New York: Longman.

Graber, Doris (1988) *Processing the News: How People Tame the Information Tide*, New York: Longman.

—— (1990) 'Seeing is remembering: how visuals contribute to learning from television,' *Journal of Communication* 40: 134–55.

Hinckley, Ronald H. (1989) 'American opinion toward the Soviet Union,' *International Journal of Public Opinion Research* 1: 242–57.

Hoge, James (1997) 'Foreign news: who gives a damn?', *Columbia Journalism Review* 36(4): 48–53.

Holsti, Ole R. (1996) *Public Opinion and American Foreign Policy*, Ann Arbor: University of Michigan Press.

Isaacs, Harold (1958) *Scratches on Our Minds*, Cambridge: MIT Press.

Iyengar, Shanto (1991) *Is Anyone Responsible? How the Press Frames Political Issues*, Chicago: University of Chicago Press.

Lang, Gladys Engel and Kurt Lang (1994) 'The press as prologue: media coverage of Saddam's Iraq, 1979–1990,' in W. Lance Bennett and David L. Paletz (eds) *Taken by Storm: The Media, Public Opinion, and US Foreign Policy in the Gulf War*, Chicago: University of Chicago Press, 43–62.

Larson, James F. (1984) *Television's Window on the World: International Affairs Coverage on the US Networks*, Norwood, NJ: Ablex.

Manheim, Jarol B. (1991) *All of the People All the Time: Strategic Communication and American Politics*, Armonk, NY: M. E. Sharpe.

—— (1994) *Strategic Public Diplomacy and American Foreign Policy: The Evolution of Influence*, New York: Oxford University Press.

Media Monitor (1991–7) Washington, DC: Center for Media and Public Affairs.

Mattlin, Jay (1997) 'Yes, Americans still do care about the news, but not the way they used to: behavioral evidence from television and print,' Paper presented at the *52nd Annual Conference of the American Association for Public Opinion Research*, Norfolk, Virginia, May 15–18.

Moisy, Claude (1996) *The Foreign News in the Information Age*, Cambridge: Joan Shorenstein Center on the Press, Politics and Public Policy.

Mowlana, Hamid (1984) 'The role of the media in the US–Iranian conflict,' in Andrew Arno and Wimal Dissanayake (eds) *The News Media in National and International Conflict*, Boulder, CO, and London: Westview, 71–99.

Neuman, W. Russell, Marion R. Just, and Ann N. Crigler (1992) *Common Knowledge: News and the Construction of Political Meaning*, Chicago: University of Chicago Press.

NORC (1990) *An American Profile: Opinions and Behavior, 1972–1989*, ed. Floris W. Wood, Detroit: Gale Research.

O'Heffernan, Patrick (1994) 'A mutual exploration model of media influence on US foreign policy,' in W. Lance Bennett and David L. Paletz (eds) *Taken by Storm: The Media, Public Opinion, and US Foreign Policy in the Gulf War*, Chicago: University of Chicago Press, 231–49.

Pew Research Center for the People and the Press (1999) Media Consumption, Washington DC.

—— (1988–98) *Data Base: Public Attentiveness to Major News Stories*, Washington, DC.

—— (1999) *The Internet News Audience Goes Ordinary*, Washington, DC.

Princeton Survey Research Associates (1996) 'News in the next century,' unpublished report conducted for the Radio and Television News Directors' Association, Princeton, NJ (October).

Richman, Alvin (1972) 'Public opinion and foreign affairs: the mediating influence of education level,' in Richard L. Merritt (ed.) *Communication in International Politics*, Urbana: University of Illinois Press, 232–51.

Richter, A. J. (1991) 'Enemy turned partner: a content analysis of *Newsweek* and *Novoye Vremya*,' in Everette E. Dennis, George Gerbner, and Yassen N. Zassoursky (eds) *Beyond the Cold War: Soviet and American Media Images*, Newbury Park: Sage.

Robinson, John P. and Geoffrey Godbey (1997) *Time for Life: The Surprising Ways*

Americans Use Their Time, University Park, PA: Pennsylvania State University Press.

—— and Mark R. Levy (1986) *The Main Source: Learning from Television News*, Beverly Hills, CA: Sage.

—— (1996) 'News media use and the informed public: a 1990s' update,' *Journal of Communication* 46: 129–35.

Roper Starch Worldwide (1993) Survey, New York (10–17 July).

RTNDF (1996) *Profile of the American News Consumer. News in the Next Century*, New York: Radio and Television News Directors' Foundation.

Smith III, Ted J. and S. Robert Lichter (1997) 'The people talk back: public attitudes about the news media,' Paper presented at the *52nd Annual Conference of the American Association for Public Opinion Research*, Norfolk, Virginia, May 15–18.

Tunstall, Jeremy (1971) *Journalists At Work*, London: Constable.

—— (1977) *The Media Are American: Anglo-American Media in the World*, New York: Columbia University Press.

United States Congress (1994) *Impact of Television on US Foreign Policy*, House Committee on Foreign Affairs, Doc. 79–868 CC, 103rd Congress, 2nd session, Washington, DC: US Government Printing Office.

Utley, Garrick (1997) 'The shrinking of foreign news: from broadcast to narrowcast,' *Foreign Affairs* 76(2): 2–10.

Wallis, Roger and Stanley J. Baran (1990) *The Known World of Broadcast News: International News and the Electronic Media*, New York: Routledge-Comedia Book.

Wanta, Wayne (1993) 'The agenda-setting effects of international news coverage: an examination of different media frames,' *International Journal of Public Opinion Research* 5: 250–64.

Whitney, Charles D. and Lee B. Becker (1982) 'Keeping the gates for gatekeepers: the effects of wire news,' *Journalism Quarterly* 59: 60–5.

20

PAN-ARAB SATELLITE TELEVISION

The Dialectics of Identity

Oliver Boyd-Barrett

This chapter explores aspects of the development of satellite television broadcasting in relation to the dynamics of local–global identity relations. This study is based on ethnographic observation of the feasibility planning for a new Pan-Arab satellite venture, based in Dubai, in the period Autumn 1997–Spring 1998. It focuses on the cultural, economic, professional, and political negotiation that informed the identification of the new channel's principal objectives which were: to make money, to present a family television service, to promote Dubai, and to be Pan-Arab. The findings are evaluated with reference to globalisation theory, the re-formulation of media imperialism theory, and implications for issues of democratisation and development.

EARLY FEARS OF SATELLITE TELEVISION

Since its inception, the prospect of widespread satellite delivery of television has raised a number of key issues for media scholars. It is not mere coincidence that the prospect of satellite delivery for mainstream television paralleled the development of New World Information and Communication Order discourse within UNESCO during the 1970s. These issues are discussed in relation to four categories:

- *Cultural*: fears of 'cultural invasion' were premised on the assumption that the United States would be the main actor in satellite television delivery, that it would exert its cultural muscle within a continuing Cold-War context, and that this would further accentuate what in the 1960s and 1970s was the already US-dominated character of television content in many parts of the world. The foremost spokesman for this perspective was Herbert Schiller (1969), backed by the research of many other scholars, including Jeremy Tunstall (1977), Kaarle Nordenstreng (1974), and Tapio Varis (1973). The United States was then the major supplier of international television programming, the most important actor in the production and operation of satellites and the dominant voice in forums on international satellite regulation.

- *Economic*: concern here was with the implications of a shift of television production and delivery away from an economic model of regulated scarcity to one of de-regulated profusion. Increasingly in the 1980s, satellite was at the center of key movements within the television industry: it had improved the competitiveness at home of US cable by providing alternative sources of program software, thus reducing the power of terrestrial networks, while also being a direct competitor to both cable and terrestrial broadcasting through Direct-to-Home delivery. In theory, satellite offered a practical and accessible alternative to dependence on either state or advertising revenue: namely, subscription revenue, with its promise of independence from either political patronage or advertisers. Satellite delivery spearheaded the challenge to state-controlled public service broadcasting in many parts of the world, notably in parts of Europe, Asia and the middle east. This was because the only serious challenge to public service broadcasting in many countries came from beyond national boundaries, drawing on the resources of highly capitalised international enterprises. The new profusion of channels stimulated by satellite, along with cable and digital electronics has generated increases in demand for content, with important implications for program pricing and advertising rates. It has boosted the overall market for television, helping to account for the rapid growth in the importance of the Asian television market, which is expected to account for 21 percent of the global television market by the year 2000 (Leonard and Harrison 1998).

- *Political*: the delivery of satellite channels to national markets, beamed in from external locations, roused political anxieties. Would satellite television be exploited as a direct political tool in much the same way as international radio broadcasting? And if so, could it be much more effective? Satellite broadcasting facilitated the penetration of national markets by external television signals: would this subvert the authority of existing political institutions, especially in authoritarian countries, or in countries where gender relations were characterised by patriarchy, or in countries where local cultural forms were controlled largely by elites? What kind of challenge would satellite television pose to the bureaucracy and politics of television regulation, through such means as curbs on the sales and distribution of satellite dishes? In particular how much of a challenge would it pose to state or public broadcasting systems, both in countries which had already opened the doors to commercial broadcasting on terrestrial airwaves and those which had so far resisted commercial-isation altogether? Through provision of a broader range of imagery, would satellite television contribute a wider range of frames for the interpretation of political and other events, at home and abroad, and thus be seen to contribute to democratisation? What might be the influence of global television on local television forms?

- *Global and local relations*: it was originally envisaged that satellites, with their huge geo-stationary footprints would be powerful influences of globalism and regionalism, at the expense of the local and the national. In more recent years, this expectation has been confounded, at least in some parts of the world. Increasingly, international satellite is subject to processes of controlled appropriation by nation–states, especially where: satellite providers must negotiate with local cable and other providers and where the state has succeeded in regulating cable provision and the up-linking of satellite signals; where satellite providers, in order to protect larger business ambitions must accommodate to the provisions of local states; and where the economics of competition dictate that the content of satellite services should target local linguistic and cultural markets, possibly fostering co-production agreements with local producers. At the same time, there has been a rapid increase in the development of local satellite television providers, as is particularly noticeable in India and the middle east, and governments have also set up their own satellite stations. Furthermore, satellite has added significantly to supply of alternative programming for diasporic communities around the world, with possible implications for the prospects of their integration or adjustment with host communities. The growing number of satellite channels has been boosted by the facility for digital compression of channels on transponders. Contrary to the prevailing impression in the 1970s that satellite television was primarily about the invasion of many national television markets by services located in the United States and some other powerful countries, by the 1990s we have a more diversified situation, with a few powerful international players (e.g. Sky Television, CNNI, BBC World) and many regional, national and local stations. Leonard and Harrison (1998: 35) argue that the 'satellite service market remains a market developing within boundaries set by state controls.'

SATELLITE TELEVISION IN THE MIDDLE EAST

In the middle east and throughout the Arab world there has been a notable intensification of satellite activity. Up to the early 1990s, broadcasting in the Arab world was largely characterised by state-controlled radio and television. In the case of television there was heavy dependence on US imports in the early days, which has since diminished in favor of local Arab world productions, notably from centers in Egypt, and the Lebanon, and in favor of imports from non-US sources, including Latin America. Television has characteristically become a site of tension between forces of tradition and forces of modernity (cf. Katz and Waddell 1975). The industry has attracted considerable regulation, although in the case of satellite regulation is often not acted upon. As in Asia, satellite broadcasting was boosted by the example of CNNI's Gulf War coverage in 1991, and this was followed soon thereafter by the establishment of the Saudi-backed enterprise MEBC (now MBC) operating from London. The Egyptian state broadcaster also launched its first satellite television service, ESC, in 1991. Other ventures followed, including two connected with the Saudi royal family: Orbit (operating from Italy) and the Saudi-backed ART (operating from Rome, Cairo, and Jeddah). Others included Showtime (owned by US multinational Viacom and Kuwait's public investment bank, KIPCO); and, more recently, two strong Lebanese contenders LBC and Future, have appeared, both linked to capital associated with the Lebanese Christian community. LBC had displaced MBC by 1997, within two years of its inception, as the dominant free-to-air supplier of satellite programming in Gulf Co-operation Council (GCC) countries. By the late 1990s, nearly every Arab state had at least one satellite channel, in addition to a variety of channels and 'bouquets' of channels available from external sources. Several more channels were in planning by 1998.

Gross (1995), drawing on the work of Boyd (1993), identifies the following parameters of change and development that must be taken into account in the analysis of media in the Arab world: western influence; interrelationships between countries of the middle east (one motivation for media development in the past has been to counter or compete with the influence of media transmissions from neighboring countries); government power and control; religion; cultural conventions (including the maintenance of a strong oral culture and the influence of important intermediaries such as the bazaar and the mosque); economic factors.

Marghalani, Palmgreen and Boyd (1997) studied the factors accounting for the spread of satellite television in Saudi Arabia. These included:

- a previously restricted range of heavily censored content on the two government-run channels;
- the greatly reduced cost of Direct Broadcast Satellite;
- the technological impracticality of wiring such a large and dispersed population by cable (although cable is significant in the major cities);
- the need, demonstrated by the Gulf War and the experience of CNNI provision, for alternative sources of information about world affairs;
- the earlier success of VCR technology, which may also have played a role in whetting Saudi appetite for a wider variety of content;
- the availability, twenty-four hours a day, of a 'great variety of quality programming.'

To this list must be added the growing volume of advertising revenue for satellite television, reaching $210 million by 1997. Mention should be made also of the difficulty that governments have faced in controlling satellite dishes – both because these are getting smaller and because of the strength of business interest in supplying dishes to mass markets. Marghalani *et al.* (1997) noted that 64 percent of respondents owned and/or had regular access to a satellite dish, and of these 71.5 percent had a private dish and the others shared a dish. Arabic television channels were more popular than non-Arabic. MEBC, ART and ART (Film) were the most popular; least popular were channels from Morocco, Mauritania, Oman TV, and the Sudan. International channels such as CFI, CNNI and BBC World Service ranked in between.

A study of satellite broadcasting in the United Arab Emirates conducted in November 1996 found that ESC broadcast for longer than MBC, had greater program variety, and dedicated a higher percentage of the total both to entertainment and information categories than MBC, and less time to religion (Arish 1997). ESC news was dominated by politics first, then economics, followed by military interests and sport, whereas MBC gave priority to economics, followed by sports, politics, and military interests. In terms of news spread, MBC was more balanced, awarding slightly more emphasis to GCC than other countries, while ESC prioritised Egypt, eastern Europe, Africa and western Europe. ESC used mainly voice-over film, whereas the MBC presentation techniques were more varied. MBC showed greater commitment to 'western-style' coverage of the middle east.

There are also large non-Arab expatriate audiences for non-Arabic programming. Non-Arabic sources include some twenty-five international satellite channels, among them Rupert Murdoch's Star TV network, Indian and Pakistani telecasts and various language services in Malayalam, Tamil, Mandarin, and Tagalog that are beamed to the middle east via Asiasat, Arabsat, and other satellite carriers.

MEDIA IN THE UNITED ARAB EMIRATES

Founded in 1971 out of seven sheikhdoms that had been part of the Trucial States, the UAE is one of the most prosperous of Arab countries, and enjoys the world's fourth or fifth highest per capita income, with a relatively affluent population and a high degree of adult literacy. Oil is an important industry, representing one-third of the GNP in 1994, although most of the oil is concentrated in one emirate, Abu Dhabi. A strong commercial incentive exists, therefore, for providers of all sorts of capital, durable and consumer goods, including media producers. The government is the largest spender (mostly on social services), and investment in the growing non-oil sector has a large foreign content.

In 1992 there were 11 daily newspapers with a total circulation of 335,000 or 189 copies per 1,000 population, 490,000 radio receivers (1 per 4.9

318

persons), 170,000 television receivers (1 per 14 persons) and, in 1993, 623,800 telephones (1 per 2.8 persons) (*Encyclopaedia Britannica* 1997). The number of radio receivers per 1,000 population increased from 90 in 1970, to 236 in 1980, and 326 in 1992; the number of television receivers per 1,000 population went from zero in 1970 to 88 in 1980–9, and to 111 in 1992 (*UNESCO Statistical Yearbook* 1994).

In addition to UAE laws, media are subject to a federal press law, administered by the Ministry of Information and Culture. Arab radio services were established in the late 1960s in the two largest emirates (Abu Dhabi and Dubai), later supplemented by English services and other foreign-language services. Black-and-white TV stations were also introduced in the 1960s in Dubai and Abu Dhabi, developing into nationwide networks by the mid-1970s. They started as Arabic channels telecasting mainly Lebanese and Egyptian programming, augmented by dedicated English-language channels in Dubai and Abu Dhabi (the Abu Dhabi English channel was shut down in 1995, victim of, among other things, the competition to terrestrial television from satellite for expatriate audiences). In 1994, Dubai introduced a mainly Arabic cable/satellite channel with which the terrestrial channel links up after midnight.

A 1995 article by Babbili and Hussain observes that UAE Broadcasting is a government-owned service, operating a two-tiered structure; the federal government owns and operates the broadcast industries, while allowing the individual emirates to undertake their own broadcasting. The authors note that Dubai was operating both Arabic and English radio services: the Arabic service played music, with news and brief features, and the English service played mainly popular western music. Dubai introduced commercial television in 1972, carrying imported Arabic and western entertainment programs. Its success led to the establishment of two commercial channels broadcasting in Arabic (Program One) and English (Program Two). Program One broadcasts were produced locally, and typically included a mix of humor, sports, documentary, and an Arabic play. Other broadcasts received in Dubai were from Abu Dhabi (7 channels), Sharjah (4 channels), Bahrain (2 channels) and India's national television service Doordarshan. There were three major cable networks: BBC, Star TV Plus, and MTV. By 1992, some 85 percent of households were estimated to own a VCR.

This brief survey indicates that Dubai has had a relatively long history of television, in particular of commercial television and, more recently, commercial satellite television. It has catered for an increasingly prosperous audience, and Arab members of that audience are sophisticated consumers of both Arab (local and expatriate) and non-Arab media materials. Dubai is also noted as a trading center, one of the principal attractions for the 2.5 million visitors who travel to the UAE each year.

INCEPTION OF A NEW SATELLITE CHANNEL

The idea for a second satellite television station in Dubai was mooted by sources at the highest political levels in 1997. The programming director for the existing state broadcaster (which runs a satellite television station for the domestic UAE market) was invited to develop a feasibility study. 'Dubai 2' was conceived as a new private satellite TV channel projecting 'The Spirit of Dubai.' A small core team was appointed to develop the project, housed in a private villa in Dubai, and comprising, among others, marketing, animation, production, and technical and computing experts. The staffing was predominantly Arab, drawn mainly from outside of the UAE, from other parts of the Arab world, including Lebanon, Palestine, Egypt, and Ethiopia. The team worked with a variety of consultants, including market research and marketing companies, based locally but made up, predominantly, of non-local Arab professionals, some of whom had been educated or had worked in the United States. Of particular note was the role of an American-based global investment bank specialising in media, which was assigned responsibility for the development of an overall business plan. The US-based corporation Silicon Graphics Inc. was a leading technical consultant. During the period August 1997–March 1998 there was a series of major seminars, each lasting a few days, which brought together the core team, the main consultants, and a wider range of production and other media experts. The broader advisory panel, if it could be so called, included many representatives of Arab production companies as well as representatives of western-based media groups. (Most of the statistics quoted in this chapter come from documentary evidence supplied by consultants to the advisory team).

From the core planning team there emerged a guiding concept as to the nature of the planned new station. It was to be located in a shopping mall in Dubai, showing mainly commissioned programs (in-house or from external production houses) and some acquired, with extensive use of the Internet and automation. It would target Pan-Arab viewers, representing traditional values yet with a liberal or modern style, with interactive programs that would exploit the opportunities of a mall location and also involve all members of the community, including children. The channel would promote Dubai both within the Arab world and beyond, and generate revenue, both directly through such means as advertising and sponsorship but also through related business ventures, such as the sale of commissioned and in-house programming, online shopping, telemarketing, cable networks and hotels. Dubai was to be promoted not by direct propaganda but more subtly through positive association. House style would combine credibility and balance, glamour and entertainment, fast pace and interaction, information and forward planning, and aggressive marketing. The venture would demonstrate that Arab professionals can successfully plan and consult in a team environment.

Thus, one of the objectives was to represent Arab confidence and profession-alism in the management of television. This would also boost the supply of local television resources generally, including expenditure on advertising, which traditionally had favored print media in the Gulf.

Key features of the concept of Dubai 2, while not necessarily unique in themselves (operational models were quoted with respect to a Toronto city channel and London's Channel 4) made for a very distinctive operation when put together. They included the integration of the station with a shopping mall; the linking together of key production houses through a club, which also was to be linked with a source of program finance ('the Fund'); an audience 'parliament' made up of representatives from different categories of society to assess performance, a parallel web site, and a programming philosophy designed to secure profitability, uphold family values, promote Dubai, reflect Pan-Arab sentiment, and sustain an image that was fresh, fast-moving and modern. Five main profit centers were identified: TV advertising and sponsorship, real estate, the mall, the hotel, and the fund. Other considerations included merchandising, a station shop in the mall, program sales and so on. It was envisaged that the fund could be financed partly by Dubai 2 and partly by all other interested parties, each with representation on the fund's board.

In its original construction, the concept of Dubai 2 was to have included both the television station and the mall under single ownership. This concept later changed to one in which the TV station would lease space in a mall that was to be built by a public company (EMAAR), one of whose principal investors would also own Dubai 2. The potential for symbiosis between mall and television station was seen to be considerable. The mall would occupy some 50,000 square meters. In addition, it was to form part of an ambitious larger development – in the vicinity of the Trade Center and the Hilton. The project incorporated a 300-bedroom hotel, the Millennium Building (a communications facility including teleport and cyber-cafe), an Exhibition Center, Business Park, Amusement Center, office tower and apartments, four theatres, connecting sky-bridges (one of which would connect with the planned Emirates Tower) and a 'media corridor' packed with satellite and advertising monitors. The teleport would interconnect satellites transmitting to northern and southern hemispheres, thus becoming the only private station of its kind between Rome and Singapore. There would be close consultative links between Dubai 2 and EMAAR. The publicity benefits of Dubai 2 – in effect a free source of advertising for EMAAR – would pay the rent.

The identity of the television station would be closely associated with the mall, the mall providing many televisual contexts relating both to commerce and to community and lending themselves well to interactivity. The mall would provide background passers-by and spectators, audiences, 'vox-pop' respondents, personalities and celebrities. These people would represent all age groups; that they would be physically present in the mall would in itself suggest spending power as well as community affiliation, with representation from all over the middle east and further afield. The station, meanwhile, would provide businesses and traders in the mall with a very suitable vehicle for advertising and promotion: it would act as a beacon to many other television-related businesses wanting to rent space in the mall. It would provide guests for the hotel, and tenants for office and apartment accommodation.

The integration of a mall with a television station had obvious commercial advantages. But the concept was intended to be more than purely commercial. As a representation of the modern bazaar, the mall could also stand for Arab community and civic society, for the sustenance of an oral culture which requires the possibility of face-to-face community, one which can be extended through television and consolidated through the Internet. The mall was intended to lend identity to the station, and the station to the mall. Ideally, therefore, this had implications for the design of the mall and for the character of the activities within it. Trade is itself part of the identity of Dubai, and the station exists to promote trade through positive association. The symbiosis of mall and television would help to articulate an identity for Dubai for the beginning of the twenty-first century, an identity that could also serve as a beacon for modern Arabism and an attraction to potential visitors and emulators. But in this it had to contend with competition from other pretenders to such a role.

Discussions envisaged close management relations between Dubai 2 and the mall, affecting even the range of businesses to be included in the mall, the interior and exterior design of the buildings, additional components including hotel (for visiting celebrities), heliport, cybercafe, roof gardens and restaurant, and housing complex (for station employees). The wiring of the mall would facilitate television production from any point within it. Market research indicated that the possibility of being on television would generally appeal to potential visitors to the mall. A production studio would be separated by glass from a public restaurant adjacent to it, and would also provide the setting for cultural productions such as concerts playing to live audiences that would be televised.

Having discussed the basic concept of the new station, there are three questions that arise to be explored. The first is an economic as well as a political question: what persuaded the feasibility team that in spite of the rapid increase in the numbers of satellite services in the region there could be room for at least one more? Second, how did the team set about constructing an identity for the new station, in relation to what conceptual resources of nation, region and globe? Third, is there anything here that appears to support or refute either classical theories of media imperialism, or alternatively newer concepts of international relations which stress the constraints of global commodification and inequalities of power?

A New Venture in an Increasingly Competitive Environment

I have noted the already intense activity and competition in satellite television services for the Arabic world. Why, then, start another station? The principal reasons were equally political and economic. I will deal with the economic first, noting that the main objectives for the station included a strong insistence that, whatever else it should be, the new station should be profitable. Let me make it clear that the dangers of market speculation were fully acknowledged. The following dangers were identified:

- advertising revenue might increase more slowly than the consultants' models envisaged – the market might become even more competitive;
- there could be another 'Gulf War'-type conflict which could completely undermine business confidence;
- some traditional government-owned channels, such as Saudi Channel 1, might become more competitive;
- other Arab markets might develop more slowly;
- subscription television channels might grow more quickly and/or decide not to retransmit Dubai 2;
- audience segmentation might increase with the development of niche channels;
- the supply of high quality Arabic television productions might not keep pace with rising demand, increasing the cost of such content to Duabi 2.

The team's advertising experts and business consultants produced figures to show that global spending on cable and satellite television advertising was set to increase as a share of the total, from 6 percent in 1997 to 11.1 percent in the year 2002. Furthermore, Pan-Arab television advertising spend was expected to grow from $165.1 million in 1997 to $292.5 million in 2000, at the same time as country-specific advertising was expected to fall, at least in some countries (Saudi Arabia falling from $38.6 million in 1997 to an estimated $27.8 million in 2000). Part of this development would reflect a switch away from print to televisual advertising, and a trend towards a broader spread of advertising sources, away from prestige consumer goods such as cosmetics, soaps, etc., towards a greater emphasis on consumer durables. In 1996, the single most important category of advertising revenue in the middle east was cosmetics and beauty, which totalled $8,261 million. In addition, various advertising spin-offs were expected, including sponsorship, and the display of advertised goods in mall-related programmes. The web-sites would provide a 'virtual' mall to simulate the actual mall, and even extend it, helping consumers inspect and choose goods, order and pay for them without needing even to visit.

In spite of intense competition there was a perception here of a market as yet barely developed. Interest was concentrated on the most developed markets, defined in terms of advertising spend rather than size of population. Egypt, with a population of 59 million, had a per capita income in 1996 of only (US)$1,021, and was seen to be of interest only within the context of a second tier of countries to be reached once the primary markets had been captured. This was related to the low penetration of satellite in Egypt itself, and to the fact that the Egyptian market was well catered for by its own domestic channels. Saudi Arabia, with a population of 17.8 million, a per capita income of (US)$6,745, and high satellite penetration, was considered a much more important target. Highest expenditures on television advertising in the GCC region were identified as: Lebanon (US$329.4m), Saudi Arabia (US$290.9m) followed by Egypt (US$204.5m), UAE (US$187.7m), and Kuwait (US$149.3m). Per capita expenditure on television advertising was highest in UAE (US$81.6), the Lebanon (US$77.8), Kuwait (US$71.4), but only (US)$15 in Saudi Arabia, and (US)$1.4 in Egypt. These were among the basic factors in a business plan which estimated that, for a total investment of $115m, the new station could reach break-even on its current account within three years, and actual profit (after repayment of capital) within eight years. In addition to the $115m, a further $97m was estimated for the building capital for the associated mall complex, although this would be a separate development.

Advertising, sponsorship and sales constituted by far the most important category of the anticipated revenue, although by the year 2005 it was expected that the associated web-sites would generate approximately 10 percent of total revenue. Availability of advertising money was just one component helping to explain planners' enthusiasm to enter this market. Another consideration had to do with whether the new station had the potential to forge a distinctive identity for itself in contrast with the competition, and thus to attract viewers and impress advertisers. Market researchers concluded that Pan-Arab audiences for existing channels still regarded them as nationalistic, including those of Egypt, the Lebanon and Saudi Arabia. The major competitors, in terms of reach and viewers, were MBC (Saudi), LBC (Lebanon), ESC (Egypt), Future (Lebanon), ART (Saudi) and, trailing a long way behind, Aljazeera (UAE). The marketing manager considered that LBC subtly promoted Lebanon, had flair and style, promoted casual fashion, was western more than Arab, and youth-oriented. Future he defined as a family channel, less liberal than LBC but also more frivolous. MBC targeted the older, more serious, viewer: respectable, credible, professional, with a focus on practical programmes – information more than entertainment. ESC was totally Egyptian in character, hence not Pan-Arab, with a focus on films, and serials. EDTV promoted Dubai in an obvious way, was very local in character, but lacking in flair. LBC was contemporary but neither family-oriented nor Arabic; MBC was not family-oriented, nor strong on entertainment; ESC was family-oriented, but not contemporary, more Egyptian than Arabic; and Future was insufficiently Arabic.

How would Dubai 2 be distinctive? The team's marketing manager argued that it would free-to-air, promoting the 'personality of Dubai', in a subtle manner, unique and trendy, Pan-Arab, interactive, with a good mixture of entertaining, educational, high quality programming (the product of careful selection procedures, open, employing liberal techniques, with style, and appealing to all). The key words would be *family, Arab*, and *contemporary*, and he believed that none of the existing channels responded to all three dimensions. In news, Dubai could capitalise on the relative neutrality of this city within the political panorama of the Arab world. Others cautioned that the new channel would not enjoy the same degree of 'liberality' (especially with respect to open discussion of political and social issues, and the presentation and representation of women) as some of the competitors. The commitment of Dubai 2 to the themes of family, community, and Arab values could therefore be counter-productive. Further discussion of plans for news also revealed a preparedness to think critically on the global stage, while favoring a radical 'good news' agenda for the Arab world.

Motivation for establishing a new satellite station was not exclusively or directly economic. One of the principal goals of the project was to promote Dubai. This may be construed as a macro-economic objective for the community as a whole, but one that would not directly or necessarily determine the profitability of the station as such, since the station's revenue would depend mainly on income from commercial advertisers. The desire to promote Dubai is a reflection of the source of proposed investment for the project, a political source. The intention is that by (re)constructing and disseminating an image of Dubai that positively resonates with the populations both of the UAE itself and of its neighboring countries, not to mention Arabs and non-Arabs living beyond the Arab world, more and more visitors will be attracted. The most likely reasons for visitors to want to come to Dubai would include trade, commerce and shopping – activities iconicised by Dubai's World Trade Center – sports such as horse and camel riding, desert and sea travel, and major spectacles such as the bi-annual air show. Indirectly, such economic activity for the community could likely impact on the fortunes of Dubai 2 in the form of increased advertising revenue and viewers. A stronger, modernised Dubai would in itself enhance the role of Arabs in global trade and reduce dependence on western culture. The web-sites, with moving and still images, and text-based sources, would connect searchers to sources and databases of information about many different facets of the Arab world, functioning as a gateway between east and west.

Concentration on Dubai, on the other hand, could be off-putting to at least some of the potential audience outside the UAE, and might aggravate tensions between different emirates of the UAE, impeding the development of the desired image of a 'modern' Pan-Arabism that could resonate positively with Arabs and non-Arabs outside the UAE. Situated within Dubai, such a station might be seen as too 'nationalistic', its screen crowded with images of

Dubai, of local Arabs in the mall, giving excessive weight to the voice of local Arabs in interactive shows.

Other considerations here include the existing structure of television within Dubai, and the origination of the concept itself from the ruler of Dubai – also the most likely major, if not the sole, investor – his relations with other members of the ruling family and with other powerful families within the UAE. The existing state-controlled broadcasting network, which already included a satellite station designed primarily for a national UAE audience, was seen to represent an older media political economy, one that was heavily dependent on state subsidy, was over-manned, inefficient, and unresponsive to commercial needs, especially the needs of advertisers who wanted more commercial savvy in program selection, planning, and scheduling, and more involvement of advertisers in these processes.

State control can facilitate the direct intervention of powerful interests over programming in a way that may preserve established elite values while resisting popular demand. In its resistance to commercialism and to popular demand, state-controlled broadcasting sometimes resembles public service broadcasting. State-controlled broadcasting, especially in a region such as this, is not typically associated with efforts to create an open and accessible forum for the discussion of issues of public interest. On the other hand, even acknowledged public service broadcasters sometimes attract accusations of elitism or, on the contrary, can be vulnerable to commercial pressures as they endeavor to maintain income, competitiveness, and legitimacy.

One would normally expect a state broadcaster to have the full support of the central ruling interest of the state. Here, it *was* the central ruling interest which had, in effect, stimulated an initiative that could compete with the state network. The state network itself was under the overall control of a member of the royal family, in his capacity as minister for information. The initiative threatened the existing bureaucracy, and this indeed may have been its purpose. One outcome of the feasibility project would have been a compromise resolution to situate the new station within a reformed, commercialised and galvanised state system. A further dimension here has to do with relations between Dubai and other emirates of the UAE which, as a federal structure, experiences tensions and rivalries between federal and emirate levels, and jockeying for future influence. An efficient, 'modern', international, profitable, and popular television station would reflect well on the brand of politics and trade relations for which Dubai's rulers wish it to be known, and help them develop support for their approach throughout the nation and the region.

The Politics of Identity

Identity politics in this case study can usefully be discussed with reference to both programming and audiences. The exact ethnic composition of the UAE is not precisely known and is changeable. Local Arabs are generally considered to represent less than 10 percent of the population; in addition to expatriate workers, including workers from other Arab countries, a large proportion of the remainder are accounted for by immigrant workers from India and Pakistan, laboring in very insecure conditions, and subject to the control if not the whim of their local employers or (in the case of businesses) 'sponsors'.

It is a striking feature of the dynamics of the 'Dubai 2' project that this Indo-Pakistani audience was largely ignored. There was certainly a great deal of ethnic relevance in programming available to such an audience on satellite services beamed into the middle east from Asia. But such programming can scarcely fulfill the particular 'public sphere' requirements of such a large mass of immigrant workers whose interests are barely served by local press and broadcasting, and have almost no place in the local political structure. This population remained conspicuously absent from most of the debate, but some interest was expressed by the project team in a presentation from the chief executive of an Indian production company that specialised in soap opera productions. In particular there was interest in a new soap opera, in production, that celebrated the ancient history of an Indian warrior–princess. The team's interest was predominantly practical – driven by the need to fill peak viewing hours with an essential minimum range of large-budget productions, and the insufficiency of time and resources for local soap opera production – but was justified by reference to the Moslem identity of the lead character, to cultural similarities between film traditions of the middle east and India (both feature strong emphasis on song and dance), as well as to practices of inter-marriage between local Arab men and immigrant females. There was discussion of the options for parallel shooting of the soap opera in both Hindi and Arabic, even using some known Arab actors for lead parts in the Arabic version.

A key feature of Dubai 2 planning was the assumption of a large proportion of in-house and commissioned programming, representing more than 50 percent of the total. In-house material would in the main be relatively inexpensive, day-time or off-peak programming, much of it centered on the mall, commercial for the most part but also incorporating 'public sphere' objectives, such as programming for children, women, youth, retired people, and much of it 'interactive' (a somewhat imprecise concept, but one which has increasing importance in judging the likely success of certain kinds of programming). There was a potential tension here between the heavily 'local' or Dubai-specific character of such programming and the Pan-Arabic aspirations of the strategic concept. This could be off-set by commissioned programming, of which it was expected that much would come from local, or at least from Arabic, production companies, many of which were represented on the project team. The idea of a 'club' was based on the perceived need to help Arab companies identify with Dubai 2, achieve economies of scale through collaboration, provide links with a source of funding ('the Fund') which in turn would offer competitive loans, ease cash flows (a major problem for small production companies) and contribute to the rigor of program selection and production monitoring. Although a key virtue of this concept was that it would help foster local production talent, it introduced a further potential paradox. Some 'Arab' production interests perceived to be potentially suitable members of the club were linked with multinational corporations (e.g. the Beirut bureau chief of WTN, and the senior executive of a London-based financial television news service delivering financial news services to Arabic television services), or targeted Arab audiences in western markets (e.g. the USA) or specialised in the customisation or formatting of programs from non-Arab sources for Arab audiences, including a company which specialised in translating Latin American telenovelas into Arabic. The main candidate to manage 'the Fund' on behalf of the founding owner of the new station was the Florida-based investment bank that also developed the station's business plan. Despite commitment to original and commissioned programming, there was scepticism among some members of the team as to how things would pan out once the station was running and had a fixed number of programming hours to fill. In these discussions, applause for originality gave way to imitation, parallel programming. One response – that of the designated programming manager to the market research identification of an Arab appetite for more comedy – was to consider purchasing rights to either the scripts of some successful British comedy series (re-shooting them for Arab audiences) or simply dubbing rights.

Market research evidence from comparable stations suggested that the program categories achieving highest broadcast time share (percentages) were variety (40), serials (16), film (all categories – 11) news (7) and programs for children (7). Program categories achieving highest share of advertising revenue were variety (35), serials (21), news (12), film (all categories – 12) and cultural (6). The same sources showed that 60 percent of advertising revenue is earned between the hours of 8.00 p.m. and 2.00 a.m., with 29 percent earned between 3.00 p.m. and 8.00 p.m., with only 12 percent earned between the hours of 7.00 a.m. and 3.00 p.m. The importance of the evening hours underscores the importance of having a certain number of major draws to attract viewers to the channel, encourage them to keep viewing, and to return to the same channel on subsequent evenings. These considerations, coupled with resource constraints and shortages of available artistic and technical talent, meant that in practice the new station could not afford to be too different. Main program categories were likely to be news, drama, sit-com, Arabic movies, variety shows, game and quiz shows, concerns and festivals. There would be at least two long-running serials made up of one-hour episodes. In-house and commissioned programs would generally assume short time-span concentration, highlighting new technology and interactivity.

In determining the audience reach of this programming mix, the marketing team considered that in the first stage (first three years) the focus of attention would be Saudi Arabia, UAE, Kuwait, Lebanon. These countries shared high populations, regional proximity, high potential for revenue generation – especially Saudi Arabia, then accounting for approximately 65 percent of the current advertising revenue of the GCC countries, the highest satellite penetration (around 72 percent), and a population base of 17 million, representing 70 percent of the AGCC population. A second stage (years 4–6) would focus on Oman, Bahrain, Qatar, Jordan, Syria, North Africa and the rest of the intended satellite foot-print. The importance of the Saudi market raised certain challenges to the philosophical basis of the new channel. The task of fashioning a 'family' channel for Saudi viewers, especially women, could entail a self-imposed requirement for conservatism and caution (even if some Saudi women have a strong appetite for knowledge of modernity not catered for by local television).

This had implications for the viability of the 'Pan-Arab' claim of Dubai 2, especially for the belief in the possibility of an Arab modernity. Pan-Arab ideology has a long history, and its use needs to be considered in relation to the interests of those who employ the language of Pan-Arabism. It cannot be irrelevant here that Pan-Arabism, whatever else it might signify, is also a marketing concept, probably indispensable for a satellite television venture which wants to extend beyond national territory yet also remain ethnically distinctive. The ideology suggests that there already exists a regional identity for which the station is catering, and at the same time it acts as a force for the very construction of such an identity, although the distinction between the actual and the ideal becomes confused. Supporting the view that there is already a regional Arabic identity, advocates invoke commonalities of language, religion, history and aspects of culture. Sceptics, on the other hand, attach more weight to political divisions, different dialects of spoken Arabic, significant differences of wealth and history between different countries of the Arab world and significant differences of culture, touching on such matters as gender roles, and tolerance in matters of political and social communication. On the question of language, the proponents of Pan-Arabism argued in favor of a simplified 'media' version of classical Arabic, which available market research did suggest would be acceptable to audiences in the target area. There was some disagreement on this point within the team, however, some arguing that classical Arabic, even a 'media' version of it, would seem unnatural to audiences which had grown accustomed to consuming a great deal of Arabic media material in Egyptian and Lebanese dialects.

Questions of Imperialism

Older models of media imperialism (see Boyd-Barrett 1998) emphasised the role of international dominance–dependence in media relations as these related both to older forms of territorial colonialism as well as to newer forms of global capitalism. I have argued that it would be a retrograde step to abandon our awareness of structured inequalities that determine whose voices and interests get to be heard through the media, even as we struggle to accommodate previous paradigms to evidence of the greater fluidity of movement of peoples, cultures, money, and political groupings. I would argue that Arabic satellite television is a case in point. On the one hand, this example demonstrates the extent to which satellite television has helped to reduce the strength of western media influences, at least in some parts of the world. This is manifest in terms of the capital sources most likely to finance this project, in terms of the high proportion of in-house and commissioned programming, the expected involvement of a wide range of Arab production houses and consultancies, imaginative arrangements (through the 'club' and the 'fund') for nurturing Arab production, and the relatively low priority given to 'classic' western media imports, such as Hollywood film. On the other hand, we should take full account of the forces of cultural commodification here, which in turn relate back to the media politics of US President Reagan and British Prime Minister Thatcher in the 1980s. This is manifest in the close relationship between television and commerce, best exemplified through the symbiotic relationship between the television station and the shopping mall. The principles of commerce are embedded generally within the concept although not to the exclusion of what we can also call certain 'public sphere' goals (which may be boosted by market-research findings suggesting that viewers are loyal to stations that are believed to 'care' for their audiences). There is considerable emphasis here on competing with existing satellite stations by ensuring a strong role for advertisers in the selection and monitoring of in-house, commissioned and acquired programming. Much of the advertising that is being sought here relates to luxury consumer products from global corporations. Western programming formats are likely still to play a role through the purchase of script and translation rights, and through the continuing influence of television news channels such as WTN. There is likely to be considerable dependence on western and Japanese technology. While the overall concept can be fairly described as 'Arab', and is distinctive in relation to many of the imported western channels available on some 'bouquet' subscription satellite services popular among wealthier classes in the Arab world, this does not in itself signify that the station would achieve a qualitatively different kind of relationship with its target audiences. The target audience would most likely continue to be positioned primarily as consumers. Furthermore, this positioning would discriminate in favor of certain audiences: in particular, Arab as opposed to non-Arab expatriate (particularly Indian and Pakistani) audiences, prosperous Arab as opposed to poor Arab, proximate Arab as opposed to distant Arab.

CONCLUSION

In this relatively brief snapshot of a complex feasibility study, I have attempted to contour the principal features of the deliberations of a group of serious people weighing up the advantages and disadvantages of entering an already competitive market of satellite television. With reference to the fears of cultural and media imperialism that greeted the early days of satellite television, I wanted to draw attention to the light that this case study could shine on the dynamics of identity construction, with particular reference to issues of programming and issues of audience. The case study suggests that early critical discussion of satellite television and cultural imperialism underestimated the potential of satellite television in the hands of non-western entrepreneurs, producers and markets. But this in itself is hardly sufficient evidence to be sanguine. Of particular concern is the influence of prevailing definitions of what it means to be commercial which, alongside political factors, are very constraining. Commercial goals are sought within a context that requires huge initial investment, is politically very cautious, whose agenda is set by political as well as commercial interests, and which is selectively responsive to ethnic identities.

REFERENCES

Arish, Muhammad (1997) 'Arab TV goes commercial,' *The International Journal for Communication Studies* 59(6): 473–94.

Babbili and Hussain (1995) in Y. Kamalipour and H. Mowlana (eds) *Mass Media in the Middle East: A Comprehensive Handbook*, Westport, CT: Greenwood Press.

Boyd, D. (1993) *Broadcasting in the Arab World: A Study of Electronic Media in the Middle East*, Iowa State University Press.

Boyd-Barrett, O. (1998) 'Media imperialism reformulated,' in D. Thussu (ed.) *Electronic Empires*, London: Edward Arnold.

Gross, L. S. (1995) *The International World of Electronic Media*, New York: McGraw-Hill.

Katz, E. and E. Waddell (1975) *Broadcasting in the Third World: Promise and Performance*, London: Macmillan.

Leonard, P. and K. Harrison (1998) 'The development of DTH satellite broadcasting in Asia,' *Intermedia* 26(1).

Marghalani, K., P. Palmgreen and D. Boyd (1997) 'The utilization of direct satellite broadcasting (DBS) in Saudi Arabia,' Paper presented at the *Annual Meeting of the International Communication Association*, Montreal, Canada, May 26.

Nordenstreng, Kaarle (1974) *Informational Mass Communication*, Helsinki: Tammi.

Schiller, Herbert (1969) *Mass Communication and American Empire*, New York: Augustus M. Kelly.

Tunstall, Jeremy (1977) *The Media Are American*, London: Constable.

Varis, Tapio (1973) *International Inventory of Television Programme Structure and the Flow of TV Programmes Between Nations*, Tampere: University of Tampere, Finland.

INDEX